# 'TIS THE FAR FAMOUS VALE

## National Influences on the
## Vale of Aylesbury

## Ken and Margaret Morley

The
Book
Castle

## By the Same Authors

**Ken Morley**

Voluntary Social Organisations in Redditch (with Ken Laugharne)
Communiversity
Social Activity and Social Enterprise
Some Morleys of Southwest Lancashire
One Man's Words 1894 – 1920: From Mansfield to the Marne
One Man's Words 1920 – 1946: The Road to Lunghua

**Ken and Margaret Morley**

Yeomen of the Fens
Echoes 9 and 10
The Great Upheaval
Wingrave

The jacket illustration is from a painting by Edward Stamp of Stewkley
(photograph by the artist)
The illustration on the title page is from the Buckinghamshire County Museum
(photograph by Peter Hoare)

**For our dear friend**

**Emma Bowes Romanelli:**

**so brave and steadfast in adversity;**

**finding joy and sparkle in life's simplest pleasures.**

First published November 2007
by
The Book Castle
12 Church Street
Dunstable
Bedfordshire
LU5 4RU

© Ken and Margaret Morley, 2007

ISBN 978-1-903747-86-5

Preparation for printing by
Ken Morley, Simon Jauncey and Tracey Moren (Moren Associates Limited)

Printed in Great Britain by
Antony Rowe Ltd
Chippenham, Wiltshire

# In Memory of the Vale's Greatest Fight for its Preservation

The above illustration is from an engraving of the village of Hoggeston by Edward Stamp of Stewkley in support of the Wing Airport Resistance Association, in its fight to prevent the location of a third London airport in the Vale. On its back it bears a message from Sir Colin Buchanan:

"I believe that the Vale of Aylesbury is a critically important part of this island. It is part of the fundamental hill and dale, forest and farmland break between London and Birmingham. It is of immense value to the nation. To locate the airport squarely athwart the break between the country's two largest conurbations would seem to me to constitute nothing less than an environmental disaster."

# CONTENTS

# RECOLLECTIONS

# MAPS

## Some places connected with the text, which are:

## WELL WORTH A VISIT

**Churches**
All Saints, Wing  13-16
St Michael, Stewkley  42-44
St Mary and St Nicholas, Chetwode  89 & 96
All Saints, Hillesden  88-89

**Specialised Collections**
Stoke Bruerne: The Canal Museum  148
Luton: Stockwood Park  140
      Stockwood Collection of Rural Crafts
      Mossman Collection of Horse-drawn Carriages
Hitchin: The British Schools' Museum  173
Pitstone Green Farm Museum  248
Luton: Wardown Park Museum - lace and strawplait displays  179
Aylesbury: the County Museum lace and brick displays  179
Haddenham: Museum Trust; witchert buildings and walls  112 & 211-212

**Wall Paintings**
St John the Baptist, Little Missenden  96
All Saints', Little Kimble  96
St Lawrence, Broughton, Milton Keynes  96

**Early Military Remains**
Wallingford: ramparts and motte  36
Castlethorpe: motte and bailey  39-40

**Mills**
Ivinghoe: Ford End Water Mill  248
Quainton: Windmill  248
Brill: Windmill  259
Pitstone: Windmill  accessible by public footpath from O/S 944156

**Railways**
Chinnor and Princes Risborough Railway  159
Cholsey and Wallingford Railway  159
Buckinghamshire Railway Centre at Quainton  159
The Watercress Line  159

**Other Visits**
Deserted Villages: Cublington  57-59; Quarrendon  63-68
Stowe: Landscape Gardens  69-70
Pitstone Wharf: Glebe Canal Cruises  148
Waddesdon Manor  01296-653211
Aylesbury Conservation Area: Heritage Walk; Tour of Kings Head  179
College Lake Wildlife Centre  262
Mead Open Farm  262

To avoidance disappointment check availability, opening times, etc. before travelling. For instance, some sites are only open during the summer months. Others vary their opening times from year to year. Museum's may also change their displays from time to time.

# TABLES

# Preface & Acknowledgments

When our book on Wingrave had been published, we thought long and hard as to what we should tackle next. Then we remembered "The Great Upheaval", our earlier book about the enclosure of the parish of Wingrave with Rowsham. It was clear that much of what had happened to many of the ordinary folk of the parish (the villagers who held rights of common, the smallholders and the smaller farmers, for instance) was determined by the landed interest (many of them absentee landlords) socialising mainly in groups of similar affluence and influence. In earlier times the principal social group was the royal court. In later times three interlocking groups of royal court, parliament and county flourished. We recalled that there had been other great upheavals at other times, and on a variety of issues. So we decided to examine how national events, and the decisions of those in authority, and those who sought authority, had affected the ordinary folk (the commoners, the peasants, the rank and file, the great unwashed, etc., etc..) in the Vale of Aylesbury, our home for over thirty years.

There were the invaders from Europe (the Angles, Danes, Jutes and Saxons) who, in the Dark Ages, either plundered and retreated with their loot, or slaughtered and settled on the lands they had conquered. They were followed by the Norman kings, who introduced a feudal system which turned the peasants into slaves of the soil. In late medieval times ruthless landowners dumped their tenants onto the roads in the course of medieval enclosure, destroying both their jobs and their homes. Later, King Henry VIII, in pursuit of an heir and a solution to bankruptcy, destroyed the monasteries, which were the principal source of poor relief. Henry's children were no better. They turned the peasants' religion upside down and back again to satisfy their political and religious ambitions, and enforced their preferences by branding dissidents as 'heretics' and burning them (by the hundred) at the stake. Over these centuries mass dissent was also rigorously and brutally repressed, often by guile and false promises as well as armed force. The Harrying of the North by William I, the Peasants' Revolt during the minority of Richard II, and the Pilgrimage of Grace in Henry VIII's reign are outstanding examples of repression by armed force followed by ruthless murder on the gallows or the block.

In more recent centuries the authorities, whether royal or civil, continued to disregard the concerns of 'the inferior multitude'. The aristocrats and landlords in Parliament kept the Settlement Act of 1662 on the statute book for two centuries, so tying unemployed peasants to their place of birth, even when jobs existed a few miles away. The landlords and farmers of the 19th century expected dawn to dusk labour for a pittance that brought families close to starvation, with the dreaded workhouse and emigration to distant lands as their last resorts. Happily, the extension of the franchise in the second half of the 19th century and universal suffrage in the 20th not only helped to democratise institutions like the Vestry and the House of Lords, but created a canopy of local government resting on direct popular election, which tackled long-standing problems such as sanitation, water supply, public health, transport and housing. Less happily the 21st century has seen the emergence of benevolent despotism with, for example, unelected (and thus unaccountable) members of remote committees devising policies, which central government then imposes upon local authorities with little allowance for local concerns. We touch briefly on this in respect of housing in the Vale in Chapter 20.

Throughout the preparation of this book many people and organisations have helped and encouraged us, and we are most grateful to everyone listed below. However, the following gave considerably of their time, and their expertise resolved many problems. The staff of the Centre for Bucks Studies have been unfailingly helpful. Our grandson Simon Jauncey's impressive familiarity with Adobe InDesign enabled us to begin the typesetting of the book in a form acceptable to the printers. Tracey Moren (of Moren Associates Ltd) then finalised the submission by installing all the illustrations to our very exacting requirements, and combined the various elements of the book to produce the final disks for the printers. Honor Lewington contributed not only the section on Hulcott's First School, but also made available her invaluable research into the deserted village of Burston. Dr David Noy generously allowed us to make use of information from his work on the Winslow Court Rolls, which he has brilliantly transcribed and translated. This has revealed facts about the Black Death and the tenancy of land that had been hidden for over 650 years due to the rolls' difficult medieval script and abbreviated Norman-Latin language. Edward Stamp's generous contribution of a very suitable painting for the cover, which was selected from hundreds of slides of his past work, provided us with just the right solution for a problem which had been troubling us for some time. Fundamental to the production of the book were the contributions of Paul Bowes, the publisher, and his assistant Sally Siddons: we are grateful for their assistance, encouragement and expertise.

The following list covers all contributions appearing in the text, other than pictorial material:

Aston Abbotts History Group, Wendy Austin, Stuart Bell, Maureen Brown, the late John Camp, Peggy Cattell, the Chiltern Open Air Museum, Peter Cooper, the Staff of the County Library Reserve Stock, the late Gerald Evered, Henry Franks, Prudence Goodwin, Brenda Grace, Michael Griffin, Peter and Diana Gulland, Haddenham Museum Trust, Ken Harris, Mark Harvey, David Hillier, Peter Hoare, Julian Hunt, Peter Knight, George Lamb, Marlene Lee, Leighton Buzzard Observer, David Lindsey (Ford End Water Mill Society), Trevor May, Alan Maizels, Eve McLaughlin, Prof. W. R. Mead, Mary Mountain, Andrew Muir, Michael and Phyllis Page, Bill Phillips, Neil Rees, Barbara Rodwell, Dr David Snow, Dr Michael Synnott, George Harper and Julia Wise (County Archaeological Service).

The following list is of those contributing illustrations for the book, while retaining copyright. We are most grateful to them all, but are especially indebted to Alec Bignell, Richard Daniels, Gillian Donald (Joyce Donald Collection), Norman Groom (Manager of Pitstone and Ivinghoe Museum), Tom Lawson, Edward Stamp (cover, title page, etc.), and Tony Wells, all of whom put their whole collections freely at our disposal. We were also greatly helped by Bedfordshire Record Office, Stuart Bell, Andrew Bunyard (Chinnor and Princes Risborough Railway), the late John Camp, Andy Chapman (Northamptonshire Archaeology, Northamptonshire County Council), the County Museum at Halton, the staff of Haddenham Museum Trust, Kenneth Dix, Mike Farley, Barbara Ginn, Valerie Godfrey, Prudence Goodwin, Christine Hatt, Barry Keen and Derek Pelling of The Bucks Herald, Honor Lewington, Rosemary Masters, Ron Miller, W.H.Pyne (from 'Microcosm' by kind permission of Constable Publishers), Margaret Rees, Victor and Christine Scott, Sylvia Sherwood and Carole Fryer of the Stone Local History Group, the late Gerry Tomlinson, Joan Watson, Peter Wenham and the Buckinghamshire County Museum Collections.

The word Plate followed by C and a number is the reference to a colour picture. These pictures are grouped into five blocks, which appear at intervals throughout the text.

As the notes and references at the end of the book demonstrate, our indebtedness to earlier writers is considerable. With research spread over a number of years it is possible that some names have been overlooked. If so, please accept our apologies, and inform us so that we can rectify the omission when there is a reprint.

## ’Tis the Far Famous Vale

Know ye the land where the butter's so yellow,
So rich in its flavour, so sweet to the taste –
Where the milk is so white, where the cream is so mellow –
Ah! Sweeter than nectar and thicker than paste?
Know ye the land where the dear little duck
Doth dabble about in the mud and the muck –
Where the little lambs frisk, as bright Phoebus peeps out,
And cock up their tails as they scamper about –
Where the pasture's so rich, and the cattle so plump,
And milk may be had without using the pump?
’Tis the Vale, ’tis the Vale, ’tis the far famous Vale,
Near Aylesbury town – within sight of the gaol –
The pride and the boast of the County of Bucks,
That garden of plenty, of pigstyes and ducks,
That Eden on earth, that spot ever sunny,
That place of all places for the making of money,
Which floweth with milk and with butter – not honey!

Extract from The Phantom Hound: A Legend of the Vale of Aylesbury
by Frank Percy, 1880

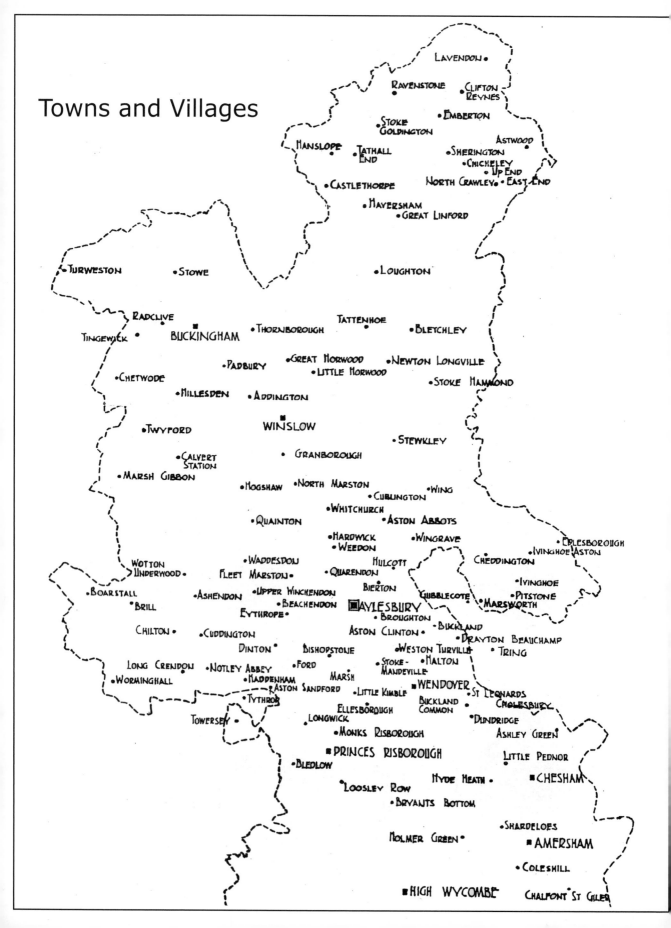

# Towns and Villages

## Introduction

# 'TIS THE FAR FAMOUS VALE

However they defined Aylesbury Vale, early travellers such as John Leland (Henry VIII's surveyor), Daniel Defoe (author of Robinson Crusoe), Celia Fiennes (inveterate traveller and diarist) and Arthur Young (secretary to the first Board of Agriculture) were all greatly impressed by its fertility, but by the mid-19th century the appearance of the Vale was also attracting attention. Thus in 1856 Clare Read wrote:[1]

> *Such a prospect, if viewed from Wendover Hill in the freshness of spring, the luxuriance of summer, or mellowed by the approach of autumn, always presents a scene of mingled beauty and interest.*

In 1942 Archibald MacDonnell enthused: [2]

> *Pasture and hedge, mile after mile, grey-green and brown and russet, and silver where the little rivers tangle themselves among the reeds and the trodden watering-pools.*

However, these quotes pale into insignificance when Sir Arthur Bryant, an outstanding Vale enthusiast, lambasts the Roskill Commission in Chapter 20.

The Vale of Aylesbury crosses the whole county of Buckinghamshire, from near Edlesborough on its boundary with Bedfordshire in the east, to Worminghall on its boundary with Oxfordshire in the west. It stretches northwards from the foot of the Chilterns but, unfortunately, to this day, writers seem unable to agree as to just how far northwards the Vale does extend. For Arthur Young writing in 1771 it stretched 18 miles from the Chilterns to Buckingham. More recently J.H.Donald [3] viewed it as extending even further: from Amersham (well within the Chilterns!) to beyond Buckingham. Our definition is firmly based on the geology of the area, because for 200 years this has been a major factor in determining the use of the land.

### Fig.1: Fruit Growing in the Vale.

In the 19th century it was noticed that fruit trees flourished on the belt of Greensand refreshed by downwash from the Chiltern Chalk. This picture of apple pickers was taken at Pitstone Green Farm in the 1930's.

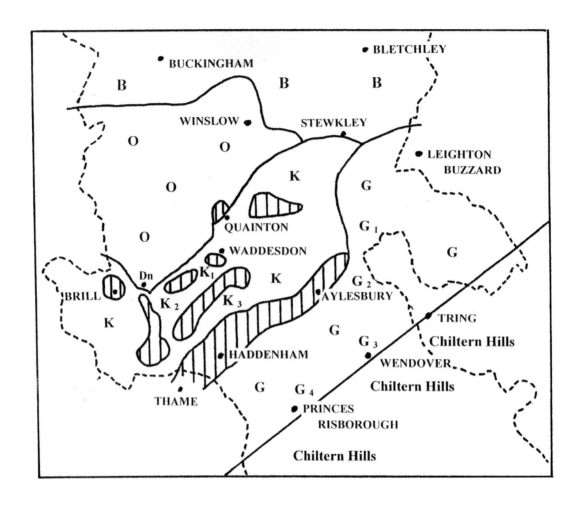

**Map 1: Simplified Geology of the Vale and North Bucks.**

G   Gault Clay         )
K   Kimmeridge Clay  ) The Vale of Aylesbury
|||  Portland Beds    )
O   Oxford Clay
B   Boulder Clay
Dn  Dorton
- - - Buckinghamshire County Boundary
     Subscripts $G_1$ etc. and $K_1$ etc. indicate a just a few of the areas
     where modifications of the Gault and Kimmeridge Clays are
     to be found (see Chapter 19)

In the south-east of England there is a strong relationship between geology, topography and land use. Relief maps reveal very clearly the chalk of the Chiltern Hills (to the south of the Vale) and the limestone of the Northamptonshire Uplands (to the north of Buckingham). Between them lies a lowland which is largely covered by thick deposits of the mud that we call clay, although from it rise the Portland Beds of limestone and sand, which create patches of higher ground. Map 1 shows the eastern part of this lowland, most of which is the administrative area of Aylesbury Vale District Council (AVDC). In Map 1 note the areas with Gault Clay, Kimmeridge Clay, Oxford Clay, Boulder Clay, and the Portland Beds.[4] Due to these differences in its geology this lowland can be divided into sub-regions, one of which is the Vale of Aylesbury, dominated by the Gault and Kimmeridge Clays and the Portland Beds.

It is important to distinguish between AVDC's area and the much smaller Vale of Aylesbury, which is the subject of this book. 'Our' Vale begins at the foot of the Chilterns, and its southern boundary is marked by villages such as Edlesborough, Ivinghoe, Tring, Wendover and Princes Risborough. It extends northwards to the northern edge of the Kimmeridge Clay, a boundary which is marked by villages such as Stewkley, Hoggeston, North Marston, Quainton, Westcott, Dorton and Boarstall. It is to this Vale that we shall be referring, when we mention 'the Vale', 'Our' Vale, or 'the Vale of Aylesbury' in chapters 19 and 20.

Most of the Vale of Aylesbury averages about 85 metres above sea level. However, four miles to the north-east of Aylesbury, taking in parishes such as Aston Abbotts, Wingrave, Wing and Mentmore, the Vale rises into a huddle of hillocks (Plate C1), which form a low watershed between the Thames, flowing to the west and the Ouse flowing to the east. To the west of Aylesbury the Portland Limestone creates an area of ridges and hills (Plate C2), including Muswell Hill, Brill, Ashendon, Pitchcott, and Lodge Hill at Waddesdon, which divide the western Vale into three parts. In earlier days this limestone was much used for building, and many boundary walls, cottages and even some churches and chapels remain to add character to the local villages. Occasionally massive fossils known as ammonites are found. (Fig. 2) In earlier times the Portland ridges became the natural choice for primitive east-west tracks, so avoiding the sticky clays of the lower land surrounding them. One such track is now the A418 linking Aylesbury and Thame.

We return to the influence of geology in chapter 19.

**Fig. 2: The Coiled Shell of an Ammonite**
The Ammonite was a common shellfish in the Mesozoic period, which began 225 million years ago. Ammonites had been extinct for 70 million years when the most primitive of early men appeared. The ammonite in our picture was found in a quarry at Stone, Bucks., and was built into the wall separating Hartwell Park from the A418. With a diameter of 18 inches it is quite a modest specimen: the largest are six feet in diameter.

## Chapter 1

## *EARLY TIMES*

The great Ice Age began roughly a million years ago. It was punctuated by warmer intervals, one of which alone extended over 190,000 years, during which Palaeolithic or **Old Stone Age** people roamed the land that is now Buckinghamshire. In the glacial deposits, and the river gravels of both the Thames and the Ouse, we find their bones and crude flint tools mixed with the bones of the animals upon which they preyed: the mammoth, (a large woolly elephant), hippopotamus, woolly rhinoceros, bison, deer and horse. These very primitive people also lived on the fruits, nuts, berries, leaves and fungi which they gathered from the forest. Because they could not fell the forest trees, or cultivate the land, any effect which they had on the landscape has been obliterated by time, and by the ice-sheets of later glaciations.[1]

About 10,000 years ago, when the ice sheets had receded, people once again occupied this area. At that time there was no English Channel: they just walked in. Theirs was still a Stone Age culture, and they were still hunters and gatherers, but over the millenia they had developed more effective weapons and tools: stone axes with which they could probably fell trees; adzes and chisels of antler and bone to work wood; sharp-edged flint scrapers for cleaning skins; choppers; and a variety of smaller flint tools. They are known as the Mesolithic or **Middle Stone Age** people. Their tools have been found at Bow Brickhill, one of the few Mesolithic sites known in Bucks..

During the fifth millenium BC they were gradually absorbed or supplanted by a new wave of immigrants. By this time the melting ice-sheets had raised sea levels, and the newcomers had to brave the English Channel. They brought with them livestock and seeds, and agricultural techniques first developed 2,000 years earlier in the Middle East. They still hunted and fished, but had domesticated sheep and cattle, and knew how to plough, select seed, sow, harvest, husk the grain, rub it between stones to make flour, and turn it into food. But, before crops could be sown, the forest had to be cleared. When the fertility of the clearing declined, more forest was cut down, while the original clearing reverted to scrub, and was used for grazing. Such groups were semi-permanent settlers for, in time, they had to move on to a fresh site, where the process was repeated. Eventually, it was discovered that manuring and fallowing would maintain fertility, and permanent villages were created. Over the millenia

**Fig. 3: An Iron-Age Roundhouse.**
This reconstruction at the Chiltern Open Museum was based on evidence from Iron-Age sites excavated at Puddlehill. More recent investigations during the building of the Stoke Hammond Bypass, have revealed post holes, pits, ditches and circular drip gullies (used to collect water from the rooves), all of which tend to justify such constructions.

this activity made significant changes in the landscape. Later immigrants included the Iberians (3000-2500 BC), whose much improved stone tools (ground and polished axes, borers, chisels, knives and scrapers) were the hallmark of these Neolithic or **New Stone Age** people. Most of their known Buckinghamshire sites are in the the south, but they have also been found at sites further north such as Wolverton, Whiteleaf and (probably) on Pitstone Hill. Quite recently neolithic flint axes were found at Stone and Hartwell.

Between about 2500 and 1600 BC they were supplanted by another wave of invaders, whose skilled use of bronze (especially for swords, axes, sickles, and arrows) marked the beginning of the **Bronze Age**. They also made decorated pots shaped like beakers, and so are known as the Beaker people. Hoards of used and broken tools and scrap metal have been found at Waddesdon, and much later at Aylesbury. There are over thirty of the round barrows which they used for burials in the Buckinghamshire part of the Ouse valley. About 600 BC the Celts began to arrive from central Europe, at first continuing in the use of bronze, but later using iron to make harder-wearing tools and sharper weapons, so ushering in the **Iron Age**, with a material which was appropriate to their war-like temperament. They occupied sites at Pitstone Hill, Boddington Hill (overlooking Wendover), Pulpit Hill (overlooking Askett) and Bledlow, while the intensive development of Milton Keynes has already revealed ten more sites, including a late Iron Age farm at Westcroft, occupied from around 100 BC to AD 50. More civilised Celtic tribes, known as the **Belgae**, first came from France circa 75 BC, bringing ploughs that could cultivate heavy soils. In 43 BC, almost a century after Julius Caesar's unsuccessful expeditions to Britain, more **Romans** arrived and stayed until AD 407. Evidence of their stay − scattered across the Vale and North Bucks − is increasing. It includes: the site of Magiovinium (a fort and small town at Bow Brickhill); the sites of villas; and a network of paths and tracks, including long-distance trade routes like Watling Street, and Akeman Street. [2] An excavation at Bierton in 1979[3] recovered such things as flue tiles from hypercausts, tesserae from a mosaic pavement, 15 pieces of Roman glass, and around 9,000 sherds of Roman pottery from platters, jars, beakers, bowls, flagons, lids and cups: see also Plate C7. Doubtless more sites will be found. The Romans also gave us a national identity: to them our land was Britannia and its people were Britons.

**Fig. 4: Iron-Age Saddle Quern c. 500 BC.**
The quern was found in Pitstone during ploughing. In use, grains of corn were put
on the large stone and then rubbed into powder (i.e. flour) by the small stone.

## THE ANGLO-SAXON INVASIONS

By the 4th century AD heathen Germanic tribesmen (Angles, Saxons, Jutes, and Frisians) collectively known as **Anglo-Saxons**, or just **Saxons**, had begun to arrive in Britain. Indeed, some came by invitation of the Roman authorities, who employed them as soldiers in return for land, on which they settled with their families, at Walton (now in Aylesbury) for instance. They replaced the Roman troops which were slowly being withdrawn to the continent, and helped to deal with the Saxon and Irish pirates, who raided the coasts of Britain, and the Picts and Scots who were creating havoc in northern Britain. These Saxon mercenaries and their families were relatively few in number, and appear to have lived peacefully alongside the Romano-British residents.

Then, from about AD 450, the number of Saxons arriving increased substantially. Unlike the pirates their main objective was not loot but land. And it was not a single, highly-organised invasion. For many years these fair-haired, blue-eyed raiders arrived on the east coast in their 'wave-horses' (Fig. 5), and established settlements. Many of the settlers were refugees due to the flooding of the coastlands of Friesland and Saxony, though others probably joined the movement out of sheer opportunism. For the whole venture (of attacking England) would attract the warrior classes, who may well have organised the shipment of the farming families which must have made up the bulk of the invaders. Young warriors especially would see the migration to Britain as an irresistible opportunity to acquire land for themselves at an earlier age than at home. From time to time, as more arrived, they would combine into a 'host' or armed band, that would move inland along the river valleys and, having found sufficient territory, would divide into smaller groups to settle the land for farming. It would have been extremely difficult for the untrained residents of peaceful farms and villages to resist these professionally trained warrior-raiders.[4] However, the Saxons did have to overcome local opposition, and at times fight against organised British forces.[5] Just before AD 500, the Britons inflicted a serious defeat on the Saxons at Mount Badon.[6] This slowed down the Saxon advance. Even so, within fifty years they had occupied parts of the Midlands, much of East Anglia, and large areas on the south coast, from which they had penetrated into the Upper Thames Valley.

Needing still more land for settlement, the Saxons moved into the area immediately north of the Chilterns. There is both archaeological and place-name evidence for the presence of Saxon settlers in the area in the first half of the 5th century, but it had remained essentially a British province.[7] The Britons fought to stem the invasion. They failed. In 571, Cutha (probably the brother of a Saxon king)[8] defeated the British at a battle near Bedford.[9] This victory began a campaign which eventually gave the Saxons control of a large area stretching westwards from Bedford to Eynsham near Oxford. Their new territory included Aylesbury, the Vale of Aylesbury, and the watershed between the River Ouse and the River Thame. Some of the defeated Britons escaped to the west, and some fled into the dense Chiltern woodlands. The remainder were either killed or

**Fig. 5: A Saxon Wave-Horse.**
They were up to 70 feet long and carried as many as 80 -100 people. The single mast carried a square sail, but the most reliable means of propulsion was the long sea oars, up to 16 pairs on the larger boats.

6

enslaved.[10] Fortunately, when developing a new area, the Saxons were short of labour, and thus were inclined to enslave the defeated Britons. Having acquired both land and slaves, the Saxon warriors rapidly switched to the clearing and cultivation of the land, and the erection of buildings. The result was *"a massive increase in new settlements in the late 6th century"*, which continued into the early 7th century.[11]

**Fig. 6: A Relic of the Wars.** An Early Saxon Spearhead found at Stone.

## THE ESTABLISHMENT AND EARLY DEVELOPMENT OF WING

Particular site features are important for the *establishment* of settlements. Thus easily cultivated and defended land particularly attracted early Saxon settlers, while a riverside site might appeal to Danes with their bias to boat transport. In practice many factors encouraged settlement: a junction of routes; a local source of stone or timber; a source of water power which could operate a mill; a pure and reliable supply of drinking water, etc., etc.. Table 1 indicates the variety of habitats which the Vale offered to early invaders.

The Saxon village of Wing appears to have been the first permanent settlement on that site, and (as Table 1 indicates) those early Saxons would have seen several factors in its favour. Largely on place-name evidence, it is thought that Wing – like Oving, Ivinghoe, Tyringham, Lillingstone and Buckingham – was settled at some time after AD 571 (when Saxons invaded the Eastern Vale), but no later than AD 650.[12]

All these names include a personal name combined with *inga* or *ingas* (the people of*)*: Oving is the place of *Ufa's People;* Ivinghoe is the *Spur of Ifa's People;* Buckingham is the *Meadow of Bucc's People;* and Wing combines *Wihthun* and *ingas* to form its ancient name *Wihthungas* meaning Wihthun's People.[15] The likelihood that the village of Wing did exist by the second half of the 7th century is strengthened by the possibility that Wing church existed by the late 7th or early 8th centuries. It was possibly the first stone church to be built in what was to become Buckinghamshire.[16] The church, its founders and its recently excavated Saxon graveyard (Figs. 7 and 8) are the main sources of information about early Wing. The establishment of its church, and the ambition and leadership of a royal tenant with a strong interest in that church illustrate one way in which a settlement could *develop* in Saxon times.

### The Founding of Wing Church

When persecution ended in the early 4th century, Christians on the continent began to build permanent churches for public worship, using a plan based upon the Roman basilica (law court). This usually consisted of a nave to accommodate the people, and at its eastern end an apse (a raised semi-circular or semi-polygonal area) for the judge. The religious version simply replaced the judge and his seat by the priest and his altar. This adaptation of a Roman building is not surprising. The influence of Rome on England's emergent Christianity was considerable. The Church of All Saints at Wing is the most complete and least changed of the basilican churches still in use in England. The question then arises, "Who founded Wing church?"

We elect Bishop Wilfrid (634-709), later canonised as Saint Wilfrid, for this role, but we agree with Jackson and Fletcher that *'speculation is all it can be'*.[17] But what a subject for speculation! For Wilfrid was a force majeure: perhaps the most militant missionary of his time. He was a powerful man: a Northumbrian nobleman; a friend of kings; a leader with a fine episcopal image, and a large retinue (said at one time to number 120) of armed supporters, including masons and artisans of almost every kind.[18] Consequently, the heads of many monasteries placed themselves under his protection, and accepted his 'rule',[19] which further increased his power. He was a very rich man: kings, noblemen, and abbots lavishly endowed him and his churches and monasteries with land and treasure. He had, therefore, not only the ambition but also the means to create institutions which would convert the heathen. And on two occasions Wilfrid was excellently placed (and in the right company) to add Wing to his monastic empire.

### Table 1 : Some Influences on Anglo-Saxon Settlement AD 500-650 [13]

| Settle-ment & O.S. ref. | Height over local base[14] | Nature of site Kms = kilometres | Arable hides 1086 | Special site factors |
|---|---|---|---|---|
| **Tetchwick** 42/6719 | 4 metres (13 feet) | On bottom contour of Sharpe's Hill, with marshy land stretching 6 kms to the west. Marshland discourages armed attacks. | 2 | Brook for water, & waste disposal. Transhumance possible between marshes (summer) and hills (winter). Woods for pigs (50 by Domesday). Fishing for eels? |
| **Bucking-ham** 42/6934 | At and above base level | Easily defended: on a hill almost surrounded by the river Ouse. Protects the upper Ouse valley. | 1 | Access to River Ouse & main routes to the upper Thames valley. Created as a major defensive site (buhr) by King Edward the Elder. |
| **Oving** 42/7821 | 50 metres (164 feet) | Hill-top site with the ground sloping away quite steeply on all sides. | 10 | Woods for pigs (200 by Domes-day). The Portland beds created fertile soils. Views on all sides gave protection from surprise attack. |
| **Wing** 42/8822 | 30 metres ( 98 feet) | Elevated tongue of land with cultivable land sloping gently into the Vale to the south and undulating land at a constant level to the north. | 5 kept low to favour royalty | Good views along and across the Vale protect from surprise attack. Water from headwaters of the Ouse. |
| **Ivinghoe** 42/9416 | 23 metres (76 feet) | At the junction of Icknield Way and Lower Icknield Way. On the springline at the base of the chalk. | 20 | Became a long narrow parish with Vale clay, chalk scarp and some dip slope, so crops, sheep & pigs possible (600 by Domesday). Increased fertility where chalk and sand washed down onto clay. |

The first occasion relies upon the fact that from 666-669 Wilfred was often invited by King Wulfhere, to visit Mercia,[20] the Saxon kingdom from which Buckinghamshire was later fashioned. Eddius Stephanus, Bishop Wilfred's biographer, tells us:

*This most kindly monarch, for the benefit of his soul, granted our bishop many pieces of land in various places, on which he founded monasteries for the servants of God.* [21]

Wing could well have been one of those pieces of land, because in the last years of his reign King Wulfhere was in firm occupation of the district which lies at the northern foot of the Chilterns.

He was also active within the area. So it was from Thame, at the western end of the Vale, that he issued the charter of Chertsey Abbey.[22] If the Church of All Saints really *was* founded by Wilfrid on King Wulfhere's land, it would mean that the building would have been completed at some time late in the seventh century.[23] The second occasion relies upon the fact that by 691 Wilfrid was back in Mercia for, after a long dispute with two Northumbrian kings, he had finally been expelled from their kingdoms.

> *For the next eleven years he lived under the protection of Aethelfred, King of Mercia, administering the whole Mercian diocese for a time . . . and he founded many monasteries in that country.* [24]

If Wing were one of these, its completion date would have been early in the 8th century.

At that time such churches were not parish churches as we understand them today. Known as minsters, they not only sheltered missionaries covering large regions, but also provided pastoral care and burial facilities for the villages and hamlets of a large surrounding area. So the feldcircans (field churches) were born.[25] At first they were just a space in the village where the villagers could gather, perhaps in the shelter of a spreading tree. For instance, at the deserted village of Burston (in the parish of Aston Abbotts) there is a bit of ground which has been

### The Excavation of a Saxon Graveyard at Wing.

**Fig. 7: Saxon Grave** with a child's skeleton on top of an adult's. Scientific analysis of the child's teeth and bones determined its age (12 years), sex (female), health (repeatedly ill) and approximate date of death (c. 1000 AD). The adult's death was much earlier. They were not related.

**Fig. 8: The Graveyard** is adjacent to the church of All Saints, and was previously part of its burial ground. In 1999 archaeologists excavated that part of the site which was to be developed for housing. The skeletal remains of 77 individuals were recovered from this area, which was utilised from the 8th century AD through to the early 13th century. However, in the 1850's other human skeletons had already been found during the building of a school.

known to generations of local people as the Hallowed Acre. Eventually a wooden or stone cross might be erected at such a spot. Here the priest would 'preach the Word of God . . . celebrate the heavenly mysteries, baptise, and teach the Creed and the Lord's prayer'.[26] However, for burial the villagers must carry the corpse, perhaps two miles or more, to the minster, for the feldcircan had no graveyard. Understandably, the hope of a joyous after-life, which Christianity offered, comforted the downtrodden, over-worked, half-starved, debilitated,[27] short-lived peasants. In time it even inspired their masters into acts of unexpected humanity, such as freeing slaves.

At or about this time minsters appear also to have been established at Aylesbury,[28] Haddenham and North Crawley,[29] each spawning a number of feldcircans in its surrounding area. In subsequent centuries the feldcircans gradually acquired churches, depending very much upon local ambitions. The first building would usually be small, which might mean a nave measuring no more than 25 feet by 13 feet as at Bradford-on-Avon (Wiltshire), or 24.5 by 14.5 ft. as at Escomb (County Durham): about the size of the living room in a modest modern house.[30] Many of these churches were built of wood, which is not surprising for a people whose economy relied so heavily on timber that their word for building was 'timbrian'. Over a thousand years later, not a single wooden church remains in the Vale or North Bucks.. Indeed, nationally, just one has survived: at Greensted-juxta-Ongar in Essex.[31] Not that the county's Saxon stone churches have fared much better. Locally, apart from Wing, Reed mentions only Hardwick, *"on the evidence of the double-splayed, round-headed window over the north door"*, and Lavendon for *"the lower part of the west tower and the main walls of the nave"*.[32]

## THE DANISH INVASIONS OF THE 9TH TO 11TH CENTURIES

Anglo-Saxon England was an age of warfare and everyday violence. By AD 600 Romano-Britain had been invaded by Angles, Saxons and Jutes, who divided the land into separate kingdoms (Map 2). Their kings were forever doing battle: with one another; with ambitious subjects who coveted their kingdoms; and for nearly two centuries with the raids and invasions of the Danes.

### 835 - 878: The Early Battles and the Creation of the Danelaw

The Danes repeatedly raided England, principally for loot and slaves, but sometimes to settle. Finally, in 865, they landed their Great Army and full-scale war began. By this time the residents (the Angles, Saxons and Jutes) were beginning to construct a common identity as *'the English'*. Unfortunately, instead of uniting against the Danes, they fought them kingdom by kingdom. Consequently, by 874 the Danes had conquered not only much of Eastern England, but also southern Mercia (including the future Buckinghamshire), and much of Wessex. With no frontier to contain them, they then roamed around England at will, living off the land, carrying off anything which would show a profit, and challenging English forces wherever they found them. Unfortunately, southern Mercia was astride the route of the Danish armies, and suffered accordingly, as the Anglo-Saxon Chronicle (ASC) confirms.

> *Then in the harvest season the (Danish) army went into Mercia and shared out some of it (ASC 877); the (Danish) army harried all over Mercia until they reached Cricklade (ASC 903); then the Danish army went into Mercia, slaying and burning whatever was in their path. (ASC 1016)*

Because they were accustomed to success in battle, the Danes seriously underestimated the skills and tenacity of the Royal House of Wessex. Consequently, the Saxons were increasingly victorious. Alfred the Great (reigned 871-899), king of Wessex, (Fig. 9) was an exceptional man. He codified laws, translated books from the Latin, and designed the ships which provided England's first navy. He also created the Saxon buhrs (fortified towns), and planned the details of their manning. His skilful diplomacy sometimes won over defeated enemies, who had expected to be slaughtered.

For instance, in 878, when King Alfred decisively defeated the main Danish army under King Guthrum at Eddington (in Berkshire), he introduced Guthrum to Christianity, arranged his baptism, and persuaded him to retire eastwards behind an agreed frontier. This ran from London to Chester, much of it along Watling Street. (Map 2) Alfred recognised the large territory north and east of that line as Danish, and it was later called the Danelaw. Guthrum agreed to share out this land, and to settle his army down to farming. This agreement became known as the Treaty of Wedmore. In the 9th to the 11th centuries national frontiers were still very variable, so map 2 shows only the approximate location of Mercia. It was probably the early 11th century before the Midland shires were named and their boundaries determined. However, for convenience, we refer to south-eastern Mercia as Buckinghamshire, as though it really did exist throughout the Danish wars.

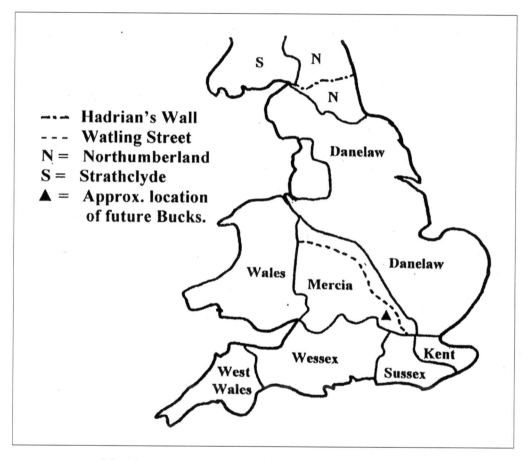

**Map 2: The Danelaw and British Kingdoms - Late 800's**

### 1878 - 906: A Sort of Respite

By 880 Guthrum's army did return to East Anglia, and settle down to farming. However, the new frontier brought the Danes too close for comfort: only twenty miles from English villages like Wing and Ivinghoe in the eastern Vale. For seasoned fighters from the temporarily redundant Danish army, these were trivial distances for raiding parties looking for some prime beef, horses, women, slaves and a good bonfire to round off the evening's entertainment. A second Danish army moved to the continent until 892, when it returned to England and resumed hostilities, harrying all over Mercia and causing havoc as far west as Wessex itself. However, with Alfred leading the English, the Danes were often defeated. For instance, in 893:

*The English overtook the Danish army . . . . and besieged it on every side in a fortress for many weeks . . . and the besieged were oppressed by famine and had eaten the greater part of their horses, and the rest (of the horses) had died of starvation. Then the Danes came out and fought . . . and a very great slaughter of the Danes was made. (ASC)*

After King Alfred's death in 899 the second Danish army – quite contrary to the Wedmore Treaty – advanced westwards towards the Vale, and also into northern Buckinghamshire. In 906 by the Treaty of Yttingaford (then 'the ford of Ytta's people', now Tiddenfoot just south of modern Linslade) King Edward (Alfred's son) appears to have accepted the Danes' occupation of west Bedfordshire, probably in return for Danish territory in north-east Buckinghamshire.[33]

## 906-24: the Buhrs Outwit the Danes.
## Alfred's Progeny Rule England

**Fig. 9: Alfred the Great:**
reigned 871-899

By 917 King Alfred and his son Edward had completed a long line of forts, known as buhrs. They stretched from North Cheshire to Essex, and formed a defence against Danish attacks by blocking important routes, and providing launching points for raiding parties and longer campaigns.[34] For example, the buhr at Wallingford helped to guard the western route into the Vale of Aylesbury. The site was roughly rectangular and guarded on three sides by ten foot high earthen ramparts and a deep ditch, while the Thames formed the fourth side. See also Chapter 4. The buhrs were usually large as they had to shelter the population of the surrounding countryside. At Buckingham 1600 men were required just to man its 2200 yards of fortifications, and that force required a large hinterland to provide both the men, and the provisions to sustain them. For peasants, often on the verge of starvation, and already occupied by hard physical labour throughout every hour of daylight, such additional demands were extremely difficult to meet. Moreover, when roads were at best signless earthen tracks, practically impassable in winter, and bullock carts were the ultimate in bulk transport, the problems of assembling men, materials, tools, food and weapons at any given point were formidable. This hinterland, with Buckingham as its administrative centre, was the nucleus of the future Buckinghamshire. Buckingham's two forts were deliberately located to block land and river traffic moving south-westwards along the Ouse valley, while the fortifications at Towcester blocked the route southwards down Watling Street.

*The (Danish) armies broke the peace and went to Towcester intending to take it by storm, but the people . . . inside defended it until more help came. The Danes then abandoned the town and went away. But soon after that they went out at night for plunder, and came upon unprepared men and captured no small number of men and cattle, between Bernwood Forest and Aylesbury. (ASC 917)*

Despite such occasional setbacks, by the time of King Edward's death in 924 all Danish territory south of the Humber was subservient to the Royal House of Wessex. When, in 937, the Danes decided to test the strength of the English, the men of Wessex led by two of Alfred's grandchildren, completely defeated them.

*King Athelstan and his brother Edmund won by the sword's edge undying glory in battle round Brunanburh. Their enemies perished. The field grew dark with the blood of men. The whole day long the men of Wessex with mounted companies kept in pursuit of the hostile peoples. Grievously they cut down the fugitives from behind with their whetted swords. They left behind them the black raven with its horned beak, to share the corpses, and the white-tailed eagle to enjoy the carrion. Never in this island before this was a greater slaughter of a host made by the sword. (ASC 937)*

A long period of peace followed.

### 980 - 1042: England Becomes a Danish Province

Then in 980 the Danish raids re-started in earnest. Once more Danish and English armies criss-crossed the country, both living off the poor peasants' livestock, corn, seed corn and hay without which famine and disease would decimate them. Even that was not the worst, for in a brutal age the Danes were simply better brutes. They were often fired by a blood lust, when whole villages were torched, and men, women and children killed, just because they were in the path of the army. The Danish raids became bigger, and culminated in 1013 in a full-scale invasion by Canute and his father Sweyn Forkbeard, who was now determined to become King of England, and:

*all (the English) submitted to Sweyn and all the nation regarded him as full king. (ASC 1013)*

Eventually, in 1014 Sweyn died and Canute succeeded him. The English tried to regain power but (after a long and bitter campaign) were completely defeated at Abingdon in 1016. By this time the English were so disillusioned with their own king (Ethelred 'The Unready'), and by the Danes repeated demands for Danegeld, that they accepted Canute as King of all England, and for the next eighteen years he brought peace to the war-weary, and impoverished English. He also restored their ancient laws, and respected their religion. The peace continued for thirty years after Canute's death in 1035. A strong king was needed to avoid further chaos. Instead England got Edward the Confessor (1042–66).

## WING BECOMES THE CENTRE OF A ROYAL ESTATE

It seems that since King Wulfhere's time the estate at Wing had remained in royal hands for, by 957, it was one of the estates of the Lady Elgiva, the estranged wife of the adulterous and ineffectual King Edwy (955-959). On his death in 959 it is believed that she retired to Wing. However, she was still the sister-in-law of Edwy's successor, King Edgar (959-975), who in 966 added Linslade and Murren (in Oxfordshire) to her extensive estates.

Elgiva (Aelfgyfu, meaning Elf-gift or Elf-grace in Anglo-Saxon) is credited with the restoration and enlargement of the minster at Wing.: see Plates C3 and C4 and Figs. 10, 11, 12 and 13. This is possible as the work has been attributed to the 10th century, and Elgiva's estate provided the wealth to fund such an expensive project. Elgiva's wealth was partly due to her extensive estates (approximately 28,000 acres) and the fact that she actively encouraged their development; and partly because – presumably as a matter of royal policy – Wing and Chesham were considerably under-taxed, while after 966 Linslade was exempt from *'all secular burdens'*, except military service and the repair of bridges and fortresses.[35] Elgiva may also have promoted both industry and agriculture on some of her estates.[36] Of the five manors in Buckinghamshire where the Domesday Survey of 1086 mentions the production of iron ploughshares, three (Chesham, Wing and Bledlow) had belonged to Elgiva. It may be that the diversion of the River Chess at Chesham, to operate a water mill, was initiated by her, and another source of her wealth.[37]

Certainly the restoration catered for the attendance at the church of someone of high social position, for two ancient doorways pierce the western ends of the north and south walls at a height of about sixteen feet. It is quite possible that these elevated doorways once gave access

**Fig 10: The Church of All Saints, Wing**

Everything of the building that you see in this photograph is Saxon and at least a thousand years old. Only the outer wall of the south aisle (just visible through the massive arches on the right) and the tower are younger, dating from the 14th and 15th centuries respectively. The great chancel arch (21 feet wide) is also Saxon, as is the double window above it, with arches of Roman tiles. Beneath the chancel arch is a much later screen supporting the 'rood' or cross. Just before the screen are the steps which give access to the chancel and its altar. In Saxon times, on either side of these steps, were steps leading down into the crypt. The Anglo-Saxons were fond of small cosy apartments attached to their churches: porticos leading from the nave; upstairs chapels; crypts; and rooms in the tower.[38]

to a gallery at the rear of Wing church to enable the Lady Elgiva to attend divine service without rubbing shoulders with the local peasants (Fig.11).The Wing minster's crypt also provided a suitable place to display her halidom (collection of relics), and being beneath the chancel, with access from the nave, it was ideally suited to this: Figs.12 and 13. Like most benefactors she sought salvation for her soul, and the restoration of a minster, especially with attractions for pilgrims, was one way of gaining merit.[39] In addition, in her will (in the form of a plea to her Royal Lord) she left her precious halidom to her mentor Bishop Ethelwold, the primate of Winchester cathedral, and also bequeathed much property to the church. This included (to Winchester cathedral) all *"the land at Risborough just as it stands save that...they free in every hamlet every penally enslaved man who was enslaved under me"*. Her conscience was ahead of her time, but seems to have established a precedent, for although enslavement continued, others followed her example.

## WING'S DEVELOPMENT & THE POSSIBLE ORIGIN OF WINGRAVE

Minster churches often provided training and education for the Christian ministry.[40] If this is what happened at Wing, then its resident population would be increased by the missionaries, the monks, their novices and those who served them. The population might also have increased temporarily for the celebration of the major Christian festivals, especially Easter, which was regarded as the correct time for Christian initiation. If the church possessed highly regarded relics, then lords and rustics alike might arrive from afar, looking for both food and lodging. The Lady Elgiva's decision to settle in Wing would also have substantially increased its resident population, for a person of her rank, wealth and enterprise would require a household of some size: domestic servants such as maids, stable boys, hostlers, butlers, table waiters, cooks, etc; workmen; a steward; reeves; a personal priest; clerks and so on. Some of these would be recruited locally, bringing unexpected job opportunities to the village, whereas others would be brought in from Wessex. There would also be

**Fig 11: Elgiva's Entrance to All Saints, Wing**

visitors to house, feed and entertain for social, business and religious purposes.

If Elgiva's precious relics were installed in the crypt (the relics of a member of the Royal Family, remember!) a steady flow of pilgrims was likely for, in an era rife with superstition and pestered by elves, spirits and devils, relics were a source of both mental and physical consolation especially

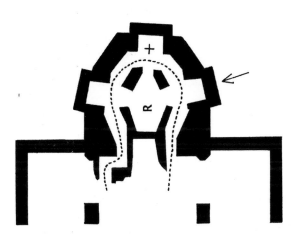

**Fig. 12: Plan of Saxon Crypt at All Saints' Church, Wing** (note 39)

\----- Route of medieval Processions
R = Display of Relics
+ = Position of camera for Plate C4
→ = Modern entry from churchyard

for the sick, the injured, the deformed, and those troubled by conscience or thoughts of death. A touch was preferable, but even the sight of a piece of 'the true cross', a thorn from *His* crown, a bone or a piece of the shroud from the burial of a saint or a martyr: what hopes they raised! what favours they might bestow!

At Wing the pilgrims descended into the crypt by a short flight of stairs at the eastern end of the nave. A semi-circular corridor (the ambulatory) gave them three glimpses of the relics, after which a second short flight of stairs returned them to the nave. Alternatively, a procession of clerics could emerge up into the nave, carrying the most important relics and other treasures, and proceed around the crowded nave before descending back into the crypt by its second stairway. All this would yield a triple benefit: the possible remission of the

**Fig. 13: Saxon Crypt below the Apse at All Saints, Wing**
The pilgrims would enter the crypt from the entreme left and get their first view of the relics through the arch nearest the camera. They would then follow the broken line on the plan of the crypt (Fig. 12) and obtain two more views of the relics before returning to the nave by a second staircase.

pilgrims' sins or ills; the receipt by the minster of the pilgrims' offerings; and a market for the food and services of the villagers.

An increased demand for food by the minster, its pilgrims and the royal household could only be satisfied by enlarging the farming area. Eventually, this could mean that the furthest strips in the great fields surrounding Wing were sufficiently distant to justify the establishment of a temporary settlement. Baines[41] speculates that an area on the edge of Elgiva's estate at Princes Risborough was cleared of woodland and scrub as a by-product of herding swine, and later settled. He bases this idea on the fact that the area's present name of Loosley Row is derived from the Saxon *hlos-leah,* which translates into *pigsty clearing*. The Grove of Wihthun's People (later to become Wingrave) would have been suitable for such treatment. To cultivate it in the absence of such a satellite, residents of Wing would have had to make a return journey of about five miles: at least two hours' time, if leading plough-oxen. Notice that Wingrave church is not central in its parish: only half a mile from its eastern boundary (i.e. with Wing), yet a good two miles from its western boundary. This minimising of the mileage between Wingrave and Wing is consistent with the assumption that they were closely related in those early times.

Pigs were perennially herded in woodland in the Autumn, when the fruit of the oak, beech, chestnut and other trees and shrubs provided fodder. In other seasons their search for food could well prepare an area for later clearance. Trees would become rubbing posts, which the pigs' strong chines would soon clear of their bark until the trees were ringed and so killed. Saplings and shrubs would meet the same fate by uprooting, and the stripping of their new leaves and tender young shoots. Eventually, the whole land surface would be effectively ploughed by the routing of porcine snouts. Anyone doubting this should take a look at modern pigs in action.

At this time, Wingrave would be merely a huddle of shelters which would be almost entirely roof, being built from saplings in the shape of a modern ridge tent. First two stout poles, each topped by a fork would be driven into the ground. They would be linked by another substantial pole which would form the ridge. On either side lighter poles would slope from the ridge down to the ground. This framework would be held together by lashings. Finally, on both sides, flexible twiggy branches would be threaded between these sloping poles to support a thatch of whatever was available: reeds, straw, grass or sods of turf. (Fig. 14) In time such an outpost could well develop into a permanent

**Fig. 14: A Primitive Rustic Shelter.**
Our nomadic ancesters used such shelters, after they changed from hunters to farmers or herdsmen.

settlement, and it is *possible* that Wingrave developed in this way, encouraged by the site's natural advantages. Its hill-top position provided good views of surroundings should strangers approach. The hill is heavy gault clay in the form of a shallow basin, which is infilled and capped by lighter glacial deposits of sand, pebbles and boulder clay. In wet seasons this infill becomes saturated with water until it reaches the edges of the basin, when it overflows as springs. Such a formation creates a high water table on the top of the hill, so that shallow wells for drinking water, and ponds for watering cattle can easily be constructed. (Fig. 15) So the hill-top has what the Saxon settler would regard as a magical combination of good access to water yet good drainage when there is persistent rainfall. Also, although the Saxons had ploughs which could cultivate the heavy clays of the Vale, they preferred the gently sloping, better-drained land and lighter gravelly soils such as are found on hill-top Wingrave,[42] these being more easily cleared and worked. From Wingrave there was easy access to the forest of the Vale, and when this was cleared the clay

## Fig 15: Section - The Hollow on the Hill at Wingrave.

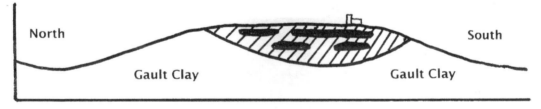

/// Light brown boulder clay with sands and gravels
▬▬ Mainly water-bearing sands and gravels

soil sustained good meadowland, while the floodplain of the Thistlebrook provided valuable water meadows. The Thistlebrook and other streams helped to define the parish boundaries, so avoiding disputes with neighbours. Our timing for the emergence of Wingrave is consistent with a chronology of settlement development suggested by Christopher Taylor in Local Historian.[43] He sees the 9th century as the *beginning* of a secondary expansion of settlement, including new

17

hamlets and villages.

**The Church of All Saints at Wing is well worth visiting**, but the crypt is open only on special occasions, or by special arrangement.

## *THE SHIRES AND THE HUNDREDS*

The shires go back well into the Dark Ages. Those of the midland shires, including Buckinghamshire, were laid out between 900 and 1016. The shires were sub-divided into smaller districts called hundreds. Each hundred held moots (meetings or courts) which were attended by the representatives from the area of the hundred.[44] These usually took place on rough benches around a table in the open air at regular intervals of 4 weeks. The Cottesloe Hundred covered the north-eastern part of the Vale and included Soulbury, Linslade, Grove, Mentmore, Wingrave, Aston Abbotts, Hardwick with Weedon, Whitchurch, Creslow, Cublington, and Wing. The meeting was probably on what is now the remnants of the main runway of the wartime airport at Cublington. It offered pleasant views on a nice summer's day, but in poor weather was a bleak, windswept spot. Not so bad if you came from nearby Wing, but an eight-mile round trip across the local clay if you lived in Hardwick. The moot discussed and tried to resolve local problems, and especially inter-village disputes. Boundaries were a perennial problem. Almost all were written, not drawn. The writer of the Linslade charter of 966 was fortunate as the boundary followed the River Ousel for half its length and so could easily be described by the Saxon *"andlang ea"* (along the river). However, the rest of the boundary ran through open country and had to be described by its natural features: *"to tumbaldes treowe"* (to Tunbeald's tree); *"to pam ealdan dic"* (to the old dyke); *"of seofon hlawan to pan anum hlawe"* (from seven mounds to the one mound).[45] This may have sounded reasonable at the time, but charters often lasted for many lives, by which time Tunbeald would be dead, the river could have changed its course, and the mounds (possibly burial mounds) might have increased in number.

The Hundred Moot was also the local law court where a man could be accused, defended and judged for his alleged misdeeds. The verdict would be determined by the cries of *"Ja! Ja!"* or *"Nay! Nay!"* from the onlookers. If judged guilty, the punishment was usually a fine, but for serious offences such as arson, slander and banditry, the penalties inflicted put most violent videos into the realm of fairy tales. For example, King Edmund required local posses to hunt down bandits, hang the leaders out of hand, flog the rest three times, scalp them and cut their little fingers off.[46] It was important, when mutilating a slave, not to deprive the owner of his usefulness!

## Chapter 2

## *AN ANGLO-SAXON VILLAGE*

The charters of the mid 10th century prove the existence of innumerable villages with a distribution in the Midlands and South little different from that later recorded at Domesday. So the Vale villages were probably typical Saxon villages, with open-field subsistence farming under a lord as the norm.

### *WINGRAVE IN THE REIGN OF KING EDWARD THE CONFESSOR 1042-1066*

Even if our supposition in chapter one that Wingrave developed as an off-shoot of Wing is correct, we still do not know exactly *when* Wingrave became independent. We cannot even be sure when Wingrave first acquired a church of its own, because a village could practise its faith without one. Wingrave could have been served for many years by priests from Wing, or even Aylesbury, providing Mass in the open air.

In her will Elgiva left Wing (including Wingrave) to King Edgar (959-975) and it appears to have remained in his family until the time of Edward the Confessor (1042-1066). Eventually, he gave Wing to a nephew, identified in Domesday Book as Young Edward, and treated Wingrave as a separate property. This was certainly before 1052, for Domesday Book makes it clear that by the time of Swein Godwine (see below), a landlord who died in that year, Wingrave was definitely an independent village.

At the beginning of King Edward's reign just three people owned the whole of Wingrave's arable land. King Edward himself held 720 acres, while Edith his Queen held a further 600. The remaining 480 acres were held by Brictric, who is described in Domesday Book as a thane of King Edward.[1] We don't know just how Brictric managed to acquire so much land, especially as he was only a thane, which was a higher social standing than that of a ceorl or ordinary freeman, but several grades below an earl. It is extremely unlikely that the peasants of Wingrave ever saw persons of such high social rank. King Edward was totally preoccupied with national and international affairs. Early in his reign, he had granted his holding in Wingrave to one of his knights, called Swein.[2] Swein was the eldest son of Godwine, Earl of Wessex, who was also the father of Queen Edith. This made Swein the brother of Queen Edith and the brother-in-law of King Edward, relationships which alone could account for the gift of land from Edward, and the earldom which Edward granted him in 1043. There is no record as to exactly how Swein dealt with this acreage. He could have sub-let it, or employed someone to manage it. One thing is certain. Whoever was responsible for his Wingrave holding would have had to apply substantial pressure on Wingrave's peasants, if the results of their efforts were to satisfy such an intolerant master. Provided they did, Swein would have had little time for Wingrave. This could only have been Wingrave's good fortune, for he was a murderous ruffian, whom King Edward eventually denounced in the Viking manner as *"nithing"* (a villain of the lowest type), and banished from the kingdom on three occasions[3] for such crimes as the murder of his cousin Earl Beorn, and the seduction of Eadgifu, the Abbess of Leominster. For quite different reasons Queen Edith would also not have been personally involved in Wingrave. For as well as her royal duties and lands in Buckinghamshire, Berkshire, Devonshire and Somerset, she held Winchester and Exeter. Significantly, she ignored her brother, Swein, and granted her 600 acres in Wingrave to Brictric, thus raising his holding to 1080 acres, and making him (for a time) the largest landholder in the village. He may well have been the same man as the Brictric who had 28 other holdings in Buckinghamshire.[4] If so, in that shire alone he would have occupied over 12,000 acres.

**Fig. 16: The Principal Holders (in bold) of Land at Wingrave in King Edward's Reign**

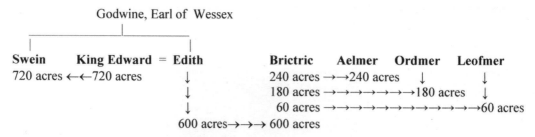

The 600 acres which Brictric received from Queen Edith was a dispensation from royal hands, a social level at which literacy *did* exist. So the occasion of the grant would probably have been evidenced by a writ or a charter, and there would also have been some sort of ceremony. Exactly what was included in the ceremony would depend upon the social standing of the main participants, and the nature of the gift. In Brictric's case Queen Edith and some of her thanes would assemble, and Brictric (probably with one or two of his supporters) would be called before them. The writ or charter or some other explanation of the occasion would be read out. We know that Brictric was receiving an outright gift of freehold property (as opposed to a tenancy), because Domesday Book tells us that 'He could sell'. So there would then be a short ceremony known as seisin, or taking possession, in which Brictric would receive a token of the gift from the Queen. In such elevated circles a dagger seems to have been popular for this purpose. Next a curse would be pronounced on anyone acting against the gift, with the assembled company chorusing, "*Sy hyt swa, amen, amen*". ("*So let it be, amen, amen.*") Domesday Book describes Brictric as '*Queen Edith's man*', so we can be sure that there was also a ceremony called homage, when Brictric would kneel before the Queen, place his hands between hers, and declare himself to be 'her man'. After this she would raise him to his feet, and he would then take an oath of fealty (loyalty) by swearing on the Bible,[5] or on some holy relic, that he would keep the faith which he had pledged.

These ceremonies were intended to publicise the Queen's action and the indebtedness of the vassal, though in Saxon times exactly what was owed was often rather vague. It might be a month's guard duty from time to time, quite possibly carried out by a substitute who was paid by the vassal; or visiting the Queen's estates, prior to a forthcoming royal visit; or accompanying her on actual visits; or by providing specified items of food for the royal larder; etc., etc..

Such indebtedness was also expressed at lower levels in the social hierarchy. For instance, Brictric gifted his original 480 acres in Wingrave to three Saxons of lesser status: Aelmer (240 acres), Ordmer (180 acres) and Leofmer (60 acres).[6] We know that these were gifts, because in each case Domesday tells us that the new occupier '*could sell*'. We also know that although they were gifts, the recipients still had obligations to fulfill to Brictric, because Domesday tells us that each of the new occupiers was still 'Brictric's man'. So, once more, there would be the short ceremonies of seisin in the presence of witnesses, probably including some of the villagers. In addition, as a visible gesture of good faith that the customary obligations would be observed by both parties, a knife might be exchanged. The new occupiers' obligations to Brictric might include ensuring: that the traditional requirements to contribute to local defence, and to maintain local bridges were encouraged; that law and order were preserved on their manors; that significant contributions were made to Brictric's larder and/or purse; and that there was cooperation with the authorities when danegeld was collected. Each of the new occupiers might work the land himself, or he might sub-let it. Aelmer, for instance, with at least 405 acres (240 at Wingrave **+** 165

**C1: Sheep on Lines Hill in the Eastern Vale**

Lines Hill near Aston Abbotts is one of the "huddle of hills" mentioned in the text. Viewed across 5 miles of Vale countryside, the hills on the skyline are considerably diminished. In fact, they are the Chilterns and rise nearly 600 feet above the floor of the Vale. The dip in the hills on the right of the picture is the Wendover Gap.

**C2: Sheep on the Portland Ridges in the Western Vale**

The sheep in the foreground are grazing on one of the ridges. Beyond is a strip of low 'Vale land'. Beyond is another ridge followed by more low land, with the Chilterns just a grey smudge on the horizon.

**C3: The Church of All Saints, Wing**

That part of the church on the right is a complete Saxon Apse. The upper part serves as the Chancel. Beneath it is an elaborate crypt, now entered from the churchyard, using the steps on the left of C4.

**C4: The Crypt of Wing Church: View from the East**

See also Chapter 1 and fig. 13.

**C5: The Church of St Michael, Stewkley – the West Doorway**

The doorway is typical of Norman masonry at its best. Look out for spiral ornament and chevron carving around the central doorway supplemented by birds, animals and dragons. See also Chapter 4 and figure 23.

**C6: St. Martin's Church, Dunton – the Norman Nave**

When visiting the nave, notice the Norman font, and the small - but definitely Norman - windows.

**C7: Roman Pottery (courtesy of the Ashmolean Museum, Oxford)**
The display includes urns, vases and amphorae unearthed at various locations at Stone.

### C8: The Norman Invasion
The Norman army with its horses and armour crossed the English Channel in small open boats and landed unopposed at Pevensey. They were confronted by - and defeated - the English army at Senlac, near Hastings.

at Soulbury, where he was already a reliable sub-tenant of Brictric's land) might well sub-let. If so, then it would again be evidenced before the villagers. Maybe a sod of turf would be dug out and turned over, sufficient to remind the new tenant and the gawping peasants that this was a serious bargain and both parties must keep to their obligations. Aelmer, as lord of the manor, must provide security and protection for his peasants by maintaining law and order on his acres, and contributing to local defence. The peasants' rent in labour and goods was considerable. However, with widespread lawlessness, and the tenancy of land bringing social and economic status many peasants may well have viewed such arrangements as a reasonable bargain.

We have now reached the peasants who actually toiled on the land, and had not only to maintain both themselves and their families, but also the layers of middlemen above them. The peasants came in four varieties: the free men; the villeins; the cottars; and the slaves. The free men were not numerous. They were not bound to the manor, and this freedom of movement was their outstanding characteristic. The Buckinghamshire Domesday ignored them, and so shall we. The villeins, (a term for peasants which the latest edition of Domesday translates as villagers) were a majority of the peasants. They and their descendants were bound to the manor for life, unless their lord gave them permission to leave, which was unlikely. The land which they farmed (typically 15 to 30 acres) was 'rented' from their lord. The cottars, whom the latest Domesday calls smallholders, usually had a toft (large garden) attached to their cottage, and up to five acres in the open fields, but they eked out a living mainly by labouring for the more affluent tenants. The slaves were generally unpopular. They ate so heartily that the other villagers called them loaf-eaters, which was soon shortened to loafers, a term still used to describe the idle. After Domesday little is heard of them, and they were probably promoted to cottager status, when they would have to work or go hungry.

### *THE MANAGEMENT OF ESTATES IN ANGLO-SAXON TIMES*

At least as early as Athelstan's reign (925-940) Saxon kings employed men that they called reeves in the control of the shires. The reeve had many duties. He assisted the ealdorman responsible for the shire, when he was known as the shire-reeve, later contracted to sheriff. He investigated claims that cattle had been stolen, supervised moneyers, dealt with powerful wrongdoers, etc., and one of his most important tasks was to manage the royal estates in that shire. The advantage of having a functionary to cope with this work was quickly appreciated by the king's tenants-in-chief, and copied by *their* tenants, and the holders of land in general.[7] As the centuries passed, this function became the reeves' most important task. So much so that by the early 11th century a short tract entitled 'Be Gesceadwisan Gerefan' (On the Competent Reeve) describes the reeve as the steward of an estate responsible for the availability of tools, and supervision of the year's work. Indeed, it has been claimed that by this time, *"each estate had its reeve or steward"*.[8]

There is no evidence that Brictric sub-let his 600 acres at Wingrave, but even if it were his sole holding, and even if he felt qualified to do the work, he would certainly have employed a reeve to manage the farm overall and probably someone to assist the reeve in supervising the labour. One of the great advantages of a substantial land holding was the fact that you did not have to rise at dawn and work until dusk, or do really hard physical work in all weathers whatever the state of your health. Moreover, if Brictric's Buckinghamshire estates really did exceed 12,000 acres he would certainly have employed a reeve who would have had overall responsibility for the management of the estate, and from experience would soon notice if a particular holding was not producing an appropriate income, and what needed to be done to remedy the matter.

As the centuries rolled by, estate management underwent considerable development, and even the nomenclature changed, as Chapter 7 will show.

## ANGLO-SAXON FARMING

Archaeological digs make it certain that the dominant occupation of the Buckinghamshire Saxon was farming. For instance, at Walton in Aylesbury, the bones of sheep, pigs, oxen, fowl and a few horses were found, together with quern stones for hand-grinding corn, and spindle whorls for spinning wool and flax. However, there is still much about which we are ignorant or uncertain.

For instance, over most of central England the regular hedged and fenced fields that we see today are the product of parliamentary enclosure in the 18th and 19th centuries, and are thus relatively modern. However, this landscape is underlain by an earlier one which is the product of open-field agriculture, and characterised by the ridge and furrow of medieval strip ploughing. A good deal of ridge and furrow is still visible in the Vale and North Bucks.. Notice how often the line of 'modern' hedges clashes with the ancient ridge and furrow. Much blood, sweat and candle-grease has been expended in an effort to explain the origin and early development of open-field agriculture, but so far no consensus has been reached. Rowley rejects the idea that the open-field system was imported by Anglo-Saxon immigrants and points to the influence of Celtic and Romano-British field systems. Stenton sees much that is *of obvious Germanic origin*. Loyn, examining the same problem more cautiously, simply concludes, *"The evidence for the existence of open-field farming in Anglo-Saxon England is overwhelming, and for early Anglo-Saxon England it is strong."* [9]

### The Subsistence Economy

The use of money had increased in late Anglo-Saxon times, partly due to King Edward's reform of the coinage, round about 975. Nevertheless, the farmer's principal aim was subsistence: the feeding and clothing of his family over the coming year. He might not have a surplus which could be marketed, or a market in which to exchange a surplus for cash. So, at local level much was bartered. Thus the lord, on whose land the village was situated, provided his peasants with a house, garden and some strips of land scattered across the two open fields surrounding the village. In return the peasant provided his lord with a 'rent' calculated in labour, or goods and labour. So a villager's rent might be two or three days' labour per week, at whatever the lord required. A specified amount of ploughing, harrowing, sowing, and threshing were likely tasks, and at haymaking and harvest the lord would require extra work. This boonwork might extend to four or five days per week just when the villager's own land needed his attention. On another manor the villagers' 'rent' might be payable partly in labour and partly in kind. Perhaps four days per week at boon times and 3 days of work per week for the rest of the year; plus twenty sesters of barley and two hens at Martinmas; and one lamb at Easter. Few cases have been recorded where cash was involved. [10] Even a peasant with several strong sons, would not find it easy to fulfil his commitment to his lord *and* maintain his family. The smallholder's burden would be smaller, but still heavy. These were pretty hefty 'rents', and when the Normans arrived they became even heftier!

### Open-field Farming

In late Saxon times the arable land around the village was divided into just two very large unfenced fields. Each year one field would be sown with crops, of which wheat (for bread), barley (for ale), and peas and beans (for the pot) were the most important. The other field would be fallowed i.e. rested, and twice ploughed. Before the plowing started, this fallow field would be open to all the villagers' animals, not only to economise on the use of precious hay by grazing the stubble and weeds, but also to add their manure, which would raise the fertility of the soil. First of all, a year's accumulated muck from the rakings of the ox-stalls, the styes and the lord's stable was carted onto the fields. Later in the year the first ploughing would turn in the manure, the stubble and roots of the previous year's crop, and the remains of the weeds. This first ploughing had to be done in time to let the buried material rot, and to let the rain and the frost break down the clods of soil left by the ploughing, while the roots of peas and beans would add nitrates. Not that the value of nitrates was realised until the 17th and 18th centuries; in earlier times there was just a suspicion that buried roots were 'a good thing'. The decomposed weeds would also increase the soil's ability to retain both moisture, and the minerals in the urine of pasturing animals. The second ploughing, followed by a harrowing, was to reduce the soil to a fine tilth in preparation for seeding. In the following year this fallow field was sown, and the field which had been cropped was fallowed and twice ploughed. This alternation continued, year in, year out, over the centuries.

Each of the large fields was first divided into blocks called furlongs, and then further divided into long, narrow, unfenced and unhedged strips (see chap. 11) separated from each other only by grassy banks sufficient in width to provide access for men, carts and ploughs. In theory, each plot was one acre (220 yards by 22 yards), but in practice the medieval 'acre' was variable both in size and shape. A family's holding consisted of plots scattered around the large fields so as to give each family an equal proportion of cropland and fallow, and a fair share of the varying soils, aspects and distances from the village. The principal landholder was the lord of the manor, who might cultivate 40% or 50% of the arable with the labour of the villagers and smallholders. [11]

### The Ploughing Problems

Two factors determined the acreage to be ploughed: the villagers' need for food; and the number of plough-teams which could be provided. This depended upon the number of oxen available, for on the clays and glacial deposits of the Vale and North Bucks each plough would normally require at least six oxen harnessed in pairs.[12] Most peasants were too poor to field a whole plough-team, so each family contributed what it could, which made the work a communal operation. So the peasants as a group had to decide by what date the grazing of the fallow field must cease so that ploughing could begin. Similarly, joint decisions about harvesting were unavoidable, because individual plots were not fenced or hedged,[13] and anyone who had not completed his harvesting by the prescribed date would find his crops invaded by the animals which his neighbours turned out to feed on the stubble and weeds, that covered the rest of the field.

**Fig. 17: An Anglo-Saxon Plough-Team** (After Saklatvala)

Oxen were the main motive power of Saxon times. They were much cheaper than horses, and at the end of their working life they could be eaten. They worked at a slower rate than horses, which was unfortunate, because there was a lot to be done. The Saxon ploughman worked from dawn to dusk for six days a week, and still had to feed, water and muck out his beasts on Sundays. Saxon ploughmen were definitely not feather-bedded. Rather, as the ploughman in Aelfric's Colloquy assures us, they were pushed to the limits of their endurance even in a normal year.[14]

> *At daybreak I drive the oxen out to the field and yoke them to the plough. I have to plough every day a full acre or more. No winter weather is so bitter that I dare lurk at home for fear of my lord ... I have a boy with me driving the oxen with a goad, who like me is hoarse with the cold and the shouting ... It is very hard work.*

The availability of oxen was critical. Therefore the provision of fodder for the winter months was critical. Consequently, to save on the consumption of hay, some villagers let their animals stray into the lord's meadow, or a neighbour's crop. This was quite illegal, but it continued over the centuries, as the earliest manorial court rolls prove. For example, in July 1290 at Newton Longville:

> *Ralph Cheeseman, Henry le fferour and Hugh Roberd put themselves in mercy for trespass in the lord's meadow with their sheep.* (fined 2d each)

On the same day this court dealt with thirty-two similar cases of trespass with a variety of animals (lambs, pigs, cows, calves, horses, geese and oxen), all for feeding animals in the corn and the hay. The importance of oxen reinforces assertions by archaeologists that there was not a wholesale slaughter of animals at Martinmas.[15] It was certainly the time when the peasant would assess his stock and - before the shortage of winter feed took the fat off their bones - cull the weak, the sick and the aged, for salting-down to stock the larder in preparation for the difficult winter months. But oxen were too valuable as draught animals to be slaughtered for food when in their prime; and, as with all farm animals, sufficient cattle had to be retained to ensure the creation of the next generation. So they had to be fed throughout the year, which explains why the hay meadows, the product of which helped to feed the stock over the winter months, were tended with such care: protected with hurdles from stray animals or illegal grazing; shared out amongst the villagers in proportion to their land in the open fields; cut and repeatedly turned to dry out the moisture which could overheat the rick; and finally carted back to the village for the rick building and thatching.

### The Other Jobs

With the fallow field organised, the strips of the cultivated field had to be sown with wheat in the autumn, and barley, peas and beans in the spring. All the seed was broadcast and, to protect it from the birds, the ground was harrowed. Even so, children would be sent out into the fields bird scaring: crow-starving as it was called in some villages. Later the strips would have to be weeded: by hand! What a job! But at least the weeds could be dried and fed to the cattle. As a result, there was actually competition for weeds, and often a village bye-law warned that: [16]

> *No-one shall gather herbage in another's grain.* ( July 1290, Newton Longville)

Weeding was one of the many jobs that required experience and judgement. Cut the thistles too early and four heads would spring up where there had been but one; cut them too late and they would have spread their seeds. Soon the year's most important event was in progress: the harvest, with its laborious cutting, stooking, carting and storing, to be followed by the interminable threshing. The straw from the threshing was used to bed down the animals, but as a last resort it could be fed to them. With the exception of barley straw, it was a poor substitute for the more nutritious hay. But *'it tided them over'*, and they could regain their strength in the Spring flush.

Throughout the year the peasants' other animals had to be tended. The shepherd took the sheep from the fold to pasture each day, and with his dog guarded them against wild animals. The ewes had to be milked twice daily, and the flock sheared in the summer. Sheep were extremely important. Besides milk and wool, they provided fleeces for bedding and winter wear, skins which could be sold for parchment, and mutton for the pot. The cowherd and the swineherd pastured their animals on the fallow, the waste, or the meadow, according to the time of year, with the pigs having the additional benefit of autumn in the woods feeding on the acorns, nuts, berries, snails, etc.. All these guardians of the village animals had to be on the look-out for thieves and wild animals. They also had to be rewarded for their services.

When the fieldwork was finished, or made impossible by the weather, there were always plenty of jobs to be done: buildings to be repaired; hurdles to be made; ditches to be dug; privies to be cleared out; flour to be ground; stock to be selected for breeding; and the hedges of the closes around the homesteads to be checked and reinforced to provide a safe place where animals could drop their offspring or receive some assistance, and be free from predators.

Farming in Saxon times was quite different from today. Most things had to be done by hand. The water-mill, the plough and the cart were the nearest the Saxons got to mechanical assistance. Practically everything had to be made and maintained within the village. So the smith would be expected to produce and repair weapons, working tools, and all sorts of domestic wares such as pots, pans, trivets and hooks for suspending the pots. The villagers also had to process their crops and animals into food, drink and clothing. That meant spinning, weaving and the preparation of animal skins to make shoes, belts, clothes and coverlets. Each family also baked bread, brewed ale, made butter and cheese, dressed poultry and game, preserved meat, and dried herbs. [17]

## *HOUSING FOR THE SAXON PEASANT*

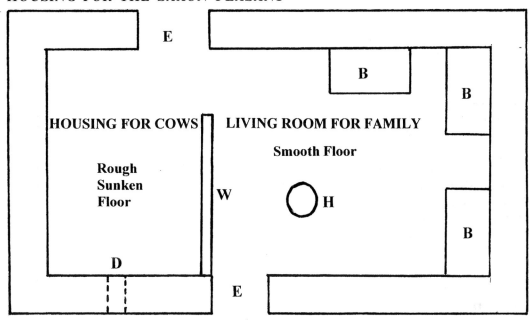

### Figure 18: PLAN OF A BASIC HOUSE FOR A PEASANT

H = hearth
B = box-bed or space for a bed-board
E = entrance
S = shit-house with cess-pit, surrounded by a wattle screen
W = Wooden divide
D = Drain
0_____10  FEET

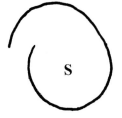

The construction of houses varied from place to place, and even from house to house. Thus the walls might simply consist of a line of close-set posts. Alternatively and more likely, they might consist of occasional posts (sufficient to support the roof) the space between them being infilled with wattle in a sandwich with turf as the filling. If stone were available, it might be used to provide a ground-cill to protect the lowest part of the wattle from rain. The roofing would consist of whatever was available locally: most commonly straw, reeds or turf.

The plan of the house was inevitably a rectangle, perhaps with an internal partition to create a byre for the cattle. Alternatively, as their family grew up, and some labour could be spared for the task, the cows might be relegated to an out-shot (or lean-to) with walls of wattle. The space which they vacated could then be converted into a bedroom. Even then, living conditions would be cramped, uncomfortable and squalid. So to reduce the draughts the walls might be plastered with some sort of mud: such as the witchert later used in much of the Vale. The rooves would be covered with straw, reeds or turf as available. The general effect in the village would be of a cluster of shallow-topped boxes, interspersed with smaller buildings like circular or ridged tents, built over shallow pits to give more headroom, and used for spinning, weaving, dressing skins, etc.. Completing the scene would be the roofless, wattle-walled shit-houses.

## VIOLENCE AND CRIME IN SAXON TIMES

The peasant looked to his lord for protection, which was very necessary, for civil violence was common. Judging from the legislation of 10th century kings, theft, murder, rape, violent assault and arson were commonplace. Travellers and traders were often attacked by roving bands comprised of outlaws from justice, escaped slaves, peasants dismissed by their lords, and those who found crime less arduous than the daily drudgery of village life. Some villages were less successful in husbandry than their neighbours, and supplemented their incomes with a little cattle- or sheep-rustling. The law itself was violent: the blood feud was a legally-approved social custom; trial by ordeal could be used to determine guilt; and a stranger who approached a village without shouting or blowing a horn could be assumed to be a thief and killed out of hand. The penalties which the law inflicted for misdemeanours were correspondingly severe, and the death penalty was common. For forging money one lost a hand, which was nailed to the smithy door. The judicial ethos of medieval times is well illustrated by the action of William the Conqueror who, in one of his more benevolent moments, decided that capital punishment was being used excessively, and replaced it (for some less serious crimes) by blinding or mutilation. And remember that, if a peasant were involved in a court case, a lord's oath counted for more than a peasant's!

## *Chapter 3*

# *THE NORMANS AS CONQUERORS*

After almost a thousand years, William the Conqueror is famous for just two events: defeating the English army at Hastings in October 1066; and creating the Domesday Book in 1087. Now we consider how our region fared under him and his descendants.

## *THE DOMESDAY BOOK*

In 1086, twenty years after he invaded England, King William decided to find out the exact worth of his kingdom, and just who "held" what. Consequently:

> *At Gloucester at midwinter... the King had deep* speech *with his counsellors... and sent men* (his commissioners) *all over England to each shire ... to find out ... what or how much each landholder held ... in land and livestock, and what it was worth.*[1]

The information which was obtained was written up in a book, which soon became known as the Domesday Book, because *"like the day of judgment its record is unalterable"*. It still exists, and is housed in the National Archive in Chancery Lane, London. Now, printed copies are available with the original script on each left-hand page, and on the facing page the translation. It is revered by historians as the first comprehensive survey of national resources ever undertaken anywhere. In Domesday Book the commissioners' reports appear in the following or similar form:[2]

> *The Archbishop (Lanfranc) holds (Monks) Risborough himself.*
> *It answers for 30 hides. Land for 14 ploughs;*
> *in lordship 16 hides; 2 ploughs there.*
>     *32 villagers with 8 smallholders have 12 ploughs.*
>     *4 slaves; meadow for 6 ploughs; woodland, 300 pigs.*
> *Total value £16; when acquired 100s; before 1066 £16.*
>     *Asgar the Constable held this manor from Christ Church, Canterbury,*
> *before 1066, on condition that it could not be separated from the church.*

The final line(s) of each entry provides the names of the Saxons who held the land before the Battle of Hastings. The King Edward, who is often mentioned at this point, is Edward the Confessor (1042-1066). The penultimate line of each entry gives us the value of the village on three dates: "total value" or just "the value" means in 1086; "when acquired" means in 1067 i.e. just after the Conquest; "before the Conquest" or "before 1066" means in 1065. If the line reads, "The total value is and always was £x", it means that the value was £x at all three dates.

## *DUKE WILLIAM VISITS THE VALE*

After the Normans landed at Pevensey (Plate C8), the Battle of Hastings was fiercely fought and narrowly won by Duke William of Normandy, the final turning point being the death of Harold, the king of England. Figure 19, based on the Bayeux Tapestry, depicts his death, but is Harold the man on the right with the battleaxe, or the man on the left plucking an arrow from his eye? Tradition favours the latter but, nearly a thousand years later, no-one is certain. After the Battle the Normans remained in the area for a fortnight. This allowed time to bury the dead; time for the dying to meet their maker; time for the superficially wounded to recover for the march on London; and, in particular, time for the Saxon earls to "recognise" William as their new lord. But this last simply did not happen. Maybe that is why William did not march directly into London. Instead he began a huge clockwise encirclement of London,

**Fig. 19: The Battle of Hastings, and the Death of King Harold**

covering at least 350 miles in seven weeks.

It had long been noticed that in the south-eastern counties of England the value of many villages fell between 1065 and 1068, and it was assumed that this was due to the Norman armies harrying villages for food and fodder. However, in 1898 F.H.Baring went a step further[3]. He decided that we should be able to trace the line of William's march from Hastings to London by recording these falls in value. Some of the results of this exercise appear in Map 3 and Table 3.

The Normans first moved westwards to the Goring Gap, where the Thames cuts through the chalk ridge which we call the Chiltern Hills, providing an easy low-level route through the heavily forested, uneven terrain of the hills, which would have been much more difficult and dangerous countryside for a large army. Once through the Gap the army could cross the river Thames by the major ford at Wallingford. A few miles further on, and the army entered Buckinghamshire, and moved north-eastwards along the Vale of Aylesbury: see Map 3. In 1066 armies, both friend and foe, still fed off the land that they passed through. Now, thanks to Domesday Book, we can better see the impact on the innocent. Most of the villages which had been pillaged by the Normans were still recovering twenty years later. It was very much the luck of the draw. Villages were to be found in every stage of pillaging from 'completely wasted' to 'totally untouched'. One village might be plundered, while the village next door escaped completely. Thus Chetwode and Barton Hartshorn suffered heavily, while just over a mile away Preston Bissett was untouched. Similarly Ivinghoe and Pitstone were severely wasted, while Marsworth, just two miles away, was completely unscathed. Only one in every five villages escaped completely. Table 2 shows the overall result.

**Table 2: Change in Value of Villages in the Vale and North Bucks. in 1066**

| | |
|---|---|
| 8 increased in value | 43 lost on average 46% of their value |
| 33 retained their pre-Conquest value | 11 lost on average 56% of their value |
| 72 lost on average 18% of their value | Stowe was completely wasted |

and there is insufficient information for 2 villages.

28

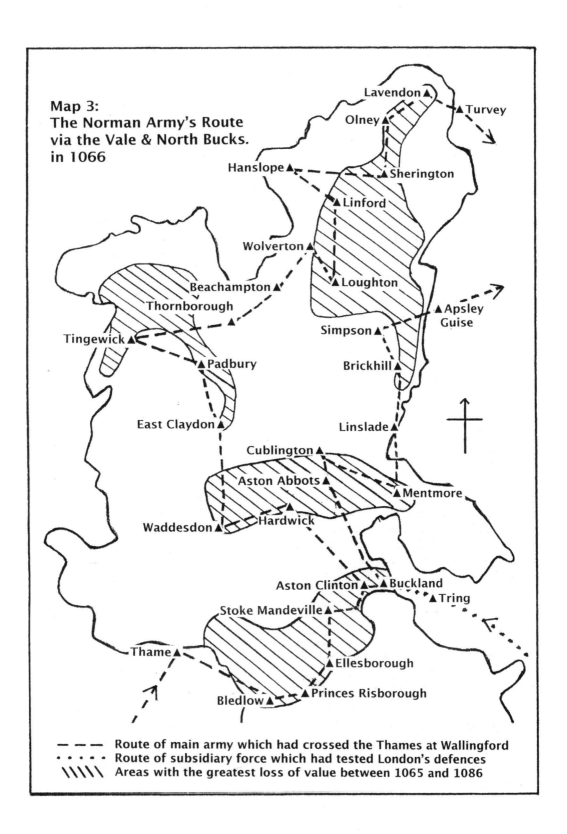

Map 3:
The Norman Army's Route
via the Vale & North Bucks.
in 1066

Lavendon ▲
▲ Turvey
Olney ▲
Hanslope ▲
▲ Sherington
▲ Linford
Wolverton ▲
Beachampton ▲
Thornborough
▲ Loughton
Tingewick ▲
Simpson ▲
▲ Apsley Guise
▲ Padbury
Brickhill ▲
East Claydon ▲
Linslade ▲
Cublington ▲
Aston Abbots ▲
▲ Mentmore
Waddesdon ▲
Hardwick ▲
Aston Clinton ▲ — ▲ Buckland
▲ Tring
Stoke Mandeville ▲
Thame ▲
▲ Ellesborough
Bledlow ▲
▲ Princes Risborough

– – – Route of main army which had crossed the Thames at Wallingford
· · · · · Route of subsidiary force which had tested London's defences
\\\\\ Areas with the greatest loss of value between 1065 and 1086

But would not the villagers be inclined to exaggerate their losses? We think that they would not, for by the time of Domesday no-one doubted that you trifled with William at your peril. In any case, he took steps to ensure the accuracy of the data:

> *Other commissioners followed the first, and men were sent into provinces which they did not know and where they were unknown, so that they could check the survey of the first investigators, and denounce any who were guilty to the king.*[4]

Even for those who escaped the pillaging of the Norman army, the uncertainty of their situation must have been extremely stressful. Thus the peasants of Wingrave, perched on their hill fifty metres above the floor of the Vale, would have followed William's progress with increasing apprehension. At first, when the invaders were in the region of Risborough, there would be just a red glow as irritated Norman outriders, foraging for supplies, torched straw rooves as a punishment to peasants trying to stop their cattle from being driven off. Later, when the two divisions of the army met at Aston Clinton and Buckland their camp fires would be clearly visible from Wingrave. Finally there were a few hours of the greatest uncertainty, when the forerunners – their pennants streaming from their lances – could easily be identified, followed at some distance by the main body of the eastern division. The mere sight of several thousand heavily armed troops would be enough to astound and terrify the villagers, for Wingrave's population was a mere one hundred and fifty. Would Wingrave be passed by, or find itself in the centre of the next night's camps? Villages which did, certainly suffered. To be completely ravaged could be a death sentence. The loss of hay, corn and animals, together with seed-corn and breeding animals inevitably put a self-sufficient village in danger of death from starvation and /or disease, unless their neighbours could provide assistance. The villagers' losses would be all the greater because William's march took place in November, when the harvest was in the barns, the hay in stacks, and meat had been salted down for the winter. Wingrave was lucky. At Aston Abbotts William's troops were less than 1½ miles away. At Cublington they were moving northwards and were three miles from Wingrave. Then, inexplicably, the whole force turned south-eastwards until it reached Mentmore, in the process by-passing Wingrave, though by no more than 1¼ miles. Fortunately it then disappeared northwards (see Map 3). The potential seriousness of Wingrave's situation is emphasised by the long time which it took the most heavily ravaged villages to recover. Table 3

### Table 3: Loss of Value due to William's March, and the Extent of Recovery

| Village | Initial loss in 1066 | Amount of loss by 1086 | Village | Initial loss in 1066 | Amount of loss by 1086 |
|---|---|---|---|---|---|
| Stowe | 100 % | 33 % | Burston | 52% | 14 % |
| Simpson | 82 | 23 | Cublington | 50 | nil |
| Bedgrove | 75 | 25 | Aston Clinton | 50 | 10 |
| Buckland | 70 | 20 | Linslade | 50 | 25 |
| M'ks Risborough | 69 | nil | Lathbury | 50 | nil +121 |
| Lavendon | 66 | 28 | Addingrove | 50 | 25 |
| Shalstone | 64 | 50 | Beachampton | 47 | 13 |
| Bradwell | 60 | 27 | Loughton | 47 | 22 |
| Wavendon | 57 | 41 | Weston Turville | 47 | nil |
| Little Woolstone | 56 | 33 | Waddesdon | 47 | nil |

records the 20 villages which lost most value due to William's march through the Vale and North Bucks.. By 1086 some (like Lathbury and Monks Risborough) had made a good recovery, but the majority still had a loss (though a smaller one), while a few (like Shalstone and Wavendon) had only slightly recovered.

In fact, as they might have realised later, the people of Buckinghamshire were exceedingly fortunate compared to those areas later punished for rebellion against King William. William's men may well have torched some Saxon buildings if the villagers were foolish enough to resist, but the speed of the march round London (50 miles per week) suggests that William did not pursue a scorched earth policy, but simply a *'living-off-the-land policy'*. There would not have been time for his troops to create *widespread* terror. Although to the peasants of particular villages it must have seemed never-ending, within a few hours William's trampling hordes had passed northwards. They then crossed into Bedfordshire, and one group even entered Cambridgeshire. Finally, William did a u-turn and moved southwards into Hertfordshire where, at Little Berkhamsted, [5] *"he was met by Archbishop Aldred, Edgar Cild, Earl Edwin, Earl Morcar and all the chief men from London"*. *"Out of necessity, after most damage had been done"*, they accepted his authority and Archbishop Aldred consecrated William king at Westminster on Christmas Day, 1066. On that occasion he

> promised Aldred on Christ's book and swore . . . that he would rule all this people as well as the best of the kings before him, if they would be loyal to him.[6]

If they ever heard of this, the people of Buckinghamshire might be forgiven for thinking that William had made an inauspicious start!

### THE FEUDAL SYSTEM

After his coronation, William's first action was to name himself as the possessor of the whole of England's land, and to begin the lengthy process of rewarding his supporters. By the end of 1068 much land in the south and east of England had already been transferred from English into Norman hands. These transfers of land were sealed in ceremonies very similar to those of Saxon times. However, the Saxons did not relate land grants to active service on the battlefield: such service was a general obligation of all freemen. Whereas, when William rewarded his knights with leases of land, the "rent" was almost invariably knightly service, very often on the battlefield. Such leases, when granted by the king himself, made the recipient a tenant-in-chief, and conveyed a much sought-after status in society. For the recipient it meant that, when required by his lord, he had to make himself available on the battlefield complete with horses, armour and weapons. For a small allocation of land William might demand no more than the tenant himself, fully equipped for the battlefield. On the other hand, for the huge allocations of land to his senior knights, he might set a "rent" of sixty knights, all mounted and fully equipped. Such knightly service was an excellent arrangement for William. As the recent conqueror of the English, he had to be prepared for challenges from abroad and for uprisings within. So he had to be able to raise an effective army at very short notice. These feudal land settlements provided this, ensuring eventually that a force of nearly 5,000 knights could be assembled rapidly. All William had to do was arrange for notices to be served upon the relevant tenants. These would be in a form similar to the following and, as in this case, might require the recipient to pass on the message to other tenants:

> *William, king of the English, to Aethelwig, abbot of Evesham, greeting. I order you to summon all those who are subject to your administration and jurisdiction that they bring before me at Clarendon on the Octave of Pentecost all the knights they owe me duly equipped. You also on that day shall come to me, and bring with you fully equipped those five knights which you owe me in respect of your abbacy. Witness Eudo the steward.[7]*

However, providing the king with knights was expensive, especially if the number was large. For example, eleven of William's lay tenants each had to provide him with sixty or more knights, while nine of his ecclesiastical tenants owed forty or more. At first landlords tried to fulfil their knightly quotas by maintaining landless knights as part of their household, and continuing the long, intensive training necessary to enable a knight in full armour to fight effectively on horseback. This was the tradition in Normandy, but it was expensive, and sometimes Norman knights-in-waiting became involved in unnecessary clashes with the English. Another way of dealing with the matter was needed.

William's land grants to his closest supporters were huge. Such estates were known as baronies or honours. They spread his supporters across the length and breadth of England, making it easier to subjugate the English. His ten most powerful courtiers – men bound together by marriage, descent, boundless ambition, and (for the time being!) total loyalty to William – shared nearly a quarter of England. For instance, Robert, Count of Mortain and a stepbrother of William, received 797 manors scattered over twenty counties. In the Vale and North Bucks. alone the Count held 18,000 acres, and just four of his Buckinghamshire manors (Bledlow, Mentmore, Marsh Gibbon and Great Brickhill) covered over 8,000 acres. Odo, Bishop of Bayeux and William's other step-brother, was similarly rewarded. Their reward was not only for loyalty to William, or performance in battle. They had also invested heavily in William's expedition to England. One of the more modest estimates claims that – as well as many small boats – William assembled a fleet of 696 ships, most built specially for the invasion.[8] Of these it is said that the Count of Mortain provided 120 ships, and the Bishop of Bayeux supplied a further 100. Walter Giffard, the Lord of Longueville in Normandy, who was closely related by blood to the Conqueror, not only helped to plan the Conquest, but also provided 30 ships and a hundred knights.[9] Another 170 of William's leading supporters were very well recompensed.[10] Even the lowliest knight had to arrive equipped at his own expense with horses, armour and weapons.

### Walter Giffard

In 1066 Walter was an elderly, balding, grey-haired man "of great kindliness".[11] Even so, he was also a fighter of great ability who, over the years, had supported William in the defence of Normandy, and particularly distinguished himself in the great battles at Arques and Mortemer. At Hastings, Walter had commanded the Norman division of William's army and his son (Walter II) had also fought in the battle. Over 33,000 acres of Walter's land was in the Vale and North Bucks.,[12] and in 1071 William created Walter's son (Walter II) Earl of Buckingham and in 1085 appointed him to be one of the commissioners who conducted the Domesday survey. Walter senior was a well-connected member of the inner circle at William's court. For instance, he was the cousin of Hugh de Bolbec (whom we shall meet again later) who was the son of Sir Hugh de Bolbec, another follower and relative of William. And the Giffards and the Bolbecs, were longstanding neighbours. Walter's holdings included land in:

> **Addingrove#, Akeley#, Ashendon, Beachampton#, Bradwell#, Bow Brickhill# Bourton#, Broughton, Chearsley, Chilton*, Long Crendon*, Dorton*, Easington#, Edgcott#, Hardmead, Hartwell, Hillesden, Great Horwood*, Great Kimble#, Lamport, Lavendon, Leckhampstead, Lenborough, Lillingstone Dayrell#, Great Linford, Littlecote, Loughton, Maids Moreton, Milton Keynes, Moulsoe#, Mursley, Newton Longville*, Pitstone, Pollicot*, Ravenstone#, Singleborough#, Swanbourne, Whaddon*, Whitchurch#, Lower Winchendon*, Little Woolstone, Great Woolstone#, and Wotton Underwood#.[13]**

The eight asterisked properties were Walter's core holdings: over 10,000 acres, which he kept entirely 'in hand'. Of these Long Crendon, Chilton, Pollicot, Lower Winchendon, and Dorton formed a continuous block of about 6,600 acres of good Vale land, which supported 159 families (over 750 people), as well as Walter's family and household. The hashes (#) identify another 12,000 acres, of which Walter was the sole tenant, but which he sub-let. The remaining properties were shared between Walter (11,000 acres) and other knights. He also had manors in South Bucks., Bedfordshire, Berkshire and Huntingdonshire.

William's policy of allocating land to his supporters explains many of our village names. For example, Lillingstone Dayrell took its name from a family which had an estate at (de) Airelle between Bayeux and Caen. Newport Pagnell was the new port belonging to the Paynell family, whose name came from its latinised form Paganellus. Newton Longville was just Newton until Walter Giffard granted it to a church in Longueville, south-east of Paris, of which he was also lord.

## Subinfeudation

Tenants-in-chief soon realised that they had a solution to the problem of paying their rent to the king with knight service. They simply followed the king's example, by offering landless knights some of their surplus land in return for knight service, which they could then pass on to the king. This created a layer of under-tenants and helped to spread the responsibility and financial burden of providing the king with his required number of knights. Walter Giffard delegated all his quota of knights to his under-tenants. For example, Walter let 3,600 acres (including the manor of Whitchurch) to his cousin Hugh de Bolbec, in return for which Hugh had to provide Walter with twenty of the knights that Walter owed the king.[14] This became known as subinfeudation. As the years passed, some of the tenants-in-chief who had previously required knight service from *their* tenants preferred cash, which enabled them to hire professional knights: men whose age, talents and general fitness for battle were more to their liking. As early as the reign of Henry I (1100-1135) knight-service was being converted into the fixed money payments, called scutage, normally 20 shillings for each knight not provided.

## The Effect of William's Land Grants on the English

William the Conqueror's land grants to his supporters almost completely replaced the Saxon aristocracy, who had previously been the principal landholders of England, by Normans. Most sub-tenancies also went to Normans. But many Normans had no wish to live in England. A lot of them already had estates in France and Normandy. Besides, living in a conquered country was dangerous and so was crossing the Channel. Henry I's only son was drowned at sea while crossing from Normandy to England. So the shortlist of Normans available to fill English sub-tenancies was short indeed. William overcame this by consolidating holdings. For example, in 1065 at Moulsoe, a village between Milton Keynes and Cranfield, eight Saxon thanes[15] had held the land. They all owned their holdings, and so could sell them, bequeath them, or rent them out without having to get permission from anyone. William changed all that. Remember that, as the self-styled owner of all England, he did not give land away, but rented it out in return for knightly or some other service. At Moulsoe, William let all ten hides to Walter Giffard, who promptly sub-let to a Norman known to us only as Richard, to hold as just one manor.[16] This was what infuriated the English nobility: eight independent farmers, including three lords of the manor, were replaced by one Norman lord of the manor, who might graciously (or otherwise!) allow the displaced Saxons to retain their holdings, but only as tenants acknowledging the Norman interloper as their lord. In 1086, in the whole of England south of the Tees, only two Englishmen – Thurkill of Arden and Colswein of Lincoln – held estates of baronial dimensions *directly* of the king in 1086. It was very upsetting, and the resentment of the displaced landowners surfaced occasionally even in the Domesday survey. For instance, we learn that in Marsh Gibbon:

> *Alric holds 4 hides from William . . . He held it himself before 1066, but now he holds it from William at a revenue (i.e. rent) harshly and wretchedly.*[17]

## THE FUNDING OF FEUDALISM

Uprisings did occur, most seriously in the north of England, where William employed both feudal knights and mercenaries, all of whom had to be paid. He faced even worse problems in Normandy, where his neighbours were trying to annex his territories and spent most of his time there, only visiting England in 1075, 1080 and 1085. War (and the royal court) were extremely expensive. Three things helped the Norman kings to remain solvent: the land tax known as the geld, which was just plain taxation; feudal incidents, which were stealth taxes in a variety of disguises; and exploiting the peasantry through fines, which were simply local taxes that the king left his tenants-in-chief to levy as some compensation for the extent of the feudal incidents.

***Levying the Geld*** was an Anglo-Saxon system of taxation. The Normans adopted it because it was so simple. All William had to do was to send a demand to each of the shire courts in a royal writ bearing his seal and stating the extent of the tax. In the south midlands (including Buckinghamshire) the assessment was in hides, and the court officials knew the number of hides for which their shire was responsible. So they could calculate the total tax payable, and divide it amongst the hundreds,[18] which divided it amongst the villages, which informed each of its villagers of their liability. It worked like a charm! A typical levy was two shillings per hide and in Saxon times that had yielded as much as 72,000 lbs of silver coin.[19]

***The Feudal Incidents*** on which kings based these demands were quite ordinary things like deaths, marriages, minorities, broken promises, ransoms following capture in war, etc.. The following are four examples of how the king turned them to his financial advantage.

When William distributed land to his supporters, he regarded them as tenants. In William's view, it followed quite properly that, if a tenant died without heirs, or was convicted of treason or other serious crimes, the land reverted to the king. And if William thought that, then that was what happened. This re-possession of lands became known as **escheat**. It happened to the lands of Walter Giffard's grandson, Walter III, 2nd Earl of Buckingham. Having died without heirs, all his lands reverted to King Henry I, who let them to Geoffrey Fitz-William at £324-15s-4d per annum. Later King Richard divided the lands between two earls both of whom paid the king 2,000 marks (£1,333) for his share. All this added nearly £3,000 to the royal treasury from just one landholding.

Similarly, if a tenant-in-chief died leaving a minor as his heir, the king would take possession of his estate, and (as a sort of tax) retain the profits from it until the heir reached his majority. This was known as **wardship**. If, however, the heir was female, things became much more complicated. For example, at Whitchurch the Bolebec family built the castle which still bears their name. On the death of her father, the Manor of Whitchurch and Bolebec Castle passed to an Isabel de

Bolebec. Being only nine years old, she became a ward of the king, and a good example of how such wardships profited him. He transferred the wardship to the Earl of Oxford, who paid the king 500 marks, so that his son Robert might marry Isabel. Later, the son gave the king a further 200 marks and three palfreys (a type of horse) for leave to marry her. Then Isabel herself gave the king 300 marks and three more palfreys to ensure that she would not be *forced* to marry. This was a bold step, because if she wished to keep the property, she was obliged to take for a husband one of the three men whom the king chose for her. If she rejected them all, then she lost the property. This was known as **forfeiture**. But if she could pay the king what he would have received from her husband for arranging their marriage, she could retain the property. This was known as **marriage**. Faced with this situation, Isabel eventually married Robert, by now the 3rd Earl, taking with her, as her dowry, the Manor and the Castle. They descended with the Earls of Oxford until 1558.

King John's repeated demands for **feudal aids**, to fund his continental wars, so incensed his barons that it was a major reason for the creation of Magna Carta and the civil war which followed it: see also under Castlethorpe in chapter 4. To cope with the king's demands, his tenants-in-chief increased the profitability of their land *"by a more ruthless exploitation of the work and 'dues' that they could extract from their peasants".*[20] In later years such 'dues' were entered (as fines) in the manorial rolls, together with any other penalties which the landlords had invented to increase their incomes. As the Anglo-Saxon Chronicle put it, *"the poor people were sore oppressed"*.

***Exploiting the Peasants*** The peasant could not do much without the permission of his lord, and that permission always came at a price in time, goods or money. The villager had to pay a fine before he was allowed to educate his son. When the villager died, the lord was entitled to a heriot, a sort of mediaeval inheritance tax, which allowed him to take for himself the best live beast or chattel of the deceased. A villager required the lord's permission, and the payment of a fine, to give his daughter in marriage. Another fine would be levied if the daughter became pregnant before marriage, and yet another if she did not marry when pregnant! Such regulations were typical of the feudal system, and they continued unabated until the middle of the 14th century, when the Black Death removed the labour surplus which was the source of the lord of the manor's authority. This finally expired in the 20th century, when heriots and copyhold were abolished. The following examples of impositions on peasants are from some of the earliest manorial court records for the Vale and North Bucks.[21]

> *Granted by the lord to Alice Bouere she may marry wherever she wishes in the lord's fee. Fine: 12 cocks* (Court of Newton Longville, 1283)
> *Richard Matheu who held of the lord one messuage and half a virgate of land has died and one ox worth 10 shillings accrues to the lord by way of heriot.* (Also Newton Longville,1290)
> *John son of Roger the cowherd, who is in the custody of Alexander le Ropere, is of full age to recover his tenements and lands. And the lord granted to him the aforesaid land and tenements, and he put him in possession of them to hold them for himself and his heirs through services on them, dues and customs. And he gave for gersuma (premium) and entry half a mark.* (6s-8d) (Court Baron of the Manor of Wynselow, 1329)
> *Ralph Adam came and made a fine with the lord so that he can live outside the lordship while it pleases the lord. And he pays 3s-4d annually at Michaelmas as poll-tax. John Maundeville to be surety and do fealty.* (Court Baron of the Manor of Wynselow, 1364)

# Chapter 4

## THE NORMAN BEQUESTS

Despite the destruction which the Normans created in the early years of their occupation, within a few decades of the Conquest every county town and many others had acquired castles, parish churches, cathedrals, and stone-built lay buildings. Their erection often destroyed parts of the towns, changing their appearance and greatly upsetting the inhabitants.

### THE NORMAN CASTLES

Castles were an essential part of the Norman military strategy.[1] The earliest were just a circular ditch, the earth from which was thrown into the middle of the circle to form a motte (pronounced mot as in cot). This was a flat-topped mound, occasionally up to 50 feet high and 100 feet in diameter at the top. At first it was surrounded by a timber palisade and crowned by a timber tower. Timber was essential due to its lightness. Only when the earth had consolidated could stone be used. So the first mottes were built cheaply and quickly by forced labour, using land and timber seized from local landowners. Buhr-work [2] (building defences for towns) had long been required of all adult Saxon males. It wasn't popular, but at least the buhr was designed to protect the town's population plus that from the surrounding countryside, whereas the Norman castle was only intended to protect the Normans from the people they had conquered. So castlework was distinctly unpopular under the Normans, *"who sorely burdened the unhappy people of the country with forced labour on the castles"*. (Anglo-Saxon Chronicle = ASC)

Initially the mottes provided a military base for a knight and a small number of soldiers. Later the motte and ditch were surrounded by a bailey, which was an open area protected by another deep, circular ditch or moat. The earth from this was used to surround the bailey with an earthen bank, on top of which a timber stockade was built, entered through a wooden gatehouse. The bailey contained accommodation for the lord, his family and the men-at-arms, a hall, a kitchen, stables, a well and a forge. To contain all this, some of the peasants' precious land, and even their houses, had to be confiscated, creating still more resentment. This was the case at Wallingford, where initially a great motte was built in a corner of the old Saxon buhr. To the inhabitants, this offence was compounded when, in the 13th century, stone fortifications were added, the bailey was enlarged and more houses had to be destroyed. The motte also served as a watch-tower, and as a final strong point. If there was an uprising, Norman cavalry could rapidly emerge from the bailey; or retire into it if an encounter did not go their way. Meanwhile, archers could deal with any of the enemy who reached the outer defences. If these were penetrated the Normans could retreat onto the motte, where its height put everyone who had got into the bailey within range of the bowmen. **A visit to Wallingford is highly recommended.** 'Historic Wallingford' is a walk-round guide with a map, obtainable from the Tourist Information Centre in the Town Hall (Tel: 01491- 826972). Don't miss stopping places 3 (for the Saxon ramparts), 1 (for the museum), between B and C (for the deep Saxon ditches now screened by surrounding trees), and F (for the huge, *conical* and densely treed, *but accessible*, motte, which is drawn but not named in the area marked 'site of castle'.

Some mottes were developed into strong castles with a stone keep and walls punctuated by stone towers to allow the bowmen to fire on the enemy, if they got close in against the walls. Some, like Berkhamsted Castle (Herts), were surrounded by a deep moat which was filled with water by diverting a river or stream. Castles and mottes were built in strategically important

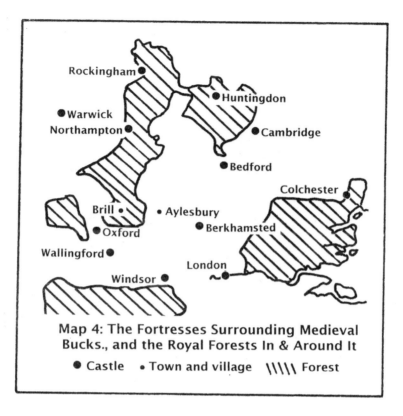

**Map 4: The Fortresses Surrounding Medieval Bucks., and the Royal Forests In & Around It**

● Castle   • Town and village   \\\\\ Forest

positions, from which they could dominate main routes, river crossings, landing places and large towns. The largest castles combined the functions of fortress, administrative centre, barracks, military storehouse, chapel and baronial (or royal) residence. The lack of castles of the first rank in the Vale and North Bucks. is probably due to the fact that, more by luck than design, Buckinghamshire was ringed by castles, blocking access to the county from all directions: from the south by Berkhamsted, Windsor and the London castles; from the west by Wallingford and Oxford castles; from the east by Bedford, Cambridge and Colchester castles; and from the north by Warwick, Rockingham, Northampton, and Huntingdon castles. (Map 4) However, although no really large castles with complex defences were built in the Vale and North Bucks., the castles at Buckingham and Whitchurch seem to have been substantial fortresses, both built of stone.

Between 1066 and 1216 over 600 motte, and motte and bailey, castles were built, mostly in four periods: 1066 to 1072 when William I completed the Conquest of England; 1088/9 when William II defeated the rebellion of Bishop Odo and the Norman barons; 1135 to 1154 when Stephen, the last Norman king, failed to keep his unruly barons in order, so creating the civil war known as the Anarchy; and 1215 to 1216 when King John fought his barons over Magna Carta.

At Domesday Walter Giffard sub-let Whitchurch manor to his cousin Hugh de Bolebec, whose descendants built Bolebec Castle close to the village during the Anarchy (Map 5). One entrance to the castle was in Weir Lane, and old people living at the end of the 18th century could remember an ancient drawbridge there. In earlier centuries the castle probably earned tolls from travellers on the main Aylesbury to Buckingham road, and from users of the local market on Market Hill. It also provided a secure residence for the tenant and his household. There is good building stone in the parish of Whitchurch, and it is claimed that the castle once had walls of stone, and a stone keep, *"the foundations of which are said to exist"*.[3] However, the buildings were largely demolished during the 17th century Civil War, and a later owner let villagers use the

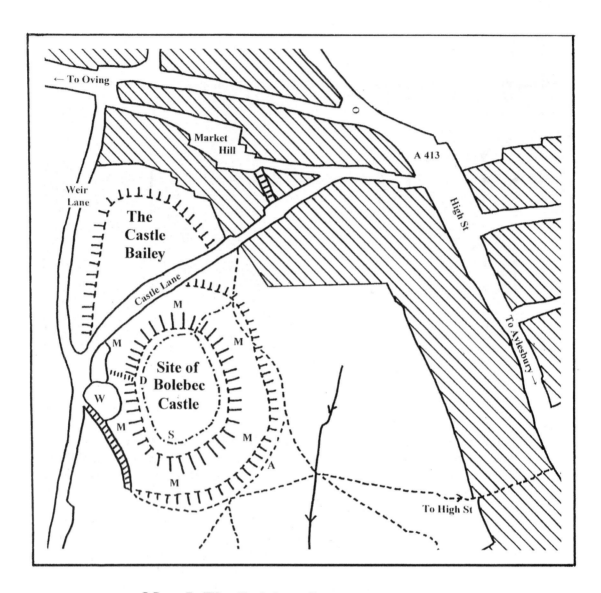

## Map 5: The Bolebec Castle at Whitchurch

A = Spring of Fair Alice
W = site of weir pond
D = ancient entrance via drawbridge
M = moat
S = note steepness of slope

|||||||||| buildings, gardens, etc.
⊞⊞⊞⊞ pedestrians only
- - - - - public footpath
O = mini roundabout
—·—·— best access to top of motte
〰➤ stream feeding Dunn Mill

**Fig. 20: Margaret on top of the Bolebec Motte.**
Not the sort of slope to run up in full armour, with the defenders waiting for your arrival at the top.

stone for building and road mending. The earthworks are over-grown but still conspicuous, and the spring of "Fair Alice", which supplied the castle with water, still runs.

The earthworks of the motte and bailey castle at **Castlethorpe** (Map 6), west of Newport Pagnell, were probably thrown up as a baronial stronghold in the 12th century by a William Mauduit. Enough earthworks remain to indicate that it also had both inner and outer baileys, the whole covering ten hectares (24.7 acres). The motte is still substantial: 40 metres long and 20 metres wide, but with no sign of a tower. The inner bailey alone is 100 metres in diameter, but the outer bailey now contains Castlethorpe village, and a stretch of the Birmingham to Euston railway. All was peaceful until King John tried unsuccessfully, but very expensively, to recover England's lost territory in France. He returned to England to find his earls and barons furious with his endless demands for money. They were still recovering from a punitive tax of a seventh on their moveables in 1203.[4] Faced with rebellion, John agreed to a list of his barons' demands. This list was the Great Charter (the Magna Carta), which became a vital part of England's largely unwritten constitution. It included a demand for more consultation over government.

But no sooner was Magna Carta agreed than King John persuaded the Pope to declare it invalid, and took up arms against his barons. Robert Mauduit, a descendant of William, joined the confederacy of the great barons opposed to King John, whose forces very quickly besieged, overcame and slighted[5] the castle. For his treason, as the king called it, Robert Mauduit forfeited his lands and his castle. However, in 1216 King John died. He was succeeded by his son Henry III, to whom William Mauduit, the son of Robert, promised allegiance, thereby regaining his barony and his father's estates, including the site of his castle, though this was never rebuilt. **Castlethorpe is worth a visit**, if only to marvel at the amount of labour needed to create the motte.

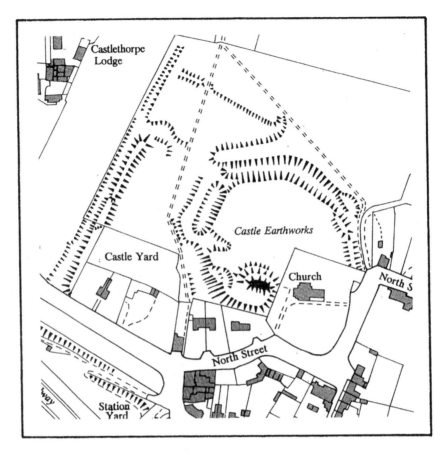

**Map 6: The Castlethorpe Motte and Bailey**

=== Public footpath ⚝ Highest point of motte

### Table 4: Some Mottes and Mounds in and Around the Vale [6]

| Location | Name of Site | Feature | * | O/S ** |
|---|---|---|---|---|
| Brill | Castle mound | motte | vis | 655138 |
| Castlethorpe | Castle | motte + baileys | PF | 799446 |
| Cublington | The Beacon | motte + deserted village | PF | 833222 |
| Ellesborough | Cymbeline's Mt | motte + bailey | vis | 832063 |
| Little Kimble | | motte + bailey | nil | 827063 |
| Old Wolverton | | motte + bailey + d. village | PF | 802413 |
| Oving | | ringwork + bailey | vis | 782214 |
| Weston Turville | Manor House | motte + bailey | vis | 859104 |
| Whitchurch | Bolebec Castle | motte + bailey | PF | 799208 |
| Wing | Castle Hill | an insignificant motte | vis | 881230 |

\* = Access;  PF = public footpath;  ** O/S = Ordnance Survey Ref; vis = visible from  road or path

40

## THE NORMANS AND THE CHURCHES

In 1070 the papal legate, Bishop Ermenfrid, prescribed penances for the Normans who had fought at Hastings:

> *Anyone who does not know the number of those he killed or wounded must ... do penance for one day in each week for the rest of his life; or, if he can, let him redeem his sin by perpetual alms either by building or by endowing a church.*

In the days when Heaven and Hell were stark realities to most people, the Vatican's message was a call to action which few ignored, and something of this sort was a time-honoured way of smoothing the route to the Golden Gates. Perhaps this accounts for the contradictory attitude of the Norman knights for, as they conquered England, these often brutal men plundered the land and showed little mercy to its population. From the blood of their opponents came the booty of war. From the sweat of their peasants came the marketable surpluses of corn. From such doubtful enterprises they funded on the one hand castles, and on the other hand cathedrals, churches and monasteries. And all the latter were built in stone. Expediency required that castles had priority, but cathedrals, churches, monasteries and other religious houses eventually outnumbered them. Between 1066 and 1100 around 1,750 churches are thought to have been built in England.[7] This means that on average, somewhere in England, one church was being completed per week (every week!) for 34 years. No wonder that William of Malmesbury is said to have commented in 1125 that one might see *"churches rise in every village ... you do not know which to wonder at more, the beauty or the speed"*. In the Vale and North Bucks. (1066 - 1189) [8] at least 52 churches were completed in the Norman style: roughly one church every 2½ years.[9] This was no small achievement for a small area with no large towns, especially as the supply of masons lagged behind the demand, due to all the newly imported bishops desperately wanting their pet projects to have priority.

**Fig. 21: Norman Font at St. Mary's, Aylesbury**

As in Saxon times, so in Norman times, all sorts of people and organisations built churches: kings, barons, archbishops, lords of the manor, abbots, the minsters and anyone who was so minded and could afford to do it. Many of the new Norman lords had such large estates and had so increased the surpluses from them, that they certainly could afford to build churches. Or re-build them, for the Norman belief that "He destroys well who builds bigger", particularly applied to Saxon buildings, of which the Normans had a low opinion. Due to this the Normans demolished and replaced most of the Saxon cathedrals, churches and abbeys in the forty years following the Conquest. The style they created was based on the ideas of the Romans, and so the replacement was always larger and 'heavier' than the original. Thus their walls are exceptionally thick, the columns are massive and support heavy semi-circular arches, which are often combined to create large vaults in the ceiling. Even the carved decoration of the stonework is bold and

41

vigorous. All this enabled wider floor spaces to be created, and so was ideal for building churches. Initially, most lords who built churches did so on their own estates, primarily out of concern for the salvation of themselves and their household, which might be quite substantial: family, servants, slaves, resident knights and visitors. A priest was employed to offer prayers for their souls, and their hopes of Heaven. He might also be allowed to serve the local villagers, and even to commute between the lord's estates. Such beneficence was also a demonstration of wealth and social status. Churches like this were widely recognised as private property. They could be, and were, bought and sold. They could be used as security for the repayment of money borrowed. They could also be a source of income: churchscot (payable at Martinmas by all landholders, and usually consisting of grain); soulscot (a medieval burial fee); plough alms (a small charge on the peasant's plough); and offerings from the congregation at major feast days, weddings and funerals. Most important of all were the tithes, for these were one tenth of each farmer's annual income. No wonder the bounds of the parish were beaten so thoroughly, for the larger the area of the parish, the larger the tithes. By the 11th century these often ill-afforded contributions to church funds were being rigorously enforced, and the Catholic Church was soon insisting that such income was for the clergy and not the lay owners. Consequently, the lay owners of churches found it increasingly difficult to make a worthwhile profit on their investment. So in the 12th and 13th centuries many lay lords granted estate churches to monasteries. For example, at Wingrave the church of SS Peter and Paul dates from the latter part of the 12th century and was probably built by William son of Alured de Wedon not long before he gave it to St Albans' Abbey. At Great Horwood the church of St. James was granted *with the manor* to Longueville Priory in France by Walter Giffard II, the first Earl of Buckingham. It is said that he also granted the Priory the church of Long Crendon. Before his death in 1091, Robert of Mortain gave by charter the Rectorial Manor and the church of Bledlow to the Benedictine Abbey of Crestain in Normandy. The monasteries welcomed such additions to their income, and also valued the influence and status which they gained when they acquired the advowson of the church: the right to appoint a priest to the living.

**Fig. 22: The Norman Content of Churches in the Vale & North Bucks**

| | |
|---|---|
| Entirely or very substantially Norman | 1 |
| Definite and easily recognised Norman features | 30 |
| Slight Norman features | 16 |
| Present church known to have been preceded by a Norman church | 5   52 [10] |

### Saint Michael's at Stewkley

Pevsner describes it as, *"The most splendid piece of Norman parochial architecture in Buckinghamshire"*. Apart from a modern porch and vestry, and the pinnacles and gargoyles of 600 years ago, the church is still just as the Normans left it. It is late Norman and was built of stone, probably around 1140-50. Its walls are exceptionally thick, and are pierced with small windows. At the foot of the splendid west front are three semi-circular arches, each decorated with zig-zag (i.e. chevron) moulding, and birds and animals on its columns. The central arch contains the doorway which, in the Norman fashion, is deeply recessed to take the place of a porch. It has two shafts on either side, the inner ones having spiral ornament running up to their richly carved capitals. (Plate C5) The interior is impressive, with unusually sumptuous decoration everywhere. From the south entrance one can look through the two great central arches supporting the tower. Their west fronts are richly carved with triple mouldings, the lower one consisting of beak-heads, cats' heads and grotesque figures with their tongues or beaks lapping over a large bead moulding. These massive semi-circular arches spring from piers nearly four feet thick: a marriage of strength and elaborate decoration. Beyond the arches is the chancel with its rib-vaulted ceiling. Finally

**Fig. 23: Norman Grandeur at St Michael's, Stewkley (Edward Stamp 1971)**

there is the altar, beneath a deeply splayed window, elaborately framed in zig-zag. Round the whole interior runs a line of intricate moulding, and every window is bordered with zig-zag. The amount of carving is bewildering in its opulence and variety: look out for dragons' heads, and dragons with twisted tails.[11] **St Michael's is well worth a visit.**

However, not all Norman churches are on the scale of Stewkley. Nearby, at tiny Dunton, is a delightful little church with a medieval tower and chancel, and in between them a genuine Norman nave with a Norman font and somewhat younger, but very ancient, box-pews: see Fig. 24 and Plate C6.

## *THE NORMANS AND THE MONASTERIES*

The Normans also encouraged a considerable development of monasticism, and foundations from the continent expanded into England. Between 1066 and 1154 the number of religious houses rose from 48 to nearly 300. Just as the Normans founded churches to gain merit in the after-life, so also some founded monasteries. Bradwell Abbey was such a case. [12]

For his support in subduing the English, William I leased over 12,000 acres in North Bucks. and the Vale to a Breton known as Mainou. He made Wolverton his home and base, and his motte and bailey still stand by Old Wolverton Church and the now deserted village. When he died, his son Meinfelin inherited the barony. Clearly, he had much to be thankful for, but he was getting old and, like many Norman barons, he feared that his soul would be banished to purgatory, where his sins would be slowly purged with fire, before being admitted into Heaven. However, he had been told that these sufferings could be lessened by regular prayers and masses to the Virgin Mary. So – probably in 1154 – with a gift of 450 acres of land at nearby Bradwell, he persuaded the prior of Luffield Priory to build a monastery on it, which later became known as Bradwell Abbey. Shortly afterwards Meinfelin died, and the monks began regular prayers for the souls of him and his wife. This was typical of the way in which many Norman churches and monasteries originated. However, it was a small monastery, and typical of the houses in the Vale and North Bucks., financed by Norman lords unable or unwilling to afford the cost of a large abbey. The sites of 15 are known, but only five retain buildings: see Table 5. The rest have

**Table 5: The Remains of Religious Houses of the Vale and North Bucks** [14]

| Name | Found'n | 0/S Ref. | Remains | Dissolution |
|------|---------|----------|---------|-------------|
| Bradwell Abbey | 1154 # | 827394 | A small chapel with wall paintings, and a tithe barn. | 1524 Given to Cardinal Wolsey to fund a new college at Oxford. |
| Chetwode Priory | 1245 | 640298 | The only monastic church still in use in Bucks. | Absorbed by Notley Abbey in 1460. |
| Newton Longville Priory | Circa 1150 # | 847313 | In the manor house are *"the remains of a Norman priory"*. * | Granted to New College, Oxford in 1441. |
| Notley Abbey | Before 1164 # | 715093 | Now, after restoration, a venue for weddings. | Surrendered Dec. 1538. |
| Ashridge College | 1283 | 994121 | Re-built in 1814. Only a fine vaulted cellar remains. | 1538/9 |

* Mee, Arthur: The Kings England, Buckinghamshire, pp. 160-1.    # Norman foundation

**Fig. 24: St. Martin's Church, Dunton**

**Fig. 25: Notley Abbey Dovecote**

The dovecote housed hundreds of doves. The birds grew fat on the villagers' crops, and the monks grew fat on the doves. It annoyed the villagers, for they were not allowed to kill the birds.

disappeared except for occasional earthworks, fishponds and fragments of masonry embedded in nearby buildings. Even at the Reformation, the Vale and North Bucks. had only two slightly larger but still modest houses: Notley Abbey (early-mid 12th century), and the College of the Bonhommes at Ashridge.[13] Both feature in chapter 8.

Although they often departed from their own high ideals, the monasteries brought a little humanity into the harshness of medieval life. They provided parish priests, they relieved the poor and comforted the sick. Being literate and numerate in an ignorant world, they provided some education, reproduced books and manuscripts before the invention of printing, serviced the courts of the numerous manors which they had been given, and kept records of events both local and national.

Of course, the overall wealth of the monasteries and churches did not escape the eyes of the Norman kings. From around 1070, William the Conqueror applied feudal principles to the bishoprics and monasteries, and required knight-service from them in return for their occupation of his lands! William II also coveted monastic wealth. He reasoned that the services of an estate could not be rendered by a minor, and so neither could the services of a bishopric or an abbey be rendered if the bishop or abbot was not in post, so he could justly take its income instead. One didn't argue with William II any more than with his father!

### BRILL AND THE FOREST OF BERNWOOD [15]

Although it did not consist entirely of woodland, Bernwood was a substantial forest, extending in the west to the edge of Oxford, in the east to Bletchley, in the north to Tingewick and in the south to Chearsley and Quainton. Although William the Conqueror claimed ownership of the whole of England, with the royal forests he went further, insisting upon exclusive rights of hunting for himself and his court. For, next to fighting, the Normans loved hunting. Much forest was already available, but the Normans extended it until by the reign of Henry II it covered almost one-third of England. And it included *any* area where the king hunted, so if, during a hunt, their prey strayed into the villagers' crops, the whole hunt would follow, often doing enormous damage.

To ensure the pleasures of the chase, the Normans introduced Forest Laws enforced by forest wardens. For carrying a bow and arrows in the forest one could be fined. To stop it from chasing game, a hunting dog must have three claws cut off each of its front paws, leaving only the ball of the foot.[16] Otherwise the owner would be fined 3s-0d for each animal. To preserve the low-level vegetation on which the deer fed, only the inhabitants of Brill, Boarstall and Oakley, were allowed to graze private animals in the forest, unless licensed by the king. Although the deer, rabbits and hares would feed in the villages' open fields, causing considerable damage, *"only the favoured and well-connected"* such as Chetwode Priory were allowed to enclose their fields.[17]

The penalties for disobedience were harsh. Early punishments for killing game included death, blinding, and mutilation. There were also lesser penalties for lesser offences, of which there were many, and they brought in a substantial income. In 1176, in Hampshire alone, they yielded £2,093.[18] In fact, under the Normans the royal forests became *"a nice little earner"*. In addition, for a price, most things could be arranged. Thus special licences might be granted for the king's favourites to hunt, or fell timber. The royal larder benefited from the supply of venison, and other woodland fare, which was greatly appreciated by the royal court as an alternative to salted beef and fish. It was cheaply obtained too. Of course, all the restrictions, innovations and penalties considerably disadvantaged the English nobility, to say nothing of the English peasants. It certainly soured the already brittle relationship between the conquerors and the conquered. As the Anglo-Saxon Chronicle put it:

> *He ( William the Conqueror ) made great protection for the game*
> *And imposed laws for the same,*

*That who so slew hart and hind*
*Should be made blind.*
*He preserved the harts and boars*
*And loved the stags as much*
*As if he were their father.*
*Powerful men complained of it and poor men lamented it,*
*But so fierce was he that he cared not for the rancour of them all.* [19]

## THE BEGINNING OF AN ERA

William the Conqueror died in Normandy in 1087. About forty years later Ordericus Vitalis reported what he believed to be William's death-bed confession:[20]

*I have persecuted the natives of England beyond all reason. Whether gentle or simple I have cruelly oppressed them; many I have unjustly disinherited; innumerable multitudes perished through me by famine or the sword . . . I fell on the English like a ravening lion. I commanded their houses and corn, with all their implements and chattels, to be burnt without distinction, and great herds of cattle and beasts of burden to be butchered wherever they were found. In this way I took revenge on multitudes of both sexes by subjecting them to the calamity of a cruel famine, and so became the barbarous murderer of many thousands, both young and old, of that fine race of people. Having gained the throne of that kingdom by so many crimes I dare not leave it to anyone but God.*

William's reign was the beginning of an era. William's third son William Rufus, who reigned as William II (1087-1100), *"was even more savage than his father. He lived entirely for the battlefield:. greedy, immoral and fearless, he eliminated anyone who defied him"*.[21] Neither was Henry I (1100-1135), the Conqueror's youngest son, much better *"for he too was a cruel and violent man, who spent his life either fighting or hunting"*. Stephen (1135-1154), the last of the Norman kings, and a grandson of the Conqueror, was described by contemporaries as good humoured, kindly and easy-going; a good knight, but as a ruler a weak fool. His reign was plagued by nineteen years of civil war. Some of his subjects are said to have expressed a preference for his predecessors!

# Chapter 5

## *THE DECLINE OF FEUDALISM*

The essence of feudalism was simply the payment of rent for the use of land, by providing the landlord with some sort of labour service. At the highest level of society the king required his tenants-in-chief to pay their rent by providing him with knightly service in the royal army. At the lowest level of society the lord of the manor required his tenants (the peasants) to pay their rent by providing him with manual labour or with a combination of labour and goods. The decline of the feudal system began when the king became willing to accept his rent in cash for, in the long run, it stripped the transaction of its feudal trappings of chivalry, homage and fealty at a time when such matters were sworn on the Bible, and were thus taken very seriously. These cash payments, called scutage (literally 'shield money'), began as early as 1100. They enabled the king's tenants to avoid the battlefield while, with cash in hand, the king could hire just those knights whose age, fitness, skills and enthusiasm for battle were most to his liking. For his tenants-in-chief this converted a transaction often complicated by personal relationships, accidents, age and illness into a simple matter of cash, which the lord's clerk could pay direct to the king's exchequer. However, the lord had to obtain the cash. There were three possible sources. Firstly there was the booty from wars, but this was irregular and uncertain. Secondly, there were the many fines, which the lord could extract from his peasants as payment for *"due and accustomed services"*, but the sums involved were small and uncertain. Finally, there was the lord's land (his 'demesne') which traditionally was cultivated by the unpaid labour of his peasants, who did this instead of paying cash rents for the land which they held from the lord. Some lords began to wonder whether charging the peasants cash rents for the land which they occupied, and using that cash to employ waged labour on the demesne, might increase productivity and so create a bigger surplus which could be sold to obtain cash for the king.

### *THE INTRODUCTION OF CASH RENTS INTO THE MANOR*
Peasants and lords both saw advantages and disadvantages in such a change. Several factors would particularly concern the peasants. Many felt that the labour rent was one of the things that was responsible for their lowly status in life. They were resentful and tired of being at the beck and call of the lord's reeve, who was only of peasant birth like themselves, but who – himself under the sharp eye and tongue of the lord's steward – ordered and chivvied them, and accepted no excuses if the allotted tasks were not completed by the end of the day. They also found that it was difficult working for the lord and cultivating their own land at the same time, because the precise timing of jobs such as sowing, harrowing, weeding, reaping, stooking and carting was determined not by the whim of the lord, and certainly not by the convenience of the peasants, but by 'windows' in the weather, which were common to both. Consequently, too often the peasant needed to be in two places at the same time, and the lord's work always had priority. In addition, disputes with the lord or the manor's officers were too frequent for comfort. For instance, there were always arguments as to whether time lost through illness, bad weather or holy days had to be made up later or done by a substitute at the peasant's cost. Some stewards would not accept sickness as an excuse unless the last rites had been administered! Moreover, a change to cash rents would leave the peasants with more time to attend to their own affairs. Time perhaps to take on more land, if the opportunity arose. On the other hand, some peasants worried that at the end of the farming year they would not have a sufficient surplus of crops to take to the market, or that the market price would not yield them sufficient cash with which to pay the rent.

Some lords of the manor also favoured a monetary regime, though for rather different reasons. Many felt themselves served by half-hearted and lazy workers, and that consequently their land under-produced. There was also the problem of undisciplined workers, for manorial officials wasted much time directing and supervising workers, and resolving disputes with them and even between them. And if the result of a dispute did not go their way, disgruntled peasants could create a considerable and expensive nuisance for a lord. For example, trespassing in the lord's meadow with cattle was an offence presented at manorial courts with astonishing regularity. At Kingsey (south of Haddenham) in 1322 the whole body of tenants committed this offence, and were fined by the manorial court. Theft was another problem: a pocketful of beans or grain, a few eggs here and a sheaf of corn there. And if the lord's acres were scattered amongst those of the villagers it was not difficult to steal a furrow when ploughing or reaping. As Walter of Henley, a contemporary commentator on agriculture, warned:

> *Customary tenants neglect their work, and it is necessary to guard against fraud.*

A major advantage of cash rents to the lord of a manor was that it left him with several options. He could continue to farm his demesne as arable, but with paid labour which could be dismissed if it was not sufficiently productive. Alternatively, he could convert the demesne arable into pasture and install a flock of sheep, for wool was a very profitable crop, and the towns were a good market for meat. The only labour needed would be a few shepherds. Another possibility was for the lord to rent out the demesne to the highest bidder, and leave him to exploit the situation to his best advantage. An increasing number of lords were prepared to see a weakening in the feudal system in return for a higher income, even if much of it had to be paid over to the king. However, some lords were reluctant to lose the tight control over the peasants which the forced labour of the feudal system gave them.

Despite the reservations of some lords, significant changes began to take place, and by the end of the 13th century, when the manorial records of Buckinghamshire begin, the conversion of the peasants' manorial obligations from personal services into cash rents, and the parallel change of the lords hiring labour in return for wages, was already under way, though it varied from manor to manor. Thus:[1]

> *At Brill by 1251 the lord paid in cash for all work connected with the harvest, but the rest of the year's work was done by tenants in lieu of rent.*
> *At Westcott in 1336 and 1337 all the work at harvest was paid for in cash, and the tenant of a small-holding paid a rent of 12d a year.*
> *At Wendover in 1338 men were hired to help with the hay-making, but all the reaping was paid for by the acre.*
> *At Ilmer in 1342 only the reapers, swineherd and a maidservant were paid in money, whereas in 1343 wages were paid to all labourers.*
> *At Whaddon it was 1356-7 before the tenants paid their rent in cash, instead of performing services in person.*
> *At Haddenham in 1625, the new manorial management tried to reimpose labour rents. However, the tenants were determined to end the custom once and for all. They raised what was then the enormous sum of £1,532, and this was accepted. Of course, they still had to pay a cash rent: the lord wanted 6d per acre; the tenants offered 3d; the vicar was asked to make the decision, and he discreetly struck the bargain at 4d.[2]*

**The Manor of Winslow**

Winslow was certainly not amongst the earlier manors to change from "due and customary services" to cash rentals. It was 1341 before the lord of Winslow manor (the Abbot of St Albans

Abbey) broke with tradition and rented out for cash a few acres from his demesne, but after that the amount increased from year to year. Thus, in 1345 a further 116 acres of demesne arable and 3 pieces of pasture were rented out to 7 tenants. Still more of the demesne was leased out in 1347, when 43 villagers took over a massive 300 acres. Over the 12 years for which the leases ran, the cash rentals raised £240-17s-5d for the lord of the manor, and at the same time freed 51 peasants from customary services. It was another significant erosion of feudal restrictions. However, much more change was in the offing.

## POPULATION, PLAGUE AND THE ENGLISH ECONOMY

By the early 14th century England's population had increased considerably to around four million, and England was over-populated to the extent that diminishing returns had begun to operate. For example, to feed the additional population, less fertile land had to be brought into cultivation, *despite its lower productivity*. And the demand still exceeded the supply, which kept prices up and the living standard of the peasants down, thus maintaining the power of the landlords.[3] A peasant with an empty belly was far easier to discipline! Then in 1349 the Black Death arrived and, in a short but startling interlude, labour became scarce, and the relationship between lords and peasants changed to the peasant's advantage.

'Black Death' was the medieval name for bubonic plague, which was caused by a bacillus not identified until 1850. A feature of the disease is the bleeding beneath the skin causing dark blue or black bruises. The plague came in three forms. The most common form was called 'bubonic' because bubes (dreadfully painful tumours on the lymph nodes) developed in the early stages of the illness. The plague is believed to have originated in the heart of Asia, from which it was carried to the Crimea by the Tartars, who in 1346 were besieging the trading city of Kafka. When the siege army was suddenly stricken by disease, the commanding Khan used catapults to hurl infected corpses over the ramparts of the city. The disease entered Europe when, in October 1347, trading ships from the eastern Mediterranean put into the harbour at Messina, Sicily, with dead and dying men at the oars. By August 1348 the plague appeared at Melcombe Regis, now a suburb of Weymouth. It reached Bristol in September, and London in November. It then advanced relentlessly northwards. It was at its peak in Buckinghamshire from May to September 1349. Centuries later it was discovered that the carriers of the disease were the fleas which lived on the black rats, which thrived in the wattle and daub walls and the turf rooves of the medieval cottages. Until then, speculation about its origin was just a bizarre guessing game in which the cause was blamed on everything from immorality to astronomical spectacles.

### The Black Death Arrives

From the historian's viewpoint the snag about the Black Death of 1349 is that the manorial records of that time are usually too sparse to allow precise conclusions to be drawn. In the Vale and North Bucks. few records have survived for the 14th century, but even less for the critical years affected by the plague. Thus Chilton's manorial rolls survive for the courts held in 1347/8, and for the courts held in 1553/4, but none have yet been found for the intervening years. Similarly, Hartwell court rolls survive for 1344/45/47/48, and for 1356/58/59/60, but the critical years from 1349 to 1355 are missing. This is not too surprising. In mediaeval times most folk could not write their own name, let alone record court proceedings in abbreviated lawyers' Norman-Latin. And the few people who could do this, mainly lawyers and priests, were as vulnerable to the plague as anyone else.

However, where information is available it is quite startling. In August 1349 at the manor of Salden in the parish of Mursley, a jury declared under oath that the mill was of no value, for not only was the miller dead, but there were no tenants left to want any corn ground. In the previous year the total rents of freemen and serfs had amounted to £12. In the current year nothing had been collected, and the land was uncultivated. In 1349, in the diocese of Lincoln, of which Buckinghamshire was a part, 77 deceased clergy had to be replaced instead of the usual 13 or 14.[4] In the same year Leighton Buzzard church ordained three successive vicars! The lack of manorial rolls also indicates the disruption caused by the plague, for they were vital to the efficient administration of the manor. They recorded the peasants' holdings: the length of their leases; and their responsibilities as tenants. Most peasants were *customary* tenants, and it was to the manorial rolls that the lord turned when he needed to enforce customs. Fortunately, Winslow's manorial records were kept by the cellarers of St. Albans Abbey, the custodians of the Abbey's wine and provisions. Being clerics they were literate and used to keeping records in Latin. So Winslow's manorial records were maintained even during the Black Death.[5]

Winslow's court rolls reveal the drastic effect of the plague on its labour supply. Over twelve years (1327/8 to 1338/9) *before* the plague, the rolls record – *in connection with the occupation of property* – an average of 4.75 deaths per year. In just the first year of the plague (1349/50) the rolls list 161 deaths. The plague returned in 1361/2 to add another twenty-nine. The outbreaks of 1369 and 1371 passed Winslow by, but that of 1375/6 claimed a further sixteen lives. Since these are only the deaths of property-holders (plus, in a few cases, their nearest heir) the total death roll was undoubtedly very much higher, for when the Black Death entered a household it was so contagious that it was rare for just one person to die. While some of the unrecorded deaths would be of young children and the elderly, a significant number would be of men of working age, but who had not yet obtained their own acreage, and whose deaths were therefore not entered in the manorial records. So we shall never know the final total of Winslow's dead, for nearly two centuries would pass before churches had to record all burials.

## THE RECORD OF THE PLAGUE IN THE WINSLOW ROLLS

Note especially the heriot (the lord's death tax), and the fines paid by the new occupiers of the holdings, and in some cases the difficulty of finding guardians for an under-age heir to a property.

> *Geoffrey Mager has died. Held 1 messuage and 17 acres 3 roods of land and meadow. Heriot 1 horse worth 3s-4d. John his son is nearest heir, of full age. He came and paid a fine of 13s-4d.*

However, in twenty-five cases the heir to the dead person was under age. In those circumstances, if a parent survived, custody would normally be granted to that parent. For example:

> *Henry Cooc has died. Held 1 messuage and 18 acres of land. Heriot one ox worth 4s-0d. Alice his daughter is nearest heir, aged 9. Custody granted to Henry's wife Matilda until the heir's coming of age . . .*

With several deaths in the same family, a more distant relative had to be identified as the heir. Thus:

> *Ralph Kyng has died. Held 1 messuage and 1 virgate of land. Heriot one bullock worth 2s-0d. Walter his brother is nearest heir (but) has died. Heriot 1 brass pot worth 12d. Agnes his sister is Walter's nearest heir and has died. Heriot 1 bowl worth 6d. Her heir is John Kyng her uncle, who came and paid a fine. To hold by the rod. The fine was waived because of poverty.*

Soon the plague was killing people so quickly that more distant relatives had to become involved:

> *John Cherdesle has died. Held 2 messuages and 18 acres of land and more. Heriot one ox worth 4s-0d. Agnes his daughter is nearest heir, aged 15 days. Custody granted to Master John Isonde chaplain, until her coming of age . . . Because both the said Agnes and the said John the Chaplain died, the lord put the said land into his own hands, because Richard son*

*of John atte Halle is Agnes' nearest heir and under age, namely aged 12. Custody granted to Richard Martyn junior until Richard's coming of age. If the heir should happen to die under age . . .* [6]

If all the extended family had died, the manorial court had to look outside the family for a guardian. So:

*William Kyng has died. Held 1 messuage and 1 virgate of land. Heriot one ox worth 8s-0d. Ralph his son is nearest heir, aged 12. He came and paid his fine. Fine 26s-8d and no more because of poverty. He is under age so custody of the heir and holdings was granted to Geoffrey Kyng Vicar of Greneburgh until he (i.e. Ralph) comes of age . . .*

## THE EFFECTS OF THE PLAGUE ON THE MANORIAL SYSTEM

The restrictive, expensive and degrading regime of the typical manor was increasingly resented by the villagers. However, some regulations were considered especially servile, and so were particularly resented. Winslow's villagers hated the rule which compelled them to have their corn ground at the lord's mill for a payment (called multure) in cash or flour, for medieval millers had a reputation for fleecing their customers. Non-compliance resulted in a fine. The brewing of ale was similarly restricted. At just one Winslow court no less than 46 villagers "brewed, and broke the assize", and were fined. Another major source of resentment was the rule that villagers had to live and work "within the lordship". He or she could not leave the manor unless a fine was paid for the lord's permission, which had to be renewed annually, and which was very carefully recorded. Thus at Winslow in 1364:

*Nicholas Thornbrugh made a fine with the lord so that he can live outside the lordship while it pleases the lord. And he pays 6d annually as poll-tax.*

Anyone who left without permission was condemned as a fugitive, and could be taken into custody and forcibly returned to his or her lord. In addition, at Winslow, *except for the demesne land leased at an annual rent in the 1340's,* each villager still had to *'hold himself and his heirs in villeinage at the lord's will through the due and accustomed services'.* Of course, these services still included both weekly and boon work on the lord's land which, from the villagers' viewpoint, were just as inconvenient as ever.

Overall the mortality from the plague was immense: there was no known cure. In England as a whole probably a third to a half of the population perished. In the many very badly affected settlements the death rate was so high that burial became a problem. In one parish the priest had to add half an acre to his graveyard without proper authority. Naturally agriculture suffered. In the worst affected areas the harvest rotted in the fields. Cows, oxen and sheep strayed through the fields and wandered among the crops, for there was no-one to drive them off, or herd them, or milk them. Many animals died of hunger, neglect and disease in remote lanes and copses. Henry Knighton, a churchman of the time, tells us: [7]

*Even in the following winter there was such a shortage of servants for all sorts of labour as it was believed had never been before.*

At Cuxham, a few miles into Oxfordshire, not only was the field labour disastrously reduced, but also the supervision: the reeve died in March 1349, his successor died in April, another successor in June and yet another in July. Although for most manors the shortage of labour quickened the change from payment by labour to payment by cash, all the restrictions and the fines on customary tenants (at death, marriage, grinding corn, etc.,) were still enforced. This increased the villagers' discontent. [8]

## REBELLION WRIT LARGE

Obviously the impact of the plague on Winslow was severe. Its labour supply had been horrendously reduced. It was now inadequate to carry out the fieldwork necessary to maintain the villagers and the lord of the manor at their previous standard of living. Most villages in England were facing the same problem, but lords of the manors were reacting to it in different ways. Some were determined to maintain the discipline of the feudal system. Others were more pragmatic and prepared to welcome fugitives from other manors with concessions, which would improve their status and standard of living, while at the same time helping their new manor to bring back into cultivation some of the land abandoned due to the plague. Such news spread quickly. Soon it was being whispered around Winslow.

In 1351, just as Winslow was beginning to recover from the Black Death, eight tenants of the manor refused to go to the woods and collect nuts for their lord. Tenants often broke the rules, but usually meekly paid a fine as punishment. The nut gathering was different because the tenants claimed, *"that they were never accustomed to perform the work . . . nor ought they rightly to do it"*. To settle the matter the next manorial court was held under a great ash tree near St. Albans Abbey, which held the manor's records. These proved that the villagers were wrong, They acknowledged their error and were fined, and their lord assumed that discipline had been restored. So he was surprised and annoyed to discover that four of his villagers had absconded. He was even more upset to learn that the his manorial jury knew all about it. At its next meeting the manorial court noted:

> John, Ralph and William Adam and Alexander Horsemeleward who are living at Swanbourne are the lord's villeins, and are staying outside the lordship without licence. Therefore it was ordered to seize their bodies, and bring them to St. Albans.

For this was rebellion writ large: a blow to the authority of the lord, and a breach of feudal discipline. It could set a precedent. The jurors were fined 2d each for concealing the fact that villagers were living outside the lordship. Then the lord sent his servants to Swanbourne where they arrested William Adam and brought him back to Winslow. But not for long! For:

> Richard le Barn came from Swanbourne to Wynselow and forcibly seized and abducted William against the will of the lord and his servants. Advice is to be taken and a writ procured, etc..

Brave words! But nothing seems to have come of them. In the meantime:

> The jurors reported that Henry Boveton had arrested John Adam, a villager of the lord. Henry released him of his own accord, against the lord's will. And Henry was accused on this account, and put himself at the lord's mercy for contempt. And Henry undertook to make John come to the next court . . .

Unfortunately, Henry couldn't deliver, which embarrassed both him and the manorial jury, which had supported him. The failure to retrieve these early fugitives, who had easily found employment elsewhere, encouraged others. By the end of 1358 thirty-eight young men and women had left Winslow, never to return. And twenty years after the first visitation of the plague, the total of absconders reached fifty-six, including ten females. The failure to bring them back to Winslow is the more remarkable because the new locations of about half the fugitives were known, and for some even the name of the person with whom they were staying. These were fugitives who had gone to nearby manors like Nash, Claydon, Swanbourne, Mursley, Great Horwood and Waddesdon. A few went further afield, to London, Kent, Reading, Lincolnshire, Woburn and St. Albans. For the rest there are no precise records.

None of the fugitives returned to live in the Manor of Winslow. Obviously they had found manors where concessions were available, such as cash payments of rent, free entry into property, no forced labour, and fewer permissions to be obtained, most probably because the lords of those manors were desperate to attract labour to replace the victims of the plague. Such concessions would be seen by fugitives as a definite advance in status. With such freedom from the lord's whims, a new day had dawned. Historically, it was yet another step towards the end of the feudal system.

### A Further Decline in Labour Rents

Although in the 1340's part of the lord's demesne had been let out for cash rents, the rest of Winslow manor's land was still held in return for labour rents. Indeed, the mantra, *"due and accustomed services"*, was repeated in the manorial rolls with monotonous regularity until November 1363, when an entry about property to be occupied by a William Robyn states that it is to be held simply:

> *in villeinage, at the lord's will, paying the lord annually the whole rent . . . and he (Robyn) will find in the Autumn two men while the lord has need for harvesting.*

All the other entries in the manorial rolls at that time still require not only boon work but the *due and accustomed services*. So what next? An entry for July 1364 granted a William Bate 3 acres to be held:

> *in villeinage, at the lord's will performing annually one boon service with one man for a day while the lord has need for harvesting . . . The fine was waived.*

Only one man for one day for boon work! No fine, and no "due and accustomed services"! Then the dam broke. At the court of July 1370, under the heading "Demising (i.e. transferring ) of Demesne Land", 26 tenants were all granted land solely in return for cash rentals yielding a total of £5-16s-0d per annum. This was followed (Court of May 1371) by a general relaxation of boon work:

> *the lord granted to his tenants of Wynselow, Shipton and Horewode a relaxation of their boon-works from Michaelmas before the date of the court to the end of 21 years, at the instance and petition of those going to continue as the lord's tenants, so that any tenants who were accustomed to perform boonwork should pay the lord annually for each boon-worker 2s-0d.*

Of course, much of Winslow's land was still held for "due and accustomed duties" (i.e. labour rent), but leasehold for a cash rental had been conceded. Winslow's 14th century rolls do not extend beyond 1377, so we do not know how much more leasehold tenancy was created at this time.

By 1600 [9] land held for "due and accustomed duties" still existed, but was regularly termed copyhold, because such holdings were evidenced by *"a copie of the appropriate entry on the court roll"*. At this time there were at least 155 copyholders in Winslow Manor. They still faced fines for entering property, and the lord was still entitled to his heriot. They were still dissatisfied with their lot, and in dispute with the Lord of the Manor, although there is no mention of regulations on marriage, place of residence or the education of children, and despite the fact that they now had the right to lease out their copyhold lands for up to 21 years *without licence of the lord*. Freehold, leasehold and copyhold were clearly distinguished by name. Arthur Clear [10] tells us that by 1900 in Winslow:

> *many of the worst features of serfdom and villeinage have been allowed to lapse, or remain dormant, yet fines and heriots are still pretty rigidly enforced.*

He quotes from Winslow records of the 18th and 19th centuries seven cases of fines for admissions to property, and ten cases of heriots, including in 1885 a heriot of £84 which had to be paid to obtain entry to the quarter acre upon which the new Congregational Chapel was to be built.

These relics of the past were finally disposed of when copyholds, heriots and other relics of feudal times were abolished by an Act of 1924/5.

### *The Response of the Landlords*

The shortage of labour due to the Black Death increased the bargaining power of the peasants, and reduced that of the landlords. So shortly after the end of the plague the wages of labourers and craftsmen rose significantly. Naturally, landlords tried to prevent this, and in 1351 Parliament passed a Statute of Labourers in an attempt to freeze wages. It failed. In fact, it would have made no difference to the landlords if it had succeeded. Well paid or poorly paid, labour was in short supply. And without an adequate labour force, landlords could make little or no profit from arable farming. Landlords responded in a number of ways. Many welcomed new peasants, not only to keep the land under cultivation, but also to keep down the wage demands of the peasants already resident, by showing that there was no shortage of labour on their manor. Some lords economised on labour by converting arable to pasture and rearing cattle and/or sheep, both for the meat market and in the case of sheep for their wool. So popular did this become that nearly 9% of Buckinghamshire (mainly north of the Chilterns) had been enclosed by 1607.[11] Other lords were more adventurous. They rented out the demesne and became absentee landlords, either making politics (i.e: attendance at the royal court) their principal occupation, or joining the army, which was fighting the French in what we now call the Hundred Years' War, in the hope of plunder. Whether it was politics or war these lords' most pressing need was for cash rather than agricultural produce, a situation which hastened the conversion of their manors to a monetary economy. Some landlords even enclosed the open fields farmed by the peasants, and turned them out onto the roads: a problem to which we shall return in chapter 6. Despite all the above, many landlords tried to continue as in earlier times, but they were desperate for labour, so wages continued to rise, which did curtail their profits and therefore their lifestyles. Moreover, during the next century the population continued to fall, which further increased the bargaining power of craftsmen and labourers.

Some peasants were also stimulated by the new situation. The more ambitious, especially those whose sharper minds and more temperate natures had enabled them to save for the future, could buy or lease more land. The more successful of these would emerge in the next century as the yeomen. Many peasants would never reach that state, and would have to sell out in the 14th century and become labourers in order to survive. Both developments are well illustrated by what happened in Sherington.[12]

By removing the labour surplus, the Black Death reduced the overwhelming power of the lords, and the Feudal System had to adjust, as has been indicated in this chapter. However, the changes came gradually, and at different times in different places.

### *THE PEASANTS' REVOLT*

By 1377 the feudal system was further weakened by an unexpected development. Due to the extravagance of the royal court and the exorbitant cost of the wars with France, the government was bankrupt, and a new parliament was desperate for money. So the poll tax was invented: a levy of one groat (about 4d) on everyone over 14 years old, male and female, rich and poor. In 1378 there was a further levy of 3 groats from everyone over 15 years, with a maximum of 20 shillings from households with over twenty members, a provision which greatly reduced the burden on the rich. No-one was surprised that the government was desperate for money, or that it was relying upon taxation to provide it. What was unexpected was the extension of the tax to every citizen over the stated age, *irrespective of their personal wealth*. This was a new development, and for many peasants it was the last straw.

We mentioned earlier that the restriction which the peasants of Winslow most resented was the obligation to pay for their corn to be ground at the Lord Abbot's mill. So Winslow's peasants were furious when, in order to enforce use of his mill, the Abbot confiscated the handmills which his men had found by searching their homes, and used them for paving the abbey cloisters.[13] This coincided with the series of uprisings known as the Peasants' Revolt. The poll tax was the spark that started the fire, but it was fuelled by all the other grievances. So, when they heard that the men of St. Albans had risen against St. Albans Abbey, releasing the Abbot's prisoners, seizing his grain reserves, decimating his fishponds, and burning his records, the men of Winslow hastened to join them. Under the leadership of one William Gryndecobbe, they tore up their millstones and carried them home in triumph, having extorted from the terrified monks *"charters of liberties such as were never before held by bondmen"*.

The monks had reason to be terrified, for this uprising included much mob violence. Monasteries, abbeys and the houses of repressive landlords were attacked, and some buildings were burnt or pulled down. The palace of John of Gaunt, King Richard's uncle, who was the power behind the throne (the king was only eleven years old), was ransacked and reduced to ashes. Old manuscripts and manorial records were destroyed in the hope that this would end the oppressive old customs. No mercy was shown to clerks and lawyers, who were regarded as the main enemies of the common people. The few that had not run away were beheaded. Then, due to treachery in which the young King Richard played a leading part, the government's troops brought the revolt to a bloody end:

> *Never before had there been such a slaughter of the commons of England. All over southern England the gallows sprouted and the blocks ran red.*

To add to the horror, the authorities disposed of some of the leaders by the bestial process of part-hanging before drawing and quartering. The death toll has since been estimated at seven thousand.[14] The survivors returned to their manors, to the same endless days of labour, the same miserable hovels, and still too many fines and restrictions. Doubtless they felt that things would never change.

Of course, things did change. With nearly 700 years of hindsight we know that the Black Death and the Peasants' Revolt were turning points, which showed for the first time that the powers of the lords were finite. Progress since then has been infinitesimally slow, and the ups and downs have been boundless, but progress has been substantial. Royalty still reign, but they are less spendthrift, and no longer omnipotent. The aristocracy is still with us, but its role in government is being curbed. A pseudo-aristocracy (the life peerage) has been invented, to allow exceptional public service to be recognised, while any power which it endows is restricted to one lifetime. The suffrage is universal, and personal freedom taken for granted. The conditions of employment are closely controlled. The poverty of the 21st century would not be recognisable as such to a medieval peasant. There is greater equality of opportunity than ever before. And since the Law of Property Act was passed in 1925, even the most persistent remnants of the feudal system have been relegated to the history books.

## Chapter 6

# DESERTED VILLAGES

One of the strangest relics of medieval times is the deserted village. At first sight it is often little more than a collection of grassy mounds and hollows. Especially in summer, when the grass and weeds are high, many people walk through a site without realising what lies around them. Long broad trenches, as much as ten metres across, known to archaeologists as hollow-ways, were formerly the village streets and lanes. Alongside them are slightly raised rectangular areas which have clearly been levelled. These house platforms are all that remain of the cottages of the villagers. The buildings have long since disappeared, their thatched rooves sometimes torched to make them immediately uninhabitable, while years of weather soon demolished what remained of the timber and mud walls and partitions. Only where stone was used in building the cottages, and the land is under the plough, is there a litter of broken blocks to help identify the site. Often there is still a pond, or at least a reedy hollow where it once existed. Sometimes, wet or dry, we can see the moat which helped defend the manor house, and the large rectangular hollows, where fish were farmed to eat at Lent and on fish-days. Occasionally a motte or mound dominates the site, once the basis of defensive works and later perhaps partly excavated to obtain sand or gravel.[1] There may be one or two stone buildings or (more likely) just the remains of them, usually a church, or manor house; or buildings of more recent date, but incorporating remnants from earlier stone buildings. On some sites, as at Stowe, Tyringham and Fleet Marston, a solitary church is the only sign of the lost village (Fig. 27). Sometimes, as at Quarrendon and Burston, there are earthworks which are the remnants of formal gardens, once the landowner's pride and joy. Around the site of the village, traces of ridge and furrow still identify the medieval ploughed fields.

The sites of eighty-three deserted villages had been identified in Buckinghamshire up to 1997: about 13% of the English total. The vast majority of these are in the Vale and North Bucks.. Historians, archaeologists and geographers have long puzzled over the reasons which caused villages to be abandoned. We consider four possibilities: the Black Death; the enclosure of arable for pasture; landscaping for parkland or gardens; and soil exhaustion.

### THE BLACK DEATH
The Black Death, which was at its height in Britain in 1349 is estimated to have killed *nationwide* between a quarter and a half of the population. At one time it was thought to have been a principal cause of the desertion of villages. Beresford [2] considers this idea in some detail. His research shows that, of 230 villages present in Buckinghamshire in 1334, only 10% were subsequently deserted. He also shows that these deserted villages tended to be weaker economically than the norm *even before the Black Death.* Thus in the tax assessment of 1334 the average for all Buckinghamshire villages was 74 shillings, while the average for villages later deserted was only 44 shillings. Beresford concludes that the poorer they were, the easier prey villages were to developers, to whom sheep were more important than people. This was simply because the development of new markets for English wool, and the massive reduction in the labour needed when sheep replaced crops, enabled ambitious and ruthless landowners to enrich themselves by converting arable to pasture.

### Cublington
This is a village with a record of depopulation and increasing poverty, which points suspiciously towards the Black Death as the final blow. Certainly its demise was *not* due to enclosure of the

**Fig. 27: Fleet Marston Church of St. Mary**

Once the heart of a small village, St Mary's now stands in complete isolation upon a small hillock, half-hidden amongst the trees and surrounded by the deserted fields created by early enclosure. Only a litter of broken stone, still visible on the ploughed fields, remains as one walks up the path to the church. It was declared redundant in 1933. Its parish, with a population of 34 in 1997, has been united with Waddesdon. The key to the church is available from the farm shop on the main road.

arable fields, for these remained 'open' until the parliamentary enclosure of 1769. The site of medieval Cublington, which lies to the west of the present village, has the usual remains of hollow-ways and house platforms, and a fair-sized fish pond. Although the church has vanished, its approximate site is known, for at least sixty skeletons have been exhumed from what was once the churchyard. Perhaps stone from the old church contributed to the construction of its successor, built a few hundred yards to the east, at the beginning of the 15th century. We know the date because a brass plate in the new church records the burial in 1410 of the first rector. On the original site is a defensive mound or motte, known locally as the Beacon: thirty-five metres in diameter and eight metres high it is roughly conical, though with a flattened top, and is still largely encircled by a ditch, which was once a defensive moat, ten metres wide. The motte is listed in the schedule of ancient monuments as a motte castle, *"thought to have been constructed by Gozelin the Breton at the time of the Norman Conquest, or by the de Chesney family who held the land in the 12th century"*. [3] **It is worth visiting,** but can be very muddy in winter.

The Domesday Book tells us that in 1086 Cublington was valued at ten hides, had land for nine ploughs and supported twenty-one households. Eight families were villagers (the larger land-holders), a further eight were cottagers (smallholders), while five were families of slaves. This suggests a population of about a hundred. By 1283 the village had increased to 39 households, but by 1334 had declined to only 16 households. [4] By 1341 it was reported that:

*there are two carucates of land which lie fallow and uncultivated, and thirteen houses stand empty and their tenants have gone away because of their poverty. Sheep and lambs are few and no-one in the parish is substantial enough to be taxed to the Fifteenth.* [5]

Manorial surveys show that there was also a reduction in Cublington's demesne (i.e. the lord of the manor's arable): 1283 - 394 acres; 1304 - 300 acres; 1346 - 160 acres. It is certainly possible that a village which had reached this state could not withstand the loss of population that the Black Death created. Yet despite the abandonment of its ancient site, a new Cublington soon arose almost adjoining the old one. Perhaps the marshy nature of old Cublington's site prompted the move. Maybe the surviving population was reluctant to continue living on a site which had been devastated by plague. Whatever the reason, the new Cublington appears to have thrived. By 1428 it was *not* included in a list of villages with fewer than ten households.

### *Winslow*

Chapter 5 showed the drastic effect of plague on the labour supply of Winslow. Deaths as recorded in the manorial rolls [6] were considerable. However, to fully appreciate its impact, the figure for plague deaths must be increased by adding the number of fugitives and the unrecorded deaths of landless peasants. We know of no source for the latter. However, the unrecorded deaths included not only landless labourers, but the very vulnerable (babies, children and the elderly) all of whom, in most families, would be living and sleeping in one room. So, especially if Winslow had the pneumonic variant of the plague, which involved continuous coughing, the sick would be highly infectious and a guesstimate of one *unrecorded* death for every two *recorded* deaths does not seem unduly high.

| **Table 6:** | Deaths | 1349/50: | 161 |
|---|---|---|---|
| **The Loss of** | Deaths | 1361/62: | 29 |
| **Population** | Deaths | 1375/76: | 16 |
| **at Winslow** | Fugitives | 1349/58: | 38 |
| **due to the** | Fugitives | 1359/69: | 18 |
| **Black Death** | Total recorded: | | 262 |
| | Estimated deaths unrecorded: | | <u>103</u> |
| | Overall total: | | <u>365</u> |

Despite these serious losses due to the plague, not only was Winslow village not deserted, but very few holdings went out of cultivation. Several factors were in its favour. It had been a well-established Saxon village of moderate size, and it claimed [7] the distinction of having been the site of a palace of Offa, King of the Mercians (757-796). Offa is said to have founded St. Albans Abbey and to have granted it the royal manor of Winslow. As late as the 14th century, the Winslow court rolls mention 'The Royal Road'. At Domesday, Winslow's population was around 125, and it was definitely in the lordship of St Albans, an abbey noted for its wealth, strong leadership and ambitious plans. By 1349, Winslow was quite a large manor, and was certainly growing, for according to its records it had a 'New Towne' as well as the original settlement, and in 1235 King Henry III had granted the manor the right to hold a weekly market. An annual fair was also held. The manor not only contained Winslow village, but also two hamlets: Granborough and Little Horwood. The total acreage vacated in 1349 due to the Black Death was 1805 acres compared with 200 acres or less in a normal year. Fortunately, Winslow Manor had a significant number of landless labourers anxious to take on land, and others pleased to enlarge their holdings. Also, some families were willing to hold land in trust for the next generation. This was quite a demanding task as they would be expected to cultivate (or hire labour to cultivate) the lands in trust, in addition to farming their own holdings. Of course, they kept any profits generated by the lands in trust. A smaller village, or one with a different lordship, might have been more seriously, or even fatally, affected by the plague as were 10% of those villages which had existed in 1334. Despite its tribulations, Winslow survived and today the parish has 4,519 inhabitants.[8]

### Most Villages Survived

Reed accepts that mortality from the plague was high in some places, but assures us that, *"in Buckinghamshire . . . no village was deserted permanently as a **direct result** of the plague".*[9] Generally this is correct. For instance, at Kimble in 1349 all the tenants died and the land was not cultivated. Even so, as the years passed, new tenants were found and the village gradually revived. Again, according to a court roll of July 1349, the majority of the Bledlow tenants had died of the plague, and their tenements had reverted to the Lord of the Manor. He also managed to find new tenants, and so Bledlow survived. In May 1349 Nicholas Passelewe, Sheriff of Buckinghamshire, died of the plague as did all but two of his tenants: one in Mursley and one in Salden. Somehow Mursley revived. Presumably, 15 year old Robert Passelewe (the surviving son and heir of Nicholas) offered new tenants very favourable terms that attracted families anxious to improve their standard of living. Salden did not recover. By the 19th century just two farmhouses remained. [10]

## THE ENCLOSURE OF ARABLE FOR PASTURE

Due to the shortage of labour after the Black Death, the wages of peasants and tradesmen were increasing significantly, while the prices obtained for the products of the manor were at best stationary. Consequently some lords were either renting out their demesne for cash or enclosing it and converting it to pasture, usually for the much more profitable production of wool. This trend is evidenced by the rising price of sheep. In the 13th century, on royal manors, sheep were valued at 4d per head, but by the 14th century they generally sold at 2s-0d a head, though prices varied widely: 1s-1d at Wendover; 1s-6d at Winslow; [11] yet 2s-8d at Whaddon. Such enclosure meant that the manorial demesne only required a few shepherds and their dogs. Obviously, this caused unemployment amongst the local villagers. However, things were far worse on some manors where ruthless landlords enclosed not only the demesne but also all the open fields. In such cases the surplus labourers and their families were often driven off the land and their houses destroyed. There were also partial depopulations due to the move from labour rents to cash rents, a change which alerted the more enterprising peasants to the financial advantage of larger-scale arable farming. As they expanded their holdings, the number of tenants was reduced. Unless the displaced tenants could get work locally as labourers, they would have to move elsewhere. The problem is well illustrated by Haversham, just north of Wolverton. In 1305/6 it had 52 tenants of all kinds, whereas in 1458/9 several men were occupying two holdings each and the number of tenants had fallen to 35. By 1497/8 only 14 tenants were left, of whom just 10 occupied most of the land. Chibnall noticed a similar reduction in peasant holdings in Sherington.

As early as 1414 there were complaints about landlords who were converting their arable to pasture, so as to profit from the high prices fetched by sheep's fleeces. Consequently, in 1488,[12] a law was passed to stop "the decay of houses of husbandry". Unfortunately, the law was badly drafted and it was not until 1515 that a further Act quite specifically made the conversion of arable to pasture an offence. Even so, to make this law effective, Cardinal Wolsey had to establish a Commission of Enquiry in 1517 to enquire into specific cases. In the next fifty years the Commission referred 583 cases of depopulation to the Court of the Exchequer. Of these, seventy-nine (14%) were from Buckinghamshire and were mostly for small-scale enclosures. Beresford believed that the Commission's enquiries only caught the small fry, most large depopulations having already taken place by 1485, before which the Commission's writ did not run, evicted tenants had no legal remedy, and determined landowners could do what they liked. However, once the Commission was operating, its direct interference in particular cases, and the example this set for other landowners, did have some effect. Most landowners were very conscious of their social standing and had no wish to find themselves being investigated, and later in court charged with breaking the law. Even so, some of the enclosers knew one another socially as well as in the course of business, and so could rely upon at least some local sympathy.

### Burston (Byrdyston, Byrdeston, Birdston, Birdstane)

In 1086 Domesday Book records Burston as possessing about 600 acres plus meadows, and supporting 14 families. It was valued at 90 shillings. In 1489, as was later reported to Cardinal Wolsey's Commission:

> *John Swafield has lately gained possession of the fief [13] of the manor and farm of Byrdyston and of seven messuages with four hundred acres of arable land which he turned into grazing for sheep . . . On the occasion of the enclosing, eight ploughs were put down and sixty people evicted. From that time tears and wretchedness caused them to remove . . . from the whole hamlet of Byrdeston en masse, so that only sheep graze there [14].*

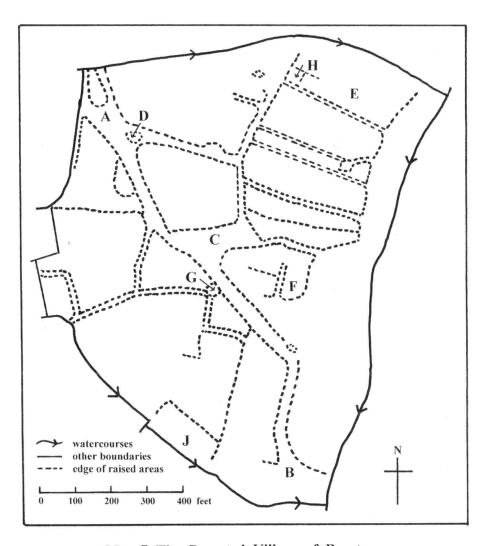

**Map 7: The Deserted Village of Burston**

61

**Fig. 28: Burston's Main Hollow-way A - B**

What are hollow-ways really like? On soft ground (as this picture shows) they can be difficult to identify, and often show up better on aerial photos. At the bottom of this hollow-way the tracks of a vehicle travelling from B to A are just visible in the frosted grass. The hollow-way is 10 to 15 feet wide, but looks wider because its sides have been worn down into quite gentle slopes by over 500 years of weather and grazing animals.

**Fig. 29: Burston's Cattle Pond**

It silted up long ago, and eventually acquired some trees, a few stumps of which could still be seen in the 1980's in the shallow layer of water. Now so much reedy grass has invaded it that very little water is visible, and the frost dominates the landscape.

After this rapid depopulation the manor prospered, almost trebling its value to 261s-8d. In 1516, Robert Lee bought the estate, and in 1526 received a royal licence to create a park. Leland visited Burston round about 1540 and praised the house with its orchard and park.[15] In 1563 an ecclesiastical survey found only three families living there. In the early 17th century Robert Lee's descendant Sir Henry Lee built or rebuilt the manor house and improved the park. He could afford such improvements, for sheep rearing was still very profitable. By this time the estate supported 1200 sheep, and was worth £520 a year.[16] The field to the south of the present Lower Burston Farm contains numerous earthworks, some of which are thought to be the remains of a formal garden established in the 17th century. To protect them from the deer, the gardens were divided from the park by a ha-ha six metres wide, the remains of which are still visible. [17] So are the hollow-ways and tofts of the long-deserted village just to the east. On Map 7 notice the main street of Burston:[18] a broad hollow-way, 3 to 4 feet deep in places, which crosses the site from A to B (see also Fig. 28). At C this street opens out into a large irregular space covered with small mounds. As it is virtually in the centre of the village, it has been suggested that it was the village green.[19] At D there is a a low flattish triangular mound, with a hollow in the centre. Could this have been the "hallowed acre" that parish tradition insists once existed at Burston? Such a feldcircan would have been used by visiting preachers from Wing or Aylesbury. From E to F there are at least six rectangular plots and a block of three smaller plots. These were the tofts: peasant holdings each comprising a homestead with a piece of cultivable land, often referred to as a garden. At Burston the largest of the plots measures 0.9 acres, while the smallest measures only 0.33 acres.[20] In addition most peasants held land in the three great fields. There are no bona fide house platforms, but G and H are possibilities, and surface variations at the western ends of the tofts may indicate the location of buildings. The rectangular area at J was a pond, fed at its northern end by a drainage ditch. However to the east there is a fast-flowing stream, which would supply cleaner water for domestic use, so the pond would be for the cattle and sheep (Fig. 29).

## *Quarrendon*

It is now believed that the depopulation of Quarrendon began in the 15th century due to the enterprise of the Lees. The example was set by Benedict Lee (died 1476), who converted his Warwickshire lands from arable farming to the grazing of sheep. He also farmed lands in the Vale of Aylesbury, which were managed by his sons. Their development of commercial grazing was very successful, and produced large quantities of fine fleeces. So, when the manor of Quarrendon reverted to the Crown in 1499, it was immediately leased to Benedict's son Richard, who had already farmed it for some years. Richard died in 1512 and his son Robert inherited the estate.

Robert Lee was summoned before Wolsey's Commission, but this was with regard to his involvement with enclosures and evictions at Fleet Marston and Burston. Although there had been enclosures on the family lands at Quarrendon, resulting in the depopulation of the village, which we now call Quarrendon One (Map 8), Robert was not accused of infringements there. This was probably because Quarrendon was a royal manor, and royal lands were excluded from the Commissioners' investigations. In any case, Quarrendon One enclosures were almost certainly carried out by his father (or grandfather) *before* 1485, which was the earliest date for retrospective investigations by Wolsey's Commission. [21]

Indeed, the evidence suggests that Sir Robert's own enclosures (he was knighted in 1522) came later. For we know that there was arable at Quarrendon in 1512, and that it still existed as late as 1524/5, when there were 20 households there to be taxed, a figure which suggests (when the non-taxpayers are taken into account) a total population of nearly 200. A village of this size would need a lot of arable to support it. So the enclosure, which obliterated the village now called Quarrendon Two, probably took place between 1525 and Sir Robert's death in 1540, when his will revealed that while at Quarrendon he had created an additional 960 acres of pasture, *and some*

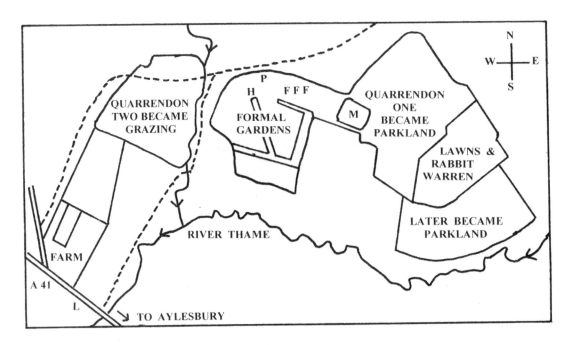

**Map 8: The Sites of the Deserted Villages and Other Remains at Quarrendon**

| | | | |
|---|---|---|---|
| H | Possible site of almshouses | L | Layby |
| M | Site of moated manor house | F | Fishponds |
| P | Ruins of St Peter's Church | | |

- ⌒Უ Watercourse
- - - - Public footpath

*land formerly occupied by dwellings!* Significantly, by 1563, the Bishop's Returns recorded just four families, which is totally consistent with a major conversion from arable to pastoral farming. The way was now open for Sir Henry Lee (1533-1611) to convert the Lees' large farm into a country estate (Map 8). The result was a large, moated country house with views in all directions. To the east, where once stood Quarrendon One, was parkland. Deer and sheep grazed on it, providing meat for the household and for sale to local butchers, while the rabbit warren, stretching away to the skyline, yielded both meat and fur. To the west, undoubtedly at great expense, Sir Henry had 22 acres of water gardens laid out for his visitors' entertainment. By 1636 Quarrendon village was just *"a small hamlet anciently enclosed and depopulated"*. Some impressive earthworks remain: a moat (Fig. 30) surrounding the foundations of Sir Henry's mansion, three fish ponds (Fig. 31), and the dried-up site of the water gardens (Fig. 32), a spectacular memorial to the commercial greed and social ambition of Elizabethan gentry, for in 1592 Sir Henry is said to have entertained Queen Elizabeth and her court with a masque of "great splendour and magnificence". Her maid of honour, Ann Vavasour, later became his mistress. The only building which remains is a very small part of the ruins of St Peter's Church (see Figs. 33 and 34, and Recollections B). Its demolition did not begin until some time after the Lees' main line had died out. For the Lees had been strong supporters of the church. Benedict Lee had left a bequest in his will which established the family's burial rights, and Sir Henry is credited with refurbishing it after it was badly damaged by a major flood in 1570. Both Sir Henry and his mistress were buried there, and commemorated with elaborate alabaster and marble tombs, while Lady Lee and her children were buried at St. Mary's, Aylesbury where a monument survives.

Unfortunately, the humps and hollows, which are all that remains of the two village sites, are only meaningful to the trained eye. They have been interpreted by Everson [22] as

**Fig. 30: Sir Henry Lee's Moat**

Rushes have taken over much of the water area, and only the whitened bole of a tree bridges it.

**Fig. 31: Sir Henry Lee's Fishponds**

The church forbade the eating of red meat on Fridays and in Lent. However, fish was allowed, but for inland places like Bucks. this meant poaching fish from a river, and risking being punished by the landlord, or buying salted herrings, unless you were wealthy enough to own fish ponds. Most peasants could not afford herrings, so fish days would usually mean more of the endless vegetable stews, or bread and ale.

## Recollections B: The Destruction of Quarrendon Chapel – J.K.Fowler

When I first saw this church in the eighteen-fifties, there then existed some remarkably handsome tombs in the chancel, but there was no roof left, neither a door nor a window in the place. When I visited it, there were eight or ten great Hereford oxen sheltering themselves from the sun in the nave, and the chancel was hurdled off for sheep. Yet there were men living who remembered marriages being celebrated in the church, and an occasional service performed by the clergyman from Bierton.

At this time there were only five tenant-farmers residing in the parish, and one labourer, who called himself clerk and sexton. It will thus be seen that everyone was interested in permitting this church to fall into ruin. When one of the tenants wanted a gatepost, a beam was taken from the roof, and when railings to mend a fence were wanted many rafters were carried off. When the farmyards or gateways required stoning, part of a wall was pecked down and carted away, and occasionally the roads were also mended with its ruins. This is no exaggeration, and I can vouch for the following as a fact. I was visiting a highly respectable farmer in the parish, who said that he was going to build a summer-house in his garden, and make it a sort of ruin, and that he could get two or three windows and other ornamental stonework from the chapel, and one of the doorways, and build them into the walls and when covered with ivy it would look very well. I expressed my horror at his suggestions, but when I visited his place a few months later, there was the summer house.

There was also a man, residing in Aylesbury, a turner by trade, who made ornamental candlesticks which were at that time popular decorations for the mantel-shelf. And this worthy was accustomed to go to Quarrendon Chapel when he had an order, and break off an arm or a leg from the alabaster figures, and then turn them with his lathe into candlesticks. I once saw a leg broken off in this manner, with the garter in rich blue enamel, and the legend in gold letters, "Honi soit qui mal y pense", still visible. No-one attempted to prevent the barbarous destruction of this ancient structure, once dedicated to the service of God and used for many centuries for that purpose.

J.K.Fowler: Recollections of Old Country Life, Longman, Green & Co., 1894.

loose groupings of farmsteads, farm buildings and cottages around open greens rather than the tightly grouped buildings more typical of medieval villages. Quarrendon One was the more substantial of the villages, and appears to have comprised four or five quite large farmsteads surrounded by closes, gardens and platforms, which were probably the sites of cottages, barns, stables and other farm outhouses, all linked by a network of hollow-ways. Quarrendon Two has similar elements but is on a smaller scale. **The site as a whole is well worth a visit.**

### Creslow (Kerselawe, Kerslowe)

Situated in an isolated spot, about a mile north-east of Whitchurch, the site of its deserted village is marked by a tumbled landscape of grassy mounds and hollows in a field just north of Creslow manor house. Only the manor house remains, much altered and reduced, though a tower with a turret, and narrow pointed lancets has survived to remind us of the uncertainties of life in the early 14th century. Built around 1330, this is one of the oldest inhabited buildings in Buckinghamshire. It remains an impressive building (see Plate C9), and has distant views over a huge green bowl, the flocks and herds from which once supplied the royal table. The Antiquarian and Historian, William Camden (1551- 1623), noted that Creslowe's "rich meadows feed an

**Fig. 32: A Corner of the Water Gardens**

Sir Henry's elaborate water gardens extended over 22 acres, which were reshaped to provide massive embankments, channels, ponds and islands. All this was done when wheelbarrows and shovels were the principal tools.

**Fig. 33: St Peter's Church, Quarrendon in 1846**

**Fig. 34: St. Peter's Church, Quarrendon in 2003**

**Fig. 35: Creslow's Redundant late Norman Chapel**
From the appearance of the window it was either very late Norman or very early English.

incredible number of sheep", and "consisting of around 500 acres (327 of them in one huge field) hath yielded a rent of £800 a year and upwards". Even in its truncated modern form, the manor house's sturdy structure reflects this wealth, for its tower is 43 feet high, its stone walls are 6 feet thick, it has mullioned windows, and a superb cellar with a vaulted roof. Close by are the remains of a chapel which once had a chancel and a small tower. Until the reign of Elizabeth I it was the parish church. Since then it has been used as a dovecote, a barn for feeding cattle, and later as a coach-house and stable (Fig. 35).

## LANDSCAPING FOR PARKS AND GARDENS

In Norman times parks were created by the very wealthy: as status symbols; to provide enjoyable exercise; and for a supply of venison. For the tenants of a manor, a particular problem arose when emparkment reduced their 'common rights', this meaning their right to pasture their livestock in woodland, on waste land, or on fallow land. There were complaints about this problem as early as 1254. Tenants often had pasturage in their lord's park *provided they paid for it*. Of course, if before emparkment they had had *free* pasturage they would obviously regret the loss, which could be considerable. By the 15th and 16th centuries wealth from sheep farming, from well-remunerated government appointments, and from industry and trade was becoming more dispersed. And for those who had money but no estate, the dissolution of the monasteries made a great deal of land available. By the 17th and 18th centuries some families had amassed large fortunes with which they acquired land, and built mansions. And then re-built them as even bigger mansions. It was in this context that a fashion for landscaping and large-scale gardens developed. Of course, the very profitable grazing of sheep, deer and cattle was quite compatible with a landscaped park, and the invention of the ha-ha protected gardens from the stock in the park. Such landowners did not want the hovels of the local peasantry on their doorstep, or as a blot on their carefully contrived vistas.

### Stowe

In the 16th century the parish of Stowe comprised the four settlements of Boycott, Dadford, Lamport and Stowe, the latter being roughly 2½ miles north-west of Buckingham. Towards the end of the century, Peter Temple, a wealthy grazier of Warwickshire, purchased the manor of Stowe and carried out a limited amount of enclosure in 1587 and 1599. By 1637 his grandson (another Peter) had inherited the estate, which already included a deer park. To extend it and re-fashion the landscape, he enclosed the commons of Lamport and Stowe. Later, in 1649, he enclosed the common fields of Stowe, destroying at least seven houses and ten or twelve of its farms, and turning out the occupiers, some of whom moved to Dadford. He re-stocked the park with deer, which multiplied so rapidly that they destroyed both crops and woods, further depriving the villagers, of firewood, for instance. All this incensed the Dayrells of Lillingstone, who had an estate at Lamport, and a bitter quarrel ensued, which spread to other local families.

In 1680 Peter Temple's great-grandson, Sir Richard Temple (1634-97), returned rich from the wars and built '*a great messuage or house of brick*' a little to the north-west of the old family home, which was demolished. In 1694, Celia Fiennes, the tireless traveller, visited Stowe: [23]

> *Stowe House stands pretty high. You enter into a hall, very lofty with a gallery round the top. Thence to a great parlour with a balcony that opens onto the garden. And there is a vista through the whole house, so that on one side you view the gardens which are one below another, separated by terraced walks. Beyond them are orchards and woods. From the other side (of the house) you see the park with an avenue of trees. . . . A good staircase takes one to the gallery which leads through a large cupulow to the ledds, from which there is a prospect of the whole country.*

When Sir Richard died in 1697, he was succeeded by his son, also Sir Richard, but later Viscount

Cobham (1675-1749). Convinced that he could improve upon his father's achievements, he spent the rest of his life re-building and extending the house, the park and the gardens, which eventually occupied 400 acres. In the process, the remains of Stowe village were finally swept away. [24] Today, apart from the church, there is no sign of it except for scraps of tile and pottery. In 1989 the landscaped gardens were taken over by the National Trust. They are said to be the largest in the world and contain monuments, temples, ornamental lakes and spectacular views. Stowe House, now Stowe School, is also open to the public. For details phone 01280 - 818166 (house and events), and 01280 - 822850 (gardens and activities). **Stowe is well worth a visit.**

## SOIL EXHAUSTION

According to Reed,[25] a tax return of 1341 reveals that some villages in the Vale and North Buckinghamshire had abandoned arable land due to soil exhaustion. For example, Ellesborough had 300 acres uncultivated, though the village was not deserted. Thornborough also was said to have a large area of sterile land, which had ceased to be cultivated. Here, the village moved slightly eastwards to an adjacent site. This may indicate re-settlement away from ground tainted by the plague, or because of superstition about inhabiting ghost houses. Of course, if plague had reduced the population, perhaps the village could survive without the sterile land. One thing is certain: one way or another these villages did survive.

## THE FATE OF THE EVICTED

The enclosure of land usually increased its output and its value. Sadly, in the process, it often created a human problem: the homeless, jobless peasant, and his family. More precisely it added the refugees from enclosure to the existing problem of the wandering poor: the professional beggars, criminals, wandering tradesmen, homeless old soldiers, fencers, minstrels, common players, jugglers, tinkers, actors, bear-leaders, Egyptians (gipsies), etc.. Most of these wanderers survived by begging. As Thomas Bastard (1565-1618) wrote: **"*The pining labourer doth beg his bread. The plow-swain seeks his dinner from the town*"**. This continued until the Elizabethan Poor Laws came into force at the end of the 16th century.

## Chapter 7

# *LIFE IN A MEDIEVAL VILLAGE*

Over the centuries – at least in one respect – governments have not changed at all. They are always short of money. It was just the same in 1332. When the King required money, Parliament would grant him a subsidy, which was a tax on the land or personal property of the people. Thus in 1332 Parliament granted Edward III a Fifteenth and a Tenth. This was a tax of a fifteenth part of the moveable goods of those living in rural areas such as Wingrave, and a tenth part of the moveable goods of those living in urban areas. By a fortunate chance the detailed records of this tax have survived for Wingrave.[1]

## *WINGRAVE IN 1332*
### *The Taxman Cometh*

In the autumn of 1332, John le Ladde and Andrew Symond were selected to act as local sub-taxers and to make a house-to-house valuation of everyone's moveable goods. The sub-taxers required each householder to declare the amount of these goods, and also to provide information about his neighbours' goods! The following examples are typical of the final list of the 32 villagers due to pay tax:

**Thomas Frambaud** had 2 beasts 6s-8d; 4 oxen 32s-0d; 3qrs. wheat 10s-0d; 4qrs. drage 10s-0d; and fodder 2s-7d. Sum: £3-1s-3d. Tax: 4s-1d.

**John de Wengrave** had 2 beasts 6s-8d; 1 ox 8s-0d; 1 pot 2s-6d; 40 sheep 40s; 2qrs. wheat 6s-8d; 1qr. beans 3s-0d; and fodder 12d. Sum: £3-7-10d. Tax: 4s-6¼d.

**Hugh Edward** had 1 beast 3s-4d; 1 steer 6s-8d; 1 cow 6s-8d; 1 pig 17d; 6 sheep 6s; 1 qr. wheat 3s-4d; 2qrs. drage 5s-0d; Sum: £1-12s-5d. Tax: 2s-2d.

**William Dameris** had 1 beast 3s-4d; 1 cow 6s-8d; 1qr. drage 2s-6d. Sum: 12s-6d. Tax: 10d.

The complete list provides useful insights into life in a medieval village, but its value is restricted by the many exclusions. To start with, all the poorest people in the village (those with under 10s-0d worth of moveable goods) were completely excluded. Also, by custom, the tools of a trade (small carts, rakes, spades, hammers, pincers, adzes, etc.) were exempt. This exemption included *"the implements of husbandry"*: ploughs, plough-oxen, harrows, flails, pitch-forks, seed-corn, a year's supply of animal fodder, etc.. There was also no tax on those goods which would be *consumed* by the family during the taxation year: clothing, boots, cooking utensils, the year's supply of food, etc.. In addition, some young animals (lambs, calves and heifers) were exempt. The well-to-do were also excused tax on their military equipment. All the above were regarded as necessities. However, one can well imagine what arguments there could be if the lord of the manor claimed that his wife's jewels and their silver dishes and cups should be classified as necessities for the maintenance of their position in rural society. Tax *was* levied on all moveables that were surplus to basic needs, and which could be sold, if required, in the local market: animals not needed for food, crops not needed for the family's food and drink, etc..[2]

The tax assessment shows that Wingrave's field crops were typical of the Cottesloe Hundred: wheat, barley, oats, beans and peas. The barley and oats were sown and grown as a mixture, known as dredge, but in the Bucks dialect called drage. Some villages specialised: Linslade was one of the few to grow much rye; Cublington grew more rye that wheat; and Weedon grew no rye, but produced a substantial amount of barley. Such differences imply specialisation for the market, for there had long been local markets. Aylesbury had a market before 1066. More convenient for

Wingrave was the market at Wing which was granted in the 13th century. Money had long been required for the purchase of essentials (such as salt and iron) which had to be imported from a distance. Now, with the increase in local markets, the use of money was replacing barter in local trade, as it had already replaced goods and agricultural products for the payment of manorial fines and taxes, and was increasingly used for the payment of manorial rents. Even so, the 14th century was still essentially an era of subsistence farming, and each village's priority was to produce sufficient crops to make basic food-stuffs: a bread corn; a broth crop; a beer corn; and animal fodder. So while wheat was strongly preferred for bread, other grains could be used: barley; rye; a mixture of barley and rye; or a mixture of wheat and rye, called maslin. There is no mention of rye or maslin in the Wingrave assessments, so Wingrave's bread was probably made from wheat, which was generally thought to produce the choicest loaves. Barley was the preferred grain for malting, but drage was also used: 25 of the 32 Wingrave tax assessments mention drage. Fodder crops, like oats, beans and peas, could be added to a broth or stew to make an excellent filler for hungry peasants after a hard day in the fields.

By 1332 there had been poor crops nationally for several years and the price of wheat had risen sharply. In the 14th century it was priced in quarters, each weighing 28lbs. In 1330 a quarter cost 7.3 shillings, in 1331 it was 8.25 shillings, but in 1332 there were slightly better crops and the price fell to 6.4 shillings.[3] The lower price would have brought groans from those villagers with surpluses of wheat, while the cottagers, who at best had only small acreages, and who had to buy in some of their wheat, would be cheered by the fall. In fact, as the decade wore on the groaners would groan louder and the cottagers would become more cheerful. For over the next five years the price fell steadily until by 1337 wheat could be bought at 2. 92 shillings a quarter. It was not until 1346 that the price (at 6.96 shillings per quarter) recovered sufficiently to please the producers. It was 1350 and 1351 before the price (at 8. 8 and 9. 3 shillings) reached the giddy heights of twenty years earlier. That it did so was probably because the harvest was smaller, due to the loss of labour caused by the Black Death and the higher wages demanded by the labour which was available.

Only 14 of Wingrave's 32 taxpayers had surplus little piggies that *could* go to market. Pork being the cheapest meat to produce, most Wingrave families would have kept a pig for their own consumption. Ironically, the poorest families could not afford to rear one! One problem was that before you could have a little bacon, you needed a little pig and, unless barter was possible, or a kindly neighbour played Santa Claus, little pigs cost money. And being greedy, omnivorous, and possessed of a cast-iron constitution, the pig scavenged for its food so aggressively and with so little discrimination that it often caused considerable damage. Manorial records are full of warnings about pigs:

> *Every tenant shall cot his hogg in the nyght time . . .*
> *Every man shall keep his hoggs in his stye untyl such time as the hoggerd shall goe.*
> *It is ordained by the lord that no one of his tenants shall have his pigs or piglets outside of his house except under good custody (or) he shall lose his pig together with a substantial amercement. (1342 Newton Longville, Bucks.)*
> *No one shall enter the stubble with his pigs or sheep while the large animals are pasturing there. (1387 Newton Longville, Bucks.)*
> *By the assent of the whole homage it is agreed and ordered that no one shall enter the meadows with pigs or sheep before the end of autumn . . . (1391 Great Horwood, Bucks.)[4]*

So a hogherd had to be employed to restrain the pig's activities in the daytime (Fig. 37). Wingrave had no substantial woodland or heathland where the hogherd could take his charges, and the common pastures were usually reserved for "the great beasts". So the hogherd would have to use the fallow field when allowed, or the common wastes. Where there was woodland the hogherd would help the pigs to put on weight with the autumn 'fruits' of the trees: acorns, chestnuts, hazel nuts, berries, etc.. Herding the pigs was a full-time job, and the hogherd had to be paid. For night-time a stye had to be constructed in the garden to restrain the pig. Mature pigs being demolition experts, if the stye was to do its job, stout timbers were required for the corner posts and thick saplings for its sides, materials which – in woodless Wingrave – nature only provided after a violent storm felled a mature tree. Otherwise more pence must be spent. As the pig grew bigger and stronger, the smith would put a ring through its nose to curtail its foraging: for a small payment, of course. Without a ring there could be a bill for damages. Despite all

**Fig. 37: The Hogherd**

the warnings manorial courts still had to deal with porcine problems:

> *Alice . . . complainith of her neighbour that . . . his pigs entered her garden and rooted up her beans and cabbages, so that she would not willingly have had that damage for 2s., nor that shame for 12d., and she demandeth that amends be made.* [5]

Fortunately, at the end of its life, everyone agreed that if you could afford it, the pig's advantages exceeded its disadvantages. True that, like all medieval pigs, Wingrave's pigs were scrawny-looking creatures with less meat on them, which was much less succulent than the flesh of modern pigs for, in the 14th century, grain and skimmed milk could not be spared for them, and they were usually left to find their own fodder. Even so, the peasant's pig conjured up for him the comforting sight of hams and flitches of bacon hanging from the rafters, safe from the rats and mice. And when he thought of the rare treats that the slaughter of the pig would bring – the liver, the kidneys, the chawl, the tongue, the trotters, the chitterlings, the blood – the peasant could only think

kindly of his pig. Not one bit would be wasted. In an age when a simple pot was an important possession, even the pig's stomach was valued as a receptacle for storing the lard made from the pig's fat. The meat could be salted down, but the offal must be consumed before it went 'off'. So some of this would be given to those relatives and friends, who could be relied upon to return the favour, when they killed their own pig.

In terms of sheer numbers, sheep were the dominant livestock in Wingrave, as they were in both the Cottesloe and Chiltern Hundreds. In both hundreds sheep rearing may have been encouraged by the undulating

**Fig.38: The Shepherd**

nature of the countryside which marginally increased the drainage, thus improving the pasture and reducing the incidence of foot rot. Given such conditions the sheep was ideally suited to peasant needs. Alive it yielded one fleece per annum, the wool of which could either be sold as such, or spun into thread and woven into cloth. The ewe's milk could be drunk, but it also made a tasty cheese, which kept well. Ewes produced at least one lamb annually. The sheep's droppings were an important source of manure. A dead sheep provided meat for the pot, and still more of that tasty offal. Its skin with the fleece attached made an excellent bed cover and a warm and near-waterproof jacket. Alternatively, the wool and the skin could be sold separately, the latter to be converted into parchment. Despite these advantages only 223 *surplus* sheep were listed in the Wingrave tax roll. They were owned by only twelve (37½%) of the 32 tax-payers, who were thus the only villagers rearing sheep *for the market*. In some villages this was much more widespread. Around 80% of the tax-payers at Mursley and High Wycombe, and 70% at Linslade, raised sheep for the market, and the total numbers were much greater. Consequently, at Wingrave, sheep made a smaller contribution to the manuring of the arable, and in medieval times lack of manure could be a major cause of low crop yields.

Consequently, the shepherd was an essential member of the manorial work-force. By the late 1300's the wolf, the principal predator of sheep, had been killed off in Britain. Even so, with open-field farming, shepherds and their dogs were essential to ensure that sheep did not invade the growing crops, and that they could easily be rounded up for shearing, washing and lambing. At lambing time it was also very necessary to guard the lambs from lesser predators.

The 23 oxen on the Wingrave taxation roll were also surplus animals,[6] some of which could be intended for the market, for the larder, for extra plough-teams to extend the acreage of arable, or as replacements in case any of the plough-oxen already working in the fields went sick or lame.

### Fig. 39: The Medieval Plough-team

This ploughman and his 'boy' illustrate the typical features of medieval dress: the use of the skirt by both sexes; turned-up toes to the shoes; straw leggings; girdle; and hood-like head gear. From the girdle a knife and leather pouch usually hung, the latter serving as a pocket. Their clothes were home made from home-produced materials and were designed to give protection from the weather, for these people spent most of their time working in the fields.. There was no place for fashion. The upper classes wore better material and longer skirts, but the styles were similar.

There had been an epidemic of murrain (cattle plague) only a dozen years earlier, so the village herd had either had a lucky escape or made an excellent recovery. This was very important, for oxen were absolutely essential to the village's production of field crops.

### Managing the Manorial Economy

In chapter 3 we saw that William the Conqueror rewarded his supporters by granting them the tenancy of large, and sometimes huge, areas of land. Most tenancies consisted of many pieces of land scattered across the English countryside. The recipients were known as tenants-in-chief. As the years rolled by, many tenancies changed hands. Some tenants-in-chief returned to France, some families died out, and some lost their lands through offending the King. So in 1248 the family of Fiennes was able to take possession of a tenancy which included a holding of 720 acres at Wingrave, 17 holdings in Northants. and holdings in four other counties. The Fiennes occupied one holding and rented out the rest (a process then known as 'granting lordships') to sub-tenants. Sizeable holdings such as that at Wingrave were known as manors.

At the end of the 13th century the Fiennes were still tenants-in-chief. At Wingrave three of their sub-tenants were Bennet Rolleston, John de la Chapelle and John Okholte (Table 7). All three rented out their Wingrave holdings to one Nicholas Fermbaud. These holdings totalled 283 acres, and the entry fines alone (in modern parlance, key money) cost £60, a huge sum in those days. The records do not explain how Nicholas came by it, but presumably he managed, over a long period, to save the

#### Table 7: The Evidence of the Feet of Fines

| Date | Tenancy Acquired by | Tenancy Acquired from | Property ac. = acres | Consideration i.e. entry fine | Nature of Tenancy |
|---|---|---|---|---|---|
| 1284 | Nicholas Fermbaud | Bennet & Denise Rolleston | Messuage, 210 ac. arable 10 ac. meadow | £26-13s-4d | To hold of the de Rollestons |
| 1294 | Nicholas Fermbaud & Amicabel his wife | John de la Chapelle | Messuage 30 ac. arable | £13-6s-8d | To hold of the chief lords |
| 1295 | Nicholas Fermbaud & Amicabel his wife | John de Okholte | 33 ac. arable | £20-0s-0d | To hold of the chief lords |

£26-13s-4d for entry to the Rolleston's land in 1284, and then used the profits from it to finance the acquisitions of 1294 and 1295. The Fernbaud family continued to hold this land in and after 1332. The actual holder in 1332 was *Thomas* Fermbaud, and heading the Wingrave tax assessment for that year there is a Thomas Frambaud. The spelling is different, but medieval spelling was so erratic, the calligraphy so impenetrable, and surviving manuscripts so often damaged that Thomas Frambaud and Thomas Fermbaud are assumed to be the same person.

With so much of their property in tenants' hands, landlords had to find a way of keeping track of it so as to ensure that the tenants' farming was yielding the best return, and that no opportunity for raising the rent was missed. As was explained in chapter 2, the solution in Saxon times was to employ a manager, who was generally known as a reeve, simply because Saxon kings employed a servant with that name to supervise their estates. By 1332 such a servant was known as a steward, a name brought to England by the Normans who, as in William the Conqueror's household, had a servant known by this name. If William called his estate managers stewards, then so did his tenants-in-chief, and so did their sub-tenants. Life was like that with the Norman kings! And with 99% of England's land in the hands of Normans, this change to Norman terminology was universal. However, the nature of the stewards' work had also changed. By the end of the 12th century the holders of estates had begun to make and use records: particularly surveys, accounts and custumals. The latter were surveys of rents, services and other customary obligations owed by tenants to the lord of the manor, and the rights and obligations of the lord. So the new class of stewards had to act as planners, managers, advisers and organisers all rolled into one. So they had to be literate and numerate. These attributes were in short supply in late medieval times and so they also had to be well paid. In 1300 the Steward of Berkhamsted received £15-6s-8d a year, as well as two fur-lined robes, and all the hay, litter and firewood that he needed.

> The steward was in charge of the whole of the lord's estate, and as such he must travel from place to place, checking with his bailiffs on the state of each manor and the work being done by the tenant's reeves, whose temperament, knowledge and abilities he had to know if he was to ensure that his lord's business was conducted conscientiously, and that the peasants were treated impartially. The steward must have a comprehensive and detailed knowledge of agriculture. For instance he must know how many acres could be ploughed, how much seed would be needed, what the yield should be, and how many loaves could be made from a quarter of corn. He had to know how many cattle the manor's pasture could support. He must also conduct the manorial court, if the lord chose not to be there, and for this he must have some knowledge of the law, and know all the customs that regulated the relationship between the lord and the peasant. He must take responsibility for the various records of the manor, and be happy to brief his lord upon them. In particular, he must be mindful of his lord's needs both of money and kind, to ensure that they were always adequate. [7]

If the lord's estate was large. the steward would have many manors to supervise, and would only have time to visit each one once or twice a year. On such occasions he would conduct the manorial court if the lord could not be there, and he would certainly inspect the accounts. Afterwards the bailiff and the reeve might have to answer a lot of questions, for the bailiff had responsibility under the steward for several of the lord's manors, and was expected to keep a sharp eye on those servants of the manor who supervised the other peasants: the hayward, the dairyman, the cowherd, the swineherd, the shepherd, the head mower and the reeve. Of these the reeve was of particular importance. Yes, there were still reeves, but they were much lower in the managerial hierarchy than they had been in Saxon times, for now their job was to oversee the details of the farming. In particular the reeve must allocate the jobs amongst the workers and ensure that their tasks were performed efficiently and honestly. So it was his job to see that the day's work started and finished at the right times; that the threshing was done efficiently and that none of the threshers filled their boots or pockets with grain; that the dairymaids did not waste their time flirting with the cowherds, and did not lunch on the lord's cheese; and that the shepherds and herdsmen did not snooze when they should be watching their charges. Indeed, like Chaucer's reeve he must know his job and the workers thoroughly:

> Well wiste he by the drought and by the reyn
> The yeelding of his seed and of his greyn.
> His lordes sheep, his cattle and his poultrie,
> Was wholly in this reeves governynge . . .
> Ther was ne baylyf, herde ne other hyne
> That he ne knewe his sleight and his covyne. [8]

At some point in time, someone hit upon the brilliant idea of recruiting the reeve from amongst the leading peasants in the manor. Who better to know the work of the manor, the local conditions of soil and weather, and the capacity, initiative and honesty (or otherwise) of their fellow villagers? The reeve might be elected by the villagers themselves, or appointed by the steward. It was a difficult job, but some benefits came with it. He might be paid, though the pay was not generous. The Berkhamsted reeve was only paid five shillings for his year in office. However, he might well be given better accommodation, and he was exempt from actual physical labour in the field, which was a very welcome concession at a time when work had to continue even in diabolical conditions. [9]

To the villagers the steward represented authority with a capital A. However, in practice, the steward could temper his decisions with advice from the bailiff and the reeve. Working together they could maintain a balance between the lord's rights, the peasants' obligations and the customs of the manor. By such means the dictatorship of an arrogant and grasping lord could sometimes be mellowed into benevolent despotism.

# EVERYDAY LIFE IN A MEDIEVAL VILLAGE

## The Village Landscape

To modern eyes little would be recognisable in the Wingrave of 1332. Firstly, Wingrave's medieval farms and cottages were gathered together in three centres: Wingrave, Nup End and Rowsham. And within each centre the farms and cottages were intermixed. This feature only disappeared in the 20th century, when the farmhouses and farm buildings were converted into much sought-after housing for the general public. Secondly, medieval building was higgledy-piggledy and this left numerous 'windows' onto the countryside, which later development and infilling have mostly destroyed. Finally, medieval Wingrave was so much smaller. Most of its present development has happened since 1876, when the Rothschilds replaced many of the old cottages, added still more, and supplied cheap land for self-building. Even then the north side of Winslow Road was all countryside from the Aylesbury to Leighton road until you reached Parsonage Farm, by which time you were within a hundred yards of the Parish Church, the Green and the Village Pond. There was another expansion in the 1920's, when the local Council began to build houses, a process which continued after World War 2, when the large estate of Twelve Leys and much infill was also built, but this time by private enterprise. In the course of all this the hamlet of Nup End became an integral part of Wingrave, and the village began to look much less rural.

**Fig.40: Wingrave Church c.1880.**

The tower already existed in 1332, and in 1880 it was still much lower than today. The chancel had a lower roof, but was the same length. It cannot have changed very much, for where the arch of a blocked-up window is just visible from outside, there is a tiny room reputed to have been a priest's cell, the walls of which still bear traces of medieval painting. In 1332 the nave was much narrower, for the north and south aisles did not exist until 1370, and for some years the roof remained lower, so the interior was rather gloomy because there were no clerestory windows.

The only building present in 1332, and still recognisable by modern eyes, is the late 12th century church, which was probably built by William, son of Alured de Wedon. In 1332 the vicar was Walter Lokkeslie. He had only arrived in 1327, so that to the villagers he would still be 'a stranger'. As such his parishioners would doubtless have recounted in detail the story of the desecration of their church, which the older folk would still vividly recall (Recollections C). Walter only stayed for seventeen years, so he was probably still regarded as 'a stranger' when he left! By 1332 the original building had already been substantially altered. After William de Wedon had given the church to the Abbey of St. Albans very late in the 12th century, the Abbot had the chancel extended to its present length, and the west tower built. Even so the church looked very different than it does today: see fig. 40 and caption. Once inside, the differences were marked. In 1332 (and for some time later) there were still no pews, though there may have been a few benches alongside the walls, for the elderly and the sick, who needed to have their backs to the wall. And the walls were decorated with colourful paintings and inscriptions. Many details were different: for instance, it was late into the 15th century before the twelve wooden figures of men appeared in the roof of the nave. However, today's parishioners would certainly recognise the font, for it has served every generation since 1190.

---

### Recollections C: The Desecration of the Parish Church *

Oliver, Bishop of Lincoln, to the Dean of Mursley, greetings. It has come to my hearing that certain impious and unpleasant men, making little distinction between the sacred and the profane, on the Thursday night following the feast of St. Dunstan, violently and with arms entered the parish church of Wingrave about the middle of the night and on the pretext of looking for the body of one Gilbert Simon, a parishioner of the said church, broke the altars sacred to God and the images of the saints that were in the said church, defiled the floor of the church, beat the men and the clerics who were there, and dared to perpetrate other abominable and violent actions, to the great peril of their souls, in violation of ecclesiastical immunity and to the extreme scandal of many.

Therefore, lest we incur divine displeasure through negligence in allowing such heinous sacrilege to go unpunished, we order you by virtue of your strict obedience to assemble as many rectors, vicars and parish priests as you can conveniently accommodate, dressed in white, with cross and waxen tapers in front as is the custom, and in person go to the said church of Wingrave on the Sunday immediately after the feast of the Ascension and solemnly and publicly announce, with bells tolling and candles lit, that the sacrilegious offenders mentioned above, together with their instigators, patrons, and accomplices are summarily excommunicated, and on subsequent Sundays and feast days up to the festival of St John Baptist, in the aforesaid church of Wingrave and in other churches of your deanery, for which you should arrange for the declaration to be made with suitable solemnity.

* Lincoln Record Society, Rolls and Register of Bishop Oliver Sutton, Bishop of Lincoln 1280-1299, translated by Dr David Snow, June 1996

---

In 1229 Wingrave also had a windmill, and we assume that in 1332 it, or a replacement, was still there, for this was one of the lord of the manor's main perks. The last windmill to operate in Wingrave did not arrive until 1809. It was demolished in 1872, and replaced by the steam mill at Mill House in Winslow Road. The remainder of Wingrave's medieval buildings would be quite unrecognisable to modern eyes.

### Living Conditions

The peasants' cottages were so poorly constructed that none have survived to modern times. Fortunately, archaeological research[10] in other areas indicates the sort of buildings which were generally found in the south of England and which would most likely have housed the Wingravians of that time. In 1332, in rural areas, most domestic and farm buildings were single-storeyed. The poorest cottages, which still stood from earlier days, were simple buildings constructed from unsquared poles lashed together into a simple framework of rectangles which were filled with interwoven branches, sealed with a coating of mud, and thatched with straw, or turf, or whatever was available. With a good footing, an overhanging thatch, and a few coats of lime-wash these buildings lasted well by medieval standards. Even so, after twenty or thirty years they might well have to be replaced, or at least given over to storage and sheltering animals. For new cottages the cruck system was used. (Fig. 41) A cruck was formed from a tree trunk or large branch possessing a natural curve, and roughly squared. It was split vertically into two halves which were set opposite one another to form an arch, which was usually little more than 11 feet wide. Then another arch was erected at a distance of about 16 feet. The two arches were joined by a ridge-pole, or beam, and at a lower level by horizontal tie-beams. Rafters supported a roof of thatch or turf, and as before the walls were rectangles of timber, filled in with panels of wattle and daub, or with a vertical sandwich of turf between two layers of wattle. Not only was the resultant buillding single-storied, it was also single roomed and, due to the leaning crucks, even that room had limited floor space. The ruin in Fig. 41, and the simplified diagram beside it, show how the crucks were modified to improve the headroom. As the cottage only contained one room, the cattle were probably relegated to a lean-to shelter built onto its side, this being the easiest and cheapest extension that was possible. Of course, the basic cottage could be doubled in size by erecting a third pair of crucks another 16 feet from one end, but this required time and money, both very much in short supply for most cottagers. Still it could be done. At Cuxham, as early as 1304, all the villagers' cottages had at least two rooms.[11] If the extra room was completely divided off from the rest of the house, it might provide private quarters for the head of the family. Alternatively, in severe weather it could be used to shelter the cattle. If the two rooms were only divided by a chest-high partition, the cattle would also provide a primitive (albeit smelly and noisy) central heating. Not that the shifting, shuffling and grunting of cattle would disturb the sleep of peasants who had laboured in the fields from dawn to dusk. In such cottages the fire was still on a central hearthstone set on the earthen floor, and the smoke found its way into the roof-space, where a hole allowed it to escape. At any rate, that was the theory. In practice, especially on calm days, the smoke hung about in the roof space, as the blackened roof timbers of ancient cottages prove. Being so affected by smoke, the roof-space was not habitable, but sometimes a half-loft was constructed and used for storage. With a strong wind, blowing in the wrong direction, the smoke (and probably the inhabitants) escaped by the door. Glass was extremely expensive, and so the windows were simply unfilled panels in the walls. At night, or in poor weather, or when not needed to vent the smoke, they could be closed with portable panels, which were later hinged to the framework of the window to form shutters. Living conditions in these cottages were cramped, unhealthy and extremely uncomfortable: cold, draughty, smoky, leaky, damp in winter, and a fire hazard in summer.

Most houses had a piece of ground, known as a toft, on which vegetables and herbs could be grown. Beyond this were the great arable fields (the main source of the villagers' food) and the meadows for the all-important hay. Timber was also essential for a medieval village, which required it for building its cottages, making its furniture and feeding its fires. However, Domesday Book makes no mention of woodland in Wingrave, and we can only surmise that it managed to survive on timber from copses, thickets, shaws and its few hedgerows. For up-market projects, timber could be imported from the Chiltern woodlands, but this would be relatively expensive.

The poorer peasants lived in a state of considerable poverty. They owned little more than the clothes they worked (and slept) in. Some landlords provided a few items of household equipment, which had to be accounted for when the tenant left or died. It is from the lists of such articles, which appear in some manorial court rolls, that we learn something of the furnishings of a peasant's cottage: a trestle-table; one or two stools; a chest; a measure of capacity; the inevitable brass pot and brass pan; and very often a vat. The trestle-table was invaluable in a one-roomed cottage: as soon as the meal was finished it could be dismantled and stacked against a wall. Stools and benches were an inexpensive form of seating, and also took up a minimum of space. Chairs were definitely up-market, but the more affluent peasants did have them. The chest was for storing grain. Pots were commonly of one to three gallons capacity, though pots of four to six gallons were found in larger cottages, where there would be servants as well as the family to feed. Larger cottages also had enormous pans ranging in size up to ten and twelve gallons, probably for steeping grain as part of the malting process. If ale were brewed, there would also be a vat. The beds would be straw-filled pallets either placed on the earthen floor, or (such luxury!) on a board near the fire. These boards could also be cleared out of the way in the daytime, perhaps being propped against a wall, or slid into the rafters. Other possessions[12] might include a basket (worth 6d), a tub (worth 4d), a trivet (worth 1d), a ploughshare (worth 4d), and a shovel (worth 1d). Only in the larger cottages could a built-in box bed, complete with hangings, be accommodated and afforded; or a coffer (a strong box, worth 6d, for valuables); while a cart (worth 12d) would be left outside, in a lean-to, with the cow (all 7s-10d worth of it) for company. In the cottages of the poorest peasants the poultry may well have shared the accommodation

### Fig. 41: The Cruck Construction of Cottages and Possible Modification

Initially, because the crucks sloped, so did the cottage walls, and this limited the use of the floor space. The ruin pictured below was of a later design, which made vertical walls possible, as shown in the adjacent sketch.

80

with the tenants. The poor widow of Chaucer's Nun Priest's Tale lived in a "narwe cottage" of this sort:

> *ful sooty was her bour and eek her halle . . . Chauntecleer among his wyves sat on his perch that was in the halle.*

Erasmus tells us that:

> *The floors are commonly of clay strewed with rushes to keep down the dust. Under lies an ancient collection of beer, grease, bones, spittle, excrements of dogs and cats, and everything that is nasty.*

However, archaeological investigation has revealed that in some cottages the floor was brushed so clean that it acquired a U-shaped depression.

Messuages of three, four and even five bays were built at this time, but they were usually single storey. Inevitably, their size tended to reflect the economic level of the occupants. A two-bay cottage might be occupied by a peasant with a few acres of land, while a three-bay messuage might house a half-virgator or a virgator. Messuages of four or five bays, perhaps with half-lofts at each end, would usually be occupied by families with the largest acreages of land. Quite often the occupants of the larger messuages not only had more acreage to farm, but also had unpaid duties connected with the management of the manor, and a larger home was some compensation. Generally speaking, acreages in the fields, size of home, and manorial duties determined one's social standing in the manor. We have no certain evidence of the existence of superior messuages in the Wingrave of 1332, but it seems reasonable to assume that the lord of the manor would provide himself with something substantial. A four or five-bay cottage could be divided to provide more room for the family, extra storage, and accommodation for servants, with the food preparation moved into a lean-to kitchen. Such lean-tos seem to have been quite common, and were known as wattle-walled, thatched outshots.

We know that by 1367 Wingrave had at least one substantial dwelling. Margaret Pippard,[13] who had inherited Wingrave manor, had married Sir Warin Lisle.[14] According to Dugdale[15] they had a house in Wingrave, which in 1367 was used to celebrate the marriage of their daughter (another Margaret) to the future Sir Thomas de Berkeley. What excitement there must have been in the village when it became known that the lord's daughter was to be married! However, that excitement would have been tinged with amazement as more information spread through the village grapevine. For this was a marriage with a difference. While their peasants had been toiling and moiling in the fields, Sir Maurice de Berkeley (of Berkeley in Gloucestershire) and Sir Warin Lisle were negotiating the merger of their two estates, by agreeing to the marriage of their children. For Sir Maurice's health was rapidly failing, and it was probably his last chance to enlarge his estate and so secure the future of his eldest son. Before this could happen a major problem had to be resolved. His eldest son was only fourteen years old, and the intended bride was only seven. Sir Warin overcame the impasse by stipulating that his daughter continue to live with him at Wingrave for four years after the wedding, a condition which Sir Maurice accepted with some relief. Sir Maurice soon died, and Sir Warin promptly applied to the king for the wardship of his young son-in-law. For this he had to pay the king £400 per year, but in return received the revenue of the Berkeley estate until his son-in-law was 21. This revenue was about £2,400 per year, so Sir Warin made a net profit of £2,000 per year for each of the seven years of the wardship. Even so, when Sir Warin died in 1382, the 600 acre manor of Wingrave became part of the Berkeley estate, so the honours were fairly even. Fortunately the son-in-law, now Sir Thomas de Berkeley, was a very business-like landowner, rather like his ancestor, a much earlier Sir Thomas de Berkeley. [16]

Church Farmhouse in Wingrave was no peasant's cottage. It is believed to have been built in the latter half of the 14th century, and except for the church, no other building in the parish

**Fig. 42: Church Farmhouse, Wingrave**

exceeds or even equals it in age. It was probably the grandest house in medieval Wingrave. So it is *just possible* that it was once the home of Sir Warin Lisle. The original building was of cruck construction, but has been much altered over the centuries. The medieval house was *at least* a three-bay (four cruck) house. The bay to the right was part of a hall which was open to the roof, while the bay to the left still has the original heavy joists for an upper floor. This would have provided the occupier with the much-valued privacy of a separate room, though he would have to remember where he was, if he still had the medieval habit of urinating on the floor. A chimney stack and chamber floor were inserted c. 1600. In 1793, when the large gabled extension on the right (now called Yew Tree Cottage, and separately owned) was built, the ancient walls of Church Farmhouse (Fig. 42) were refaced in a mixture of red and black brick, and a gabled barn was added on the left, through which wagons could drive from Church Street, in through the large double doors, and then out into the farmyard behind. It was still a farmhouse within living memory, but is now separated from its acres and used as a private residence.

### The Diet of the Wingrave Peasant

Some early writers lamented the 'uppishness' of the peasantry in the 14th century. In his Mirour de L'Omme, the poet John Gower, a contemporary of Chaucer, clearly attributed it to the post-plague situation, when "wages doubled, then doubled again":[17]

> *The world goeth from bad to worse, when shepherd and cowherd demand more for their labour than the master-bailiff was wont to take in days gone by. Labour is now at so high a price that he who will order his business aright must pay five or six shillings for what cost two in former times. Labourers of old were not wont to eat of wheaten bread: their 'meat' was of beans or coarser corn, and their drink of water alone. Cheese and milk were a feast to*

*them. Their dress was of hodden grey. Then was the world ordered aright for folk like this.*

Other sources claim that things were not usually so bad. [18] The basic foodstuffs from the great open fields provided broths of beans or peas, and cabbage flavoured with onions, leeks, garlic and wild herbs from the toft (garden). In good times there would be a little bacon, some milk, cheese, eggs, the occasional scraggy chicken, and whatever could be scrounged from the local fields. Many a cooking pot would surely contain some illicit game, for there was no problem about finding a hare, a rabbit, a pigeon or even a pheasant. The problem was to avoid being caught with game (or evidence of it) in one's possession. In practice, much depended upon the attitude of the Lord of the Manor and his reeve. For example, rabbits were important in medieval times, both for meat and fur. *"In 1292 Nicholas and Amicabel Fermbaud obtained a grant of free warren in their demesne lands of Wingrave."* [19] This meant enclosing some land for the breeding and rearing of rabbits. Naturally, poaching would not be allowed within this area, but might be regarded more tolerantly elsewhere in the manor, especially if the game was reducing crop yields. Indeed, according to Trevelyan:[20]

> *Poaching was not only the livelihood of outlaws, but the passion of men of all classes: gentry, clerks of Holy Church, besides farmers and workmen seeking a pheasant or hare for the pot . . . But most of all did it rejoice the farmer's heart to slay secretly for his own pot one of the legion of privileged birds from the manorial pigeon-house, whose function in life was to grow plump on the peasants' corn till they were fit for the lord's table.*

The Winslow court rolls confirm his view. For example: [21]

> *John Houdeby, Rector of Mursslee church, and Geoffrey Pounteys, Chaplain, were hunting in the lord's warren, and they took hares. Therefore advice is to be taken and a writ procured.*

The problems of the peasant diet in medieval times quickly emerge when one considers it in detail. The peasantry consumed insufficient fresh fruit and fresh vegetables. Fresh fruit was reckoned to be dangerous to health, and liable to cause 'putrid fevers'. Such vegetables as were consumed were added to the regular broths and stews. For the poorer peasants it was more likely to be a broth with beans than a stew with meat. Beans were a staple of the peasant diet, and broths were the preferred way of using them. Broths without beans were like mash without sausages! 24 of the 32 Wingrave taxpayers had a surplus of beans. It was another 350 years before vegetables appeared as a separate dish, probably because in 1332, and for long after, only the richer households could afford several cooking pots. And in peasant households the 'cooker' was an open fire, so there was only one 'burner', unless the householder could afford (and many couldn't) an iron frame-work, called a brandreth, which could be placed over the fire for grilling fish and meat, or used as a resting place for additional pots. However, cookery in one pot had definite advantages. It required no cleaning at the end of the meal. It was much simpler to add water and ingredients, and to put the pot back over the fire, when it was time to prepare the next meal. Such slow cooking and re-heating is now regarded as a classic recipe for increasing tummy upsets, and reducing the vitamins, minerals and trace elements in the food. Partly as a result, the peasants' diet was particularly deficient in vitamins A, C and D. These were in especially short supply in the winter when there was a shortage of fruit and green food, eggs, milk and butter. A severe deficiency of vitamin A led to reduced resistance to infection, and to stunted growth in children. A severe deficiency of vitamin C led to scurvy and anaemia. Lack of vitamin D caused rickets in children, and fragile bones in adults. It reduced the resistance to infection, so increasing the incidence of disease. Ironically, in those days, these were minor matters.

Even in good times many families were poor and *"fared hard"*, while others were paupers *"that really pinched and suffered"*. In bad times, when crop yields were low, such people faced slow starvation. Despite this, in bad times as well as good, every labourer had to contribute a tithe, or tenth, of all he produced to the maintenance of the local church. The whole range of agricultural products was involved, from live animals (like lambs and poultry) to crops of all sorts, and even perishable goods like eggs, milk, cabbages and cheese, while cash in lieu would always be accepted.

**Fig. 43: Peasants Deliver Their Tithes in 1479** [22]

These included a small bag, presumably containing coins, a lamb, and a goose. Notice the difference in clothing between the two social levels. The payers are peasants, who wear a close-fitting short coat, whereas the principal recipient wears a long gown. Their clothes would also differ in quality. Under the sumptuary laws of 1363, richer knights, lesser knights, merchants and yeomen were all prescribed different qualities of cloth. Peasants were not allowed to wear cloth, but must make do with garments made from 'blanket or russet wool'.

## THE COUNTRYSIDE

The countryside of the South Midlands, of which the Vale is a part, was the product of the Saxon system of open-field farming. In addition to its two or three huge arable fields for cereals and beans, all unfenced and unhedged, each village had a considerable acreage of meadow: sometimes – as in Wingrave's case – mainly one long, sinuous belt following the course of the Thistlebrook; sometimes – as at Chearsley – in smaller areas, but always clinging to the Thame and its tributary the Wattesbrac, and in the process surrounding much of the parish. Somewhere within each parish, surrounded by its little hedged closes and half-hidden by its wealth of trees, was its village, half-camouflaged by its thatched rooves. This was the landscape which – with the addition of a lot of churches, and the eventual substitution of tiles and slates for much of the thatch – would survive in essence until the open fields were enclosed, mainly between 1750 and 1850.

84

## C9: Creslow Manor House

Before the dissolution of the monasteries, this 14th century house was occupied by the Knights Hospitallers. It is now just a farm house. Despite some demolition, it is still deceptively large. The tower is 43 feet high and there is a substantial cellar.

## C10: Notley Abbey

After the dissolution, occupation of the Abbey was granted to royal favourites as a reward for services rendered. Later it went into private ownership, and for a long time was a farmhouse with the monks' refectory converted into a barn and the cloisters into a piggery. The church and other buildings were demolished to obtain their trimmed stone. More recently it became a country retreat for such people as Sir Lawrence Olivier and Vivien Leigh.

**C11: The Church of St Mary and St Nicholas, Chetwode**

The huge chancel of the former Chetwode Priory church (built about 1250) is now Chetwode's parish church. Seen on a sunny day the five stepped east lancets are magnificent. Elsewhere in the church there is stained glass dating back to the 13th and 14th centuries.

**C12: A Wall Painting in the Church of St Lawrence, Broughton, Milton Keynes**

St George is destroying a particularly fearsome dragon, breathing fire and fumes. Nearby is the Lady Cleodelinda, with her little lamb, just waiting to be rescued.

**C13: Wall Paintings of Saints in the Church of St Lawrence**

St Helena's T-shaped cross is its original Latin shape. St Eligius was the patron saint of farriers and blacksmiths.

**C14: Winslow's Early Baptist Chapel, erected in 1695**

This chapel is often called Keach's chapel. In fact, his persecution occurred 30 years before it was built.

**C15: Old Princes Risborough**

Walking from the quaint market house to the church gives one some impression of Risborough's ancient charm.

# Chapter 8

## THE REFORMATION

**Fig. 46: Henry VIII**

The Reformation of the church under Henry VIII was largely due to personal and political motives. Henry had two problems. He desperately wanted a son to succeed him as king, but although his first wife (Catherine of Aragon) bore him five children only one (Mary) survived. So Henry decided to divorce[1] Catherine and marry Anne Boleyn, a maid of honour in the royal court for whom he was (as he put it) *"stricken with the dart of love"*. The Pope refused to authorise the divorce, and so Henry secretly married Anne, whilst the Archbishop of Canterbury declared Henry's marriage to Catherine invalid. The Pope promptly excommunicated Henry who, in return, persuaded Parliament to pass two Acts: one stated that the Pope had no authority in England; the other made the English Church a separate institution, with Henry as its supreme head, *"God's deputy on earth"*. For Henry was still at heart a staunch Catholic with no sympathy with Protestants, whom he regarded as extremists. Indeed, he had written a book against Protestantism and had sent a copy to the Pope, who had promptly dubbed him, 'Defender of the Faith', a title which Henry and his successors were pleased to adopt. Henry's other problem was a shortage of money, due to having spent on foreign wars the immense fortune of his father Henry VII. Taking advantage of the indignation created by corruption in the Catholic Church, its immense wealth, and an alleged decline in the morals of the clergy, Henry dissolved the monasteries, and sold their property to reward his friends and replenish his treasury.

### THE MONASTERIES

Over the centuries more than 700 monasteries (including abbeys, friaries and priories) were founded in England. In Buckinghamshire as a whole, at the time of the Dissolution, there were 17 monasteries, a friary, 12 hospitals, several smaller religious houses, and a number of granges (monastic farms).[2] Each monastery followed the 'rule' of its founder. For example, the Benedictines were confined to their monasteries, and devoted their entire lives to prayer and attendance at as many as ten religious services per day. These services were interspersed with periods for reading, discussion, meditation, and practical work such as gardening, writing, copying and illumination. The Augustinians were not so strictly confined for – besides their religious devotions – they were expected to contribute to the life of the local community by maintaining the churches under their care; conducting religious services and confessions; treating the sick; and teaching.

The monk's coarse clothing, restricted diet and mainly unheated accommodation put him on the same level as the peasant. However, the monk gained because he did not have to endure the back-breaking, dawn to dusk toil of the peasant. Whether it was the live-in labour, or the lay-brothers, or local villagers, who did the farm-work, it was not the monks. Organisational and supervisory tasks would be shared out, but in either case the monk was still in the role of employer or lord, which was a very different situation to that of the peasant. Neither did the monk do the housework or the cooking: servants were hired for that. In winter and Lent, there would only be one meal a day, but in peasant terms it would be substantial: a pound of bread per person per day with cheese and vegetables, and two dishes made from cereals, beans or eggs. In summer there

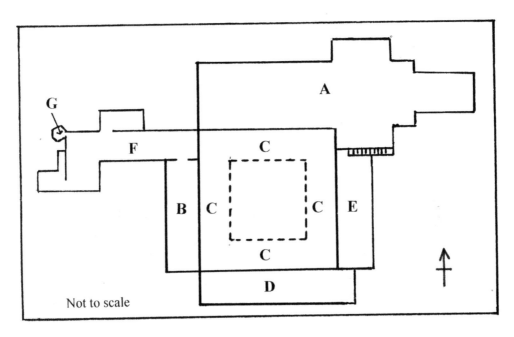

**Map 9: Plan of Notley Abbey**

### Key to Plan of Notley Abbey

A. Approximate position of the Abbey church. The interior would be carefully planned to allow for processions, which were a feature of monastic services. The nave was 100 feet long, and later extended to 120 feet.

B. Known as the West Range. The ground floor, which was used to store wine and provisions, was the responsibility of the cellarer. On the upper floor was accommodation for guests.

C. These were the covered cloisters where the monks could walk, meditate, read, write or pray. The cloisters were built so that the monks were sheltered by the church from cold north winds.

D. The frater was the refectory or dining hall. At one end was a high table for the Abbot, senior canons and guests. Down the sides were tables for junior canons. There was also a pulpit from which passages from the Bible or other religious works were read during meals. After the Reformation the building was converted into a barn.

E. On the ground floor was the Chapter House, where most of the monastery's business was transacted, and the parlour where the monks might enjoy conversation, and meet visitors. Above it was the dorter (dormitory), where the monks slept. At its northern end was a staircase by which they entered the church, when they left their straw-filled mattresses for the nightly services. At its southern end was the rere-dorter (the washroom and lavatories). This building no longer exists.

F. There were separate lodgings for the abbot or prior, and any special guests. This was built partly in the 15th century, and partly by the last abbot shortly before the Dissolution. Note the hexagonal stair turret at G.

There would also be a kitchen, bakery, brew-house, wash-house, servants' quarters, and barns. Large abbeys might also have special rooms for the tailor, cobbler and tanner. In the grounds were also gardens, stables, a dovecot, fish ponds (Fridays were fish days), a farm and an orchard.

**Fig. 47: Notley Abbey between Chearsley and Long Crendon.**
Viewed from the west (see Map 9), the Abbot's Lodging (F) is at the front of the picture, including the hexagonal stair turret (G). Beyond is part of the West Range (B) pictured in full in Plate C10. The Abbey has now been converted into the ultimate venue for weddings.

would be two meals per day at midday and 6 pm. So the monks ate well and rarely went short as did most peasants. Lack of exercise, large meals and a generous ration of ale or wine was not a healthy life-style, and monasteries usually had an infirmary, if only to accommodate the monks who had been bled to compensate for the leisurely life-style and the generous diet. [3]

Notley Abbey was an Augustinian monastery, built on lush meadows about a hundred metres from the River Thame, and surrounded by the scattered villages of the Vale of Aylesbury, of which the nearest was Chearsley. The Abbey came into existence in 1162, when Walter Giffard III, the second and last Earl of Buckingham of that family, and Ermengard his wife, founded the monastery in their park near Long Crendon, and endowed it with the park and other property:

> *in perpetual alms for the health of their souls and the souls of their ancestors, and of King Henry, Queen Eleanor and their issue, their ancestors and successors.*

By the time of the Reformation, Notley was the largest and wealthiest of the religious houses in the Vale and North Bucks. (Plate C10). Its annual income was nearly £500. [4] Much of it came from the churches appropriated to it. Appropriation meant that some of the tithes and endowments intended for the maintenance and ceremonies of the churches were diverted to religious houses such as Notley. It was just one of a number of things about religious houses that irritated the general public. By 1535 Notley received income from the churches of Ashendon, Barton Hartshorn, Brill, Chearsley, Chetwode, Hillesden, Long Crendon, Lower Winchendon, and the manors of Long Crendon, Chilton, Chearsley, Canonend and Stragglethorpe (Lincs.).

## CHETWODE PRIORY
Smaller religious houses, like the Augustinian Priory of Chetwode, were more typical of the Vale and North Bucks.. Chetwode Priory was built around 1240, and a copy of the original plan

is displayed in the church. At that time it was a large church with a nave which stretched back perhaps thirty metres to the present village street. The cloisters and monastic buildings adjoined it to the south where Priory House now stands. In contrast to Notley, Chetwode was under-endowed. The original endowment was 250 acres, the priory site, the churches of Chetwode and Barton Hartshorn, and a carucate of land [5] from King Henry III. Probably there were never more than 3 or 4 canons in residence, and by 1460 the Priory was so poor that it was dissolved and its property was transferred to Notley Abbey. In 1480 Chetwode's parish church was so decrepit that it was abandoned, and the priory church was given to parishioners as a replacement. Around 1600 its nave was demolished and a new wall and tower (Fig. 53) were built to close off the west end. So the present *parish* church is the ancient chancel of the priory church, the only surviving monastic church in the county still in use. There is some wonderful stone carving and beautiful stained glass from the 13th century (Plate C11). The north chapel was long ago converted into a family 'pew' complete with fireplace, and known locally as the 'loosebox'.

### Worldy Concerns and Religious Responsibilities

A monastery's function depended upon its endowment and upon the 'order' or 'rule' to which it belonged, and it was greatly affected by the leadership of its abbot and the authority of the bishops in the diocese of Lincoln, who occasionally inspected its religious houses. [6] It is mainly from their reports that we know something of institutions like Notley and Chetwode. The reports make it clear that monasteries were expected to do something in return for the income provided by the churches appropriated to them. For example, they should have a concern for the poor, the sick and the homeless. Thus in 1461, when the priory of Chetwode and its lands were granted to the canons of Notley, it was "*on condition that they should fulfil all the obligations attached to the suppressed foundation.*" [7] So far we have found no information as to the *totality* of these obligations, but in 1535 a dole of 2s-6d was still being paid to the poor of Chetwode, so presumably at least one obligation was being fulfilled. Responsibility for ensuring that its churches were maintained in good condition and properly served by a priest were further obligations. It is clear from the reports of 1493 and 1519 that Notley was judged to be "*sadly conspicuous*" for its neglect of its churches. For example, in 1493, the chancel at Hillesden Church (Fig. 48) was so dilapidated that the chaplain could not celebrate Mass at the High Altar,[8] while in 1519 it was reported that "*there could scarcely be any part of the country where the churches could be so forlorn and ill-kept*". [9] In particular Ashendon and Chetwode were in a ruinous condition, whilst Hillesden and Dorton were without chaplains. However, we learn almost by chance that Notley did fulfil some of its obligations. For example, right down to the 20th century, there was a small witchert cottage called Priest's Cottage, in a field at Chearsley known as Priest's Close. Locally it was believed that this was where the Notley canon lived when acting as parish priest.[10] And it is only from the fortunate survival of a letter to Thomas Cromwell, Chief Minister to Henry VIII, that we learn that Notley provided the warden for Caversham Priory just north of the centre of Reading. [11]

Despite some lapses over the centuries it seems that the reputation of Notley within political and ecclesiastical circles was good. Both Edward II and Edward III occasionally used the Abbey to house old servants. Several times during the 14th century the abbots of Notley were commissioned by the Pope to enquire into petitions and appeals from other abbeys. In 1471 the Abbot of Missenden Abbey sent disobedient canons to Notley as a punishment, its discipline being more rigorous than Missenden's. In 1529 King Henry VIII stayed at Notley when visiting the Midlands.[12]

### THE DISSOLUTION OF THE MONASTERIES

Thomas Cromwell, Henry's Vicar-General, master-minded the dissolution of the monasteries, the power-houses of Roman Catholicism. In September 1535 he organised visitations of all the

**Fig. 48: The Church of All Saints, Hillesden**

Browne Willis credited the Abbot of Notley with the rebuilding of Hillesden church at the end of the 15th century, but the celebrated Victorian architect Sir George Scott, who restored it in 1875, disagreed because the records describe faults repaired in a short time rather than a complete re-build. Having lovingly restored the church, Sir George described it as *"a cathedral in the fields, the choicest specimen of a village church in the county; very few in England of its period and scale surpass or equal it"*.[13] Hillesden is well worth a visit, as is the church of St Nicholas and St Mary at nearby Chetwode.

religious houses. Extremely quickly the visitors produced reports from which Cromwell concluded that the monasteries, though often wealthy, were corrupt, decadent, worldly and lecherous. However, in practice, the morality of the religious varied greatly, as did their service to society.

> *So after the visitations some Visitors petitioned that certain monasteries might continue on account of the ecclesiastics residing in them, the benefit derived by the poor, and the advantages of education. Bishop Latimer even moved for the preservation of some for pious uses. But Cromwell disagreed, and all (the monasteries) were involved in the common ruin.* [14]

The poor reputation of monasteries, the potential value of their property (reckoned to add over £10,000 per annum to the income of the Royal Treasury), and the persuasion of Cromwell and Anne Boleyn (another Protestant sympathiser) convinced Henry that he should proceed with the Dissolution. By 1540 the monasteries had gone. The low resistance to dissolution was due to the policy of stick and carrot which was employed. Henry was quick to execute those who opposed him. In 1539 the abbots of Glastonbury, Reading and Colchester were hanged. Robert Hobbes, the abbot of Woburn Abbey, was hanged from an oak tree growing just outside his own abbey's gate, for expressing doubts about the king's supremacy, and for declaring that Catherine of Aragon was *"the king's true and undoubted wife"*. Sir Thomas More, the ex-Chancellor, was beheaded in 1535 for refusing to recognise the king as head of the church. Many of more lowly status suffered. They included John Eynon, who was just a secular priest at Reading, and Sebastion Newdigate, who was a priest at the monastery of the Charter House in London, whose savage execution

### Recollections D : The Execution of Sebastian Newdigate *

When the king had proclaimed that profane and sacrilegious law – commanding all to acknowledge and to swear that he was the Supreme Head of the Church within his dominions – he resolved first to draw to his will such as were of note for either their good life or learning. If these were once gained . . . others might the more easily be brought and drawn to pretended submission. Upon this device, having found by trial that fair promises and sweet persuasions prevailed nothing upon men committed to God's service, the king determined by violence and cruelty to force them to it. One of those who suffered was Sebastian Newdigate, the brother of Jane Dormer of Wing. He was an early favourite of King Henry VIII. He took Holy Orders and became a Catholic priest at the monastery of the Charter House of London. In May 1535 he and two other Fathers were drawn out of the cloister with inhuman violence and led to the Marshalsea, where they were kept for fourteen days bound to pillars, standing upright with iron rings about their necks, hands and feet. This cruel usage was intended to force them to yield to the king's pleasure, and to subdue them, if possible, so that they would subscribe to the law of his supremacy . . . After finding them still constant, they were sent as prisoners to the Tower of London. The king, being there, set upon Father Sebastian with menaces and injurious words. Notwithstanding this, Sebastian listened patiently and answereth,

*When in Court I served your Majesty, I did it loyally and faithfully, and so continue still your humble servant, although kept in this prison and in bonds. But in matters that belong to the Faith and the glory of our lord Jesus Christ, and to the doctrines of the Catholic Church and the salvation of my poor soul, your Majesty must be pleased to excuse me. We must obey God not man.*

The king, having this resolute answer, would not use further discourse, but called him traitor; and marvellously enraged, told him he should suffer for such a one. On June 18th a jury of twelve men found them guilty of high treason, and they were sentenced to death. So they were returned to the prison, and the next day the sentence was carried out. These blessed Fathers were laid stretched along bound upon hurdles, and so drawn by horses through the streets of London to Tyburn, the place of execution. It was a lamentable spectacle to see innocent religious men in their venerable habits, for profession of the ancient Catholic faith, to be thus handled by such as professed themselves Christians. They untied Father Sebastian from the hurdle with the rope about his neck, and put him in the cart. The rope was then thrown over the top of the scaffold, pulled taut, and fastened securely to the ground. Then, the cart being driven away, he remained hanging in mid-air. Next he and the other two Fathers were cut down and, being yet alive, were presently disembowelled and their bowels cast into the fire. Their heads were then cut off; their bodies quartered and their quarters set up in the highways and upon the gates of London. And in executing this barbarous cruelty upon such innocent persons, also was added this inhumanity: the second that was executed was made to stand to behold the death and the bloody slaughter of the first; and the third of them both.

* Henry Clifford: The Life of Jane Dormer, Duchess of Feria, 1889

was the more surprising since he had once been a favourite of the King. (See Recollections D)

On the other hand those monastic leaders who cooperated were given a generous pension. In lieu of a pension some canons were employed as parochial clergy. At Notley the abbot received a pension of £100, while the prior, though he had signed the Deed of Surrender, received only £6-13s- 4d. However, the prior later became the chaplain of Long Crendon, so perhaps this improved his lot. At Dunstable at least ten of the twelve canons had been relocated as incumbents by 1556.

### The Disposal of Monastic Property

The considerable lands of the suppressed monasteries (their most valuable asset) were in great demand by the older titled families, by the new Tudor aristocracy and by men of business, particularly from the wool trade, who were anxious to invest their wealth. Usually its disposal was politically motivated. Much was granted or sold to the king's favourites, sometimes in appreciation of past services and sometimes because once a family had been so favoured it tended to support the monarch who had granted the favour. Thus in 1542 Henry VIII leased a mill and about 250 acres of the Notley land to Sir John Williams and others. Soon after his accession, Edward VI leased the same property to Sir William Paget, his principal Secretary of State.[15] A small proportion of monastic sales was used to fund education: a few colleges at Oxford and Cambridge, and some schools. Monastic wealth had long been used for such projects.

Unless they were sited in towns, the monastic buildings had little value and were difficult to sell or to use. The government ordered them to be demolished, but this was expensive. Most of the religious houses in the Vale and North Bucks were left to decay, and their stone, timber, lead and glass were recycled into new buildings. Thus some remains of Luffield Priory are incorporated into Luffield Abbey Farm. Pieces of carved stone from Ravenstone Priory have been found in buildings nearby. All that remains of Aylesbury Friary (originally situated alongside Friarage Passage) are two alabaster altar panels now in the County Museum at Aylesbury. Overall the dissolution caused an enormous transfer of property and wealth from the priesthood to royalty and the laity.

Before selling the contents, the monastery's church or chapel was cleared of all portable religious relics and images, while fixed images were defaced. Many relics were a preposterous exploitation of the gullibility and superstition rife among the peasantry. The relics sent to Cromwell included God's coat, part of God's supper, some of the clay from which God fashioned Adam, and a thorn from the crown of thorns. In a letter to Thomas Cromwell, Dr John London describes [16] the clearance of Caversham Chapel, which had close links with Notley Abbey:

> I have pullyd down the image of our ladye at Caversham whereunto wasse great pilgrimage. The image ys platyd over with sylver, and I have putt it in a cheste fast lockyd and naylyd uppe, and by the next bardge that cometh from Reading to London yt shall be browght to your lordeschippe. I have also pullyd down the place sche stode in, with all other ceremonyes, as lightes, schrowdes (shrouds), crowchys (crutches) and images of waz hanging about the chapel, and have defacyd the same thoroughly ... I have (also) sent uppe the principall relik of idolytrie within thys realme, an aungell (angel) with oon (one) wyng that browzt (brought) to Caversem the spere hedde that percyd our Saviours side upon the crosse. It wasse conveyd home to Notley, butt I sent my servant perposeley for ytt. I have defaced that chapel inward, and have sent home the chanon to hys master to Nutley.

When all the 'offensive' items had been dealt with, anything which might interest the king or Cromwell was offered to them. The remainder of the moveable contents was usually auctioned, often at the house itself. At the auction the public, including speculators, dealers and collectors, might acquire such things as glass, vestments, missals, jewelled and plated candlesticks, crosses and ornaments of gold and silver, censers, organs, pulpits, altars and manuscripts, usually at very modest prices. Even Catholics took advantage of the situation. After the dissolution of Woburn Abbey, Wing's churchwardens purchased *"a lowde of stoffe"* at the sale of the contents of the abbey church: enough to fill three waggons:

| | | |
|---|---|---|
| *Payd for the orgayns and the ornaments that came from Woburne* | *ix liv* | |
| *To Jhon Chappell for a lowde caryde from Woburne* | | *xvd* |
| *For mete and drynke when we went for the orgayns to Woburn* | *ijs* | *vijd* |
| *To Sir Thomas for setting of ye organs[17]* | *vs* | |
| *For a glass wyndo boght at Woburn* | *iijs* | *iiijd* |
| *For taking down of ye window and ye charges of hyt* | | *vijd* |
| *To Sir Thomas for kypping ye orgayns [18]* | *vs* | |

Though some suffered years of disuse and depredation, some of the monastic buildings were eventually converted into domestic or farm buildings, sometimes suffering many years of misuse. Around 1730 the Prior's lodging at Notley Abbey became a farmhouse, while the ruins of the frater (dining hall) were eventually re-built as a barn. The cloister garth became the farmyard, and by the end of the 18th century what little remained of the cloisters was used as a pig stye.[19] Over the years people seem to have just helped themselves to building materials. The ancient stone roof of the Notley frater was removed to Chesterton (Oxon.), and replaced with common tiles. The panelling from the Prior's lodging went to Weston-on-the-Green (Oxon.). Some of the floor tiles used for levelling purposes in the 16th century chimney stacks of Long Crendon manor are claimed to be from Notley.[20] Recently the buildings have been used as a country house, and were occupied for some years by Sir Lawrence Olivier and his wife Vivien Leigh.

## *ASHRIDGE COLLEGE*

The College of Bonhommes at Ashridge (later called Ashridge College) stands on the northern edge of the Chilterns, and so was well-placed to attract pilgrims and penitents (and their alms) from the Vale and North Bucks., especially as its relics included a phial said to contain a portion of the *"Precious Blood of Jesus Christ"*. Although the Rector surrendered the house to the king, he certainly did not do so with good grace, for after his signature on the deed of surrender he added in Latin:

> *In 1539 the noble house of Ashridge was destroyed and the brothers were driven out on St. Leonard's Day. In this year was beheaded that extreme heretic and betrayer, Thomas Cromwell, who was the cause of the destruction of all the religious houses in England.[21]*

King Henry converted the College into a royal residence in place of Berkhamsted Castle, which had become too old-fashioned and uncomfortable. He gave the building to his infant son, Edward, whose mother - Jane Seymour - had died a few days after his birth, and a year later the Prince was brought to Ashridge in charge of one Sybil Penn as nurse and foster mother. Both Edward and his half-sister Elizabeth seem to have spent much of their childhood at Ashridge, and in 1543 Mary also went there for the benefit of her health. At that time Mary was 27 years old, Elizabeth was ten and Edward was just six.

**Fig. 49: The Last of the Tudors**

Henry VIII = (1) Catherine of Aragon (divorced) gave birth to Mary I (1553 – 1558)
(1509-1547)    (2) Anne Boleyn (beheaded) gave birth to Elizabeth I (1558 – 1603)
        (3) Jane Seymour (died) gave birth to Edward VI (1547 – 1553)
        (4) Anne of Cleves (divorced)
        (5) Catherine Howard (beheaded)
        (6) Catherine Parr (survived)

## Fig. 50 : Skeletal Family Tree of the Early Dormers of Wing

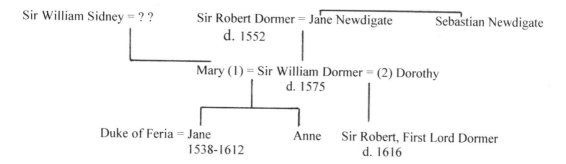

The Dormers were a Buckinghamshire family of committed Catholics. In 1515 Sir Robert and Jane Dormer (born Newdigate) bought the manor of Wing. They also owned the manors of Ascott and Aston Abbotts. They preferred to live in the country, and lived peacefully amongst their neighbours. Even so, they held steadfastly to their religious convictions, and their home was a refuge to all distressed and persecuted Catholics, both priests and laymen. They held the advowson of Wing church, and when Catholicism succombed to Protestantism it is possible that they displayed occasional conformity, for they remained on good terms with the authorities.

King Henry appointed Sir William Sidney to be tutor to Prince Edward, who was then resident at Ashridge, which is only ten miles from Wing, where Sir William's motherless grand-daughters, Jane and Anne Dormer, lived with their paternal grandparents Sir Robert and Lady Jane Dormer (see Fig. 50). In 1544 Sir William sent for his grand-daughter Jane *"to entertain some time with the Prince"*. They were both about six or seven years old, and he welcomed her company, *"taking particular pleasure in her conversation"*.

> *So thither she was sent with her governess, passing her time with the Prince either in reading, playing or dancing, and such-like pastimes, answerable to their spirits and innocency of years, and in playing at cards, he would say, as it fell out, "Now Jane, your king is gone, I shall be good enough for you."* [22]

When Jane Dormer grew older she was again commended by her grandfather, Sir William Sidney, this time to the Lady Mary herself. She became Mary's favourite maid of honour, often sleeping in her bed-chamber, joining in her devotions, taking charge of her jewels and even carving her meat for her. Jane continued to serve Mary after she became Queen until Mary's death in 1558. She then emigrated to Spain, where her home was a refuge for Catholic recusants from England. Eventually, Jane married the Duke of Feria, once the Spanish Ambassador to King Henry. [23]

Despite Queen Elizabeth's reinstatement of Protestantism as the national religion, the early Dormers seem to have continued to view All Saints, Wing, as the family's church, for they celebrated the deaths of the second and third generations of Wing Dormers by adding two more huge and hugely expensive monuments to that raised to the first generation (Fig.51). Today they still stand on either side of the chancel, a monument to a family which was noted for its charity, which reached its peak with the building of four alms-houses in Wing in 1596. There is also the charming story of Jane Dormer's paternal grandmother (another Jane) who was alarmed by the approach of a mob during a period of peasant disturbance, until its leader stepped forward and assured her that they were there to protect her, whom they regarded as *"full of pity and compassion toward the poor, and ever charitable to her neighbours and tenants"*.

**Fig. 51: Part of the Elaborate Memorial to Sir Robert Dormer in Wing Church.**

Wing church is rich in monuments to the Dormer family, and Sir Robert's is considered to be the finest of its date in England. He died in 1616 only a year after his elevation to a peerage as the first Lord Dormer of Wing. His six children, kneeling at the foot of the monument, all married into Roman Catholic families.

## THE EFFECTS OF THE DISSOLUTION UPON THE PEOPLE

In 1538, Henry approved an English translation of the Bible enabling Cromwell to order that:

> *every church shall provide . . . one book of the whole Bible of the largest volume, in English, and the same set up in some convenient place within the said church . . . whereas your parishioners may most commodiously resort to the same and read it . . .* [24]

The availability of an English Bible which the clergy could read aloud in churches meant that illiterate peasants, who formed the vast majority of church congregations, no longer had to rely on the inadequate wall paintings and stained glass windows for information about Christianity.

With the endowment of monasteries and chantries forbidden, some leading families, and the nouveau riche, eventually founded 350 grammar schools. Some sought royal approval or a more comfortable after-life, but much of this was genuine philanthropy. Whatever the motive, they made an important contribution to society, because industry and commerce were developing, and creating job opportunities for the literate and numerate. Where bequests included financial provision for poor scholars, even peasant families benefited. On Thomas Cromwell's orders, from 1538 all baptisms, marriages and burials in each parish had to be recorded weekly and these records are now invaluable to genealogists, historians and lawyers. That was the good news.

The rest was pretty grim. In England as a whole something like eight thousand monks and nuns had been either pensioned off or redeployed. However, the religious houses also employed thousands of peasants as domestic and ancillary staff, and they received no pension. Many became unemployed and homeless. The monasteries also owned a great deal of land: Notley Abbey held seven manors. When new owners acquired them many more jobs could be lost, especially if the land was converted from labour-intensive arable to sheep farming. Now, the religious houses (the friaries, abbeys, monasteries, chantries, hospitals, etc.) which had previously succoured such unfortunates no longer existed. Some found work elsewhere, or were supported by friends and relatives, or died by the roadside. The destruction of the religious houses also meant the loss of manuscripts and books from their libraries. Often these were acquired by people who did not realise their worth. Some were just burned. Fortunately, some were collected by antiquarians and eventually presented to colleges and libraries.

## THE REFORMATION AND THE CHURCHES

In medieval times church worship was very different from today. The sermon was in English and if the preacher was competent he would be listened to respectfully. However, most of the service was conducted in Latin so, with few exceptions, the congregation could not understand a word of it. Indeed, a surprising number of the clergy could not understand Latin and could hardly pronounce it.[25] As Parson Sloth confesses in Piers Plowman:[26] *"in mass-book or Pope's edict I cannot read a line."* So some of the congregation would chatter and laugh during this part of the service, hardly troubling to doff their caps and kneel at the supreme moment of the Mass: the consecration of the Host at the High Altar. Indeed, the churchwardens were constantly complaining about *"common chatterers talking and jangelinge specyally in the tyme of divine service"*.

For centuries the interior of churches had blazed with colour. There were painted and gilded images and elaborate carvings in wood or stone, both in niches in the walls, and free-standing for use in processions on special occasions. These included saints' days, when swinging censers filled with incense, flickering candles, bejewelled crosses, gleaming chalices, banners, sacred icons and the beautifully embroidered vestments of the priests would captivate both nose and eye. Even the interior masonry was colour-washed. For the illiterate majority the brilliantly coloured window glass and wall paintings relating stories from the scriptures, did homage to the Trinity and the saints; cautioned the congregation as to its behaviour; and forecast the future for the unrepentant.

**Fig. 52: Wall Painting of Saint Bernard in the Church of All Saints at Little Kimble**

Between the nave and the chancel stood the rood screen, often beautifully carved, physically and symbolically separating off the holy chancel and sanctuary from the parishioners' nave. Above it stood the Great Rood, which was a large crucifix, and perhaps behind it a rood loft, a platform which could accommodate some of the choir or some instrumentalists. As a backcloth, a doom (a Last Judgement) may have been painted. Some evidence of this is still visible today in the churches of the Vale and North Bucks.. Behind the organ at the 13th century church at Swanbourne are some badly damaged wall paintings from about 1500. They represent *"The Four Last Things"* i.e. Heaven, Hell, Death and Judgement. The demons, skeletons, and souls in purgatory must have made a fearful impression on the peasants of earlier times. The 13th century church of **All Saints at Little Kimble** has early 14th century wall paintings, *"artistically the best in Buckinghamshire"*; also 13th century floor tiles. There are excellent wall paintings in the church of **St Lawrence at Broughton**, near Milton Keynes: for key phone 01908-6750740 (Plates C12 and C13) . Outside our area, but still in Buckinghamshire, there are some excellent paintings in the church of **St John the Baptist at Little Missenden**. **Visits to the last three are well worthwhile**, provided that one allows for the fact that the paintings are up to seven centuries old, and for much of that time were white-washed out of sight. Despite all the changes the parish church was still central to the lives of most villagers even after the Reformation.

**Fig. 53: Chetwode's Parish Church**
It was once part of Chetwode Priory.

96

# Chapter 9

# THE ANGLICAN EMERGENCE

## EDWARD VI (1547-53) & THE REFORMATION

Edward was only nine years old when he became king, and a Council of Regency governed

**Fig. 54: Edward VI**

England during his minority. Most members of Parliament and of the Council were sympathetic towards Protestants, so Henry VIII's laws against heresy were at first ignored and then repealed. In July 1547 it was also required that the gospels and epistles *must* be read in English in the churches.[1]

Then, as had been planned by Henry, the chantries were dissolved. These were endowments made to finance an altar in a church or in its own chapel, or for the employment of priests to sing masses, usually for the soul of the endower. But most chantries in the Vale and North Bucks. did more than this. For instance, some funded assistant priests; some ran schools; and some distributed alms. When their endowments were confiscated, it was the ordinary people, and especially the peasantry, who were deprived. The principal beneficiary was the Royal Treasury. Not that most chantries were particularly rich, but in the country as a whole there were 2,374 of them.

This was only the beginning. From then on the pace quickened, and Edward's reign was marked by a series of changes which converted the churches from Catholicism to Protestantism. In the past many crosses and images had been illuminated by candles provided by the congregation. Soon, illumination was restricted to the rood, the sepulchre[2] and the altar cross. Even this was too much for dedicated Protestants and it was ordered that only the altar cross should be illuminated. Such a departure from customary practice must have been obeyed with reluctance and sadness, not least by Thomas Wynchester and Richard Chappman only recently *"chosyn to be cepers of the roude lytte"*, at All Saints' Church, Wing, as they returned their unused funds to the churchwardens. Later still, churches had to remove all side altars, and also the rood: the holy cross above the rood screen. Then it was ordered that the interior walls of churches must be white-limed to obliterate their rich colours and glowing paintings. Wax images must be melted down; and other images destroyed or sold after recovering any precious metal. The accounts confirm that Wing's churchwardens obeyed:

| | | | |
|---|---|---|---|
| *Payd for a quarter of lyme and the caryge* | | *ijs* | *xd* |
| *Payd to Sander and hys men for whyt lymying of the churche* | | *vs* | *vd* |
| *Payd for the wasshing out of ye dome (doom) in ye rode loft*[3] | | | *xvjd* |
| *Receyvyd for xvj pounds of wax solde* | | *ixs* | *jd* |
| *Receyvyd for the gylt of the images* | | *iiijs* | |
| *Reseyved for stuffe the whyche was sold of the churche goodes* | *xvjli* | *ijs* | |

Finally the contentious issue of the church service was addressed by Archbishop Cranmer. In 1549 Parliament approved his Book of Common Prayer, and in 1552 approved a revised version. Out went the Mass! In came the Holy Communion. Out went Latin! In came English, in Cranmer's masterly prose, and for the first time congregations knew what they were praying for. Out went the elaborately carved high altars of stone! In came simple wooden communion tables. Out went the richly embroidered vestments. In came plain white surplices. In addition ceremonials and processions were curtailed and simplified. Once more the churchwardens of Wing went to work:

> *Payd for ye takynge downe of ye aulters and ye dressyng of the walls agayne   iiijs     ijd*
> *Payd for makynge of the (communion) table                                                        iiijd*

The new prayer books introduced responses, whereby the congregation actually participated in the services by chorusing replies to the priest's declarations rather than exchanging local gossip. All these changes must have caused a sensation when parishioners first encountered them: the white walls; the empty niches; the utilitarian wooden communion table; and the plain white surplices. No flickering candles; no perfumed incense; no gleaming crosses; no magnificent robes; and no colourful banners. What emotions must have been aroused: dismay, sorrow, indignation, condemnation, bewilderment, shock … To crown it all the clergy were to be allowed to marry! To committed Catholics this was heresy, whereas to committed Protestants it was insufficient.

### The Catholics of Wing and the Reformation

The Churchwardens' Accounts of Wing provide a rare insight into this period,[4] for they reflect the many changes expected of churches during the Reformation. At this time the parish was thoroughly committed to Catholicism, for it was dominated by the Dormer family:[5] wealthy local landowners; staunch Catholics; and holders of the advowson of the parish church.[6] With their religious world collapsing around their eyes and ears, how did the pro-Catholic parishioners react? It must be remembered that the Dormers had close connections with the royal family. With a member of the family (Sir William Sidney) appointed as tutor to Prince Edward, they may well have learnt that Edward was *"a weakly child"*, and as Jane Dormer had participated in the Lady Mary's devotions she would surely have known that Mary (next in line for the throne) had *"an attachment to Rome so fervent as to be fanatical"*. [7] Certainly, the churchwardens of Wing appear to have viewed the future with some hope of change. For at the end of 1548/49, the accounts showed a surplus of £17, yet only £5 was handed over to the incoming churchwardens. Apparently, the remaining £12 was entrusted to certain parishioners until such time as the church needed it. For a reversion to Catholicism perhaps? They had not long to wait, for young Edward died at the age of 16.

### QUEEN MARY (1553-58) & THE RETURN TO CATHOLICISM

Queen Mary was the daughter of Catharine of Aragon, Henry VIII's Spanish first wife. Thus Mary was half-Spanish by birth and devoted to all things Spanish: a viewpoint which did nothing to endear her to her English subjects, who – Spain being a major sea power – feared a Spanish invasion. So when Mary became Queen she restored the authority of the Pope with difficulty. Parliament spent three months in debate before repealing the religious laws of Henry and Edward, and also refused to restore their confiscated property to the monasteries. So it was October 1553 before churches had to revert to Catholicism. Then out went the recently installed communion tables; back came the stone altars. Out went the newly purchased Books of Common Prayer; back came the Mass Books. Out went the white surplices; back came the elaborate vestments and all the other adjuncts of Roman Catholicism. Significantly, their accounts reveal that *"in joyful alacrity"* Wing's churchwardens had anticipated these requirements by several months.

> *Payd for a masse book*                                                                    *xiiijd*
> *Payd to John Lucas for ij vestments*                                    *vijs   iiijd*
> *Payd to Ellyn London for scowrynge of the sensers*                *ijd*
> *Payd to London's wife for scouring of the cannapy*                 *jd*
> *Payd for ij candlestyekes besyde the money that was gethered*   *xd*
> *Payd Edward Warde for makyng of the frame aboute the sepulcre*   *xd*
> *Payd for the rode (rood)* [8]                                            *xxixs   jd*
> *Payd for the crosse and pax*[9]                                         *ijs   viijd*
> *Payd for castyng the saunce (sanctus) bell*                           *vjs   ijd*

In all of this, speed was regarded as essential. No less a personage than 'Sir John' rode to Oxford for the blessing of the communion cup and the altar cloth. It was obviously a labour of love, for all he was paid was 2d for the *"schoynge of hys horse"*. Such prompt action was probably inspired by Sir William Dormer, who would know what was going on in the royal court, and who was the first in the county to proclaim Mary as queen.

During Mary's reign, Protestant objections to Catholicism were dealt with ruthlessly. Some of the leading Protestants succeeded in eluding the authorities by going into hiding, while over 800 fled to the continent. Even so, the heresy laws having been restored, over 300 were burned to death for their beliefs. They included rich and poor, high and low, and extended to such notables as Archbishop Cranmer, and Bishops Latimer and Ridley. Hence the Queen's nickname: Bloody Mary. For the burnings only increased public hostility both to her and the Roman Catholic Church:

> *The Spanish ambassador ... anxiously observed how the crowds gathered round the ashes and wrapped them reverently; how they uttered menaces against the bishops, or wept in compassion.* [10]

For those who publicly retracted their heresy there was usually an additional punishment, such as making a pilgrimage to a distant shrine, or wearing a jacket or gown with a faggot embroidered on the sleeve. And confession was for life. For repeated heresy, burning was inevitable. A second confession might *"bring great joy to the judges"*, but it would not reduce the penalty. Most of Buckinghamshire's heretics seem to have come from the Chilterns and the south of the county. The four persons brought to trial from Princes Risborough in 1530 were the exception rather than the rule. But the threat of burning was felt throughout the land.

So Mary converted England back to Roman Catholicism. However, it would only be permanent if she could bear a child to succeed her on the throne. Otherwise it was quite certain that Elizabeth would succeed her and return the country to the Protestant faith. To resolve the issue Mary married the Catholic King Philip II of Spain, and word soon spread that she was pregnant. But it was a phantom pregnancy that set the bells of London ringing. Disappointed, embittered and frustrated, she died shortly afterwards. As the news spread, some people celebrated by lighting bonfires.

## QUEEN ELIZABETH (1558-1603) & THE RETURN TO PROTESTANTISM

Under Elizabeth, the monarch again became the supreme head of the Church of England. Hoping to unite her subjects, she was determined to establish a truly national Anglican church. To this end she created a Protestant church which was a compromise between the extremes of both the Puritans and the Roman Catholics, and the Act of Uniformity of 1559 was carefully worded so as to appeal to many different shades of belief. Nevertheless, it was soon apparent that Elizabeth was a committed Protestant. At Christmas 1558 she ordered the Bishop of Carlisle not to elevate the host when conducting the Mass, and on his refusal she left the church. When all but one of the bishops refused to swear the Oath of (Royal) Supremacy, she promptly replaced them by Protestant sympathisers. By the end of 1559 the return to Protestantism was well under way. Mass books in Latin, stone altars and elaborate robes were replaced once more by Books of Common Prayer in English, wooden communion tables and white surplices. [11] Being Catholic, Wing procrastinated until June, when they learned that the officers of the Crown would shortly be visiting Aylesbury to require officials to subscribe to the Oath of Supremacy and to ensure that the Book of Common Prayer was being used. Only then were Wing's churchwardens activated.

> *Payd for a boke for the ministering of the sakerment in Yngllis layde owte*     vs     ijd
> *Payd at the vysittasyon at Allysberi*     xxd
> *Payd for the takyng down of the rode (rood)*     vijd
> *Payd for wyne (for the communion)*     vd

Beyond this the churchwardens of Wing still procrastinated, and it was the summer of 1561 before they were forced to act. They had greased the palm of the Archdeacon's summoner[12] who duly warned them that there would be a diocesan visitation in the near future. Out came the church box:

| | | |
|---|---:|---:|
| *Payd to ye sumner to kepe us from Lincoln for slackness of our auters (altars)* | | *viijd* |
| *Payd to him for warnyng (us of) the archdeacon's visitation at Alesbury* | | *iiijd* |
| *Payd for takyng down ye south aulter [13]* | | *iiijd* |
| *Payd for the table and other two lytle bokes* | *ijs* | *iiijd* |
| *Payd to the sexton for takynge down of our rode lofte* | *ijs* | |
| *Payd to London and Nasshe for takyng awaye the robell of ye auters and* | | |
| *Laynge downe of the stone of the auter agayne.* | | *xvjd* |

Encouraged by the moderation of the changes in the church services, and by the carefully worded

**Fig. 55: Queen Elizabeth**

Protestant communion, which allowed for some differences in belief, many Catholics continued to attend their parish church. Of course, the fine imposed on absentees may have influenced some! Unfortunately, from 1568, English fears of Roman Catholicism increased due to the military threat from Spain, the Pope's subsidies to English and Irish rebels, and the plots to replace Elizabeth by the Catholic Mary, Queen of Scots. Worse still, the Pope's edict of 1570, excommunicated Elizabeth and released her subjects from allegiance to her. It was an invitation to English Catholics to revolt, and it allowed Elizabeth no distinction between Catholics loyal to herself, and the minority whose first loyalty was to the Pope. Parliament decided to respond in kind. From 1571 it became treason to profess or promote Catholicism. Even so, hundreds of Catholic priests began to arrive from the continent. So, from 1585 Catholic priests became guilty of treason if they so much as remained in England; and it became a felony to conceal one. Despite this they did stay, they were concealed, and many paid with their lives.

Things did not quite reach this pitch in the Vale and North Bucks., mainly because, as the Justices of the Peace reported, "*There were none that refused to come to church*".[14] In 1583, in lists of persons noted as "*harbourers of Papists and seminaries*", are found only five names for this county: Gifford of Steeple Claydon, Mercer of Middle Claydon, Sir Robert Dormer of Wing, Browne of Boarstall, and Peckham. All these regularly housed certain priests (who were named, and were damned in official reports), sometimes retaining them for years as domestic chaplains, and also offered refuge to any that might pass their way. The Dormers of Wing had in their house a priest, who acted as resident chaplain. He had a room in their mansion at Wing, from which he never came out, but the family visited him. Lord Montague, who was connected wth the Dormers by a double marriage, was another gentlemen who never fell under suspicion, though he harboured some Catholics of the deepest dye, who were sought in vain for the prison and the gallows. Members of both these families entered the Catholic Society of Jesus, despite knowing what atrocities might be visited upon them. Despite this, there is no record of proceedings being taken against them, probably because they were gentlemen of undoubted loyalty to Queen Elizabeth, and attended church occasionally. In 1585, although he was in the previous list, Sir Robert Dormer (by this time Sheriff of Buckinghamshire) was ordered to draw up a list of recusants for the shire, "*that they might be compelled to pay their fines and provide horses for the Queen's service*".[15] His list of 22 names included 15 well-known families. The standard fine of £240 was beyond the total annual income of most country gentry, but ten compromised by offering lesser sums (from 10s

**Fig. 56: Medieval Woodwork in the Church of Saint Mary the Virgin at Edlesborough**
Fortunately in their effort to simplify religious services and rid them of colour and decoration, Protestants seem to have overlooked many fine examples of craftmanship, lovingly created by medieval artisans. Over five centuries later many still exist for us to enjoy, cared for in this case by the Churches Conservation Trust. The key is available from the Bell public house just across the road from the church: tel. 01525-220314.

to £100). Others could not even afford this. They included Avice Lee of Pitstone, but she solved the problem by going to church and obtaining a certificate of conformity.

So the authorities knew that there were Catholic priests in the great houses of landed Catholics such as those on the 1583 list[16] and elsewhere.[17] Such mansions lent themselves to the creation of priest holes. For example, the imposing Gayhurst House had a number of these, the last of which was destroyed in 1875. In 1860, at Claydon House near Bletchley, a long-forgotten secret room was broken into behind the Cedar Room fireplace where up to ten standing men could, and did, hide.[18] Later it was inadvertently destroyed by workmen carrying out renovations. Priest holes have been found even in smaller houses. At Church Farmhouse in Wingrave, when the owners were redecorating circa 1935, they broke through a wall to reveal a room which no-one in living memory had previously seen. It contained a chair, a truckle-bed, and a table on which was a hand-bell. The entrance was located in the loft. At Stewkley, the manor house still had secret chambers as late as 1923.[19] Priest holes saved hundreds of lives. Their construction required both originality and ingenuity. There were hiding places in chimneys, behind wall panels, and under fireplace hearths. Floor slabs would pivot, cupboards have false backs, a window seat would give access to a gable, a bookcase would swing away to reveal a recess in a wall, or a heavy oak beam might be hinged to give access to a loft.[20]

Absence from church could persuade the authorities that the truant was a Catholic sympathiser, and worth investigating. Even if there was no Catholic priest, a thorough search might yield evidence. In 1586 Sir Christopher Browne of Boarstall [21] experienced such a search.

*The house was suddenly entered by John Croke, Justice of the Peace and others, early in the morning (so that the inhabitants might have no chance of a warning) and searched from 7 a.m. to 6 p.m. the gates being guarded all the time. They searched coffers, cupboards, closets, trunks, caskets and secret places, breaking open all locked doors 'for lack of keys'. Apart from priests, they were looking for religious books, pictures, statuettes, letters, and such things as an instruction to sing the Mass.*

Even the discovery of such *objets de piété* (*"divers relicks and popish trash"* as the searchers called them) could incur a substantial fine. But if the searchers did find priests, the penalties were draconian, and included lengthy imprisonment, confiscation of property, torture and execution. In 1589 Thomas Belson of Brill and his servant were executed at Oxford for concealing a priest. In England (1577-1603), 123 priests were executed, and 60 or so men and women who had sheltered them.[22] But the authorities could also show clemency. Lady Stonor (a relative by marriage of the Dormers of Wing) astonished the judges with her frankness and the sincerity of her defence:

*I was born . . . when Holy Mass was in great reverence and brought up in the same faith. In King Edward's time this reverence was neglected and reproved by such as governed. In Queen Mary's time it was restored with much applause . . . The state would have these several changes . . . all good and laudable. Whether it can be so, I refer it to your lordships' consideration. I hold me still to that wherein I was born and bred, and find nothing in it but great virtue and sanctity. And so by the grace of God, I will live and die in it.[23]*

Despite this, judging her to be of innocent intentions, the judges did not press the charges. Consequently it all sounds very civilised, but she was risking her life, and must have known it.

## *LOOKING AHEAD*

Even after the Reformation the parish church was still central to villagers' lives, for few ventured far from home. Baptisms, marriages and burials marked the passing years, and might bring out a rare visit from relatives in a neighbouring village. The church's insistence on the sanctity of Sunday provided the labourer with respite from his six days of dawn to dusk toil. Its church services brought together families and friends and gave the lads a sight of the lasses, while festivals like Christmas, Easter, Whitsun, Thanksgiving and Saints' Days provided special occasions to which everyone could look forward. For instance, the saint to whom the church was dedicated was often celebrated by Church Ales, brewed by the churchwardens from the malt supplied by the parishioners, and sold to the parishioners at a large profit. Towards the end of the 16th century, the May Ale, *"with its feasting and drinking, leaping dauncing and kissinge in the church and churchyard"* was Wing's largest source of income, yielding from £9 to £10 yearly towards its close.

For England the future seemed clear: Protestantism with a broad appeal, a supportive government, and a national spirit evoked by the defeat of the Spanish Armada had created, in the Church of England, a distinctly Anglican institution, which has lasted to the present day. However, English Nonconformism was to become a major problem, which we consider in the next chapter.

# Chapter 10

# *EARLY NONCONFORMISM IN THE VALE*

During Queen Elizabeth's reign the Church of England was *"a broad gate through which all might pass"*. However, it was still a crime *not* to attend its church services and take the sacrament each Sunday. When Queen Elizabeth died there were several elements in England's religious spectrum. Roman Catholics had been driven underground, but were still fairly numerous among the country gentry and their households. The Protestants were those who opposed Roman Catholicism, and they were divided into two main groups: the Anglicans, who were satisfied with the reform of the Church of England under Elizabeth; and the Nonconformists, who did not wish to conform to Anglican dress, ritual, doctrine, etc.. They wished to worship and follow God as their consciences dictated which, in practice, meant a much simpler form of worship, directly with God, rather than through the mediation of a priest. Because they often used the word 'purer' instead of 'simpler', such Nonconformists were also known as Puritans. Several groups emerged, each with its own preferences as regards doctrine and religious worship. Over the years these sects gradually left the Anglican church to form the groups which we know as Presbyterians, Independents, Baptists, Quakers, Methodists, etc..

This situation was further complicated by the accession of the Stuarts, who believed in the Divine Right of Kings to rule without reference to Parliament. The Nonconformists, on the other hand, were the champions of parliamentary power, and from their ranks sprang some of the great parliamentary leaders. One such champion was John Hampden of Great Hampden, who represented Wendover in the first three Parliaments of Charles I's reign (Fig. 57). Parliament was insistent that the King must obtain parliamentary approval before declaring war, imposing taxation, etc., etc.. Hampden, for example, steadfastly refused to pay ship money (a tax that had *not* been authorised by Parliament), a stand that made him a national hero. Parliament also proposed reforms of the Church of England, to which Charles I replied by accusing five members of the Commons (including Hampden) and one member of the House of Lords of treason. So political issues became inextricably involved with religious issues. Further negotiations between the King and Parliament failed, and on August 22nd 1642, Charles' army marched on London.

In the Civil War (1642-6 and 1648) which followed, the Vale *in general* supported the Parliamentary cause with its promises of a more powerful Parliament, and a church with less pomp and ceremony and more acceptable doctrine. The war ended with the execution of Charles I and the establishment of the Commonwealth with Oliver Cromwell as Lord Protector. During the Commonwealth (1649-59), Presbyterianism supplanted the Church of

**Fig. 57: Statue of John Hampden, Market Square, Aylesbury**

England. Otherwise all religions enjoyed considerable freedom, more than at any previous time.

After Cromwell's death, the end of the Commonwealth and the return of the Stuarts were marked by a wave of intolerance and persecution created by new laws imposed by the Anglican-biased Cavalier Parliament (1661-1679). These included the Act of Uniformity 1662, which required every clergyman, schoolmaster and fellow of a college to accept the whole of the Church of England prayer book, including the Communion according to the rites of the Church of England. Some 2,000 clergy refused to conform and were ejected from their livings. This marked the beginning of large-scale Nonconformity, because the ejected clergy often remained in their former parishes, to minister to the thousands who had followed them out of the Church of England. The religious services they conducted were mostly held in people's homes and farmers' barns, and the Conventicle Acts of 1664 and 1670 were designed to suppress these gatherings. They made it an offence to attend any religious meeting of an illegal or clandestine kind, at which more than four persons were present in addition to the members of one family. The penalties for infringement ranged from heavy fines to confiscation of goods, imprisonment, and transportation. However, the authorities found it very difficult to locate such meetings, the time and place of which could vary from week to week. It was even more difficult to catch the participants with meetings in progress. Desperate to secure convictions, the authorities tended to concentrate on the open defiance of the laws and customs such as was often displayed by the Quakers. Nationally, by 1662, 1,300 of them were in prison, and in March 1685 about 1,460. In 1661, in Aylesbury gaol alone, 63 Nonconformists were incarcerated. At that time the prisons were vile and degrading places. A contemporary reported, [1]

> *The Aylesbury gaol, now so decayed that it seems scarce fit for a dog-house, has long been a centre of infection (from the plague). At this time it was crammed full of miserable Nonconformists.*

During the Great Plague of 1665 most people able to do so fled from the towns, whereas many of the Nonconforming clergy stayed in their former parishes ministering to the sick and thus earning widespread respect. To counter this, the Five Mile Act of that year forbade such clergy from going within five miles of any corporate town or their former parishes. There was also a very dubious royal initiative in 1669 when Charles II, via the Archbishop of Canterbury, instructed all the bishops to ensure that every minister in their jurisdiction reported on the current state of Nonconformity in their parish by answering eight specific questions (see Recollections E).

In 1689, Parliament deposed King James II (Charles II's brother) and replaced him by the Dutchman William of Orange and his English wife Mary. Only then was a Toleration Act passed, which granted the right of worship to Protestant Nonconformists. In particular, they were permitted to register their homes, or other meeting places, as conventicles (places for religious meetings). Despite this, their political and social rights suffered considerably. A number of Acts of Parliament (generally known as the Test Acts) excluded Nonconformists from the universities and from public office (as M.P.s, J.P.s, Judges, Mayors, Councillors, etc.), unless they signed certificates agreeing to Anglican beliefs and rites. Denied entry to public service, many Nonconformists expended their talents on industry and trade. The Cadburys, Frys, Rowntrees, Lloyds, Barclays and Darbys are just a few of the Nonconformist families who became known nationally for their industrial and commercial enterprise. Moreover, the religious trauma of the 16th and 17th centuries had deeply divided the nation, and there was no toleration for Roman Catholics and Unitarians until the passing of the Catholic Emancipation Act in 1829. Not until 1871 were religious tests completely abolished. [2]

We now consider briefly how some of the Vale's Nonconformists fared when the new movements were beginning.

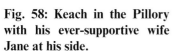

**Fig. 58: Keach in the Pillory with his ever-supportive wife Jane at his side.**
It is said that as soon as his head and hands were fixed in the pillory the unrepentant Keach preached to onlookers.

**Fig. 59 : Winslow's Humble Little Baptist Chapel**,
Built in 1695, it is one of the oldest existing Nonconformist places of worship in Buckinghamshire. The interior is said to be almost exactly as it was originally: see Plate C14. It is **well worth a visit.** For key, apply to Wilkinson, Estate Agents, 12, Market Square, Winslow (01296-712717).

## NONCONFORMISM AT WINSLOW [3]

In 1658, while still a teenager, Benjamin Keach became a member of a Baptist congregation at Winslow. He quickly developed into an outstanding preacher, who was very much appreciated by all who heard him. However, he soon fell foul of the authorities, who were implementing the repressive regime and the harsh legislation introduced by the Cavalier Parliament. Charles II had promised his subjects *"the public and free profession of true Religion and Worship"*, but it soon became clear that this applied only to those who accepted the doctrines of the Church of England.

> *Keach was often seized, when preaching, and committed to prison, sometimes bound, sometimes released on bail, and sometimes his life was threatened".*

Once a troop of soldiers discovered where Keach was preaching. Seizing him very roughly, they tied him up and threw him on the ground. Then four troopers prepared to trample him to death with their horses, but an officer suspecting their intentions rode up and prevented them. Keach was then picked up and slung across one of the horses, and so carried to Aylesbury Gaol, which was filled to overflowing with Nonconformists. He suffered considerably before he was released.

In 1664 Keach published a little book called 'The Child's Instructor' in which he argued for adult baptism as in the New Testament, rather than infant baptism. For this he was arrested and tried at the Aylesbury Assizes, for publishing *"a seditious and schismatical book"*, and sentenced (Fig. 58):

> *You will go to jail for a fortnight without bail . . . and next Saturday stand in the pillory at Aylesbury market for the space of two hours . . . and next Thursday stand in Winslow market in the same manner . . . and there your book shall be openly burnt before your face by the common hangman, in disgrace of you and your doctrine. And you shall forfeit to the King's Majesty the sum of £20, and shall remain in prison until you shall find sureties for your good behaviour.* [4]

Eventually, in 1668, Keach and his wife moved to London, and he spent the rest of his life ministering at the Southwark Meeting House.

## NONCONFORMISM AT HADDENHAM

George Fox founded the Society of Friends in the early 1640's. Its members were known as 'Friends' or very often as Quakers. At first this was a term of ridicule, but increasingly it became a term of respect. It is not until 1649, the year of the execution of Charles I, that we have the first evidence of **Quaker attitudes** at Haddenham, when one Edward Rose Junior refused to pay tithes to a church with which he disagreed on principle. At this time Edward is not described in the records as a Quaker, but refusal to pay tithes was very common amongst Quakers. His refusal cost him dear. He was taken to court, and to avoid jail had to pay £12-15s-4d costs and damages in addition to the original £6-16s tithes.

Not until 1660 was there definite evidence of a Quaker meeting in the village, when Thomas Ellwood reported: [5]

> *I went to a town called Haddenham, five miles from my father's where, at the house of one Belson, a few who were called Quakers did meet sometimes on a first day of the week.*

We also know that, by this time, a meeting for worship had already been established at the home of John White of Meadle, a small hamlet four miles to the west of Haddenham. As early as 1670, births, marriages and deaths from as far away as Haddenham (5), Thame (5), Long Crendon (4), Westcott (1), Moreton (1) and Aylesbury (1) were recorded there, despite the long distances involved. Obviously Quakerism was already evolving into an organisation where local participation would confer national membership, for Meadle was already reporting to the Luton and Leighton Monthly Meeting. Thus, although we know that in 1669 both John and Edward Rose, and Widow Rose were associating with Quakers,[6] it is from the monthly meeting register [7] that there is indisputable evidence of the involvement of the Rose family with Quakerism, and we learn that in 1694 a Jane Rose was buried in one of the Roses' closes at Haddenham: *"Jane Rose died 23.4.1694. Wife of Edward, a yeoman. Residence Haddenham, Bucks.. (Age not stated)"* Part of this burial ground is now preserved at one end of Haddenham's small shopping parade, as a memorial to these early Quakers. Later, the Rose family seem to have made themselves responsible for the continuation of the Quaker meetings, and used their thatched cottage at Fort End, Haddenham, as the venue. By this time the official threat to Nonconformists had long disappeared. It is said that by 1711 the meetings were well attended. In 1747 a later Edward Rose extended the family's existing farmhouse, and in doing so provided a venue where Quaker meetings for worship were regularly held until well into the 19th century.

**Fig. 60: The Baptist Meeting House at Haddenham**
It was built in 1809 in Stockwell, on the site of earlier meeting houses.

Quakers believed in simple living and strict honesty in business and everyday life. They did not feel the need for sacred rites such as baptism and Holy Communion, for they believed that all life was sacred. They also believed that God's spirit was in everyone, and therefore the intervention of a priest was quite unnecessary. So they refused to attend the Anglican church, or pay tithes to support it. They strongly objected to taking oaths in a court of law, for they believed that the truth should always be spoken. Nor need hats be removed before the Judges, for all men should be treated equally. These views got them into a great deal of trouble, which was recorded in a huge register that became known as The Quaker Book of Sufferings. Recollections E give us a picture of Nonconformism in Haddenham in 1689, as reported by the vicar of the parish in response to King Charles II's enquiries.

## Recollections E: The Persecution of Nonconformists

In 1669 the answers of James Stopes (Vicar of the parish of Haddenham) to the Archbishop's enquiries included the following: [9]

*There are constant unlawful meetings, and have been for many years, at the houses of Widow Rose, midwife, and Phillip Wilmot, shoemaker. The persons who frequent these unlawful meetings are some poorer, some richer, these latter being John Rose and his family, whose children are not baptised; Edward Rose and his family, whose children are also not baptised; John Plater's wife and unbaptised children; Richard Greenwood and his family; Widow Rose, the midwife; Stephen Belson and family, who are Quakers; of the poorer sort, several others at Haddenham. Their teachers are Edward Cox (glover), Phillip Wilmot (shoemaker), and sometimes others, as Mr Mariot of Aston Clinton, and Mr Parke of Grendon Underwood, ejected ministers* (from the Church of England), *and Robert Cox, a glover, who comes from Thame. If the laws were duly executed, including paying a shilling per Sunday for absenting themselves from divine service, it would much cool their heats. But they do not value excommunication, for several are excommunicated already.*

The Vicar clearly believed that the laws were not being duly exercised against these Nonconformists. If so, then they were very fortunate for – as the records which have survived tell us – many Nonconformists were being severely punished.[10] In the huge Quaker Book of Sufferings for Buckinghamshire hundred of cases are recorded. For example:

*Sarah Lamburn of Meadle widow for conscience sake refusing to pay tithes to Nathaniel Anderson, priest of Monks Risborough, the said priest cast her into the gaol at Aylesbury, where she remained a prisoner from the 6th day of the 12th month 1659 to the 29th day of the 10th 1660, she being a poor widow having 6 small children.*

*John Brown of Weston Turville for attending a meeting at Sarah Mortimer's in Tring on the 3rd day of the 7th month 1671 was fined £8. Four days later, a man was sent accompanied by a constable to demand the money. He refused to pay. They went into the fields and took 4 cows and a bull, the best they could pick out, and took them to Aston Clinton pound.*

*John Wyatt of Long Crendon for conscientiously refusing to pay tithes was thrown into Aylesbury Gaol at the beginning of the 9th month 1678. Because he would not answer the unreasonable demands of the gaoler he was forced to lie 9 nights upon the bare boards, and two of those nights was denied the benefit of a fire for his money though the weather was very cold. After he had lain a long time in Aylesbury Gaol he was at length removed to London and turned over to the Fleet Prison in which prison he remained a prisoner to the day of his death. He was imprisoned for over 3 years.*

*Thomas Olliffe of Aylesbury, having been excommunicated for not receiving the Eucharist (i.e. Holy Communion) in the Parish Church so called was imprisoned in Aylesbury Gaol on the 4th day of the 8th month 1684 where he continued prisoner until the 16th day of the second month 1686, when he with 17 more was set at liberty by the King's proclamation, having suffered imprisonment for nothing a full year and half and more.*

* The first paragraph in italics is from Broad, J: Buckinghamshire Dissent and Parish Life, Bucks Record Society, vol. 28, p.43.

We are told that in Cromwell's time (1649-59) villagers flocked to Haddenham parish church to hear the sermons of Presbyterian preachers. There were still Presbyterians in Haddenham in 1669, when Samuel Clark of Over Winchendon *"was accustomed to hold services in a house in Haddenham"*. However, around 1672 Clark moved to a church in High Wycombe, and by 1710 Haddenham's Presbyterian meetings had gone into terminal decline.

We do not know exactly when the Baptists first came to Haddenham, but we know that by 1701 they had acquired a meeting house there, because in that year it was burnt down. It was not replaced until 1734, when a small meeting house was built using the local witchert. Haddenham also acquired a group of Seventh-Day Baptists, whose pastor was a Haddenham tailor and shoe-maker named Hoare. Both groups had ceased to exist by 1760. However, half a century later the Particular Baptists established themselves. Their chapel was erected in 1809 (Fig.60), and by the Sunday of the 1851 Religious Census their three congregations averaged 500 people. Methodism did not arrive in Haddenham until late in the 18th century, as is detailed below.

## *NONCONFORMISM AT PRINCES RISBOROUGH* [8]

A Baptist chapel was built at Princes Risborough in 1705. It flourished for about 30 years. Then, a general decline in religious observance and church attendance throughout the country affected the Vale and Princes Risborough. The Baptists abandoned their church to another sect, and it was not until the end of the century that services restarted. Fortunately, a bequest left to them in 1745 by one Thomas Cartwright enabled them by 1804 to recover, repair and extend their church (Fig. 61). After this, membership revived. As Table 8 shows, by 1851 the Princes Risborough area had become a hotbed of Nonconformist worship, attracting people from villages for miles around. And, of course, all this was in addition to the attendances at the two Anglican churches. At Princes Risborough well over half the population attended Baptist chapels, but the Wesleyans and Methodists had also established themselves, and were becoming very popular. Even in the 20th century there were elderly folk who could remember with what *"fervour, enthusiasm and earnestness"* people attended chapel, which was a social as well as a religious occasion. By the 19th century there was no longer a prejudice against singing hymns in most

**Table 8: Attendance at Nonconformist Chapels in the Risborough Area - 30. 3. 1851** [12]

| Location of Chapel | Denomin-ation | Date Built | Attendance morning Cong | S/s | Attendance afternoon Cong | S/s | Attend: evening Cong | Attend: Chapels + S/s |
|---|---|---|---|---|---|---|---|---|
| P. Risborough | Baptist | 1708 | 250 | | 500 | | 150 | 900 |
| P. Risborough | Wesleyan | Pre-1800 | 60 | 35 | 50 | 40 | 30 | 215 |
| Speen | Baptist | 1802 | 55 | 38 | 155 | 40 | 95 | 383 |
| Loosely Row | Baptist | 1826 | - | - | - | - | 150 | 150 |
| Lacey Green | Methodist | 1842 | 100 | 40 | 240 | 50 | 240 | 670 |
| Longwick | Wesleyan | 1848 | - | 60 # | 80 | 40# | 90 | 270 |
| **Totals** | | | **638** | | **1,195** | | **755** | **2,588** |

# The return is not clear as to the Sunday School figures. Cong = Congregation. S/s = Sunday school.

Nonconformist sects, and when great favourites like 'Amazing Grace', 'Love Divine', and 'Guide Me, Oh Thou Great Jehovah' were included, the congregation would nearly raise the roof. Chapel was also a chance to wear your 'best', for almost everyone had something special for baptisms, weddings and funerals.

**Fig. 61: The Baptist Chapel at Princes Risborough**

It is a large and well-constructed building, making good use of traditional materials. Nonconformist congregations were willing to dig deep into their pockets, when better premises were needed, even though many had little to spare. However, in this case, judging by the size of both the tomb in the foreground, and the gravestones around it, some pockets were pretty deep.

## THE NONCONFORMISTS' STRICT RELIGIOUS DISCIPLINE

At this time strict discipline was a feature of all nonconformist religious sects. The following account of Baptist discipline at Princes Risborough is fairly typical. Applicants for membership were rigorously examined to ensure their suitability. Firstly, applications for membership were referred to the congregation by the pastor, and two deacons were appointed to visit the applicant and ascertain his/her suitability. At the next meeting applicants would be *"called in to give an account of their experience"* (i.e. their conversion). If this was satisfactory, on the next Lord's Day (i.e. Sunday) the applicant would be baptised, and afterwards receive Holy Communion, *"the right hand of fellowship at the Lord's Table"*.

Baptists were so-called because they believed in *adult* baptism, as recorded in the Bible. They considered that only adults were mature enough to make a conscious decision about religious matters. So baptism was the first step in becoming a member. Having been accepted into membership, it was necessary, both at worship and in one's private life, to conform to the standards of behaviour required by the pastor and the deacons. Absence from Communion, marriage to a person who was not a member, fornication, pregnancy before marriage, poor attendance, lack of punctuality at church services and drunkenness were just some of the things which were unacceptable. Even playing at dominoes in a public house was not allowed. The detailed records of those times [11] make it clear that Baptist standards really were strict and rigorously imposed. For example:

> *Sister Meakin having for some time absented herself from the Lord's Table, it was agreed that Brothers Bedford and Clark be deputed to visit her, to enquire the cause of her absence, and to point out to her the impropriety of thus neglecting her duty and privileges. (Agreed*

110

*to comply 21.1.1822)*

*Sister Hunt, having been accused of fornication, and having acknowledged her guilt, was excluded from Communion. (21.2.1825)*

*Brother Clay, having joined an Independent Church meeting, it was agreed that our pastor be requested to write to him, and point out the error into which he had fallen, expostulate with him on the impropriety of his conduct and endeavour to reclaim him. (Refused 16.5.1825)*

*Our single sister, Sophia Coles, is in a state of pregnancy, and having therefore dishonoured her profession, and brought disgrace upon the cause of Christ, it is become our duty to exclude her from our Communion.*

*Our pastor informed the meeting that scandalous reports were in circulation concerning Brother Goodchild's conduct. He spends much time in the public house till late in the evening, and as a natural consequence is sometimes intoxicated. He did not manifest a proper spirit, and was suspended for two months, pending a reconsideration (May 1842).*

## THE BEGINNINGS OF METHODISM IN THE VALE

Methodism began in April 1739, when John Wesley preached to a large gathering of working-class people at an open air service at Bristol, during a time of religious indifference. It was the start of a Methodist-driven spiritual revival. John and his brother Charles were both ordained clergy of the Church of England, and had every intention of remaining within it, for they had high hopes of reforming it into a more methodical (ie. disciplined) institution. Ultimately these hopes were defeated by vested interests. Indeed, soon after John's death in 1791, his followers completely separated from the Anglican church, and eventually sub-divided into at least eight denominations including the Wesleyans, Primitive Methodists, Independent Methodists, and Biblical Christians.

John Wesley preached wherever people would gather: a field, a market place, a busy street, or any empty piece of ground. His message was simple and direct: salvation was free to everyone through faith in Jesus Christ. He travelled on horse or by carriage all over the country, preaching several times a day. He was a brilliant organiser. Converts were grouped together into 'societies', each belonging to a 'circuit'. Wesley trained and appointed itinerant lay preachers, who travelled endlessly by foot or on horse (whatever the weather) to hold services according to their Circuit Plan. In his Journal, John Valton, a recently appointed itinerant, wrote in January 1776:

*I think I never suffered so much from cold as this day. I rode between two heaps of snow as high as me on horseback, and it blew into my eyes and I could hardly see my way.*

The services were held either in the open air, or at a house or barn, which had been registered as a religious meeting place under the Toleration Act of 1689.

Methodism came late to the Vale, during a period of religious indifference. So Methodism probably began in the Vale in 1772, when John Seamons of Weedon registered his house as a religious meeting place. For some reason, as yet unexplained, the Vale was slow to embrace Methodism, for in England and Wales there were already 35 Methodist 'circuits' with 30,000 members attending Society 'classes', but these were mainly in the more populous industrial districts. From this inauspicious beginning at Weedon, Methodism gradually spread to other parts of the Vale. Waddesdon acquired a cottage-based meeting in 1774. By 1775 Aylesbury had been visited by itinerant Methodist preachers, one of whom described it as "a place that hates the gospel". Perhaps there was a little truth in this, for it was not until 1781 that Aylesbury and Methodism were clearly linked, when one Thomas Higgins registered his house as a place of worship. In 1786 homes were registered as places of worship at Bierton (the house of the widow,

Ann Durley), Whitchurch and Wendover, followed in 1788 by Bledlow, Aston Clinton and North Marston, and in 1790 by Oving. However, it was 1822 before Haddenham Methodists erected their chapel (fig. 62). It was able to seat 500, and by 1851 they claimed to have an average weekly attendance of 550 on the basis of three services each Sunday.

These early groups did not have an easy time. Wesley wanted his followers to remain in the Anglican Church, but the dislike of Anglican ritual was so strong that in practice Methodist meetings for worship were always held either in someone's cottage or barn, or in the open air. At Weedon it was usually under a tree that was a recognised meeting place for large gatherings. However, a visiting preacher was looked upon as an intruder, and at least one had plenty of stones and clods thrown at him, while elsewhere *"the mob threw the preacher into the horse pond"*. This hostility may have been little more than horse play. Even so, it was no encouragement to those who had tramped for miles over muddy tracks to receive the preacher's message. Many Anglican clergy disliked what they considered to be an invasion of *"their territory"* by riff-raff. Waddesdon's first Methodist service, held in a local house, attracted a large crowd assembled outside specifically *"to disturb the meeting"*, encouraged (so it was rumoured) by free alcohol supplied by the Anglican vicar. Perhaps, not surprisingly, Methodist preachers were in short supply. Most converts to Methodism longed to hear regular preaching, but the islolated meetings of the Vale might be visited no more than once in three weeks. In consequence, some people, like the Goodsons of Waddesdon, walked or rode long distances in search of an inspiring preacher. More than once they walked to Wendover, a return journey of about 22 miles, to hear a Mr Williams, who had been *"in connexion"* with Wesley. At Waddesdon it was 30 years before they acquired a chapel.

Methodism was particularly attractive to working-class people. For example, the Anglican church was dominated by social rank (Archbishop, Bishop, Canon or Vicar presided at its

**Fig. 62: Methodist Chapel, Haddenham**
It was built of witchert in the High Street in 1822. In 1842 a Methodist school-room was built behind it. This has since become the home of the Haddenham Museum.

meetings), while the congregation was viewed as *"the lowly"* and *"their betters"*. In contrast Methodism was very democratic. Preachers were not ordained. They were recruited by the Wesleys from the laity, and so could be much more understanding of working-class problems. Each Methodist congregation was regarded as a "society" irrespective of the social standing of individuals. Methodism attached great importance to education, especially reading and writing, which were taught without charge in their Sunday schools. Adult converts were assigned to the Society's weekly classes (i.e. study groups) of no more than twelve to receive tuition in reading, public speaking and the Bible. In more recent times many a trade union activist and M.P. learnt to read and speak in a Methodist chapel class.[12] The encouragement of temperance was especially attractive for the women, who were tired of the poverty created by their husband's expenditure on alcohol. Hymn singing was a feature of Methodist meetings. It is claimed that Charles Wesley wrote over six thousand hymns.

# Chapter 11

# THE ENCLOSURE OF THE OPEN FIELDS

Cardinal Wolsey's Commission of Enquiry in 1517 (see Chapter 6) and various Acts passed during the late 15th and 16th centuries satisfied those who were against enclosure and the consequent depopulation of the countryside. However, they were disliked by the commercially-minded land-owners and farmers, whose main concerns were the inefficiency of open-field farming, and the need for more good grazing land. For them enclosure was a prime requirement for efficient farming.

## THE OPEN FIELDS

From Saxon times the cultivated land of each village had been farmed in vast prairie-like open fields. They were called 'open' because their boundaries, and the individual plots of land within the boundaries, were unhedged and unfenced. Originally each village had two such fields, but from the 13th century the arable area was increasingly divided into three fields, and sometimes in later centuries into four, five or even more. They were farmed 'in common', which meant that everyone had to plough, harrow, sow, reap, stook and cart according to the same strict timetable. One field remained fallow each year, so that it could recover its fertility from the manure of the animals allowed to graze on it, and the vegetation (weed roots and stubble) buried in it during two ploughings and harrowings. Even in the 18th century, the farming of some villages was little changed from Saxon times, although others had changed considerably. For instance, by 1797 Wingrave had four great open fields, and of its 2,421 acres only 114 acres were enclosed to provide gardens, orchards, and closes, where pregnant animals could drop their young, and sick animals be treated. Although it had most of the features of a typical open-field parish, Soulbury had much more early enclosure than Wingrave. As Soulbury's rare and very detailed pre-enclosure map of 1769 [1] shows, approximately a third of its 4,226 acres had already been enclosed to form what is now a country estate called Liscombe Park.[2]

As in Saxon times (see Chapter 2) the arable land of the large open fields was divided into blocks called furlongs, each with its own distinctive name, usually passed down from generation to generation: (Table 9). These were divided into long narrow strips known as lands or selions. In theory these measured 220 by 8 yards, but in practice they varied considerably in length, width and shape due to streams, parish boundaries, woodland and access roads. There were no hedges or permanent fences, so their boundaries were defined by narrow grassy areas known as baulks and headlands, which gave access for men and their ploughs, harrows and carts. One man's holding consisted of a number of separate strips, scattered amongst the open fields.

It was the ploughing of these strips which - over the centuries - created the ridge and furrow landscape, some of which is still visible today. A peasant would first plough back and forth along the centre of his strip to form a ridge, after which he ploughed in a clockwise direction along one side of the ridge and back down the other, the sod always being turned inwards towards the centre, until the boundaries of the strip were reached on either side. By this time the strip was ridged up by as much as a foot or two in the centre, sloping down on both sides to the outermost furrows, which divided it from the neighbouring strips. In many places, including the Vale, the replacement of arable by pasture has preserved this ancient landscape (Fig. 63).

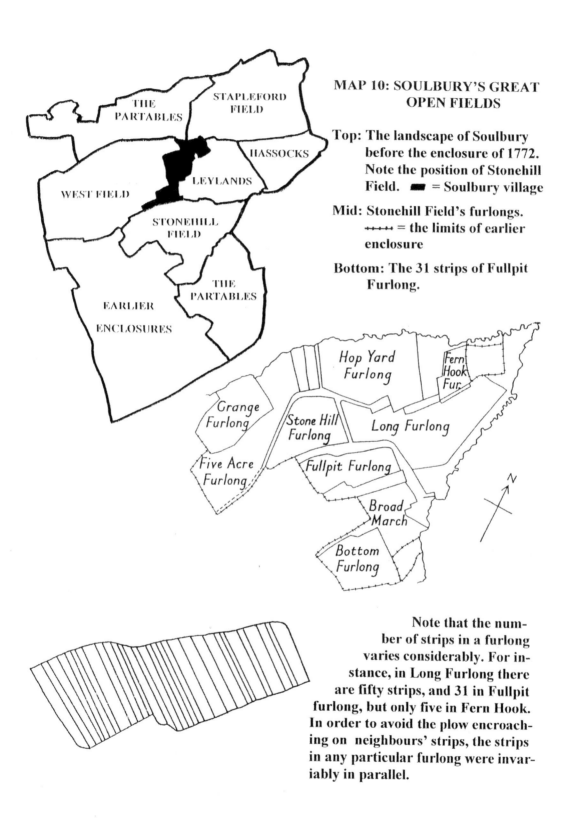

**MAP 10: SOULBURY'S GREAT OPEN FIELDS**

**Top:** The landscape of Soulbury before the enclosure of 1772. Note the position of Stonehill Field. ▰▰ = Soulbury village

**Mid:** Stonehill Field's furlongs. ╍╍╍ = the limits of earlier enclosure

**Bottom:** The 31 strips of Fullpit Furlong.

THE PARTABLES

STAPLEFORD FIELD

HASSOCKS

LEYLANDS

WEST FIELD

STONEHILL FIELD

THE PARTABLES

EARLIER ENCLOSURES

Hop Yard Furlong

Fern Hook Fur.

Grange Furlong

Stone Hill Furlong

Long Furlong

Five Acre Furlong

Fullpit Furlong

Broad March

Bottom Furlong

Note that the number of strips in a furlong varies considerably. For instance, in Long Furlong there are fifty strips, and 31 in Fullpit furlong, but only five in Fern Hook. In order to avoid the plow encroaching on neighbours' strips, the strips in any particular furlong were invariably in parallel.

**Table 9: The Holdings of John Stone[3] in Soulbury's Great Open Fields in 1769**

The numbers against each furlong identify the strips held by John Stone. The numbers in bold indicate where John Stone appears to be trying to form further blocks of land

| Stapleford Field | West Field |
|---|---|
| Long Piece Furlong: 8,10, 11 | Little White Pitt Furlong; 1 |
| Fox Hill Furlong 5 | Poor Hill Furlong: 2 |
| The Rick Furlong: **16,18,23,25** | Woolong Furlong: 2,5 |
| Burrows Hill Furlong: 3 | Great White Hill Furlong: 3,5 |
| Crockendon Furlong: 2 | Smenhill Furlong: **1,2,3,5** |
| Adjoining Crockendon Furlong: 4 | Ridgeway Furlong: 23,24 |
| Bank Furlong: 2,11 | Furlong behind Grange: 1,3 |
| Stapleford Furlong: 8,10 | Carters Piece Furlong: 4 |
| Collingsgrove Hill Furlong: 5 | Mannanell Furlong: 9 |
| Comberley Hill Furlong: 14 | Furlong below Raven's Foot: 7 |
| Debdin Furlong: 2 | Raven's Foot Furlong: 14 |
| Short Alms Hill Furlong: **2,8,13,15** | Radmoor Hill Furlong: 3 |
| **Stonehill Field** | Ballum Furlong: 3 (large) |
| The Long Furlong: **2,9,17,19,22,25** | Mole Hill Furlong: 1 |
| Line Meadow Furlong: 1 | Goss Furlong: land along the river |
| Hop Yard Furlong: 21 | Carters Piece: one block |
| Grange Furlong: 10 | Boys Piece: one block |
| Full Pitt Furlong: **17,18,20,21,23** | Two large blocks below Ballum |
| Broad March Furlong 1,4 | Brick Kiln Furlong: 4,7 |
| Hollow Bottom Furlong: 2 | **The Partables** |
| Five Acre Fg: one large block | Sandstone Furlong: 2,3 |
| Clay Hill Closes: 2,3 | Hasel Furlong: 3,6,10 |
| **Hassocks** | Great Fishpond Furlong: 11 |
| Unnamed Furlong: **6,9,13,14,15** | Furlong by Sandstone furlong: 2,3,5 |
| Lank Furlong: 1,2,5 | Lincombe Hill Furlong: 1,2 |
| Rye Slade Furlong: 2 | Collins Grove Furlong: 6 |
| Coney Mead Furlong: 3,4,5 | Fox Hill Furlong: 5 |
| Round plot | The Sedge Furlong: Stone's land |
| **Village Centre** | Summer Furlong: 3 |
| Ley Lands: 11,18, 51 | The Warren Furlong: Stone's land |
| Farmhouse, yard, 2 ponds and Kent Close. | |

## THE INEFFICIENCY OF OPEN-FIELD FARMING

The open fields of Soulbury illustrate well the inefficiencies of open-field farming. Table 9 not only records 54 of its furlongs, but also identifies the 93 strips and eleven other pieces of land which one villager, John Stone, cultivated, with the assistance of his family and hired labour. Clearly, a lot of time had to be spent just moving from one strip to another, and the baulks and headlands wasted a lot of land. Also under the open-field system the traditional crops had to be harvested by a specified date, after which the village animals were turned out to graze on the stubble and weeds, and to manure the soil. Any crops still standing at that time would be grazed out of existence. So experimentation with most of the new crops recommended by the agricultural improvers was impossible in the open fields, because they could not be harvested at the time laid down for the traditional crops. The only exceptions to this were villagers who

116

had managed to exchange strips with other villagers so as to consolidate their holdings into blocks, which could then be enclosed with hedging, fencing or hurdles. As Table 9 shows, John Stone already had blocks: the last three entries in West Field. Also in Stapleford, Stonehill and Hassocks fields notice the strips with emboldened numbers, where Stone appears to be in the process of forming still more blocks. Even so, the multiplicity and dispersion of John Stone's strips complicated the day-to-day management of his holding. Some of his land was close to his farmyard, and some distant, a factor which he would have to bear in mind when allocating jobs for the day. Also some strips might be of easily-worked loam, and others of intractable clay, which would have to be taken into account when considering each worker's output, and the best use for each plot. And each worker would be expected to be watchful that the neighbours' ploughing and harvesting did not encroach on his master's land, or allow their animals to graze on his master's crops, for this could easily be done by providing them with long tethers. There was also the perennial problem of the neighbours' weeds, for if these were not pulled or cut at the right time their seeds could infest his land and add to his workload.

**Fig. 63: The Ridge and Furrow Field Pattern Highlit by Snow at Soulbury.**
The pattern is highlit due to the snow on the ridges melting earlier than snow in the furrows.

## THE SHORTAGE OF PASTURE

All open-field villages had a large area of meadow for hay and pasture. There were also the uncultivated commons, waste and woodland. Despite this, by the 18th century, many parishes were struggling to find sufficient common pasture. True, the village meadows provided hay for the winter months, and each year's fallow field was good for autumn grazing, but overall there was just not enough fodder. 'Common rights' (the right to pasture one's cattle and sheep on the village commons) were a valued element in the village economy, and were especially important to the cottager, whose small acreage left him struggling for survival. Unfortunately, in some parishes, the demand for pasture now exceeded the supply. The answer was rationing, known to the villagers as stinting, and fines for those who defied the Field Orders which imposed the stinting.

### The Field Orders of the Village of Dunton [4]

Dunton was Soulbury's neighbour to the west, and from time to time a meeting of the landed interest was held, when the rules for stinting were debated and revised as necessary. In 1652 twenty-eight bye-laws were agreed. For instance:

> *Item: For each yardland which a man holds, no more than 20 sheep, 10 lambs or 3 beasts may be grazed on the common pasture. Item: No man shall keep geese in the common field. Item: No flock of sheep shall go in the field without a keeper, and he that have two flocks shall have two keepers; no sheep shall come upon the bean field after the peas are sowed, but be pounded by the Hayward. Item: The Hayward shall be the teller of the field, and if any keep more upon the commons than his stint, he shall pay him 2d for every sheep, and 6d for every cow or horse that is kept there three days.*

## THE PROBLEM OF THE TITHES

The parish priest received his income from four main sources: christenings, marriages and funerals; the Easter offering; the profits from the glebe lands; and the tithes. The latter were very much resented. Even the clergy found them something of an embarrassment. Enclosure provided an opportunity to get rid of them. The levying of the tithe for the maintenance of the church dated back to the Dark Ages. By the time of the Saxon King Edgar (959-975) it consisted of the Great Tithe which was 10% of the cereal crops, and the Lesser Tithe which was 10% of the value of the poultry, vegetables, young animals, etc.. Over the centuries, in some parishes, part of the tithe had been awarded to some person or body other than the parish priest. This was the case in Stewkley, where the Bishop of Oxford had acquired the right to the Great Tithes. By the 18th century the tithes were increasingly paid in cash (known as a modus), but many parishes still paid in kind. In such cases there was often some distrust between the farmers and the Vicar, and the latter might well go into the farmers' fields during harvest and mark every tenth stook of corn, before sending a cart to carry 'his entitlement' back to the tithe barn. In some places an elaborate set of rules was devised by the parishioners[5] to regulate the tithing. Dunton's tithe procedure was almost hilariously complicated:

> *Lambs are tithed in this manner. First the owner takes two, then the parson or his deputy standing without the pen must touch with his stick one, and then we take seven to make it tithe even. And then we take nine more and the parson the tenth until we have done. And if we have seven we pay a tithe lamb and* (are given) *1d ob (=1½d) and (if we have under seven) we pay the parson for everyone an ob (=½d). We begin to pay tithe milk ten days after St. Mark's Day (25th April), and continue until Martinmas (11th November), and the parson ought to fetch his milk when we milk in the Town upon the Green, and when we milk in the field at the place where the herdsman doth gather his beasts together, and not to have it brought to any place.*

## THE PROCESS OF ENCLOSURE

The enclosure of open-field farmland, which was completed in the Vale and North Bucks. between 1738 and 1856, reflected a number of national events in Britain dating back to at least 1642. The long and bloody Civil War (1642-1646), the final expulsion of the Stuarts in 1689 and the eventual accession of the Hanoverians in 1714, ensured that Britain was ruled by a Parliament which was sympathetic to landowners, and thus favoured property and wealth. The increase in trade and industry during the 18th century created a class of wealthy merchants and industrialists seeking long-term investments such as land. From about 1740, population growth and the increased size of towns established large markets for agricultural produce, and held out the promise of increasing prices. Because the social hierarchy was based upon land ownership, its acquisition also conferred social prestige. Finally, the development by the agricultural pioneers of new crops, machinery and methods augured well for future profits.

## New Methods in Agriculture

The findings and inventions of the agricultural pioneers in the 18th century convinced ambitious landlords and farmers that agriculture could be revolutionised. For instance, root crops such as mangolds and swedes provided invaluable winter fodder, ensuring the survival of livestock in good condition over the winter months. Consequently, fresh meat could replace much of the salted meat previously so dominant in winter meals. These wintered cattle also created additional manure for the fields. The pioneers showed that clover and lucerne not only supplied nutritious grazing, but stored up nitrates in their roots, which if ploughed into the ground in the following year added a valuable fertilizer to the soil. Moreover, these crops could be grown in what would have been the unprofitable fallow year, thus making all the land productive throughout every year. Jethro Tull's invention of the seed drill eliminated wasteful broadcast sowing and hand-weeding

**Fig. 64: Hensman's Patent Bedfordshire Drill**

Following in Tull's footsteps, William Hensman of Woburn invented this drill at the beginning of the 19th century. It was manufactured by George Brown's Implements of Leighton Buzzard up to 1926.

by seeding the land evenly and in rows, which could then be weeded quickly and regularly by his invention of the horse-hoe. In essence, this was a miniature plough that cut through, and broke up, the earth, but without turning it over. Use of the hoe also benefited later crops by improving the tilth of the soil, reducing weeds and adding humus in the form of dead weeds. Eventually a number of specialised hoes were invented. Thus Garrett's Patent Hoe could easily be adjusted for depth and width, while the Steerage Hoe hoed several rows at a time. Meanwhile, James Smith showed that efficient drainage alone could double crop yields. Gradually the more progressive farmers realised that the open field system was hopelessly inefficient. For instance, selective breeding, as demonstrated by Bakewell, would produce cattle of greatly improved weight and quality, quite unlike the small bony creatures then to be seen on the common fields. The new ideas had powerful advocates, especially in Arthur Young, the Secretary to the Board of Agriculture, who published a monthly magazine, The Annals of Agriculture. In 1771 he wrote, *"What in the name of wonder is the reason for the landlords (of the Vale of Aylesbury) not enclosing?"* The reason was that many farmers distrusted the new ideas, and favoured traditional methods. However, even in villages where only a minority favoured the innovations, it was still possible for land to be enclosed if that minority had the largest holdings of land, plus the wealth, literacy and the legal and political influence which were essential to ensure change. In 1794 the Board of Agriculture Report for Bucks. hoped that in a few years' time all the county's remaining 91,000 acres of open fields would have been enclosed.

## PARLIAMENTARY ENCLOSURE OF THE 18ᵗʰ AND 19ᵗʰ CENTURIES

In the Vale and North Bucks. the earliest *parliamentary* enclosures were at Ashendon (1738), Wotton Underwood (1742) and Shipton (1744). These were enclosures which had already been agreed by the various landowners, and the private Acts of Parliament simply legitimised the agreements. After 1760 the request for an Act had to be agreed by the holders of at least 75% of the land by value. Usually, *"attempts to coax and cajole support for an enclosure could go on for many years, the lobbying continuing up to and including the eleventh hour".*[6] These later Acts also appointed commissioners to be responsible for surveying each parish, obtaining the claims of all those who believed that they held land and/or common rights in the parish, and creating for each owner a single holding which could be fully enclosed, in place of the numerous unenclosed strips held previously (Fig. 65).

## THE ENCLOSURE OF THE PARISH OF STEWKLEY

Sadly, very few enclosure documents have survived for Soulbury, whereas the neighbouring parish of Stewkley is much more fortunate for it has: a printed copy of the Bill; the surveyor's book; details of claims and petitions; the account books; the Enclosure Commissioners' calculations; the pre-enclosure map; the Minutes of Enclosure Commissioners' meetings 1811-1817; and the Enclosure Award and maps of the four manors, all in a beautiful leather-bound volume. For this reason we have moved to Stewkley to describe the actual process of enclosure.

In the 18ᵗʰ century the 3,872 acres of Stewkley were divided into no less than eight great open fields: Mill Field, Longland Field, The Dean, Foxhill Field, Wolds Field, Millway Field, Thorn Slade Field, and Folding Field. It also had four manors: Sir Thomas Sheppard was Lord of the Manor of Littlecote; William Wodley had the manor of Vauxes; William Ward, gentleman, was Lord of the Manor of Stewkley Grange; and the Deans and Canons of Windsor claimed to be the Lords of Stewkley manor. Their names were known, but not one of them resided in the parish.

In 1772 many of the smaller farmers in Stewkley were concerned to learn that a group of the larger farmers headed by Sir Thomas Sheppard, Lord of the Manor of Littlecote, were planning an application to Parliament, for the right to enclose the whole of the parish. Concern was heightened because between 1494 and 1507 an ancestor of Sir Thomas had completely destroyed Littlecote, one of Stewkley's hamlets, by enclosing 310 acres of open fields, and converting the land to pasture. In the process five homes were destroyed, 32 people of all ages evicted and their four ploughs destroyed. Cublington and Soulbury, two of Stewkley's immediate neighbours, had been enclosed only recently. So Stewkley's farmers would already have heard (often at first hand) both the advantages and the disadvantages of enclosure. The latter included the trials and tribulations of the smaller farmers. Consequently, some of Stewkley's very independent farmers made clear their opposition to enclosure, by having a leaflet printed which concluded: [7]

> *We do agree that in case such application be made to Parliament ... then all the said persons shall and will present their petition in opposition to the said application thereby praying that the persons named hereto may have an opportunity to offer their reasons against such application or Bill.*

So the matter was dropped. Temporarily!! For elsewhere enclosure was proceeding with the inevitability of a tsunami. By 1800 a further 43 of the county's parishes had been enclosed. Then in 1803, though it was obtained with great difficulty, a petition was presented to Parliament for the enclosure of Stewkley parish. By this time, Parliament required that public notice of an intended enclosure should be given both in the local press (the Northampton Mercury) and by fixing a notice to the door of the parish church for three successive weeks. However, when John Roberts, a solicitor's clerk, appeared in the churchyard, he was met by a great crowd fifty or sixty strong, who tore down the notice. On his second attempt, with a constable in attendance, he was pelted with stones, accompanied by shouts from the mob, *"Damn them! Turn them out! Kick them out!"* The petition was eventually presented to Parliament, but on its third reading a counter petition from the opponents was presented. It must have been extremely persuasive, because the proceedings were suspended at the Bill's committee stage.[8]

At Quarter Sessions in 1804 three yeomen of Stewkley, William Windsor, George Belgrove and John Webb together with William Foster, were found guilty of causing a riot and assault upon John Roberts. The Court ordered that they be imprisoned in the County Gaol for three months, and then continue in gaol until they agreed to keep the peace and be of good behaviour towards all his majesty's subjects for the space of three years.[9] So, for several more years, Stewkley continued with open field farming. Not until 1811 was a third attempt at enclosure successful, despite yet another counter-petition. The petition for enclosure simply asked that "leave be given to bring in a Bill". Accompanying it were consent forms signed by landowners whose land was valued at £290–11s–7d., while the opponents' land was valued at only £58–1s–0d[10], and this determined the issue. Finally, on May 3rd 1811, the Act received the Royal Assent. [11]

### Implementing the Act

On the 10th June the first public meeting was held at the Cock Inn, Wing. Four Commissioners, (a land surveyor, a banker, a solicitor and [in case of intractable problems] an umpire) were appointed. Each of the Commissioners swore that he would:

> *faithfully, impartially and honestly, according to the best of my skill and judgement, execute the trusts reposed in me . . . without favour or affection, prejudice or ill-will, to any person or persons whatsoever. So help me God.*

Firstly, owners were required to mark out their strips and leys, and bring to the next meeting a written and signed account of their claims to arable, pasture and meadow ground. 95 proprietors successfully claimed their right to a portion of the open fields. No wonder that the solicitor responsible for dealing with the parliamentary aspects of the enclosure reported, when sending in his bill, that the work had been *"altogether of a most complicated nature"*. The claimants also had to indicate whether their land was freehold, copyhold or leasehold, and whether there was

**Fig. 65: 18th Century Surveyors at Work on Enclosure at Hanlow, Bedfordshire.**

any entitlement to cow or sheep commons. Then the surveyor's work could begin. His first task was to survey the whole parish, showing both the enclosures of 1,116 acres in earlier centuries, and the 2,710 acres now to be enclosed.

Many meetings followed, and by November an alphabetical list of Claimants and their Claims was pinned to the church door. A meeting was then arranged at which objections would be heard, and witnesses examined under oath. At a further meeting landowners were given the opportunity to request exchanges of land with neighbours, and to suggest where their new allocation should be situated. The formula would be as follows:[12]

> *Joseph Mead requests his allotment may adjoin his farmhouse and old enclosures, situated on the north side of the Dean, including part of Dean Fens as far as Mr Bull's gateway.*

Now all the land had to be valued for quantity, quality and situation. Using information from the pre-enclosure map, and from the farmers, a large and detailed schedule was compiled.[13] On the left of this document were listed the names of the 95 farmers. The information was then analysed into 44 columns. The first five dealt with previous rights to pasture animals on the common land. Next came a section on the arable: the acreage of open field land; the acreage of enclosed land; the tenure (freehold, leasehold or copyhold); quality and final value. Similar information was then recorded about grassland: meadow, pasture or ley; whether mown each year, or two out of three; tenure; quality and final value. Were tithes payable in cash or in kind? The 44th column recorded the total value of each claimant's holding.

For local people critical questions about the allocation of the 2,710 acres of unenclosed land were still unanswered. Would the new holdings be close to the farmsteads and cottages? Would they be of acceptable quantity and quality? Would requests for exchanges have been granted? Would there be fair compensation for the loss of common rights? What would be the cost of enclosure? Who would survive and who would go under?

### PRIORITIES IN THE ALLOCATION PROCESS

Before the land from the open fields could be distributed amongst the farmers of the parish, the Commissioners had to reserve land for other purposes. At Stewkley, the sponsors of the enclosure had agreed that some land from the open fields could be used to abolish the hated tithes. So the Commissioners began by taking a fifth of the total acreage of the open fields, and a ninth of the open pasture and meadow, with which to compensate the Bishop of Oxford and the Reverend Ashfield (Vicar) for the loss of the Great and Lesser Tithes, the parish glebe and all their rights of common. The Bishop received 386 acres, and the Vicar 288 acres, which in total was a quarter of all Stewkley's open fields. Many parishioners thought that this was extremely generous.

Allowance also had to be made for all the newly-established roads and footpaths. These had taken 46 acres of the Award. There was even an allowance of 9 acres to compensate the poor for the loss of their right "to cut, take and use peat, fern and other fuel from the said commons". The 9 acres was to be let out and the rents distributed in coal at Christmas.[14] Due to these priorities, the claimants on the open-field acres were allocated substantially less than they had expected, but an invitation to view the plan and voice objections appears to have settled matters, for there is no record of the umpire having to be called in to arbitrate on this matter.

Details of Stewkley's Enclosure Award of 1814, which included five maps, are to be found in a large leather-bound book now housed in the County Archives.[15] It is the source of all the detailed information which follows. Stewkley's landholding following enclosure is shown in Table 9. By then there were three landowners owning 200 acres or more: the Bishop of Oxford (386 acres) and the Vicar (288 acres) were joined by Sir Thomas Sheppard. With his new allotment added to his 203 acres of old enclosures, the latter had 422 acres in all, the largest holding in the parish. The principal reason for the increase in the number of cottagers was the inclusion of 25 cottagers who had never held land in the *open fields*. The Coles' family is an example. William Coles, the village wheelwright (a 'wheeler' as they were known in the village) died in 1813, a year before the publication of the enclosure award. He left the family cottage and the adjoining wheelwright's workshop with its garden of 20 perches to his two eldest sons. The family had

**Table 10: Stewkley - Ownership of Land by Size of Holding after Enclosure**

| Classification of Landholdings | Size of holding (acres) | Number of owners of new allotments | Total of owners of new allotments, and old enclosures |
|---|---|---|---|
| Very large | 200 and over | 2 | 3 |
| Large | 100 - 199 | 5 | 7 |
| Upper medium | 50 – 9 9 | 8 | 10 |
| Lower medium | 10 – 4 9 | 2 8 | 37 |
| Smallholdings | 1 – 9 | 3 9 | 50 |
| Cottagers' plots | Under 1 acre | 9 | 34 |
| | Total | 9 1 (2710 acres) | 141   (3826 acres) |

occupied the property since the late 16th century, and in 1814 its site and garden were regarded as an earlier enclosure. They occupied no land in the open fields, so they received no allotment, and therefore they faced no costs. The cottage still stands, but the wheelwright's shop (until recently a garage) has been demolished and replaced by living accommodation linked to the cottage, the whole being known as Stonhill House.

## THE HEAVY COSTS OF ENCLOSURE

**Table 11: Total Cost of the Enclosure of Stewkley** [16]

| Expense | Cost | % |
|---|---|---|
| Roads | £4385-9s-3d | 33.9 |
| Commissioners' and Clerks' fees | £3212-0s-9d | 24.5 |
| Legal fees | £1698-10-9d | 13.0 |
| Surveyors' fees | £1500-0-0d | 11.6 |
| Fencing for the Improprietor & Vicar | £1506-18-0d | 11.6 |
| Drains | £346-19-2d | 1.6 |
| Grass seed | £ 87-15-6d | 0.7 |
| Miscellaneous | £214-1s-2d | 3.1 |
| Total | £12,951-14-7d | 100.0 |

In August 1814, the final cost was calculated as £12,951, or 95.6 shillings per acre. At that time, this was one of the highest charges in Buckinghamshire, and a heavy burden for the individual farmer. Sir Thomas Sheppard's bill was £728, but much of his land was already enclosed, otherwise his bill would have been much larger. Joseph Mead's was £229. Several landholders, who were eligible for an allotment, made no payment at all. Presumably they sold their land, for we hear no more about them. Of course, those who possessed old enclosures were able to retain them, even if they could not afford their new allocations.

The Commissioners' accounts were closed in 1815, but their final bill was by no means final! A little later the Commissioners received additional bills and had to set a further rate in October 1816. Moreover, the allottees had the worrying knowledge that they still faced the costs of fencing, hedging and ditching those boundaries of the land for which they were responsible, a task which had to be completed within six months, if they were to receive their certificate of ownership. This requirement did little to enhance relationships between the parishioners and the parish church, for the fencing of the Bishop and the Vicar would be done for them by the Commissioners *at the expense of all the other allottees*. The costs of fencing were considerable, because the nature and quality of the fencing was specified in some detail by the Commissioners:

> *Allotments are to be enclosed round with quickset (hawthorn) hedges and ditches, with substantial posts and rails on each side thereof, with good and substantial gates and stiles where necessary, and thereafter supported and maintained for five years until the quicksets shall have become sufficient fences of themselves.*

For example, the fencing for the allotments of the 668 acres of the Bishop and the Vicar cost £1,506-18s-0d, or approximately 45s-0d per acre. However, these costs included labour, which most farmers would reduce by employing themselves and their families on the work.

Using the account books which have survived for certain parishes, Turner calculated the average costs of enclosure in Buckinghamshire. Notice the steep rise in costs for 1800-1819. Turner considers that this was partly due to the general inflation while Britain was involved in the French Wars, and the fact that fencing costs were not included until the 19th century. At Stewkley the large number of property owners would create more administrative work: more claims to verify, more correspondence, and more problems to resolve. For instance, the Commissioners

### Table 12: Average Costs of Enclosure Per Acre in Buckinghamshire [17]

| 1760's | 16s-9d | 1790's | 39s-2d |
| 1770's | 21s-2d | 1800-1819 | 81s-9d (Stewkley 95s-6d) |
| 1780's | 24s-1d | 1820-1845 | 71s-7d |

had held no less than 38 meetings, some lasting for several days. After the execution of the Award in 1814, much work still had to be done: the completion of the roads, the improvement of defective fencing, and the widening of ditches to the specified four feet, for instance. The problems of those with financial difficulties had to be resolved. After the further rate was imposed, they were duly warned:

> *In consequence of your not paying the amount of your proportion of the Rate as requested, the Commissioners have directed me to inform you that considerable inconvenience and expense will be incurred by your delaying to do so, and as you must be aware . . . it must fall upon you and other defaulters.[18]*

This was followed by an even blunter warning that Warrants of Distress would be obtained so that sufficient of the defaulter's goods and chattels could be seized as would cover his share of the unpaid rate plus interest, and the cost of doing this. Most had paid by the 16th April, but a few had requested extra time, and eight had failed to respond to the threats. On 28th May 1817, as most had paid, it was decided to enforce all outstanding arrears immediately by prosecuting the offenders.

### THE FATE OF JOSEPH MEAD

Joseph Mead of Stewkley had farmed 78 acres mainly in the open fields, but including 11 acres of old enclosures. His account book [19] suggests that he was much more the farmer, and far less the peasant, than the text books sometimes envisage. For one thing he employed a labourer at 8s-0d per week. For another he could afford to board his three sons, William, John and Thomas, at Thame School, which together with their books cost him £43–18s–4d in the year 1788/89. For yet another he was not a subsistence farmer relying mainly upon the arable to maintain his family. His inventory of stock (Table 13) indicates that he was raising animals for the market. In the enclosure of Stewkley Joseph had claimed 44 acres of freehold open-field, 26 acres of copyhold open-field plus 8 acres of land enclosed earlier, and upon which his farmstead stood. To this 78 acres, he added a claim for the loss of grazing rights on the commons for 71 sheep. So it was some

**Table 13: Joseph Mead – Inventory of Stock 29th May 1804**

| 36 cows at £15 each | £540 | 3 bullocks at £5 each | £15 |
|---|---|---|---|
| 60 sheep at £2 each | £120 | 4 cows at £3 each | £12 |
| 5 horses | £120 | 1 bull | £10 |
| 17 hogs | £55 | Hay | £50 |

thing of a shock to Joseph when he received a mere 61½ acres: just 76% of his claim. It meant that his potential for raising animals was substantially reduced. He was also left in no doubt about his responsibilities for enclosing his share of the boundaries with hedges and ditches, for the Commissioners detailed them in writing. [20]

Of course Joseph's farmland was now in one piece, conveniently adjoining his homestead. In open-field times this land would have been in at least 50 strips. Enclosure meant a substantial saving in time previously spent walking to his scattered strips. It also meant that – once his neighbours had erected *their* boundary fences – he would no longer be hampered by their activities. But, if he was to take full advantage of the enclosure, Joseph would also need to get busy dividing his allotment of land with internal fencing, which was entirely his responsibility and his expense. Until then he could raise *either* crops *or* cattle. Otherwise, his crops would be consumed and trampled by his own animals! However, Joseph was fortunate compared with some smallholders and cottagers: see Recollections F.

## *LOCAL REACTIONS TO ENCLOSURE*

In general, the large landowners and farmers were well pleased with the immediate results of enclosure: high rents for the landlords; and high profits, well able to cover the increased rents, for the farmers. However, there would be some grumbling at the expense of the enclosure, and the increase in the poor rates necessary to support those impoverished by the changes. And, as the years passed by, they would gradually realise that enclosure had put them firmly in the grip of market forces, and that *"the value of their investment could go down as well as up"*. Everyone would regard the compensation for loss of tithes as over-generous, but the smallholders and cottagers would particularly resent it, especially if they had opposed enclosure, or had been forced to borrow money or sell land to finance its costs. For now – lacking common rights – they had to struggle even harder to scrape a living from their reduced acreage. A few supplemented their incomes by labouring, which was a social demotion, as well as a loss of independence. And their entry into the job market displeased the regular labourers, with whom they competed for a supply of work reduced by the change from arable to less labour-intensive pasture.

Immediately after enclosure, the landscape was new and seemed very strange. The recently planted quicks were scarcely visible, and the landscape was dominated by the post and rail fences, which created a chequer-board of fields. Often the new field boundaries ran right across the old furlongs, which was heresy to the older villagers. And after enclosure many farmers turned their land over to pasture, so that summer's rippling gold became a perennial green. But time is a great healer, and as the hedges grew and thickened, there was the sight and scent of the May blossom, and the song of the hedge-nesting birds to enjoy. After fifteen or twenty years there was another change, when the hedges had grown tall, and had to be layered into stock-proof barriers. Later, they would be punctuated by the saplings that had grown wild, or been planted deliberately by discerning farmers and landlords, but it would be many years before mature trees graced the landscape. Several generations were required to produce what we think of as the traditional country scene. Even now, most of it is less than 200 years old.[21]

### Recollections F: The Plight of William Plaistow of Haddenham

About 1830 some notices were pinned to the church door, announcing that Haddenham's fields were going to be enclosed. When the news spread about the village, people went and tore them down. They were put up again, but people tore them down again. It was no use though! The commissioners still came down and started to enclose the fields. It was such a long time before anything was finalized that for a whole year the parishioners didn't know in what part of the parish their new allotment was placed. So for a year nothing was sown, and nobody had any crops at the end of it. Nearly every small man was practically ruined. Nothing had come in, and the expense of their families was going on all the time. In the following year, when people were informed as to the location of their new holding, there was the expense of enclosing its boundaries with quicks (hawthorn hedging plants) protected on both sides by wooden fencing. For the commissioner wouldn't give you a proper title to the land if the job wasn't done exactly as required. On top of this, new roads had to be made, the expense of which was all charged to the farmers. Due to the year without crops, and the change of some fields from crops to sheep, there was less work for the labourers, many of whom had to depend upon poor doles for their bread. So the poor rate rose to over a pound in the pound, most of which was paid by the farmers. So many of them went to the wall. Some took mortgages on their land, but couldn't pay the interest and had to sell up. And a few years later the price of corn fell, and most of those who had struggled to keep on could keep on no longer, and they fell out too.

It was a crying shame for the hard-working man to lose his land and become a labourer, but after the enclosure Haddenham was full of them. They searched everywhere for employment, but few could get it. There was great distress and want all through the place. The worst of it was there weren't any allotments then. They came later. Nobody can realise what a blessing it was to have a good crop of potatoes stored in your barn for the winter. When you've got them, they are yours, and you can go and get them whenever you want them. There were some fine strong men in Haddenham then, who left the village. Some went to Lancashire and Yorkshire, besides other places, and some emigrated.

At the time of the enclosures my grandfather, James Plaistow, got about 20 acres at Round Hill for his lot. He kept 16, but sold the others to pay his debts (2 acres 13 perches to Thomas Rose; 1 rood 20 perches to Joseph Plaistow; 2 acres 2 roods 11 perches to William Clawson). But the rates for the new roads, and the expenses of quicking and enclosing were too much for him, and reluctantly he sold his remaining acres. He found a man named Cross of London to buy 16 acres for £22 an acre. Sadly, nearly all of this went on the further costs of enclosure. So my grandfather was left at last with only his little cottage and an acre of ground, and after his death in 1865, I got married and lived in it.

Based, with only slight clarifications, on BRO/DX/783 by kind permission of the
Centre for Buckinghamshire Studies

# Chapter 12

# *THE REVOLUTION IN TRANSPORT*

## *The Roads*

The English road system of the late Middle Ages was an extension of the Roman system but, while the quantity had increased, the quality had seriously declined. Even so, travel was more common than is usually supposed. Merchants moved about incessantly, as did the agents of the aristocracy: their stewards, bailiffs, rent collectors, etc.. Medieval roads were close to impossible for unsprung medieval carts, so highly-placed clerics spent much of their time on horseback, visiting their dioceses to ordain clerics, bless new and extended premises, and shrewdly appraise churches and religious houses. Carters from Haddenham Manor drove surplus crops to markets at Oxford and Wallingford. Fugitives from Winslow Manor reached places as distant as Lincoln and London. Members of families like the Pastons and the Celeys were always making journeys from their home shires, not only to London, but also to the West country to recruit servants, and across the Channel to generate business. Even kings were peripatetic, visiting hunting lodges, eminent aristocrats and regional assemblies. A royal progress was a logistical nightmare. Henry III's (1216-1272) entourage on a visit to the royal hunting lodge at Brill included 6 long and 7 short carts, each with a carter and fore-rider, 41 packhorses, all the courtiers on their mounts, and covered waggons for the women and children. Usually the Royal Household alone numbered 150 plus the carters and fore-riders. Normally even the king travelled on horseback, although over long distances such travel was uncomfortable and even dangerous. Apart from holes created by the passage of carts, horses and cattle, the digging of holes on the public highway was a common medieval fault:[1]

> *In 1499 a glover from Leighton Buzzard travelled with his wares to Aylesbury for the market before Christmas Day. The same day an Aylesbury miller, Richart Boose, finding that his mill needed repairs, sent servants to dig clay called ramming clay for him on the highway. He was in no way dismayed that the digging of this clay made a great pit in the middle of the road ten feet wide, eight feet broad, and eight deep, which pit was quickly filled with water by the winter rains. But the unhappy glover, making his way home in the dusk, with his horse laden with paniers full of gloves, straightway fell into the pit and the man and his horse were drowned. The miller was charged with his death, but was acquitted by the court on the grounds that he had had no malicious intent, and had only dug the pit to repair his mill, and because he really did not know of any other place to get the kind of clay he wanted, save the high road.[2]*

### *THE ROADS AT THE BEGINNING OF THE INDUSTRIAL REVOLUTION*

By the middle of the 18th century, just as the Industrial Revolution was beginning, and the need to transport large quantities of raw materials and manufactures was becoming clear, England's roads were antiquated and inadequate. Most were just earthen tracks, or bridleways for pack horses and riders. Most were *"very much cut through"* by the increase in wheeled traffic and thus *"too wretched for wheeled vehicles"*. Every traveller could nominate a road *"which disgraced the kingdom"*. For instance:

> *Between Hockliffe and Stony Stratford the Roman road now known as Watling Street (A5) was in such a bad state that by 1705 it was almost impassable, especially in wet weather when parts were two to three feet deep in mud.[3]*

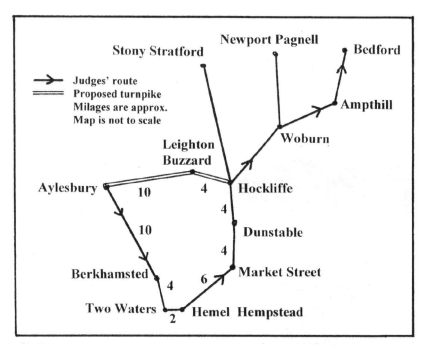

**Map 11: The Judges' Route from Aylesbury to Bedford before the Aylesbury to Hockliffe Road was Turnpiked**

The journey from Edinburgh to London could take two weeks, and the prospective traveller was advised to make his will and take a loving farewell of his family before departing. One stage-coach was advertised under the legend, *"London to Brighton in Four Days (If God be Willing)"*. The stagecoach which left Aylesbury at 6 a.m. arrived in London 14 hours later. At the end of the 18th century the road between Aylesbury and Hockliffe (incorporating parts of the present A418 and A4012) was in such bad repair that assize judges travelling north-eastwards to Bedford had first to proceed south-eastwards via Berkhamsted before continuing to Bedford, more than doubling the length of their journey: see map 11. Some roads were so bad that the inhabitants of the towns dependent upon them expected to have difficulty in obtaining supplies in winter, and stored up provisions as if for a siege, while the inhabitants of outlying farms and country villages could be virtually cut off for months. It is difficult to picture the isolation which fell upon country districts in winter. In 1792 it was said, [4]

> *You know too well that in winter when the cheerless season of the year invites and requires society and good fellowship, the intercourse of neighbours cannot be kept up without imminent danger to life and limb.*

These problems arose mainly because the maintenance of the roads was the responsibility of the parishes in which they were situated. According to a statute of 1555, the roads should be kept in order by the parishioners, who must provide labour for four (later six) days per year either personally or by paying someone to do the work. Moreover, if a parishioner's income exceeded £50 per year he or she must also provide the services of a horse and a cart. Finally, the Parish Vestry must appoint one or more surveyors who, without recompense or any training or experience of road construction and repair, must:

> *view all the common highways, trunks, tunnels, plats, hedges, ditches, banks, causeways, bridges and pavements; ensure that the owners and occupiers of adjoining land do cut, and plash their hedges, and scour their ditches; and organise the repair of the parish roads.*

**Fig. 69: Paying the Toll**

**Fig. 68: Turnpike Gate and House (Chiltern Open Air Museum)**

In practice most parishes did nothing until the road surface had deteriorated disastrously, and then used gangs of unemployed labour to tip cart-loads of gravel or stone – usually gathered from the surrounding fields – into the worst of the holes. Underpaid, underfed and inadequately supervised they effected purely temporary repairs, which rapidly degenerated into a quagmire. It was a system which had operated unsuccessfully for centuries! As early as 1373 the Fenny Stratford court roll has a long list of fines on local landlords for neglecting *"to cleanse and repair"* the highways near their land.[5]

### *The Demand for Better Roads*

This came from several quarters. Members of Parliament complained of the time wasted in travelling to and from Westminster. Landlords complained of the difficulties and dangers of inspecting their properties, which were often scattered around the country. For instance, in 1810 the Earl of Chesterfield owned 49 properties (7,269 acres) in Buckinghamshire alone.[6] All over Britain farmers had to walk their cattle to market. *"Highland cattle marched in their thousands . . . to London"*,[7] but lost so much weight in the process that they had to be fattened en route. A Creslow farmer, faced with the weight loss problem in a bull, which he was entering in a competition at Smithfield Market in London, chose to send it by canal boat. Manufacturers were also concerned because the state of the roads made it impossible to move masses of raw material and manufactured goods. In some places away from the coalfields, the coasts and the rivers, coal simply could not be obtained due to transport problems. Even the government, for military reasons, was concerned at the state of the roads, but due to the prevailing philosophy of laissez-faire it was unwilling to interfere in what it still regarded as a local responsibility.

### *THE TURNPIKE TRUSTS*

Eventually the turnpike trust was invented as the agency of improvement. It was controlled by a Board of Trustees, who employed engineers, surveyors and legal counsel to put its policies into effect. The first trust was formed in 1663, but they did not become common until after 1700. The first Act for Buckinghamshire, covering a stretch of Watling Street immediately south of Stony Stratford, was only passed in 1706. These "pikes" considerably improved roads, but they did have disadvantages. For example, eventually Britain had about 1100 different trusts, all of which maintained their small lengths of road (typically about twenty miles) at different times, and with varying efficiency. Thus the road from Aylesbury to Buckingham was improved in 1721, but if the traveller wanted to proceed from Buckingham to Northampton via Towcester he would find that that road had not been improved, and would not be improved for another 23 years. Neither would he fare better if he decided to go to Northampton via Old Stratford for that road would not be improved for another 94 years!

Initially the tolls were so deeply resented that *"ill-designing and disorderly persons pulled down, burnt and otherwise destroyed . . . turnpike gates and houses"*. Following this an Act of 1734, which imposed harsh penalties (from 3 months hard labour and a public whipping, to death without the benefit of clergy), seems to have discouraged the rioters.[8] Undoubtedly, tolls were inflated because each small trust employed its own surveyors, engineers and legal counsel, and of course, if you

### Table 14: Typical 18th Century Turnpike Tolls

| | | | |
|---|---|---|---|
| *A coach drawn by 6 horses* | *1s-6d* | *Any other cart* | *8d* |
| *A coach drawn by 4 horses* | *1s-0d* | *A horse, or mule (laden or unladen)* | *1½d* |
| *A coach drawn by 2 horses* | *6d* | *A score of cattle* | *10d* |
| *A waggon* | *1s-0d* | *A score of calves, swine, sheep, lambs* | *5d* |

travelled by coach, there was also the fare. Typically, an inside seat cost 3½d to 4d per mile. However, in the early 18th century, passengers who could not afford or stomach an inside seat

**Fig. 70: Post Coach**

These coaches operated primarily to carry mail and official despatches, but also conveyed passengers for the service was fast and reliable.

**Fig. 71: Full Speed Ahead**

Strong nerves were required by passengers seated on top of the coach, especially at night.

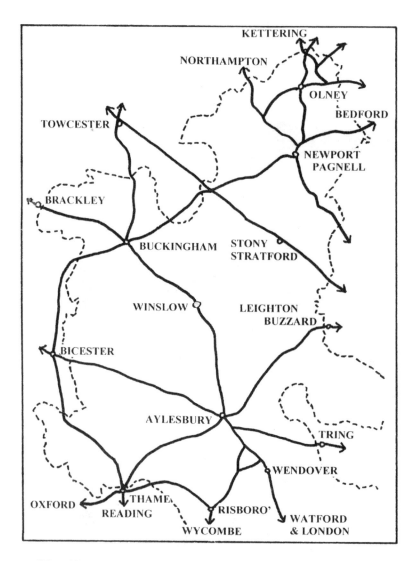

**Map 12: The Turnpiked Roads of the Vale and North Bucks.**
in 1834 at their greatest extent.

were invited to sit on top of the coach, where they were soaked by the rains, buffeted by the winds, scorched by the sun, and always in danger of being thrown onto the road below. Handles were not provided for topside passengers until 1753. Even then an outside seat still cost 2d to 3½d per mile. Small wonder then that agricultural labourers, on a weekly wage of 96d, did not travel far afield. Coach travel was not cheap.

Unfortunately, the trusts only improved the main roads, while the by-roads remained as treacherous as ever until late into the 19th century. In 1815 Gibbs reported that: [9]

*The byroads of Buckinghamshire . . . have ruts so deep that, when the wheels of a chaise fall into them, it is with the greatest danger that an attempt can be made to draw them out, for the horse and chaise must inevitably fall into a bog. Riding from Risborough to Bledlow, I turned my chaise out of the road to avoid a waggon, and my horse fell into a bog up to his chest.*

### Road Building Becomes Scientific

The turnpike trusts did make some improvements, but until the early 19th century their roads were at best indifferent, and at worst bad. After 1815 the time-honoured practice of tipping any old rubble onto the road surface began to be replaced by the more scientific methods of pioneers like Thomas Telford and John MacAdam. Telford insisted that roadstone must be tough, the best being basalts, granites and cherts. Where such stone was not available, other materials could be used, which he specified in similar detail. Thus, "picked field flints" were preferred to "dug flints", because the former, having been exposed to the weather, were judged to be less brittle. The pioneers also insisted that the stone must be reduced to angular fragments of no more than 2½" in diameter, which must be set in place on a level surface to form a close, firm pavement with a slight camber at the surface, to help drain away water into roadside ditches. Earlier road construction had made the camber of the road too steep, probably in order to drain water from the road more quickly. Unfortunately, it meant that vehicles kept to the crown of the road, and all the ruts, potholes and mud were concentrated there. After numerous experiments MacAdam improved on Telford's surface. The result was not only a smooth surface but one with excellent drainage. This revolutionised road-building, and others followed in their footsteps.

In addition to repairing and re-surfacing their roads the Trusts had to erect toll houses, toll bars and mile posts (Plate C16), build substantial bridges, re-align roads, and reduce gradients. Some of these were major works as at Shipton near Winslow, where the turnpike crossed the Claydon Brook, and a substantial bridge had to be built. At Tring Hill thirty-six feet had to be trimmed off the steepest and most dangerous part. Road construction and maintenance of this quality was expensive and over the years the tolls were increased, sometimes irrespective of the quality of the road! [10]

## THE AYLESBURY TO HOCKLIFFE TURNPIKE

In September 1809 a notice appeared in Jackson's Oxford Journal announcing that:

> in the next session of Parliament a petition will be presented for leave to bring in a Bill for more effectively repairing the road from Aylesbury to Hockliffe, which passes through Bierton, Hulcott, Wingrave, Wing, Linslade, Leighton Buzzard and Eggingon.

The petition was duly presented to Parliament in the names of George Grenville Nugent (Marquis of Buckingham), the Right Honourable Robert Lord Carrington and others. It claimed that:

> The proposed turnpike will be a great benefit and attended with much Convenience and Accommodation to your petitioners and others by affording a more easy conveyance of Goods.

The reception of the petition varied. The assize judges supported it, (Map 11) observing that the turnpike would greatly reduce the journey from Aylesbury to Bedford, whereas Soulbury, Drayton Parslow, Stewkley, Stoke Hammond, Newton Longville, Water Eaton, Bletchley, Grove and Fenny Stratford opposed it, fearing that they would have to pay a toll in going to Leighton Market even though they would only use the turnpike for a short distance. The promoters of the Bill promised *"to remedy the matter"*.

The Bill submitted to Parliament ran to over sixty manuscript pages of double foolscap and dealt, in minute detail, with everything that might cause the Trust problems, but little about things that would concern the public. The Act, which received the royal assent in May 1810, authorised the Trust, inter alia, to borrow money and collect tolls from travellers. This enabled work to start: the toll-houses to be built; the toll-gates, weighing machines and milestones to be installed. The collection of the tolls for the first year was auctioned off to the highest bidder. The road had to be surveyed, and the cost of repairs (about £2,000) estimated. Some of this could be funded by the monthly rents paid by the successful bidder for the collection of tolls, but the

**Fig. 72: Stage Coach with Basket**

**Fig. 73: Local Traffic - The Water Cart**

rest had to be borrowed. In fact, as tolls were the life-blood of a Trust, the Aylesbury and Hockliffe gates and toll-houses were made ready as a matter of urgency. Gate-keepers were installed by 13th August, and the collection of tolls started on the 17th. By the end of 1813 much had been done to improve the road but, as the surveyor reported, much remained to be done.

### Turnpike Repairs: the Parish System

Despite the criticisms of the parish system of road maintenance and repair, the Aylesbury/ Hockliffe Turnpike (like many others) still used it, each parish being paid annually by the turnpike in proportion to the amount of work done on its section of the road. Even with only nine parishes involved, this took some arranging! The two turnpike surveyors[11] had to measure the exact length of turnpike passing through each parish, and agree this with each parish surveyor. For example, Wingrave's length was agreed as two miles, one furlong, and 123 yards.[12] Next the turnpike surveyor estimated how many days' work would be needed to keep each section of the road in good order for another year. The Justices of the Peace then determined the obligation of each parish. For instance, in 1813 Aylesbury had to provide 90 days of labour, Bierton 198 days, Hulcott 108 days and Wingrave 252 days, all the work to be done under the direction and inspection of the surveyor of the turnpike road. Finally, the surveyor of each parish, in discussion with the Vestry, had to decide which parishioners must contribute labour. Then waggons and horses had to be

**Table 15: Wingrave and Rowsham: the Provision of Labour for Turnpike Repairs**

| Farmer | days | Farmer | days | Farmer | days |
|---|---|---|---|---|---|
| Joseph Lucas* | 60 | John Green | 16 | Hannah Seabrook | 7 |
| Thos. Middleton | 34 | Mary Cook | 14 | Mr Baker | 6 |
| William Payne | 30 | John Bailey | 8 | Edward Lucas | 5 |
| Thomas Purcell | 21 | Hannah Cook | 8 | John Grace | 5 |
| * = Parish Surveyor | | Wm. Maltby* | 7 | Thomas Keen | 5 |

found. Mattocks, hoes, shovels and spades had to be acquired, and sharpened where necessary. Since the Turnpike Trust would reimburse the parishes for repairing the road, the total cost of labour, transport, tools and materials had to be calculated. All the persons listed in Table 15 as liable to contribute labour were farmers, and had no wish to spend their time, or that of their labourers, in repairing roads. However, an alternative supply of labour was available in the form of the able-bodied unemployed parish paupers who, in Wingrave, in 1813, each received 8 shillings per week from parish funds. Admittedly, their productivity was much lower than that of hired labour, but its cost was reimbursed by the Turnpike and this helped to reduce the parish Poor Rate. Waggons and horses had to be found and their use costed. For example, the carting to Wingrave of one load of flints from Wendover or Tring was reckoned as 1½ days labour. Fortunately the glacial gravel, which occurred locally, was to be found – in places such as Wingrave – close to the turnpike. It had to be dug and screened, but it could be taken quite freely for roads, merely on payment to the farmer for any damage done. Indeed, when Thomas Fleet, who occupied a piece of gravel-bearing land refused to cooperate, he was ordered to appear before the magistrates.[13] The total payments to the parishes were not insignificant. Between 1817 and 1820 Bierton, which had the shortest length of pike, received £758 for repairing its section.

The office of parish surveyor was generally taken in turn by the farmers of the parish, and held for one or two years.[14] It was a thankless task. Much depended upon the surveyor's willingness to take action against uncooperative parishioners. It often meant getting work out of the work-shy, and this effort was not appreciated by the work-shy, or by their relatives and friends. Many

**Fig. 74: Local Traffic - The Village Carrier**

**Fig. 75: The Local Scene - The Kings Head, Aylesbury**
The Kings Head was a coaching inn, easily recognised as such by the 'tunnel' which admitted coaches to the stabling at the rear (see also Plate C17).

136

and bitter were the complaints against the surveyors: *"those spiritless, ignorant, lazy, sauntering people called Surveyors of the Highways"*, cried one of the kinder critics. Of course, if the parish surveyor really was so indolent, then the rest of the parish would blame him for the poor roads. It is therefore pleasant to record that – according to village records – the parish surveyors of Wingrave (see Table 15) were leading members of the community, successful farmers of substantial acreages, and highly respected for their considerable abilities. Happily, the turnpike surveyor's reports on the Wingrave section of the turnpike were usually complimentary.

## TRAVELLING BY STAGE-COACH

The early stage-coaches were a severe test of the travellers' stamina. Space was at a premium. The two bench seats were narrow and wooden with no upholstery. They each accommodated three passengers, who sat facing one another. Consequently, a tall gentleman might well find his knees bumping against those of the lady opposite him. He might also find his head hitting the roof of the coach as it pitched and plunged from pot-hole to pot-hole. Neither did coach builders make allowance for the girth of passengers. Stout persons could only hope that some of their companions would have more slender figures than themselves. The slimmer person could only pray that the 12-hour journey would not be spent, as Dean Swift found himself, *"squashed between two aged matrons of excessive bulk"*. There was no glass in the windows so, when the coach was moving briskly, summer heat was no problem. Leather curtains were intended to give some protection from cold and wet weather, but strong winds and driving rain soon found ways round them. This was when it was best to be seated in the middle of the coach, for passengers with window seats were soon very cold and very damp.

Its primitive suspension caused the coach to jolt and sway on the uneven road surfaces, which made many passengers feel sick. This mal de rue was increased by the confined space in the coach, which concentrated its smells at a time when personal hygiene, especially of travellers, was not a priority. Stale sweat, bad breath, cheap scent, dirty linen and stinking pipes combined with the smells of old leather and damp straw of ancient vintage to pollute the atmosphere of the coach.

*"What addition is this to men's Health or Business,"* demanded John Cresset,[15] *"to ride all day with strangers, oftentimes sick, ancient, diseased Persons, or young Children crying; to whose humours they are obliged to be subject? And is it for a Man's Health to be laid fast in the foul Wayes, and forced to wade up to the knees in mire; afterwards to sit in the cold, till Teams of Horses can be sent to pull the coach out?"*

Less affluent assengers could (if they dared) travel in *"the conveniency behind"*. This was an enormous wicker basket *"fixed onto the hind axle of the coach"* by leather straps, originally used for carrying passengers' luggage. For a reduced fare the passengers could squat uncomfortably in it. The superabundance of fresh air would certainly dispel the claustrophobia and sickness of inside travel, but there was no protection against the weather.

The stages covered by stage coaches were on set routes, and almost always between inns, so that travellers whose journeys extended over several days could feed and rest each night. Unfortunately, in the early days of coaching the quality of the accommodation varied greatly. Even if they were available, beds were often verminous, and had to be shared, even with strangers. Too often travellers had to sleep on a table or on the floor, or snooze upright in a chair. Food at its best was variable in quality. If your house or village was on the coach's set route, and you greased the coachman's palm, he might drop you off at your door. If not, then even when the coach reached its destination the traveller might still not have completed his journey.[16] For instance Sir John Verney, who was staying in London in June 1698, took the public coach to Aylesbury, having instructed his agent to meet him there with two horses so that he could ride

**Fig. 76: The Wheelwright's Shop c. 1800**

**Fig. 77: The Wheelwright's Shop c. 1900**
This particular wheelwright was located at Haddenham

home to Claydon the same night, if he was not already too exhausted.[17]

Road surfaces are usually blamed for the problems of road travel in the 18th and 19th centuries, but another hazard faced by coaches was winter snow. In the winter of 1814 there was a great frost. Even in the towns the snow lay four feet deep. Everywhere the mail coaches had to cease running, and often were abandoned in the snow, the letters being sent on by the guards on horseback. The Christmas of 1836 was even worse. A blizzard swept across England for three nights and days. By Boxing Day more than forty coaches were buried in drifts, some up to twenty feet deep. The London Mail was fixed in the snow at Broughton, and the coachman, guard and passengers all got down to help. They could not move it, so they obtained five plough horses, and drew the coach to Aylesbury with nine horses. It was nearly 24 hours late. One of the worst spots was at Little Brickhill, on Watling Street. Here, on the 27th December 1836 travelling southwards from Fenny Stratford, the guard of the Holyhead Mail saw the the rooves of three coaches just visible above the snow: the north-bound Holyhead Mail, the Chester Mail and a stage-coach which had lain there since Christmas Eve. As the guard shouted a scornful remark to his coachman regarding the plight of the other coaches, they were suddenly thrown headlong into deep snow, as their coach ploughed into the drift. Despite all their efforts the coach remained immoveable, for it was tilted sideways in a ditch. They could only cut the horses free, sling the mail bags across their backs and struggle back with the passengers the two miles to Fenny Stratford.[18]

A more unusual hazard was racing. Normally, this didn't cause problems, but it could! One such race, which took place on Watling Street, south of Newport Pagnell, resulted in the death of one passenger, and the injury of others. It occurred because the Holyhead Mail attempted to pass the Chester Mail by racing furiously alongside it on the wrong side of the road. The Chester coachman resented this and pulled his leading horses across his rival's path. This forced the Holyhead coach off the road where an unnoticed heap of stones ensured a collision which – in a moment – converted both coaches into a mass of splintered wood. Both drivers were indicted for manslaughter, and spent the next eighteen months tramping the treadmill in Aylesbury jail.

## THE STAGE-COACH AT ITS PEAK.

By the 1820's coach travel was much more comfortable. English coach building was the envy of the world. The seats of coaches were now upholstered. The coach suspension had been improved, and the leather used in it was specially dressed during tanning to increase its durability. The wheelbase was widened, and the body strengthened. Thanks to the turnpike roads travelling times were reduced. Large new inns provided better accommodation and refreshment for travellers, and more stabling for horses.

At the peak of the coaching era (the 1820's and 1830's) The Vale and North Bucks were well provided with road transport. For instance, four mail coaches from London crossed the county. One came up Watling Street on its 258 mile journey to Holyhead. Another followed a roughly parallel route, but passed through Newport Pagnell on its 190 mile journey to Chester. The Oxford Mail went via High Wycombe. The Birmingham Mail left London at eight every evening, reached Aylesbury just after midnight and arrived in Birmingham just before 9 a.m.. Besides the mail coaches, a number of stage-coaches catered solely for passengers. Not having to deal with the mail cut their running times so that, for example, London to Birmingham was cut from 13 to 12 hours. On Watling Street the Shrewsbury Wonder was probably the fastest. Using a stud of 150 horses, it reached Shrewsbury from London in just fifteen hours. In 1820 the people of Aylesbury were startled by the announcement that the 'Old Aylesbury Coach' would run to London and back the same day. This was thought to be amazing. On the evening of the first day a great crowd gathered at the Bell corner in Aylesbury, and some could scarcely believe their eyes when the coach first came into view. By the mid-1820's Aylesbury had twelve coaches passing through it every twenty-four hours. As early as December 1821, coaches on some routes were travelling at the extraordinary rate of twelve miles per hour, though it meant changing horses every eight miles.[19] By 1836 Wyatt's coach starting from the George Inn at Aylesbury reached the Kings Arms in London in three hours and thirty-five minutes. There were also local coach services linking towns such as Northampton and Bedford with Buckingham and Aylesbury. These services would include key stopping places like Stony Stratford and Newport Pagnell in their itineraries in the hope of picking-up or dropping-off long distance passengers. Cross-country travellers were also catered for. The Oxford to Cambridge coach still ran via Thame, Aylesbury and Leighton Buzzard. Other routes included Oxford to Kings Lynn via Buckingham, and Reading to Aylesbury. There were also the private coaches and especially on market days, numerous waggons and carts. By 1864 thirty carriers operated within a six-mile radius of Buckingham, a third of them calling on four or more days per week.

In the 1820's Watling Street was the principal artery for coaches, and Stony Stratford was a major staging post, as it had been since the 17th century. Since then business had boomed. By 1820 about forty coaches a day stopped there. It was noted for the number and quality of its inns, which graced the High Street and the Market Square. Two of the most famous have survived. The Cock and the Bull are typical of the coaching days when they were centres of news and gossip, giving rise to the Cock and Bull stories, which were often repeated, but believed by few. Little Brickhill was also an important coaching stage. Much of the traffic on Watling Street was servicing the Grand Junction Canal, which was extremely busy. By 1833, 18 mail and 176 other coaches were using this stretch of Watling Street regularly.[20] Other routes also had inns which catered for travellers. In 1806 Aylesbury was a small market town with numerous hostelries, so the George with its overnight accommodation and its stock of ale (7,136 pints), rum (424 pints), port (700 pints and 460 bottles) and brandy (336 pints) was clearly providing for more than the local trade. The White Horse was also recommended. At Buckingham Lord Cobham's Arms and another White Horse were well regarded. The later years of the 1830's saw the beginning of long-distance railways which would quickly destroy the long-distance coach trade.

**A visit to Luton's Stockwood Park is strongly recommended** for the Mossman Collection of horse-drawn carriages, and its Stockwood Museum of Rural Crafts (Tel: 01582-738714).

## *The Canals*

In the first half of the 18th century the means of moving heavy and voluminous goods on land were limited to the horse and cart and the packhorse. They could not cope. These goods, the raw materials for major industries, included coal, iron ore, china clay, and raw cotton.[21] The despatch of the finished products to customers posed a similar problem. The import of raw cotton illustrates its extent. In 1751 the traditional means of transport had struggled to cope with an import of three million pounds-weight of raw cotton. By 1830 the industry was using twenty times that amount. This would have been impossible but for the horse-drawn barges on the new canals. The Duke of Bridgewater built the first canal at his own expense, to link his colliery at Worsley with Manchester. It opened in 1761. It was such a success that he built a second canal connecting Manchester with Runcorn and so with Liverpool. The pottery, salt and other producers then combined to finance several canals in the Midlands. This led to a plan to link the manufacturing Midlands to the great purchasing power of London, and in 1793 the Grand Junction Canal was authorised. By 1830 England and Wales had nearly 2,000 miles of canal, and over 2,000 miles of improved and open rivers. The genius behind this was James Brindley, a millwright who, as the Duke of Bridgewater's foreman, implemented his employer's visions. This meant designing and building barges, locks, aqueducts and reservoirs, for which he was paid £1-1s per week. The results were spectacular. Distribution costs fell sharply. Towns grew due to better supplies of food and building materials. Ports developed and exports grew. Industry and agriculture, in previously isolated areas, prospered as new markets became accessible.

## THE GRAND JUNCTION CANAL (Now part of the Grand Union Canal)

In 1792 a group of canal consultants and surveyors called a public meeting at the Red Lion in Stony Stratford with the intention of building a canal from Braunston on the Oxford Canal to Greenford and the Thames in what is now west London. So much interest was created that the meeting had to be transferred to the parish church, where the proposal was agreed and a committee formed to implement it. The cost was estimated at £500,000, much of which was provided by the Marquis of Buckingham. The project was authorised by an Act of Parliament in 1793.

For most of its length, routine canal building sufficed. It was just laborious pick, shovel and wheelbarrow work but, although the flattest route was chosen, a considerable number of gradients had to be overcome. For the smaller of these the now familiar canal locks were constructed. However, at four places the gradients were so steep that they required expert and costly engineering work. For example, in Bucks., the Ouse Valley had to be crossed. [22] A firm at Stony Stratford constructed an embankment topped by the canal right across the Ouse Valley, with an aqueduct of three masonry arches to bridge the river. It was opened in August 1805, only for a section of the embankment to collapse in the following January. The canal company and the contractors were still arguing as to who was responsible for repairing it, when the aqueduct itself collapsed, much to the consternation of the inhabitants of Stony Stratford who, after a report in the Northampton Mercury of 28th February 1806, expected the whole town to be flooded to a great depth. Fortunately, one arch was still standing, and provided a passage for the Ouse, so there was only minor local flooding. The dispute between the contractors and the canal company went to court, where the canal company was awarded £9,262 and costs. A new cast iron aqueduct was opened in January 1811, and is still in use. There is an information panel at the site.

### The Early Development and Impact of the Canal

As a major link between the industrial areas of the Midlands and the North, and the vast market of London, the Grand Junction Canal was cheaper and quicker than the older route via Oxford and the Thames, and trade quickly built up. However, for most of its length the new canal passed through agricultural areas where production was traditionally geared to a limited local market. It took time to create new industry and build up the canal traffic, but coal was an immediate success, even though the large hearths of country cottages were designed to burn logs, and were inclined to waste coal. Eventually the canals created changes in the country building trades. New houses were roofed with the more durable and fireproof slates or clay tiles. Smaller grates and chimneys became fashionable. Stone to re-face buildings could be imported cheaply from as far away as Nuneaton in Warwickshire. Cheap and plentiful coal meant cheaper bricks, so builders used more of them and brickmaking increased. For instance, by 1819 Gregory Odell Clarke had opened a brick works and lime kiln at Fenny Stratford, just where Watling Street crosses the canal, and the canal had a wharf with a crane for unloading barges. Later more brick kilns were built by the wharf at Linford, just to the north. These and similar wharves elsewhere in North Bucks. and the Vale were not only used to import coal, iron, clay tiles and pipes, but also to export bricks, grain, hay and manure. With a plentiful, regular and cheap supply of coal passing through the town, the Leighton Buzzard Gas and Coke Company was created, though at first it served only the centre of the town. The canal not only stimulated industry, it also competed with it, and sometimes killed it. Joseph Coleman, Bedford's largest grocer, would import 54 large Leicestershire cheeses in a single load and have them brought to Linford by canal, and then onwards by waggon to Bedford, where they competed with the local cheeses. Pottery from the Midlands soon replaced the products of Potterspury and Brill, which had formerly cornered

**Fig. 78: The Grand Junction Canal at Wolverton c. 1900**
**X** indicates the position of the aqueduct, which carries the canal over the River Ouse.
The first barge is towing a smaller barge known as a butty. The cart-horse is the sole source of power.


**Fig. 79: An Empty Barge Waits for a Load at Linslade**
A loaded barge would be much lower in the water, and its cargo would usually be protected
by sheeting from the rain, and the wash from other boats as in Plate C18.

the local market.[23] The increase of traffic on the Grand Junction Canal was reflected by the dividends on its shares. By 1832, although the £100 shares had slipped from £290 to £242, the dividend had risen from 10 to 13%. The transport of people by canal was tried on a number of occasions. As late as 1832 eighty paupers travelled from Aylesbury to Liverpool by canal, en route for North America. No-one who tried it seems to have liked it. At two miles per hour it was too slow, too uncomfortable and too exposed to the weather.

## THE BRANCH CANALS IN THE VALE

There are numerous branch canals feeding into the main canal. Just two of these are in the Vale: the Aylesbury Arm and the Wendover Arm.

Work on **The Aylesbury Arm** did not start until August 1811, and was not completed until 1815. Although only 6¼ miles long, there were three problems. A potential water shortage had to be overcome by building two new reservoirs just north of Tring. For a short canal the Aylesbury Arm was rather expensive, as it required 18 bridges and 16 locks. The company was not sure of its financial viability, and had to seek reassurance from the Marquis of Buckingham. Despite this, the Arm prospered, long after the railway had reached the town. For a time, it paid dividends of up to 12%, which was more than the Aylesbury branch railway line ever managed. Most cargoes were destined for Aylesbury. Imports included wheat, coal for home fires and industrial use, timber, wire, strawboard, and other building materials. Canal transport reduced coal prices from 2s-6d to 1s-3d per cwt.. Exports included straw, hay, and food produced locally such as flour, livestock, butter, cheese, fruit and evaporated milk. The latter was produced by Nestle, whose factory backed onto the canal with a chute to the wharf, down which boxes of canned milk could be slid for loading onto the barges.

After World War I canal business declined, and in the 1930's the government gave financial backing for improvements. A plant to supply the concrete piles used to reinforce the banks was established at Marsworth at the junction with the Aylesbury Arm. Nearby, at Bulborne, lock gates were manufactured. Fortunately for the Aylesbury Arm several firms remained loyal to it. In addition, in 1923 the firm of Harvey-Taylor established itself at a wharf at Walton Street, almost in the centre of Aylesbury. In 1939 the firm still carried coal from Warwickshire to London, as well as transporting sand and ballast. Hills and Partridge of Walton Roller Mills (on the canal-side just off Park Street) continued to import grain and ship out its flour. R.P.Richards, the timber merchants of Exchange Street, were still unloading timber straight from the boats onto their wharf. But when Harvey-Taylor ceased trading in the early 1950's the end was clearly in sight. In July 1964 the Aylesbury Arm received its last commercial traffic. Despite this it survived, mainly because the potential of canals and their towpaths for boating, angling, water supply, cycling and walking were becoming appreciated. In 1959 the Aylesbury Boat Company opened a marina at Aylesbury, and the Arm is now a centre for recreational cruising in narrow boats. This has generated boat moorings, boat chandlers and boat builders and repairers. Such is the current usage of canals that AVDC's local plan (2004) proposes extra facilities for the Aylesbury Arm.

**The Wendover Arm** was intended simply to convey water from the springs of the Chiltern Hills near Wendover to the locks on the main canal at the Tring Summit, this being the canal's highest point. However, it was found that it would add little to the cost to construct it as a navigable canal. Authorisation was obtained and the 6¾ mile branch was opened in March 1797. It quickly attracted considerable use by boats. Nevertheless, its crucial job was still to supply water to the main canal. Unfortunately it simply didn't supply enough. Lengthy investigation revealed that a section of the canal arm leaked so badly that it not only squandered its own supply of water, but also additional water from the main canal. In 1904 this problem was overcome by abandoning the 1¼ miles of leaking canal, and building a pipeline to a new pumping station near Little

**Fig. 80: The Wendover Arm**
This is how it looked for much of the 19th century, before (in 1904)
over a mile was closed to reduce leakage.

**Fig. 81: The Wendover Arm in 2007**
Silted up by over a century of falling leaves and small branches falling from the over-hanging trees,
and no dredging, the Wendover end of the Arm is now so shallow that it can support reeds.
However, it is a haven for wild ducks and a variety of birds. Herons fish there.

144

## Recollections G: Life Aboard a Narrow Boat – Henry Franks *

Henry Franks, born in 1932, lived on a barge for the first eight years of his life. At this time the Grand Union Canal was a hive of industry with hundreds of barges transporting bulk materials such as coal, grain, sand and timber. Many came to Leighton Buzzard for sand for the London building industry. Much of this was loaded at Tiddenfoot tip. His father's barge had a diesel engine, whereas his grandparents' was pulled by a cart horse. Consequently, Grandfather had to "leg" the tunnels, lying on his back and pushing with his feet against the roof, whilst the family led the horse round them. Henry's father, Benjamin, was named after his father's barge. He worked for A. Harvey Taylor in Aylesbury, and was paid for loading, transporting and unloading the cargoes which the firm provided, with the rest of the family helping out without extra pay. So both Henry's parents were very strong, for most loading and unloading had to be done by hand. His father could carry two and a half cwts of coal on his back. Beside transporting sand from Leighton, his father also had contracts for taking timber from Brentford to Market Harborough, and coal from the Midlands to the Ovaltine factory at Kings Langley.

Everyday living on the boat was cramped. The total living and sleeping space was 8 feet by 7 feet, including space for food storage. Cooking was done on a coal fired stove, and a cupboard front came down to form a table. There was a double bed which folded into the wall, and beds for the two children, which also folded away. Legally, this space was supposed to cater for a maximum of three adults, or two adults and a child, but families with 7 children were not unknown! The cabin was decorated with ornate plates, and his mother's crochet work. Often barges were decorated externally with paintings of roses and castles. The toilet was a stout bucket, which from time to time was emptied into the canal, even though the canal also supplied the water for most cleaning jobs. Fortunately, at intervals, taps had been installed beside the canal, and about ten gallons of mains water was stored on the roof of the cabin. Some hand-washing of clothes was done in the washing-up bowl in the cabin, but a full clothes wash had to be done on the canal bank, where there was room for a tin bath, and a full-sized washing tub, which would enable a 'dolly' to be used. Barge people were remarkably healthy, probably because they were exposed to so much dirt and germs that they became immune to common complaints. This was fortunate because if the parents became ill there would be no earnings.

The bargees were a close-knit community, who socialised mainly in canal-side pubs, like the Bedford Arms in Linslade. Given provocation they were tough and argumentative. The women, their muscles developed by years of helping with the loading and unloading of cargo, were quite able to floor their man if he became obstreperous through drink, though they were not averse to a pint or three themselves! If possible, boat people, all dressed up in their best clothes, would attend a friend's or relative's marriage or funeral. Old Linslade church was a popular venue, being close to the canal. Later, the churches became concerned for the boat people, and set up canal missions. In 1850 a floating church was opened on the Aylesbury Arm, specifically for them.

As a child – until he could swim – Henry was often harnessed to the cabin top, just in case he fell into the canal. But canal boat children soon grew up, and at the age of six he could steer the boat, help to load and unload the cargo, collect 'provisions' from the local fields, keep the water cans on the roof of the cabin topped up from the taps by the canal, and – with a metal bowl – dip water from the canal for washing dishes, vegetables and the smalls. Most bargees had no schooling, and so hardly any of them could read or write. In 1939 Harry's parents decided that he and his sister should be educated, and not grow up illiterate like themselves. They settled in Leighton Buzzard, and his father worked for a builder. Within 3 years Henry passed the 11+ and later became a builder.

* Based on an article in the Leighton Buzzard Observer by permission of the Editor, with additions from 'Travelling the Canals' by permission of Eve McLaughlin.

**Fig. 82: Canals as a Commercial Facility**

In the early 20th century commercial traffic dominated the canals. This boat's horse has been replaced by steam power generated by the compact engines and boilers developed especially for narrow boats. The steamers were so powerful that they could tow two butties, where conditions permitted it. Unfortunately for the horse-towed older boats, tow-paths deteriorated from the wash of the more powerful boats.

**Fig. 83: Canals as a Recreational Facility**

From the middle of the 20th century recreational traffic increasingly dominated the canals. The picture shows a mid-week scene on the Grand Union Canal in the winter of 2007.

Tring, which lifted the water straight into the main canal. Throughout this time the short section between the main canal and Little Tring was operational: canal boats serviced the New Mill (Mead's flour mill), while next door to it (until 1948) Bushell's boatyard built and serviced many of the flour, grain and other barges. In 1959 the Wendover Arm Canal Trust was formed with the aim of reopening the branch between Little Tring and Wendover. So far the road bridge at Little Tring and a short stretch of canal have been rebuilt, at a cost of £420,000. Another short section, where the new Aston Clinton by-pass crosses the line of the canal, has been restored as part of the cost of by-passing the A41. Further restoration depends upon successful fund-raising.

## A CATALYST FOR CHANGE

Eventually, by introducing industry to the countryside of the South Midlands, the canals helped to break the farmers' virtual monopoly of countryside jobs, because the canals gradually provided some alternative employment for agricultural labourers, with somewhat higher pay, if only due to more regular work. For example, someone had to repair the 25,000 barges, and eventually replace them. As well as pick and shovel men, skilled labourers were needed to build the endless bridges and locks. Then men were needed to distribute their cargoes: coal, sand, lime, timber, manure, stone etc. were useless until they reached the consumers. Very often their cargoes created other demands. Iron fire baskets were needed if the new-fangled coal was to be burnt economically in the large old-fashioned cottage grates, scuttles were needed to hold the coal, and tongs with which to handle it. Farmers' markets were extended because crops like corn, hay, milk and even animals could be exported by barge.

## WORKING ON THE CANALS [24]

Working and living on the canals was a very hard life. All the family had to help run the boat. This included the opening and closing of the lock gates. In just one stretch of 160 miles a boat passed through 197 locks (see Plate C19). Loading and unloading cargo could absorb much time. Some cargoes, like sand, stone, gravel, grain, ash and coal could be tipped straight into the holds of the boat from tipper trucks, and later from the backs of lorries. At Leighton Buzzard sand was taken from the pits in trucks on a light railway to a gantry, where it was dropped straight into the waiting boats. Even then the cargo would need to be levelled by hand, before being *"sheeted up"* with side cloths and tarpaulins to protect it from the weather, and to prevent water from splashing onto the cargo, when the boat lay low in the water. Domestic coal soaked by water was not popular with customers, and brickies would complain that *"over-washed"* sand had *"too little fat in it"*. Unloading was an even bigger chore, since it relied mainly on a shovel, a barrow and a stout plank to bridge the gap between boat and wharf. A narrow boat carried 30 tons of cargo. When engines replaced horses, the narrow boat could also tow a loaded "butty" (as the second boat was called) with an additional 24 tons of cargo. Of course, this meant that loading and unloading took even longer. Imagine unloading 54 tons of sand – by hand! If the load had to be barrowed away from the canal bank, the job could take two men a good eight hours. It was even worse if the customer wanted coal not just unloaded but bagged. Worst of all was the buyer who not only wanted the coal bagged, but bagged selectively, with sacks of large lumps reserved for specially favoured households. Of course, the boatman could refuse the work, but it was a very competitive trade. Not that everything was that difficult. For instance, wheat for the Tring flour mill was usually delivered in bags, which the boat's crew simply emptied down a chute into a silo. Even so, the shifting, lifting and tipping of a thousand or so hundred-weight bags was a formidable task. Fortunately, boatmen were usually paid by the ton of cargo delivered, but it often meant working very long hours. In later years the facilities for loading and unloading improved. Some customers acquired hand-cranked cranes based on ground rails or gantries, and these speeded up the unloading. At intervals along its route the canal spawned flour mills, the raw materials for which were well suited to boat transport. In this middle region of the canal the boats serviced mills at Aylesbury, Little Tring, Leighton Buzzard and Kings Langley.

## MORE RECENT TIMES

By 1898, despite intense competition from the railways, 1,820,552 tons of cargo was carried on the Grand Union Canal. However, by the 1920's the traffic had declined. Post-1945 several factors combined to end the canals' traditional role as a large-scale carrier. Road transport, which eliminated the expensive and time consuming business of trans-shipment, increasingly poached the canals' customers. The incredibly confined living quarters on canal boats were increasingly unacceptable to boating families as national living standards rose. The reduced use of coal robbed the trade of one of its principal cargoes. In 1962/63 the canals were ice-bound for eleven weeks, during which the boatmen didn't earn a penny.

**Do visit the excellent Canal Museum at Stoke Bruerne** (Tel: 01604 862229). Typical narrow boats are moored there, and – subject to the availability of staff – it may be possible to inspect the living quarters. **Glebe Canal Cruises at Pitstone Wharf provide regular cruises** (including 2 locks) in modern narrow boats to Marsworth Village: 90 minutes there and back. (Tel: 01296-661920) Walk or cycle the 6 mile re-surfaced tow-path between Bletchley and Leighton (Tel: Sustrans 0845 1130065).

## The Railways

No sooner was the canal system established than someone had to improve on it! Primitive railways had long been used by collieries. Iron rails were in use in Cumberland as early as 1738. However, it was George Stephenson who revealed the commercial potential of railways: firstly, by developing the steam locomotive; and secondly by building (1821-5) from Stockton to Darlington the world's first public passenger-carrying railway. Its commercial success, and Stephenson's successful trials of the Rocket (Plate C20) at the then fantastic speed of 30mph, converted consideration of a London to Birmingham railway into action, and a precise route was surveyed, which included Aylesbury, Wendover and the Misbourne Valley. It was not the townspeople who objected to the route, but the coaching trade and the large landowners such as Drake of Amersham (over a distance of 45 miles!), Lord Carrington, the Smiths of Wendover, and the Duke of Buckingham, plus all the squirearchy who were under their influence. They subjected the whole idea of railways to a torrent of prejudice, ignorance and nonsense. The weight of the engine would prevent it from moving. The human body could not withstand speeds as high as 12 miles per hour. Sparks would set fire to houses next to the line. Horses would become extinct, so there would be no market for oats, hay and straw. Consequently, land would go out of cultivation, and farmers would be ruined. Iron would be doubled in price, and supplies would soon be exhausted. All the inns would be tenantless and in ruins. Thousands of people would be unemployed. One writer ended:

> *When we reflect we cannot but wonder at the blindness that has countenanced the growth of this monster, which will soon eat up the vitals of those by whom it was fostered.*[25]

Naturally the coaching companies were concerned for the survival of their trade, and the threat to their capital. They had invested heavily in coaches, horses, accommodation for passengers, and stables. For example, at Lathbury, a tiny settlement on the Newport Pagnell to Northampton road, the Inn Farm had built stables for 70 horses, while the Bull and Mouth in St. Martin's-le-Grand (London) had recently built extensions which included underground stables for 700 horses. W.J.Chaplin's business, which provided 106 coach services, employed over 2,000 people and by 1838 had 1,800 horses.

To left
**C16: Turnpike Trust Milestone**
This typical milestone still stands by the A418, just outside the Bugle Horn public house at Hartwell, near Stone.

Below
**C17: Red Lion Hotel, Wendover**
Men as disparate as Oliver Cromwell and Robert Louis Stevenson are said to have slept there. As the high-ceilinged entrance confirms, it was a regular halt in the stage-coach era.

**C18: Loaded Barges**
A heavily-laden barge and its butty on the Grand Union Canal.

**C19: The Three Locks near Soulbury**
Even now, when the canals are just a recreational facility, the locks are usually busier, but this picture was taken at 9 am on a Sunday morning in March 2007.

**C20: A Replica of George and Robert Stephenson's Rocket photographed at Quainton**
On its trial run in 1829 it reached a record speed of 29.5 miles per hour.

**C21:The Chinnor and Princess Risborough Railway's Passenger Train.**
Special wild-life-watching train trips are sometimes available: see also Fig. 90.

**C22: Ducks Thrive on Haddenham's Pond in the 21st Century**

**C23: The Waddesdon Almshouses**
They were built in the 17th century, and renovated by Baron Frederick de Rothschild in the 19th.

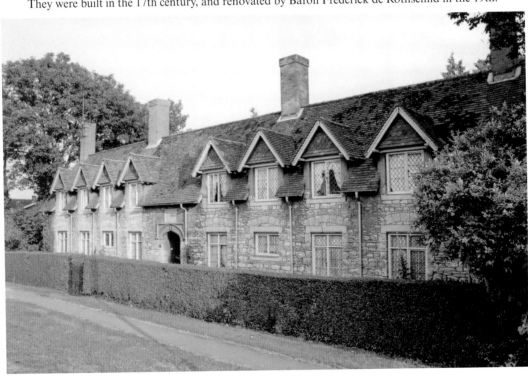

## Recollections H: The Battle for Access – J. K. Fowler *

Amongst the most bitter opponents of railways was the Duke of Buckingham. One of the projected lines went through his property at Stowe, near Buckingham, and he raised a small army of his labourers and dependants to prevent the proposed route being surveyed. The engineer of the railway line was an Irishman named Oliver Byrne, and there were numerous clashes between his chain-men and assistant surveyors, and the Duke's men. There was many a fight and breaking of heads, and every obstacle was raised to prevent a survey being made and the levels taken. Large sheets and tarpaulins were suspended on poles, and stretched across fields and roads in the hope of preventing the theodolites being used.

At last, one night, Oliver Byrne galloped up to the White Hart Inn in a chaise and four, shouting, "I've done the Duke! I've done the Duke!" Overjoyed at his success, he celebrated with a bottle of champagne. It appears that he obtained two moderately-sized ladders and, with a strong body of men, planted one ladder on a footpath which became the base line of his survey, stationing there one surveyor with a theodolite firmly attached to the rungs of the ladder. He then stationed another surveyor with a similar arrangement fifty yards off. By this expedient he succeeded in taking his levels, looking over the obstacles erected by the Duke's men. He repeated this for more than half a mile over the protected property. The survey was carried out by one group of men, while other groups took up positions on other parts of the estate, to divert the attention of the Duke's men. This is one instance of the difficulties which many of the railway lines had to overcome, caused by the blind opposition of landowners.

* Source: J.K.Fowler, Echoes of Old Country Life, Edward Arnold, 1892, pp. 153-4.
At one time Fowler was the proprietor of Aylesbury's White Hart Inn.

This opposition forced Stephenson to find another route, and at the suggestion of the Countess of Bridgewater he followed the line of the Grand Junction Canal across her land at Tring and Berkhamsted, which was already gashed by the canal. Even so, further south, the landowners forced the line over to the east of Watford necessitating a tunnel over a mile long, twenty-five feet high and thirty-four feet wide, while further south in the Colne valley an embankment seventy feet high was needed. The whole scheme was approved by Parliament in 1833. Having lost the fight to stop the railway from being built, the landowners demanded excessive prices for their land, which averaged out at £6,300 per mile. Altogether the cost of the entire railway rose from £2½ million to £5½ million. In his novel *Sybil* (1845), the politician Disraeli explained the landowners' attitude:

**Lord de Mowbray**: *I suppose your husband gives the railroads all the opposition in his power.*
**Lady Marney**: *There is nobody so violent against the railroads as George . . . He organized the whole of the district against our Marham line.*
**Lord de Mowbray**: *I rather counted on him to assist me in resisting this joint branch line here, but I was surprised to learn that he had consented.*
**Lady Marney**: *Not until the compensation was settled. George never opposed them after that. He gave up all opposition to the Marham line when they agreed to his terms.*

**Fig. 84: Clearing the Route (with dynamite) near Linslade 1837**
Dynamite had to be used due to the large concentrations of ironstone in the sandstone of this predominantly sandy area. The artist has illustrated the moment when the dynamite exploded and split up a large rock.

## THE EUSTON TO BIRMINGHAM RAILWAY AND ITS EFFECTS

Construction began in May 1833, but the full line was not open until September 1838 due to engineering difficulties. These included the crossing of the Northampton Uplands, where the Kilsby Tunnel (lined with 34 million bricks) and the huge Blisworth Cutting had to be excavated with pick and shovel plus a little dynamite. This was followed – just after entering North Bucks. at Roade – by the Ouse Valley crossing, which required an embankment 1½ miles long and 48 feet high to carry the line southwards across the water meadows of the Ouse. During construction it suffered from a serious land slip, and finally caught fire due to the presence of alum shale in the earth.[26] It led onto a viaduct 220 yards long, carrying the line 57 feet above the River Ouse, just north of Wolverton station. Having made a grand entry to the county, the line made a grand exit (just south of Pitstone) via the spectacularly deep Tring Cutting. Euston to Birmingham took 4¼ hours. It was quicker and cheaper than the fastest coaches, and in the first full year, passenger receipts amounted to over £500,000, with a further £90,000 from goods traffic.[27] In 1842 it carried 767,594 passengers. By 1862 sixty to seventy passenger trains passed through Bletchley station daily. By 1860 the fares from Wolverton to London were 9s-9d 1st class, 6s-8d 2nd class and 4s-4½d 3rd class.

Consequently, whenever the roads and the canals were in direct competition with the railways, the roads and canals had to meet the cheaper railway rates by immediately reducing their own

**Fig. 85: Clearing the Route (with a steam shovel) near Haddenham c.1906**

rates, or else they lost the traffic. The railways were also faster, which was especially important for merchants, who could reduce their costs by carrying smaller stocks, knowing that they could rely upon regular and speedy delivery. However, it was only the *long-distance* coach traffic which was quickly and completely eliminated, and with it most of the trade of the inns and stables on the main routes. Most of the canals' suppliers and customers occupied premises on or near the canals and so avoided trans-shipment costs. And, for some, a personal relationship with the carrier was more important than speed. So the canals retained a useful portion of their trade until well into the 20th century, though it declined as a percentage of total trade. The local traffic of carts, vans, waggons and coaches actually increased.

> *Nationally, between 1851 and 1900 the goods carried by rail increased from 60 million to 410 million tons, while those carried by carts, vans and waggons increased from 106 million tons to 671 million tons,* simply because these lesser vehicles *were the only means of conveying people and goods between homes, factories and railway stations.* [28]

So the railways did not, as feared, displace the horse. Quite the opposite! During Queen Victoria's reign the number of horses doubled. In fact, the railways employed a large number for their delivery services.

### The Aylesbury Branch

Between the main lines of the early railways there were huge gaps, which were only gradually filled in by branch railways. Meanwhile the turnpikes and lesser roads bridged the gaps. The

**AYLESBURY RAILWAY.**

The Public are respectfully informed, that this Line of Railway

**WILL BE OPENED**

ON

**MONDAY, 10 June 1839**

For the conveyance of

**PASSENGERS and PARCELS,**

In conjunction with the

**London and Birmingham Railway,**

TO AND FROM

**AYLESBURY AND LONDON.**

Until further Notice, the following will be the
TIME OF DEPARTURE OF THE TRAINS.

**UP** - - Leaves *AYLESBURY* for LONDON.
*Morning,* 10m past 7, half-past 10. *Afternoon* 10 m past 6.
On SUNDAYS, Morning 10 m. past 7. Afternoon, at 5.

**DOWN** - Leaves LONDON for AYLESBURY,
*Morning,* half-past 7. *Afternoon,* 2 and 5.
On SUNDAYS, Morning, half-past 7, Afternoon, at 5.

FARES:
To or from Aylesbury and London, - - First Class, 11s. Second Class, 7s. 6d.
3 JUNE 1839.

HOWSON, Printer, 38, Barbican.

**Fig. 86: The Opening Timetable of the Aylesbury/ Cheddington Branch Line**

first feeder railway in Britain was the Aylesbury to Cheddington line. Prominent citizens of Aylesbury were aggrieved that *"the most important town in Buckinghamshire"* had been by-passed. Fortunately, the route to the main line at Cheddington was straight and level. It required no bridging, and was only seven miles long. The Aylesbury Railway Company led by Sir Harry Verney and one of the influential Carringtons employed George Stephenson's son Robert as engineer, and construction started in December 1837. There was great excitement in Aylesbury when the line officially opened on 10th June 1839. A public holiday was declared. No business went on, and the shops were all closed. The town was decorated, bands paraded the streets, there were amusements in Market Square, and people flocked in from the surrounding villages to enjoy the occasion. Passengers swamped the terminus, and the first train out to Cheddington was packed. It consisted of an engine pulling five elegant first-class carriages, and several second-class carriages all full of excited passengers, dressed in their Sunday best, to and fro between Aylesbury and Cheddington. The Buckinghamshire Gazette reported:

*It was a lovely morning. Seven o'clock was the time appointed for launching the first train. Away it went and surely so much beauty and fashion were never before congregated at Cheddington. The first trip was accomplished in fourteen minutes, the distance being seven miles. The views are exceedingly beautiful. We have no hesitation in saying that in some few years, when railroads will have intersected our entire kingdom, no seven miles will be able to boast of fairer attractions to the admirers of 'nature unadorned' than ours. At every accessible spot on the route, groups of people waited to view the horseless carriages as they passed. In the evening there were fireworks, and a banquet was held at the White Hart, where the health of Robert Stephenson was proposed. He replied most genially that whatever might occur in the future, his audience could rely upon it that the London and Birmingham Railway would never forget its eldest child, the Aylesbury Railway. The assembly was much moved! But how they roared with laughter when Dr Lee of Hartwell House prophesied that the day would come when there would be more railways, for example to Thame (more laughter), Princes Risborough and Wendover (absolute convulsions).*

The Aylesbury line was a great success: in the half-year ending December 1839 over 20,000 people paid a total of £7,455 at the High Street ticket office. One wonders just where all the travellers came from, for by 1830 Aylesbury's population had not yet reached 5,000. The journey to Cheddington only took about ten minutes, but then it was "All change" and even if the main-line train was ready and waiting (which it never was!) it took another two hours to reach London. Even so, these times completely outdid the local coach services from Aylesbury, which took four hours to reach London at greater cost and less comfort. The days of long-distance coaching were

**Fig. 87: The Aylesbury/Cheddington Line as it passed along Stocklake.**

**Fig. 88: Aylesbury's Day Out to the Great Exhibition of 1851**

almost over. Indeed, the railway remained so successful that only seven years later, the mighty London and Birmingham Railway purchased the Aylesbury Company and merged it with the main line system. Another big attraction for passengers was the specials and excursions which the railways ran. For instance, capital punishment was still on the statute book, and very popular with the masses. It is said that in March 1845 ten thousand people witnessed an execution on the new 'drop' in front of Aylesbury's town hall. People would secure their places for as long as twelve hours before the execution. Every available place which provided a view of the gallows was taken. The railways exploited this craze by running cheap 'pleasure' trains to view executions. In April 1849 special trains were run as far as Norwich to see the public execution of a murderer. The Great Exhibition of 1851 was held in Joseph Paxton's magnificent Crystal Palace[29] at Hyde Park in London. It was designed to showcase Britain's achievement as the world's leading inventor and manufacturer, and it thrived on excursions. A special 'through' train of 30 carriages took a thousand passengers from Aylesbury to the exhibition. It raised the number of visitors for just that one day to 70,640. Specials were also run for prize fights.

There were several minor accidents on the Aylesbury line. Twice trains ran through flocks of sheep, which had wandered onto the line. Twice cows belonging to Thomas Cook of Wingrave strayed onto the line and were cut to pieces. He claimed £45 in compensation, but *'did not obtain a verdict'*. In 1842 an engine ran off the rails, though little damage was done. In 1846 the keeper at the Marston Gate level crossing went to sleep with the gates closed**.** A train went straight through and carried them away.

It was not until 1860 that Marston Gate (halfway between the main line at Cheddington and Aylesbury) opened as a station. A station master's house and a booking office were built alongside a timber platform on the southern or 'down' side of the track. On the northern or 'up' side was the milk loading platform, the cattle dock and a small weighing frame. In its heyday Marston Gate was a busy little station, and a great convenience to farmers. Like Cheddington and Aylesbury it had cattle pens, and farmers soon discovered that it was more profitable to send cattle to London by train, instead of walking them there. *"The butchers say that they save a stone in weight, and arrive very fresh in the market so that they are all the more saleable"*. On Wednesdays the 9 a.m. passenger train collected cattle for the Aylesbury market. There would be one van for cows and a second one if there were also sheep. A little later the farmers, in their best tweeds, would line the platform, all headed in the same direction. Each week about ten waggons of 'London Sweepings' arrived at Marston Gate, for the horse droppings from London's streets were so popular that local farmers competed keenly for a load. Another regular delivery was the chaff of barley, which Aylesbury Brewery Company sent to Marston, for local farmers used it as cattle feed. Farmers collected sweepings and chaff from the station yard, and emerged onto the Marston road with their carts swaying under their loads. Hay and coal were other regular loads. By the 1880's the Anglo-Swiss Condensed Milk Company at Aylesbury was consuming annually 1¼ million gallons of Vale milk, ¼ million gallons of which went via Marston Gate.

### *The Later Lines in the Vale and North Bucks. (Map 13)*
Due to the success and profitability of the first few lines, all sorts of schemes were devised in the Railway Mania of the 1840's, but most were never constructed. Even so, lines from Bletchley to Bedford, Bletchley to Oxford, and Buckingham to Banbury did get built. By 1851 the last two were merged as the Buckinghamshire Railway, which was in operation by May 1851. By 1866 it had been extended to Aylesbury, and renamed the Aylesbury and Buckinghamshire Railway. All three schemes met at Verney Junction, named after Sir Harry Verney, vice-chairman of the company.

In 1863 the Great Western Railway (GWR)was extended to Aylesbury via High Wycombe and Princes Risborough, providing farmers in the western Vale with access to new markets. To serve

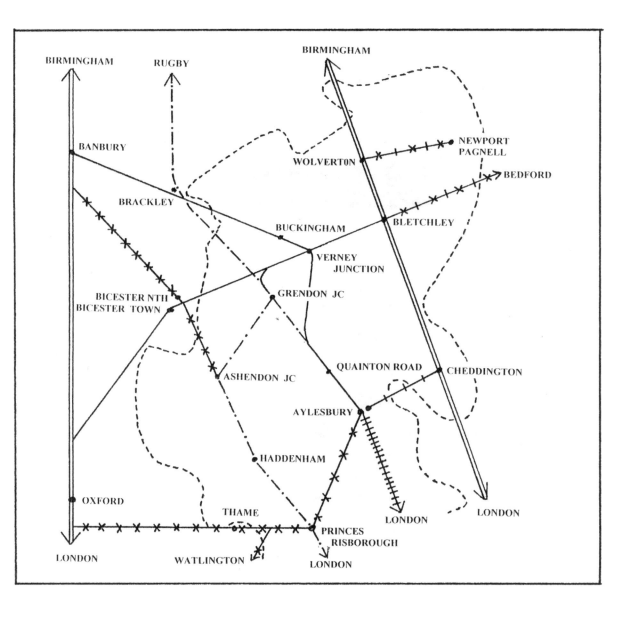

**Map 13: The Railway Lines of the Vale and North Bucks c.1912 (Not to scale)**

| | |
|---|---|
| ═══════ | The original main lines |
| ┼─┼─┼ | London and B'ham Railway: Aylesbury to Cheddington (open 1839) |
| ─────── | The Aylesbury and Buckinghamshire Railway (open 1850-66) |
| ╫╫╫╫╫ | The Metropolitan Railway (open 1892) |
| ✕✕✕ | Great Western Railway: Aylesbury to Oxford (open 1861); Ashendon Jc to Aynho (open 1910) |
| ─·─· | Great Central Railway: Risboro' to Grendon Jc (open 1906); Grendon Jc to north (in use 1906) |
| ┼✕┼✕┼ | Other lines (opened 1846) |
| ------ | The boundary of the County of Buckinghamshire |
| N. B: | The names of the companies are as at the inception of the lines |

155

it a second station (Aylesbury Town) was built, and from 1866 was shared with the Aylesbury and Buckinghamshire Railway. Roughly half a mile away, the existing station (Aylesbury High Street) continued to serve the Aylesbury-Cheddington line. In 1892 the Metropolitan Railway reached Aylesbury from London (Marylebone), and joined up to the Aylesbury and Buckingham Railway, meaning that Aylesbury's new station now gave direct access to both Birmingham and London. All these changes further widened the farmers' market, as Mark Finch, a Rowsham farmer found: see page 238.

Between 1861 and 1910 a further 44 railway schemes totalling 829 miles were planned just for Buckinghamshire, but only one was constructed. The Great Central, whose trains from London passed through Bucks. via Aylesbury, found the route too slow due to its use by leisurely local trains. Great Central felt that a new line with improved alignments and better gradients could improve running times. For example, between Saunderton and Princes Risborough a short tunnel reduced the gradient from 1 in 88 to 1 in 167. Princes Risborough acquired a new goods yard and became an important junction. Its North Signal Box had over 100 levers in a frame as long as a cricket pitch, and a second box served the goods yards. A completely new station was built at Haddenham. From there the line ran northwards to just south of Banbury, where it joined the GWR's Oxford to Birmingham line. The new route was in operation by 1910. Otherwise, this was a period of consolidation: new stations were built; second class disappeared; and third class was provided with upholstered seats. From 1881 toilets and corridors were increasingly provided.

### The Effect of the Railways on the Local Economy

The railways reduced the farmers' transport costs for fertilisers, feed, seed and implements, and in later years enabled them to exploit the growing urban demand for perishable foodstuffs: milk, butter, cheese, eggs, fruit and vegetables. Railways were also well-suited to the carriage of large quantities of heavy industrial goods like coal, sand, building materials and road-stone. In addition, the railways added an entirely new section to Britain's engineering industry, and North Bucks. was fortunate that one of the London and Birmingham Railway's works was located at Wolverton. The site had been acquired for engines to take on water, and passengers to take on refreshment. The refreshment rooms became quite famous, and the company even ran a pig farm nearby to ensure supplies of fresh meat. The site was developed into the Wolverton Railway Works, which built and repaired locomotives. In 1852 a single locomotive was said to contain 5,416 components, the vast majority of which had to be made by hand. By 1862 the Wolverton works employed over 2,000 men, mostly from agricultural employment.

### THE DEMISE OF THE RAILWAYS IN THE TWENTIETH CENTURY

After World War 2 the increased use of motor cars and motorised road haulage severely reduced the railways' business. In the 1950's the railways' share of national goods traffic fell from 54% to 44%, with annual losses of nearly £89 million. Neither nationalisation nor de-nationalisation resolved the problems. The forecast efficiency did not materialise, and the public constantly complained of poor services and the continual financial losses. In 1961 Dr Richard Beeching (chairman of British Rail) concluded that 80% of the traffic was carried on just 20% of the network, with much of the rest operating at a loss. 3,105 miles had been closed between 1950 and 1962, including the Aylesbury to Cheddington line, which was limited to freight in 1953, and dismantled ten years later. Beeching proposed closing a further 4,265 miles, and over 2,000 stations, with some lines limited to freight traffic. The government accepted this, but rejected further savage cuts. Beeching resigned. His annual savings were a mere £7 million, while annual losses had increased to over £100 million. So what went wrong? Much of the cut mileage consisted of branch lines which fed the main lines. When the branches closed, the feeder traffic was lost, reducing the income of the main lines. Over-manning and old-fashioned working practices

**Fig. 89: Full Steam Ahead**
A coal train passes through Wendover Station.

**Fig. 90: Full Steam Ahead**
The Chinnor and Princes Risborough Railway tank engine is pulling a passenger coach.

persisted, and it was incorrectly assumed that buses could replace trains. It is also claimed that increases in passenger fares were kept below the rate of inflation to please the electorate. By 2005 the system had shrunk to 12,000 miles of track and 2,000 stations. It is still subsidised by the tax-payer, though this also happens in a number of countries. More recent reorganisation has yet to justify itself. Despite government neglect of the roads and the increased taxation of cars and car usage, the public's love affair with the internal combustion engine continues.

There are steam-driven railway engines and their carriages at **Buckinghamshire Railway Centre at Quainton,** (800 metres of line) Tel: 01296 – 655450. To steam further visit **the Chinnor & Princes Risborough Railway: 7 miles round trip** *always starting at Chinnor*. Tel: 01844 – 353535; website at www.cprra.co.uk. (See Plate C21)Further away is the **Cholsey and Wallingford Railway** (2½ miles): tel.01491-835067. It could be combined with a visit to the Saxon town of Wallingford. Still further away in Hampshire is the **Watercress Line** with a round trip of 20 miles, and unlimited travel on that day's ticket. Contact 01962 – 733810; or www.watercressline.co.uk.

industries. Despite this, most children found four hours at Sunday School was a light load and much more varied and interesting than lace, straw and jobs at home. As for the adults, most of them agreed that *'the Devil finds work for idle hands'*. A Sunday School was cheap and easy to provide: some corner of the church or chapel could provide accommodation; and the teaching would be provided free by the vicar's family, or some worthy villagers. Many parents, who could not afford day school, were grateful that Sunday School was free. The main aims were *"the religious observance of the Sabbath and the improvement in virtuous habits"*, due to a knowledge of the Scriptures. However, the ability to read the Bible for oneself was considered to be very important, so basic reading skills were also taught. Often this extended to writing, spelling and even simple arithmetic, usually called summing or 'figgering'. Over ten million reading and spelling books were sold by the Sunday School Union during the first half of the 19th century. Most Church of England Sunday Schools also included the Prayer Book, and especially the Catechism, in their teaching. At Hardwick Church the Vicar proudly recorded that:

> *After the second lesson thirty boys recited the Catechism, which they did without a single mistake, and next Sunday as many of the Girls' School are preparing for the same.*[5]

Not all children were able to attend Sunday School. At Hulcott, for instance, older boys working on farms during the week were required to work on Sundays too, scaring birds and feeding the sheep and the pigs. As one official of the Sunday School Union lamented:

> *Such a lad never cleans himself, never puts on best clothes, loses all reverence for the Sabbath, loses any opportunity of education and severs his links with school-fellows and teachers.*

In 1837 the Revd. Thomas Hayton, Vicar of Long Crendon, had difficulties with accommodation.

> *When I first came, the Sunday School had 27 scholars, now it has 100 and more to come. I am now teaching the children close to the altar table and down the aisles, which is very inconvenient, troublesome and improper . . .There is virtually no day school in the place and the Baptists want to wean away my scholars: but with assistance I shall prevail.*[6]

Prevail he did. Only fifty yards from the church was the old Court House (Fig. 92). It had an upper room which was in a dilapidated and filthy state, and only used once a year. With the agreement of the Lord of the Manor, and help from the National Society, it was refurbished for use as a schoolroom (Fig. 93). In 1851 a national Religious Census was carried out by the Home Office. It surveyed church and chapel accommodation and attendance at worship. It showed that over two million scholars attended Sunday School on that day.

**Table 16: Religious Census of Long Crendon (Population 1700) March 1851**

|  | Morning | | Afternoon | | Evng |
|---|---|---|---|---|---|
|  | Scholars | Adults | Scholars | Adults | Adults |
| Parish Church | * | * | 115 | 160 | --- |
| Baptist Meeting House | 140 | 200 | 140 | 230 | 360 |
| Primitive Methodist |  | 12 |  | 12 | 12 |
| Wesleyan Methodist | 80 | 100 | 80 | 150 | 100 |

\* Neither the usual Sunday Service nor the Sunday School were held that morning. No reason is known.

Numbers for Buckinghamshire were high. As Table 16 shows, on that afternoon 552 adults attended a religious service, and 335 children attended Sunday School: 887 persons in all; well over half the total population of Long Crendon. However, the vicar would have been disappointed that his congregation that afternoon was outnumbered by his Baptist rivals who also turned out in astonishing numbers for their Sunday evening service.

**Fig. 92: Long Crendon Court House Before 1885**
The date is known, because in 1885 the cottage at the extreme right of the picture was demolished.

**Fig. 93: The Upper Room of Long Crendon Court House**
In the 19th century it was used by the Anglian Church Sunday School.

## VOCATIONAL TRAINING IN THE 18ᵗʰ AND 19ᵗʰ CENTURIES

Fortunate indeed were those children able to become apprentices, as at Lovett's Charity School. At Quainton a book listing apprentices between 1805 and 1843 gives details of parents, masters, residences and trades. Well over thirty trades are recorded: [7]

> *Bricklayer, cordwainer, blacksmith, butcher, cooper, confectioner, tailor, breeches maker and glover, miller and baker, carpenter and joiner, wheelwright, turner, grocer and shopkeeper, brazier, collar maker, hairdresser, draper, bookbinder, basket maker, plumber, glazier, plasterer, framework knitter, basket and sievemaker, cabinet maker, saddle and harness maker, ploughmaker, wheelmaker, printer, and chairmaker.*

In those times vocational training for children was quite different to its modern counterpart. The numerous lace and strawplait 'schools' were more like workshops than schools: see Chapter 14. Agriculture had the typical 19ᵗʰ century apprenticeship in that the youngster started at the very bottom (scaring birds, and taking food and drink to the field workers, for instance), and learned by watching and assisting the older men. In 1867, when asked about his son's job, George Stokes, a farm labourer of Great Horwood, replied:

> *Our boy, 9½, is at farm work and gets 2s-6d a week. He was at school till he was nine. I wish he could have kept on, but we can't do without his 2s-6d with bread so dear.* [8]

At busy times even younger boys were employed full-time: weeding, stone-picking, and bird scaring. Extremely long hours were worked at haymaking and harvest.

---

**Recollections I: Portrait of a Bird Scarer ***

In the country lanes we have met young gentlemen of tender years, whose general appearance and 'get-up' have excited our attention. For instance, there is no proportion between their feet and their boots. The former are small, weak and tender. The latter are of thick leather, studded with huge nails, caked with great clods of dried mud; so heavy that one wonders how the little chaps manage to drag them about; so spacious that one fears their little contents will be hopelessly lost. If they catch your eye they always speak, and their utterance never varies. In a thin, dreary voice they ask, "Plase, master, can you tell us wot toime it is?" And if you pass them seven times a day, they will seven times repeat their enquiry.

Who are these little men on whose hands time hangs so heavily? These, sir, are the noble army of British bird scarers: the field police who guard the germinating seed and tender growth against the depredations of our winged predators. Theirs is a lonely occupation, wandering across the fields from dawn to dusk, whirling their rattles at the feathered fiends.

\* Based on a passage from "Joseph Arch" by the Revd. F.S. Attenborough, 1872.

---

## THE GOVERNMENT ACTS

In the early 19ᵗʰ century much discussion was taking place on a difficult and thorny subject: the education of the masses. Reformers considered this essential. Few people could read, and even less could write, despite the fact that Britain was becoming an industrialised society and desperately in need of literacy and numeracy. In addition, the children of the poor deserved an opportunity to better themselves. Some hoped that education would reduce crime and immorality. "Isn't it dangerous?" asked others, remembering the French Revolution. Farmers declared,

*Going to school is idleness compared with working . . . For men who are to end their days in a tiresome and painful 'station in life', the sooner they are upon it, the more patiently they'll submit to it for ever after.*

Some parents were convinced that they would never manage to feed the family, unless their children were earning. Learning to read at Sunday School was fine, but no more was needed.

In 1833 the government finally undertook some responsibility by granting £20,000 to be shared between the two major religious societies founded earlier that century: the National Society for Promoting the Education of the Poor in the Principles of the Established Church (i.e. the Church of England); and the British and Foreign Schools Society (i.e. the Nonconformists). This annual grant (raised steadily over the years) was to be used to build new schools, provided that at least half of the cost was raised by voluntary contributions. In 1839 the Committee of the Privy Council on Education was set up to oversee education. This included the right to inspect these schools, and so Her Majesty's Inspectors of Schools (HMI's) were appointed. The onus, however, was still on voluntary effort. The vicar, a non-conformist lay preacher, or local benefactor would have to apply for a grant, find a suitable site, raise the funds, appoint an architect and builder, and cope with all the paper-work.

### HULCOTT'S FIRST SCHOOL (Contributed by Honor Lewington) [9]

One applicant for a grant was the Reverend William Morgan, the newly appointed rector of Hulcott, a small hamlet to the east of Aylesbury. He was aged 70 when he commenced his time-consuming and at times frustrating project, but throughout he showed remarkable persistence and patience in a story spanning the last six years of his life. In January 1852 he wrote to the National Society about the possibility of a grant:

*Having been recently appointed to this parish, I was greatly surprised that there is no schoolroom in it. About 40 children, boys and girls, are taught on Sundays by two or three teachers in the church. But I am truly sorry to say that not one of the children can read a chapter in the Bible, nor repeat the whole of the church Catechism. Having been engaged in the instruction of children of the poor for over 45 years I am grieved to find such a deficiency in their instruction in a parish within 40 miles of the Metropolis!*

He explained that Hulcott was a small country parish of only 800 acres with a population of approximately 160, all farm labourers, straw plaiters and lace makers apart from himself and four farmers. Unfortunately, there were no resident gentlemen who might help bear the financial load. The road to the nearest school at Bierton was almost impassible in winter. Hulcott was in dire need of a room which could be used for day, evening and Sunday School, and also for missionary and other benevolent meetings. The National Society responded favourably, sending him an application form. By May 1853 he had received the approval of the Bishop of Oxford, had estimated the cost of the new building and submitted completed application forms to the National Society, and the Committee in Council for Education.

The following year was spent raising funds and finding a suitable site. Both proved extremely difficult. The vicar had sent a printed circular explaining the pressing need for contributions to influential people and to his friends near and far, and to Hulcott's inhabitants. There was a generous response, but not enough. Even so, he persevered. In May 1854 he contacted the National Society admitting that he had exhausted all his resources, but was reluctant to give up the project after getting so far. The Society regretfully declined to help. His search for a site was also proving unsuccessful. No farmer was able or willing to provide one. At last in November 1854 both problems were solved. A rood of land in Hulcott Lane would be assigned out of the Glebe, and the non-resident Lord of the Manor and his sister contributed £20.

**Fig. 94: Hulcott School at the beginning of the 20th Century**

**Fig. 95: The Cuddington National School**
The pupils make their way to school along Church Street.

166

So now Mr Durley of Bierton was asked to submit building plans. The standards required by the Committee in Council were exacting and it took another six months before approval was granted, but at last all was well and a handsome grant of £84 was awarded which was added to the £10 promised by the National Society. Building work started and on January 8th 1856 the school was opened, almost four years to the day from the first correspondence.

### The Vicar's Message to the People of Hulcott

*It now only remains for the inhabitants of Hulcott to show their gratitude to their numerous benefactors by availing themselves of the inestimable advantages which a well-conducted school offers to all classes:*

*<u>Parents</u> – Be careful that every child be sent, as soon as the children's early age permits, constantly to the school-room. Let not the young children waste their precious time, as hitherto, in idleness, and in contracting bad habits.*

*<u>Masters and Mistresses</u> – Afford your young servants time in an evening to perfect themselves in reading their Bibles and good books in the school. Is it not better and far cheaper for you to prevent vice than to punish it by law, prisons, unions, etc.?*

*<u>Farmers</u> – The master manufacturers in our commercial towns have long ago found that well-ordered education is the only way to secure honest, upright, diligent and clever workmen. I hope you will soon learn the same salutary lesson. Give us your good wishes, your help and your prayers.*

*<u>Mothers</u> – especially, are much concerned in this good work, for on you mainly depends the success of this school. I am sorry to say that I have had more trouble with you than any in the parish. Let me faithfully warn you that you do not frustrate our endeavours to teach your children, by your needless interference and sinful indulgence of them.*

*<u>Dear Children</u> – I must say a word to you . . . you shall have, by God's blessing, a school in your own parish. Go to it thankfully, joyfully, constantly. Be assured that they are your friends who teach you, restrain you, correct you and lead you. Here is instruction for infants, children, young men and women, fathers and mothers, servants, parents, masters, the poor, the rich, for ministers, for the people, for all.*

*Let us all pray for God's blessing.     W. Morgan, B.D., Rector of Hulcott.*

Only four months later it was clear that all was not well, as the rector explained to the National Society and the Committee in Council:

*In this uncivilised part of the County of Bucks. we unfortunately find that a house for the master of our new school is absolutely necessary to DEFEND THE PROPERTY as well as to ensure a good master.*

His blunt words seem to have struck home. A government grant of £44 was awarded, plus £10 from the National Society and £30 from the Diocesan Board, which together with private subscriptions of £86 raised a total of £170. The house was completed in December 1857, but the Reverend Morgan's signature on the deed was very faint and shaky. A few months later he was dead, but his six years' work for Hulcott was complete. Throughout the county, similar burdens were voluntarily undertaken by those devoted to the welfare and education of the young.

### Payment by Results

Since 1846 the Government had granted annual maintenance funds to the 'National' and 'British' schools. But the total expenditure was rising alarmingly, from £150,000 in 1851 to £541,233 in 1858. Despite this the pupils' attainments were still low. To remedy this, payment by results was introduced in 1861. In future, the grant would be based on two factors: the pupils' attendance and the results of annual tests in reading, writing and arithmetic by visiting HMI's. To implement this, attendance registers were to be strictly kept and systematically checked by someone in authority, such as the vicar. For assessment, pupils were to be grouped into Standards: Standard 1 including children aged 6 and 7 years; Standard 2 including children aged 7 and 8 years; etc.. In Fig. 96 notice the emphasis placed on the 3 R's. Anglican schools also included religious knowledge. Finally, a grant would be awarded based on the performance of each child: 4s-0d for regular attendance; 2s-8d for each of the 3 R's passed, making a maximum of 12s-0d per pupil. Both the schoolmaster's salary and the funding for the school depended upon the results of the HMI's annual examination, so rote learning and endless repetition prevailed: multiplication tables were chanted, and spelling corrections written out many times. Over the years, to increase enthusiasm for education, the curriculum was broadened and optional subjects were introduced, which also qualified for an increased government grant. By 1890, payment by results was judged to be a failure, and was replaced by grants for discipline and organisation.

### School Versus Work

During the 1860's, 1870's and 1880's the conflict between school and work was still a major issue for labouring families. For 'learning school' parents had to pay weekly pence for each of their children, whereas those working on farms or in the cottage industries would be supplementing the family's meagre income. The 1867 Enquiry into the Employment of Children, Young Persons and Women in Agriculture, revealed many conflicting opinions: [10]

> W.G.Duncan, J.P., and Chairman of Newport Pagnell Board of Guardians: *I do not think that legislation is required to fix the age below which children should not be allowed to work on farms. I never knew a boy kept at school until he was 13 that was any use as a labourer, when he grew up.*

> Reverend J.W.Wing of Broughton: *The Factory Act should be extended to our lace schools, for children of the tender age of 7 or 8 ought not to be confined at work for many hours each day in small close rooms. If the educationalists could have them for up to ten years of age, then with a night school and Sunday School, we might give them all the education needed for their station in life.*

> Reverend F.Faber: *So far as the boys are concerned, I don't think that anything but compulsory education will be of any avail.*

In 1873 the Agricultural Children's Act forbade the employment of children in agriculture under the age of 8. However, the system was very difficult to enforce, as the problems of the Cuddington school show.

### The Education Acts

Meanwhile the Government had decided at last that elementary education should be provided for all: a momentous decision. **The 1870 Act** divided the country into districts. If existing schools were unable to meet the needs of a district, a School Board, elected by the rate-payers, would have to be established. It would have the power to build and manage its school, and would be financed from the rates. As it would be non-denominational, it was viewed with horror by church schools, and every effort was made to avoid this. Nevertheless, Board Schools (as they became known) *were* built e.g. at Linslade (1873) and Chearsley (1880). Now that sufficient schools had been provided, **the 1880 Act** compelled all children up to the age of ten years to attend school full-time. Between 10 to 13 they were permitted to leave once they reached Standard 5. **The 1891 Act** made elementary education free at last. No longer was there the problem of collecting the school pence. Attendance immediately increased. Meanwhile, the National and the British schools were still being financed by the Anglican and Nonconformists respectively. Realising that the financial strain was too great for parochial resources, the government passed the Education **Act of 1902,** which made local authorities responsible for providing education. Block grants would be paid to the County Councils and County Boroughs which would administer the scheme. At last the government had taken overall responsibility for education.

## CUDDINGTON'S EARLY SCHOOLS

The Lambeth Palace Library holds the records of the National Society. On a visit to the Library, we discovered that Cuddington had had an earlier National school built on a different site.

### Cuddington's First National School

This opened in 1845, thanks to the initiative and perseverance of its curate, Henry Meeres. It was he who obtained the site: a small piece of glebe land at the northern end of the village.[11] Its early years were made difficult by a number of factors. Cuddington had never had a school of any sort, so there was no tradition of education. It had a population of 626, but no resident lord of the manor or resident clergy to take, or support, an initiative. Its population comprised just four or five farmers, the farm labourers and their families. *"Consequently a spirit of insubordination and ignorance prevailed"*. The school consisted of only one room 18 feet by 25 feet, to accommodate all ages from infant upwards, and (from the first) was too small for its purpose. It had just one earth closet to be used by *both* boys and girls. It bore the title "National School" over the doorway, without the addition "to promote the Education of the Poor in the Principles of the Established Church", which the curate feared would only cause opposition in a village *"already too apt to find fault with our church and its instruction"*. Just before its completion he wrote to the National Society appealing for additional funds in order to provide an efficient master. *"I may be wrong, but I believe that the success of our undertaking will greatly depend on the choice of our master"*. Wise words, but the Society made no concession. Not until 1887, forty-two years and at least seven schoolmasters later, did Cuddington's first really able schoolmaster, Robert Allen, overcome all the difficulties and obstacles that had beset his predecessors.

Tragedy, in the form of cholera, struck the parish in August 1849,[12] when its small hamlet of Gibraltar lost seventeen of its fifty-four inhabitants in the space of two weeks to this highly infectious yet still mysterious disease. The hamlet was evacuated, and tents were provided some distance away. Mr Robert Ceeley, the local Medical Officer of Aylesbury, described the scene as the most heartrending he had ever witnessed, whilst a reporter from the Bucks Herald inspected *"the wretched abodes of the unhappy victims who have been swept away by the scourge"*. Their cottages were thoroughly cleansed by limewashing and fumigating. It was reported that:

> the pestiferous ditch behind the dwellings which has for years been the receptacle for filth of every description, has been filled up, and layers of lime have been introduced.

Since then no further cases had developed. Mr Ceeley commiserated with Thomas Holt, aged only eight, and the sole survivor of his family: he had lost his father, mother, and five brothers and sisters. The death of Richard and Ruth Betts had orphaned all their six children, the eldest of whom was only twelve years old. Many years later, Cuddington's residents could still recall the rumble of the cart wheels at dead of night delivering the corpses to the parish church where neither clergy nor mourners were present. Despite their low opinion of the local church, some villagers were scandalised that burials were not in accordance with the rites of the Church of England. Later, Bishop Samuel Wilberforce pleaded with the Dean and Chapter at Rochester: [13]

> Painful circumstances have drawn the eyes of the whole county to Cuddington. The cholera has ravaged it, and when at its worst, the sick were not visited by a parish priest, and the dead were interred without the rites of the Holy Faith . . . I ask you to give Cuddington a responsible and resident minister of God's words and sacraments.

His plea was well received. By 1855 Cuddington had its own minister resident in a newly-built rectory. The Reverend James Mansel Price faithfully served the people of the parish for the next 40 years. He and his wife actively supported the village's National School. He visited it regularly to examine the registers, and ensure that everything conformed to the attendance rules. He helped out with the teaching, taking not only Scripture lessons, but occasionally Spelling, Reading, Dictation and Arithmetic, whilst Mrs Price sometimes helped out with Needlework. His advice and support were invaluable, particularly when it was realised that Cuddington's school, although only built in 1845, was quite unsuitable. To the National Society, in 1863, he wrote:[14]

> *In the year 1845 a schoolroom was built for this parish at the extreme end of the village, but on account of its unfavourable position and miserable accommodation (there is but one privy for both boys and girls) many parents are deterred from sending their girls and younger children. Besides which the schoolroom is not large enough for the number of children, even at the present time. To remove these very great disadvantages, half an acre of ground has been given in the very centre of the village opposite the church, where we propose to build a new school and schoolmaster's house.*

## CUDDINGTON'S NEW NATIONAL SCHOOL

This was opened in November 1863. The main classroom measured 32 ft x 18 ft, and the infant classroom (for children under 6) 14ft.x11ft.. There were two playgrounds: one for the boys and one for the girls. Parents paid 2d per week for each child attending. The master's salary was £25 per annum plus the children's pence, and a rent-free schoolhouse. On moving day the children were excited to be in their new school, and when Joshua Hall and his wife arrived after Christmas they not only had new jobs, but the excitement of a brand-new three-bedroom home next to the school. Hopefully, this was a new beginning, which would issue the school into a more successful era. Soon 59 boys and 17 girls were attending, and more would follow gradually. Most were from Cuddington, but some walked from Chearsley and Nether Winchendon, where no schools had yet been built. The Revised Code of 1862 was now in operation, and all the pupils were placed in their respective 'standards' (the Victorian term for classes) ready for the HMI's inspection of the 3 R's in January. Apart from the buildings, little had changed. The school's success or failure would still be determined by the master's teaching skills, its pupils' attendance and their success or failure to master the 3R's: Reading, Writing and Arithmetic.

### Fig. 96: A Typical Morning's Timetable in the 1870's [15]

9.00 – 9.15:    Assembly with Hymns and prayers.
9.15 – 9.45:    M-W-F Scripture; T-Th Catechism.
9.45 – 10.00:   Mark the registers.
10.00 – 10.30:  M-W-F Copy Writing; T-Th Dictation
10.30 – 10.45:  Recreation in playground.
10.45 – 11.20:  I and III Arithmetic   II and IV Reading.
11.20 – 11.55:  I and III Reading   II and IV Arithmetic
11.55 – 12.00:  Tables. The Grace and Dismissal.

The Afternoon (2.00 – 4.15) was very similar, and confined to the same subjects as the morning.

This timetable was designed for a large group of pupils, aged 6 to 10 years, divided into four standards, and all taught by one teacher in just one room. The curriculum was limited to the 3 R's: Reading, Writing and Arithmetic, plus Religious Instruction. The 3 R's were vocational training for low-level jobs. Religious Instruction was to instil not only morality, but humility: the acceptance of one's station in life. Such a narrow curriculum was self-defeating. It was monotonous, and so provided no inspiration. Some Physical Education, or Singing would have been the highlight of the week! It was 1879 before Geography and History were added. Figure 96 tries to overcome the difficulty of teaching four separate year groups in the same room, by arranging for two groups to be taught Arithmetic, while the other two groups do (silent!) reading

170

from incredibly dull texts, with the groups reversed after the first 35 minutes. The problem was to keep the readers quiet!

### The Problems

From 1863 to 1887 a succession of six masters was appointed, with their wives taking charge of the infants. Their average stay was only four years. In each case the resignation followed critical HMI reports. Arithmetic was a persistent problem. One master's principal achievement was to get the annual grant reduced by 10% on the grounds of defective instruction in Arithmetic! Overcrowding was another problem until schoolrooms were built at Nether Winchendon (1875) and Chearsley (1880), whose children no longer had to walk to Cuddington and back each day, sometimes along flooded roads. Smaller numbers also seemed to help the learning process, for the 1875 Report was quite encouraging. Sadly, 1876's was damning: *"Of English nothing is known. I cannot understand why I was asked to examine it!"* If that was bad, the next report was disastrous:

> *No success attends the teaching of English. I find that Gray's Elegy was this year given to the 3rd standard* (8-9 year olds) *as a piece of poetry suitable to their capacities! As matters stand, the school can hardly be regarded as efficient.*

Although overcrowding had been reduced, poor attendance still disrupted the teaching. Parents often kept their children away from school. Girls would return with excuses like *"Poor shoes"*, *"Minding baby"*, and *"Mam was awful bad so I had to do the washing"*. Boys would return after following such mysterious pursuits as *"tattering"*, *"stubbling"*, *"awoodin"* and *"elderbloomin"*, all of which sounded much more incomprehensible in a rich Bucks. accent. As Cuddington's school was a church school, the pupils had to attend church. However, the extent of this was remarkable. During one headmaster's reign they attended on the feast days for St Andrew, St Barnabas, St John the Baptist, St Peter, St Philip, St James and St Thomas; also on Epiphany Day, Annunciation Day, Lady Day, Shrove Tuesday, Ash Wednesday and Ascension Day. After the last three, the children were given a half holiday. Also celebrated were the Conversion of St Paul, the Festival of the Virgin Mary, and even Circumcision Day! Some villages enjoyed a not inconsiderable social life in the late 19th century. So half days off school were also given for the Nether Winchendon Feast, the Sunday School Feast, the Church Choir Treat, the Haddenham Festival, a cricket match at Winchendon, and May Day garlands. A whole day's holiday was granted for a cricket match between Tetsworth and Cuddington, and also for the village's Harvest Festival of Thanksgiving, and two days for the Village Club Feast. In later years Temperance Fetes and Labourers' Union Teas were added to the programme, the schoolroom probably being the village's only sizeable room.

This was a time when children's diseases were rife: outbreaks of measles, mumps, scarlet fever, whooping cough, chicken pox, influenza, and diphtheria were common, and occasionally a school had to close. The new schoolmaster, Mr Allen, explained the problems which it created, especially just before the Annual Inspection:

> *It seems very hard that so many children should be away ill, and some of the best too. Not only are some away altogether, but a considerable portion of those present are affected by the epidemic. Being poorly they are sleepy and not up to their best form.*

In this case the disease was so rampant that the school had to close for four weeks, but much to the master's surprise the HMI made allowances for the school's problems, and was most encouraging:

> *The school has improved most creditably under Mr Allen, and is now likely to do extremely well. As an encouragement and in view of the general circumstances I recommend the merit mark, 'Excellent'.*

In half a century this was the first merit mark bestowed upon the school, and not just 'Good', but the cherished grade of 'Excellent', the highest praise available to the HMI.

### Success at Last!

This achievement was the first success of the newly appointed Robert Allen and his wife, who arrived from Durham Training College with a Certificate of Education of the second class. Only two of Robert's predecessors' certificates are on record: one had a certificate of the 3rd class, 2nd division, and the other was 4th class. At the end of Allen's first week, the school log book records, *"Have endeavoured to instil habits of punctuality by precept and example"*. Next he persuaded the Managers to replace the dilapidated reading books with new sets of 'Moffat's Explanatory'. He tested each class regularly, and recorded the weaknesses for the preparation of future lessons:

> *More attention to pronunciation in reading. The dictation did not satisfy me, so an extra amount of paperwork will be indulged in. Standard II are a sharp lot, and attend well.*

Robert Allen believed not only in hard work, but in encouragement, fun and treats. He gave each child a foolscap book, and promised that everyone who kept the book clean and did good work in it, should have it when it was filled up. *"In a good many cases this is an incentive"*, he declared. He organised a Sports Day for the children, and a concert for the parents.

> *At Christmas the children were given their promised treat, which was a great success. After tea, games such as Dumb Crambo, Judge and Jury, Buzz, etc. were played. The evening finished with Mr Green's magic lantern, which was enthusiastically received.*

Allen certainly knew how to get the pupils on his side. In December 1890 he wrote:

> *Continued severe weather has played havoc with attendance. Children have complained very much of their hands and feet being cold. By carrying buckets of water and pouring it on the ground in the evening, an excellent slide has been made in the boys' yard, which has given the older children an opportunity of gaining warmth and pleasure.*

However, throughout his years at Cuddington, he found no solution to the problem of poor attendance, though not for want of trying. He sent a list of poor attenders to the local authority. It included one lad who had made only 16 attendances out of 58, but nothing was done.

> *I consider there is a neglect of duty somewhere. The law is compulsory attendance, yet I rarely have a visit from the School Attendance Officer. Now the pupils are out, elder blooming again: just 19 out of 57 attending in a mixed school. I cannot imagine a more humiliating and hopeless position to be in than master of a small country school in an elder blooming and potato district with no power to enforce attendance. You are absolutely at the whim of the parents, and unless you can work with them, your case is hopeless. Fortunately, as a rule, I can get in with them, but sometimes they will have their way.*

The Allens' reign was too good to last. In June 1891, they resigned to move to a joint appointment in a school of 300 pupils at Greenhithe in Kent. Fortunately their replacements, Mr and Mrs Steventon, proved worthy successors. The HMI had no reservations:

> *This is one of my model schools. It has again come out brilliantly under Mr Steventon, whose work cannot be too highly praised.*

### Free Elementary Education for All

In September 1891 the Managers decided to adopt the Free Education Act, and from then on school pence were no longer collected. Soon the average attendance rose, especially in Standard I. New subjects such as History, Geography and Drawing had gradually been introduced into the curriculum over the recent past, and the log book recorded, for instance, *"Much interest is evinced by the boys as the Drawing examination draws near"*, and later, *"The result was Excellent."* A Prize

Day was introduced. This was *"A great day in the school year"*, and *"Thirty-one books, varying in price from 6d to 5/- given for regularity, etc.."* Then in October, *"All here in time this morning. It is a red letter day"*. This was written in red! And in March 1893, triumphantly, again in red ink, *"The boys have only missed 16 attendances out of the maximum 1269"*. Finally, in January 1896, *"I never had such attendance as I have at present. Out of a possible 793 attendances they have made all of them"*.

The HMI's Report for 1893 sums up this time at the school:

> *Nothing could be better than the state of this little school. All the work, elementary and class, is done with neatness, accuracy and intelligence. The children take an interest in doing it, which is most noticeable. I can find no fault, nor suggest an improvement.*

The **British Schools Museum** at Hitchin (Herts.) contains a Lancastrian school room of 1837 plus a galleried classroom of 1853, and other rooms added between then and 1905. It **is well worth a visit. Tel: 01462-420144**

### Fig. 97: The Cuddington National School
In the school log-book for 19.7. 1898 the Headmaster commented: "Last week an itinerant photographer called and photographed the pupils and teachers in 4 groups. We received copies today. They are exceedingly good, as good as anything I have ever seen at this time".

## Chapter 14

## *THE RISE AND FALL OF THE COTTAGE INDUSTRIES*

Local production was a feature of the Vale villages: straw plait, lace, needles, ducks, bricks and ironware were all made in and around the workers' cottages. This industry eventually declined due to competition from large-scale producers, usually employing machines. The changes are well illustrated by lace-making, needles and duck rearing.

To find employment in one's own cottage was of great value to a busy housewife and mother. To be able to supplement the meagre income brought in by an agricultural labourer was a godsend, especially when trade was brisk, and it was possible to earn considerably more than one's husband! In addition, home industry was far more convenient. For instance, no time was wasted walking to and from work. Indeed, one's work could be taken up at any spare moment, even whilst keeping an eye on the children.

### *Lace-Making*

Lace-making was an important cottage industry in Buckinghamshire, Bedfordshire and Northamptonshire. During the 18th and early 19th centuries important centres for Bucks lace-making included the villages around High Wycombe, Newport Pagnell and Olney, and the Vale of Aylesbury. As early as 1697 Celia Fiennes noticed the lace-makers of Stony Stratford sitting and working *"all along the street as thick as can be"*. [1]

**Fig. 98: Lace-making at Long Crendon in the 19th Century**

Thomas Pennant, another early traveller, recalled in 1782 that there was:

> *scarcely a door to be seen during summer in most of the towns, but what is occupied by some industrious, pale-faced lass, her sedentary trade forbidding the rose to bloom in her sickly cheeks".*[2]

It was certainly not a healthy trade.[3] Lace-makers were often deformed due to the stooping position in which they worked. Indeed, to support themselves in this position, young girls wore a strong wooden busk in their stays, which injured their soft bones, contracting their chests for the rest of their lives. It was vital that lace-work be kept scrupulously clean, so the fireplaces in the small cottage living rooms were blocked for fear of smoke and dust soiling their work. In winter, windows would be kept tightly shut, and the only warmth would be provided by the heat from the bodies of the workers, and from the 'dicky pots'. These rough brown pots were filled with hot wood ashes from the local baker, and placed around the room, even tucked under the women's skirts to warm their feet. So, with no ventilation the small crowded rooms soon became very stuffy and unpleasant.[4] Working with fine lace thread in poor light could and did strain their eyes, and even ruin their sight. Good light was vital but, candles being expensive, rushes were peeled and coated with fat. If several lace makers were working together on a dark winter evening, a tallow candle could be shared. It would be set centrally on a stool around which were fitted several glass globes filled with water. These acted as reflectors magnifying the soft light. As Mrs Harris, a lace mistress at Newport Pagnell, explained:

> *Them as sit first light can see; them as sit second light can't very well; but twelve can sit round one candle, and do at times.*

As good light was so important, the lace-makers sat at their doorways whenever possible, enjoying the fresh air, the bright light, the warm sunshine and the company of their neighbours. They could more easily see their intricate work. They could have a good gossip and chant or sing their traditional lace songs. So the summer days were much more pleasant than dreary winter days.

### The Workhouses

Lace was made at many workhouses, the income from it being used to reduce the parish poor rate. As early as 1672 at Aylesbury Workhouse a Mary Sutton was paid five shillings to teach the workhouse children lace-making.[5] An unexpected and joyful entry in the records tells us that three whole shillings had been set aside to celebrate the traditional 'Caterns', on November 25th, the feast of St. Catherine, the patron saint of spinners, who was also associated with lace-making. Catern cakes of dough and caraway seeds would be baked, and there would be feasting, merrymaking and dancing: an unforgettable treat in their hard, monotonous lives.

### The Lace Schools

Lace schools abounded in Buckinghamshire, not only in the towns but also in the villages. Girls, and sometimes boys (like it or not! ), started young, usually at six or seven years, but sometimes as early as four or five. *"Six is the best age for starting; you can beat it into them better then,"* declared one lace mistress. *"If they come after they have begun to run in the streets, they have the streets in their minds all the time,"* declared Mrs Sanders, a lace mistress at Princes Risborough. Mrs Hazard of Winslow, who had kept a lace school for 45 years, reported that her hours were from 8 to 5 with an hour at home for dinner; but for the first year she did not keep them so long by two hours: *"Cos the little things get so tired."*[6]

Very little 'book-learning' took place, though a few verses from the Bible might be recited, for the lace mistresses were usually only semi-literate. 'Schooling', which meant learning the trade, was carried out in the cottage living room: small, stuffy, badly lit and often insanitary. Discipline was maintained by the liberal use of the cane. Hands had to be kept very clean, and hair tied back

**Fig. 99: A Fine Example of Hand-made Lace**

**Fig. 100: The Lace-maker's Bolster**

or plaited. Tuppence a week was the usual fee.

Bobbins held the fine linen thread which was to be worked into lace. At first these were made from the small bones of birds and rabbits (hence the term bone-lace) but soon wooden bobbins became common, all in different sizes, shapes and colours, which made them easier to identify whilst working. Along the shaft many were ornamented with inscriptions to a loved one, whilst fixed at the bottom was a wire ring, the spangle, threaded with seven beads, coins or charms, which prevented the bobbins from rolling along the pillow, and added tension to the thread. A bobbin-winder was indispensable at a busy lace-school, winding the thread evenly onto the children's bobbins. Each child had her own 'pillow' upon which to work: a hard, heavy, round bolster packed with straw, well-hammered, and firm as a rock. It was covered with a pillow cloth, for cleanliness was essential. The maker sat on a four-legged stool, and bent over the pillow, which rested on a wooden frame known as a 'horse'. A pricked parchment pattern, usually fourteen inches deep, was fastened to the pillow and then pins were placed through the specified holes, around which a net of threads would be woven. In this way the pattern was followed, with the thread twisting, crossing and inter-weaving until the 'down' (ie. the bottom of the parchment) was reached. Then the pins had to be 'set up' again, before the twisting and crossing could be resumed. As the lace was made, it was continuously folded up in clean paper or linen cloth to protect it from dirt or damage.

As the children worked, they sometimes chanted or sang their favourite lace songs. One of these came into popular usage, although many people did not know its meaning. [7]

> One, two, buckle my shoe (= set off for work)
> Three, four, knock at the door (of the lace school)
> Five, six, pick up sticks (the 'sticks' were the bobbins)
> Seven, eight, lay them straight (ie. the bobbins)
> Nine, ten, a big fat hen. (a lace-making pattern)

> *It is said it took half a lifetime to become a skilled worker. The rapidity of such lace-makers was, however, amazing: their fingers and hands flew, tossing the bobbins from side to side, twisting the threads over and over again with lightning rapidity. The sound of the clicking bobbins, and the shaking of the beads, was very pleasing.* [8]

Sadly lace-makers were considered as of low status! Their work was regarded as the meanest type of labour, particularly for women and children, who had no other means of subsistence.

### The Market for Lace

At its height in 1800 it is said that 150,000 lace-makers, designers, agents and dealers were involved in the trade in the counties of Bucks., Beds. and Northants.. Despite its lowly image, a full-time worker could make as much as twelve to eighteen pence a day. Very often a village lace-maker used the village grocery and drapery shop when selling her work. She was usually paid in goods: fresh thread, bobbins or pins, plus her choice of groceries. Usually, she would have preferred cash, but this was only possible when trade was very brisk. These small shopkeepers then sold to a wholesale dealer, who regularly visited a local market, or the London market at Aldersgate. There were also large-scale dealers, who began to call themselves 'manufacturers'. In 1863, just one of them – Mr Thomas Gilbert of High Wycombe – employed about 3,000 persons. [9]

### The Decline of the Industry

After the end of the Napoleonic Wars in 1815, further prosperity was questionable. Firstly, new lace-making machinery had been developed in Nottinghamshire, and by 1830 it included the whole production process. This 'new-fangled' method was very much faster and cheaper, and the beautiful hand-made lace simply could not compete on price. Nor could it compete with

**Fig. 101: Duck End, Aylesbury**
Many of the cottagers reared ducks for the London market.

**Fig. 102: Some of Long Crendon's Witchert Cottages c. 1900**
There are no vehicles: just one ancient cart. A cottager, carrying two buckets of water back home, walks down the middle of the street.

the continental lace, which was also cheaper, and could be imported now that the war was over. Import duties were raised in 1819, but smuggling was a serious problem. As pillow-lace had been the staple manufacture of Aylesbury, any candidate for Parliament had no chance of election unless he supported the trade and denounced machine-made lace.

> *His election procession had to be preceded by a lace pillow mounted on a high pole 'like the head of a traitor', and his banners profusely trimmed with Aylesbury lace: 'Support Bobbin Lace! Down with The Machine Stuff!'. The successful candidate was chaired round the town in a chariot, again literally covered with pillow lace, preceded by a band, and followed by a great crowd.* [10]

Nevertheless, the trade gradually dwindled. Cheap imported lace flooded the market as import duties were gradually reduced, until in 1860 they were abandoned and free trade reigned. Meanwhile, the Nottingham machine-made lace was becoming increasingly popular.

> *The machine-made lace is now so good and answers most purposes so well, that the pillow-lace seems to be dying out in this neighbourhood . . . A girl of thirteen, a fairly industrious worker, working for ten hours a day cannot now get 2s-6d a week at the pillow, and in preference to working so hard for this, the girls all go out to service as soon as they are old enough.* [11]

Even so, hand-made lace was still highly esteemed, and greatly valued. *"No comparison,"* claimed its admirers, when comparing it with machine-made lace, because the latter was absolutely uniform, perfectly regular and flat, whilst the hand-made was bound to be slightly irregular and these imperceptible unevennesses, by catching the light and casting little shadows, created individuality in the product. So various organisations were formed. The North Bucks. Lace Association, for example, was founded in 1897, with Queen Victoria as its patron. During the 20th century there was a revival of interest in pillow lace, and the handicraft became a popular pastime. Elsie Turnham of Waddesdon (1885-1953) was an ardent collector of lace and its traditional working tools. Her collection included hundreds of patterns (also known as 'prickings'), many being one-off designs, jealously guarded secrets, handed down from one generation to another. Every Wednesday and Saturday, from before World War Two until her death in 1953, she would sit in the County Museum at Aylesbury, making lace on a pillow, which she kept there for the purpose. An old Buckinghamshire lace-maker once told her:

> *On winter morns, when the hoar frost was thick upon the ground, my grandmother told me that her grandmother used to go, in company with the village folk, and draw the frosted cobwebs, trees, leaves and ferns in the fields and woods (see Fig. 99), and return home and make new lace designs.* [12]

**Aylesbury Museum's lace display** is well worth a visit. Before leaving do view the Aylesbury duck and drake in their glass case. This can be combined with a tour of **the 15th century King's Head** (National Trust), and/or **the self-guided Heritage Walk** through the town's Conservation Area. Leaflets are available from the **Tourist Office** at the King's Head (01296-381501). **The Wardown Park Museum at Luton (01582-546722)** has a fine display of straw plaiting and lace-making.

## The Aylesbury Duck

The Aylesbury Duck industry began in the 18th century at 'Duck End', then considered the poorer end of Aylesbury town. With its clay soil this low-lying, well-watered but poorly drained area lay at the bottom of Castle Street near a stream called the Bear Brook. This severely over-crowded area had no sewerage system, and no good supply of drinking water. Open ditches and stagnant pools prevailed. No wonder its name was Common Dunghill. However, its ponds and streams

**Fig. 103: The Duck Pond at Long Crendon**

**Fig. 104: Plucking Ducks at Askett**
All the ducks are held head down, to prevent blood running into the body and discolouring it.

were perfect for the water-loving ducks, and by 1750 a small trade had developed. *"The poor people of the town are supported by breeding young ducks. Four carts go with them to London every Saturday. They hatch 'em under hens."* [13]

Aylesbury specialised in a new strain of duck called the English White. It was white as snow, highly prized, and much more popular than the common brown or grey varieties. The English Whites were large birds and fattened quickly. Within eight weeks they would reach 4 lbs and were ready for the market. Their delicate white flesh was *"the sweetest in the country"*. In addition their pure white downy feathers were ideal for filling quilts, cushions and pillows. The birds had a distinctive shape. The under-sides of their long broad bodies were almost parallel to the ground, and their heads were held high on their long necks. Their long bills were flesh-coloured, and their feet and legs bright orange.

### *The Breeders and the Duckers*

There were two distinct branches to the duck industry. Firstly, there were the Breeders who bred the English Whites, and sold their eggs. Secondly, there were the Duckers, who hatched the eggs and reared and fattened the ducklings for the market. At the start of the season each ducker would contract with a breeder for their whole supply of eggs: usually between two shillings and three shillings and sixpence per sitting of 13 eggs. Both breeders and duckers realised that they were fortunate to be reasonably close to London and its wealthy customers. They also appreciated that it was important to catch this market at its best seasons: Christmas, early Spring and Easter. Early Spring was especially important, when the game season had ended. At these times high prices could be obtained, rising to as much as 21 shillings a pair, whereas prices would fall later in the year.

During the 18th and early 19th centuries it seemed that every householder at Duck End bred ducks, usually with six drakes to twenty ducks. These stock ducks were carefully selected the previous year, using the breeder's skilled knowledge developed over the years. A good drake was essential, and worth spending extra money on, for his qualities would be transferred to the broods of all the ducks with which he had mated. [14] The ducks and drakes lived and mated on a nearby pond, each with its owner's marking on its head or neck. Once the egg-laying season had begun (brought on early with rich feeding), they would be driven home each afternoon to an outhouse. Ducks usually laid their eggs at night or early morning, after which they would be allowed to make their way back to the pond. A drake always led the way, his clutch of ladies following in line.

*It was delightful to watch that waddling line of white passing over the carpet of deep green, every neck and body zig-zagging with every step.* [15]

### *The Duckers*

Duckers were considered a better class of labourer. They had managed to save enough from their hard-earned income to set themselves up in the business of ducking. A successful ducker needed a hard-working wife, who could – during the season – take over the onerous responsibility of rearing the delicate young ducklings and preparing them for the market, whilst her husband continued his part-time or full-time labouring. Perhaps some day they would be able to buy a cottage, and move into small-scale farming or some sort of trading, for conditions were grim at Duck End. Large families occupied dilapidated cottages, some with just one room up and one down: damp, gloomy, insanitary and very crowded.

Ducks were poor, unreliable sitters, so the Aylesbury duckers scoured the countryside for broody hens. Once the eggs had been collected from the breeder, they were placed as quickly as possible under a broody hen, 13 to a sitting, for an incubation period of 28 days. At this early stage the ducker's bedroom was usually the only suitable place for a row of nesting boxes! Each day the hens would need feeding, and their nests would be checked for broken eggs. During the final week the eggs were sprinkled with luke-warm water to soften the shells, hopefully making hatching easier. In a day or two the ducklings would be strong enough to be moved into a larger group after which the hen's duties were temporarily over. These poor creatures were rarely allowed to keep the young ducklings for more than a day or so, and soon they would be used for further sittings.

Now it was the turn of the duckers to provide the skilled care and attention needed to bring the ducklings to maturity in just 8 weeks. The first few days were particularly crucial. These newly-hatched ducklings with their soft yellow down were delicate, and susceptible to cold, cramp and all sorts of mysterious illnesses. They needed warmth, and it was rumoured that sometimes even the bed was used! After all, their hard-earned investment was at stake. Ducking was indeed a speculative cottage industry compared to the lace or the straw-plait trades. If all went well in the next few days, the new brood would probably be reared in the living room. The Rev. John Priest reported: [16]

> A poor man whom I visited in January 1808 had just one living room. In it were ducks of three growths: in one corner were 18 about four weeks old; at another corner was a brood a fortnight old; and at a third corner a brood just a week old.

Other sources tell us that two hundred ducks in a room twelve feet square was common. It was impossible to house-train them, yet no proper water supply was available for cleaning up. Drinking water for the ducks was very often provided in low troughs so that they could both drink and paddle. But, oh dear, the mess!

During their first week of life, the ducklings were fed several times a day on hard-boiled eggs chopped finely, together with boiled rice and bullocks' liver, cut up small. Then the fattening began in earnest. Three times a day barley meal and 'tallow greaves' (the dregs of melted fat) became their rich diet. A special grit, found locally at Long Marston and Gubblecote, was added to their drinking water which, it was claimed, would aid their digestion, keep them healthy and also clean their bills. The remaining weeks of their lives were spent drowsing, lazy with weight. Gorging themselves they soon put on flesh. Some cottages had a backyard or garden, to which the rapidly fattening ducks could be removed. The garden could be divided up into pens using planks placed edgeways across the ground. Here the young ducklings were divided up into batches according to their age. This must have been far nicer for the ducks, and the ducker and his family, but other problems arose:

> A cottage garden given over to duck breeding was not an inviting sight, and the stench after a warm June shower was even worse. For no matter what efforts were made to keep them clean, the paddling feet of young ducks and their continual need for water caused the pens to be always dirty with slime. And one ducker would say to another over the duck pens, "I wonder what those who'll eat them would say if they could see the places where they are bred." [17]

Before long the ducks reached maturity, and were ready to market. Killing and plucking took place in the early morning. Swiftly the duckling's neck was broken back, and its body was held upside down so that the blood ran back into its head, ensuring that the flesh remained white. Women were sometimes hired to help with the plucking. The ducks were kept cool until the carrier's covered waggon arrived, when they were packed into hampers, known locally as 'flats', ready for their journey by road to the London market at Smithfield.

### 1840 – 1850: The Development of the Trade
During this period important changes took place in the size and location of the Aylesbury duck

industry. London's population was increasing rapidly, and with it the number of its wealthy inhabitants, prepared to pay for luxury foods like duck. The opening in 1839 of Aylesbury's branch railway link to London, which replaced the slow horse-drawn carriers' carts was a big stimulus to the trade, for the railways provided a fast and easy connection to London's expanding market at Smithfield. By 1850 it was reported that, *"often in the Spring, in one night, a ton weight of ducklings are taken by rail from Aylesbury and nearby villages to the metropolis"*. Until this time the ducks from Aylesbury were just called English Whites. However, in 1851 they were exhibited at the Crystal Palace under the name "Aylesbury Ducks", and the name stuck. Changes were also being made in the location of the industry, because problems were increasing at Duck End. Although a hardy breed, the artificial conditions needed to fatten the ducklings quickly made them delicate and prone to disease. Various ailments could result in the ducklings dying by the score, and many a ducker was ruined by duck fever. A speck upon the eye was the first symptom, which then spread over the whole eyeball. The duckling soon lost its appetite, and died. Restocking was useless, for years of rearing large numbers of ducklings in cramped quarters had fouled the soil. So gradually ducking moved to the surrounding villages, where fresh ground and larger gardens reduced the problem of disease. For instance, during the season, the village of Weston Turville was overflowing with ducklings, and out of season the breeding stock happily explored the local streams and ponds.

### 1850 - 1900: Prosperity

In 1891 Kelly's Directory reported, *"More than 25,000 ducks of the Aylesbury breed are sent annually to London"*. By 1895 there were no less than 27 duckers in Weston Turville, 7 in Bierton, 3 in Aston Clinton and 1 in Buckland. Haddenham, with 9 duckers, was the centre of a second area, which included Dinton and Ford with 3 duckers, Cuddington 1, Winchendon 1 and Bishopstone 1. This area used the Haddenham and Thame stations to reach London. A delightful description of Haddenham and its ducklings can be found in Walter Rose's 'Good Neighbours'. In the early 20th century a third area developed in and around Pitstone. In 1915 it had 4 duckers, Ivinghoe 3, and Edlesborough 2. Pitstone with its orchards, giving protection from the sun, was said to be, *"a very fine place to bring up young ducklings"*. [18]

A very helpful sales system had been arranged by the railway companies. The plucked and trussed ducklings, packed into the 'flats', would be collected regularly from the ducker's home. Onto each flat the ducker would attach a consignment label stating his name and the number of birds he was sending to a particular Smithfield salesman. The railway company would be responsible for its delivery, and would later receive payment from the salesman. After deducting the cost of carriage, and the salesman's commission, the ducker would receive his cheque. Thus all the work and worry of collection, delivery and marketing was undertaken by the railway. Its charges for this service were very reasonable: at most 3d a duckling, hopefully leaving a generous profit for the ducker.

By 1870 duckers in the Vale had been receiving £20,000 annually, and by 1900 this had probably increased by 50%. However, the costs of the eggs, the broody hens, the duck food, the losses due to infertile eggs, broken eggs, and ducklings killed by disease were considerable. Despite all this it was a lucrative industry especially in the second half of the 19th century, and for many duckers, whose families assisted with the rearing, a very worthwhile part-time occupation, when combined with regular or part-time work. However, large duck farms developed during this period, using modern methods in keeping with the new sanitary regulations. John Kersley Fowler, whom you will meet again in a later chapter, and William Weston both bred ducklings in large rearing sheds. It was found that a new breed from China, the Pekin duck, was a very hardy breed and a prolific layer, whose ducklings matured quickly and yielded a white tasty meat. It crossed well with the Aylesbury duck, and this gave added vitality to the young birds.

### The Decline of the Industry

For years the Aylesbury area held a monopoly of the Aylesbury duck, but gradually this broke down, as the industry developed first in Bedfordshire and later in eastern Oxfordshire. By the early twentieth century entirely new areas had developed large-scale duck farms: Lancashire, Norfolk and Lincolnshire, for example. In response to this, production in the Vale decreased, and World War I hastened the decline. The cost of duck food soared. The railways no longer provided cheap transport. Now duckers had to provide their own flats, deliver them to the station, and deal directly with the markets. The Aylesbury ducker could not accept that only large-scale production would yield profits; that to buy stock locally was to risk in-breeding and consequent degeneracy of the breed; and that tainted soil could not be tolerated. As early as 1911 a writer observed:

> *Aylesbury men still maintain that their birds are the finest in the world, but their pre-eminence has been lost, and birds from other districts now compete with them successfully . . . Soft bill, which appears to be the result of close breeding, and other weaknesses are now seriously prevalent in Bucks., whilst they are practically unknown elsewhere.* [19]

So, large duck farms prospered, but small-scale ducking had almost vanished by the end of World War One. Of course, in villages with a suitable pond, some ducks were still kept (Plate C22).

## The Needle-Makers of Long Crendon

This highly specialised industry was concentrated along both sides of Long Crendon's High Street. Tradition has it that its founder was Christopher Greening, born in 1587, for beside his name in the parish register has been added, " *This man first in Britain brought out needle-making* ". He died in 1664, a blind man due, it was commonly believed, to using an emery wheel for pointing the needles. In these earlier times iron wire had been used for needles in Britain. However, on the continent steel needles were common, and later were imported into Britain. Religious persecution forced some of the continent's skilled craftsmen to emigrate, and some sought refuge in Britain, to which they brought their trade secrets.

We know that a John Warwick of Long Crendon was apprenticed to a John Jones of London, a freeman of the Needle-makers' Company. He returned to Long Crendon with a colleague, and it seems probable that the knowledge which he had acquired put new life into its industry for, during the next 100 years, many new surnames appeared in the records: Turner, Gregory, Friday, Scott, Wheatley and above all Harris and Shrimpton, as the village became the centre of British needle-making. In 1736 Henry Young of Long Crendon wrote,

> *In most cases the living rooms of the workers were their workshops. The industry prospered, and at times some of the needle-makers made themselves merry at the alehouse. Inevitably this upset some of their more peaceful neighbours, so much so that the parish constable was obliged to take the ringleaders into custody, and they found themselves with their feet in the stocks, where they were jeered at by their boon companions.* [20]

By 1798 the Buckinghamshire Posse Comitatus for Long Crendon listed twenty-one needle-makers in the village, including eleven Shrimptons. Remember, too, that this was a roll-call for military purposes, and excluded those under the age of 15 or over 60.

In the 18th century needle-making was still a cottage industry, but division of labour had arrived. Each worker concentrated on just one process, and then put the needles in the big cupboard beside his fireplace. The worker in the adjoining cottage had access to this same cupboard, and could help himself to the needles as soon as he had the time and the inclination. The various stages of production included 'soft work' such as cutting the wire into the exact lengths required for the finished product, and very dangerous work like dry grinding to point the needles. This process produced tiny specks of steel which caused serious lung and eye trouble. Intermediate processes included hardening, when the needles were placed on an iron plate, which was held over a charcoal fire until it was red hot, before plunging the needles into cold water. Scouring followed, when the needles were placed on a sheet of buckram sprinkled with sharp sand from the River Thame, covered with soft soap, before being rolled into a package and well tied. This would be rolled back and forth under the feet of the workers, or given to some children who, for a halfpenny, would kick the package up and down the street. Finally the needles were packaged and dispatched to the customers.

The Shrimpton family dominated the Long Crendon industry and, for them, large families were the norm. The baptismal records reveal that 204 Shrimpton children were born between 1754 and 1835. Old Thomas Shrimpton boasted eight daughters and eight sons, six of them needle-makers. Two Shrimpton brothers, William and Thomas, produced 15 sons between them, twelve becoming needle-makers.

At the beginning of the 19th century there was increasing competition from Redditch in Worcestershire. Not only were they selling needles, but also manufacturing them. They had the advantages of water power, cheap coal and an enthusiasm for new machines and progress generally. For example, at Redditch the needles' eyes were being stamped out by machines, rather than fashioned by hand. Scouring was done in the water mills, which not only saved labour, but also gave a much brighter finish. And measures were being taken to combat the dreaded "miner's asthma". By 1807 the exodus to Worcestershire had begun: some to Redditch; some to Alcester. Solomon Shrimpton and his family were amongst the first to leave, and founded the Redditch needle firm of Shrimpton and Hooper. In 1814 two of Solomon's sons set up in business there, making sail needles, while in the 1820's a third son moved to Alcester where he also made sail needles, and in 1830 a fourth son started a factory at Redditch making surgical needles, which later became Shrimpton and Fletcher. The success of these early birds persuaded others to migrate. For instance, in 1844 a party of 18 left Long Crendon for Redditch amid many sorrowful good wishes, and not a few tears. They included John Shrimpton, his family and his apprentice; Ephraim Harris and his family; and John Solomon Shrimpton, his family and apprentice. Farmer John Kirby provided the two horses and covered waggon that conveyed the adults and children, and farmer William Carter provided the four horses and covered waggon that conveyed the whole of John Shrimpton's household furniture, stock in trade and trade supplies. The journey to Redditch took 3 days. [21]

Back in Crendon life continued slowly and complacently. However, there were some efforts at modernisation. In the 1830's a post windmill was erected at Crendon to mechanise the scouring operation. It failed for lack of wind and was demolished in the 1920's. Also in 1844 a John Harris and his three sons leased the thatched witchert cottage called Harroel (now Shilling Cottage) left empty by the Shrimpton removal. A steam engine was installed in an outhouse, and the business was given the grand title, 'Harris and Sons, Albion Needle Works'. Two more cottagers followed suit in 1848. Shortly afterwards, Kirby, Beard and Company, needle merchants from London set up a factory on the Chilton Road, Long Crendon, with an 8 h.p. steam engine and modern machinery. Nine workers from Redditch were imported to teach the local workers new skills. The 1851 Census was encouraging: 47 men, 9 women, 22 boys and 24 girls were employed in the village workshops and cottages. Also, due to Kirby, Beard and Company's stand at the Great Exhibition, the demand for needles had increased substantially: it was hoped to employ 200 workers. In 1856 John Harris was able to buy his little factory, and travelled far and wide with his sample books. Unfortunately the boom did not last. The 1861 Census recorded only 53 workers, and in 1862 Kirby, Beard and Company closed down and moved to the Redditch area, taking two thirds of their workers with them. It was virtually the end of Long Crendon's 300 year domination of the industry.

**Fig. 105; A Passing-Hole between Two Cottages**
Where two needle-workers lived side by side, a worker at an early stage of production could pass his partly finished needles to his neighbour through the hole.

**Fig. 106: Cottages at Church End, Long Crendon, towards the End of the 19th Century.**
The church tower can just be seen over the rooves of the cottages. The building beyond the cottages is Long Crendon's famous Court House.

It seems that several factors contributed to the needle industry's demise at Long Crendon. The offer of the water mill on the Notley Abbey site for scouring was refused, despite the fact that it would have given the needles a better shine, and required less labour. Unlike Redditch, Crendon lacked cheap coal to generate steam power. Its nearest source of coal was the Midlands, but it had to be brought to Crendon: first by barge to Oxford, and then by waggon, which greatly increased its price. No real interest was shown in modernising production, despite offers of financial help from London dealers. It is also thought that the Crendon producers relied too much on their past reputation.

# CHAPTER 15

# DESPERATE TIMES

In 1801 there were 9 million people in England and Wales. By 1851 there were 18 million. By 1911 there were 36 million ! However, while the supply of labour increased, the demand for labour actually fell in most of southern England, including the Vale of Aylesbury. Enclosure was one reason. Much of it replaced arable cultivation by pasture for the production of meat, milk and wool, and pastoral farming required far less labour. For instance, at Aylesbury in 1808, due to enclosure and a switch to animal products, wheat growing was halved. Labour-saving machinery was another reason. As early as 1809 it was said of Buckinghamshire, *"Thrashing machines are becoming more common every day"*. Yet another reason was the ending of the French Wars (1793-1815), during which the English navy ruled the waves, and severely reduced the import of cereals from the continent. With less competition, British prices had risen. It was only in occasional years that a bumper harvest caused prices to slump. So farmers had become used to higher incomes, which few shared with their labourers. After the war, to protect the farmer by stabilising the price of wheat, Parliament passed the Corn Law of 1815. Under it, foreign wheat was excluded when the price of home-grown wheat was low i.e. *at or under* 80 shillings per quarter. But when the price of home-grown wheat was high (*above* 80 shillings per quarter), foreign wheat was allowed in duty free. It sounded very reasonable but, in practice, far from being stabilised, the price of wheat fluctuated violently, and in the long run fell. With their income falling, farmers economised on labour, only to find themselves paying increased unemployment doles through the poor rate. All this was specially noticeable in 1815/16 when, at the end of the French wars, 400,000 servicemen returned from the continent looking for jobs[1], while at the same time competition from foreign wheat reduced farm incomes. To reduce expenditure, still more farmers reduced labour costs by employing machines, especially for the labour-intensive threshing. Meanwhile, the 1662 Settlement Act made the employment situation even worse, because it still prevented the labourer from leaving his parish. So even when jobs existed, the unemployed labourer could not move to fill them.

The result was low wages for those with a job, and unemployment for the rest. Even regular work was so low paid that the labourer and his family had insufficient food, fuel and clothing, and could only afford inadequate and dilapidated accommodation. These were the Poor *"that fare hard"*, and they were poor to a degree which we find difficult to understand. The rest were the Paupers, *"that really pinch and suffer"*. They included the unemployed and the unemployables: the old, the infirm, the cripples, the harmless lunatics, the handicapped, the senile, and the widows, especially those with children. The paupers' plight was desperate. With little or no income they suffered at best from hunger and deficiency diseases, and at worst from starvation. Both the Poor and the Paupers relied, to some extent, upon female and child labour for essentials like boots and breeches, and a little extra food or firing. For this the women and children plaited straw or made lace while, for a pittance, the younger lads went on the farms, working long hours crow-starving, or as general drudges.

## THE ADMINISTRATION OF POOR RELIEF BEFORE 1834

The Landed Interest dominated Parliament, and was well aware of the excesses that starving peasants had inflicted upon their lords and masters during the French Revolution. Parliament feared a repetition of this in England, and used the product of a compulsory poor rate to relieve the worst sufferings of *"the inferior multitude"*. The poor rate was levied upon the owners or occupiers of property in each parish, and collected by two or three members of the parish Vestry, known as the Overseers of the Poor. It was the landowners (or occupiers) who paid by far the greatest poor rate. Thus, at Princes Risborough in 1826, James Grace's farmland was valued at £313-6s-0d and rated at £15-13-3½d, whereas the Cross Keys public house plus an allotment was only valued at £15-18s-6d and rated at 15s-11½d, and the Rev. Meade's parsonage, valued at just £10, paid a mere 10s. [2]

The Overseers also delivered the proceeds to the impoverished in cash or in kind. These doles were called 'outdoor relief', to distinguish them from 'indoor relief', for which the claimant had to leave home and go into the parish workhouse, a step only contemplated by the really desperate. Parish vestries tried various methods of calculating the doles, but from 1796 to 1834, the Speenhamland System of poor relief was widely adopted. It supplemented the low wages received by the agricultural labourers by varying the amount of the dole according to the size of the labourer's family and the price of bread. When studying Tables 17 and 18 remember that the doles were given to all those who, for whatever reason, earned less than the dole. So a man with a wife and four children was entitled to a dole of 9s-6d per week, but if he managed to earn 5s-0d in a week would only receive a dole of 4s-6d (i.e. 9s-6d less 5s-0d) per week. Of course, everyone worked a six day week. Besides funding the doles, the poor rate was also used to help the poor in all sorts of ways as the examples of supplementary assistance in Table 19 indicate.

**Table 17: Weekly Scale for Poor Relief (Doles) at Aylesbury: Nov. 1829** [3]

| Recipient | s - d | Recipient | s - d |
|---|---|---|---|
| Man and wife | 5 – 6 | Man, wife and 3 children | 8 - 0 |
| Old man | 4 - 0 | Man, wife and 4 children | 9 - 6 |
| Old woman | 3 - 6 | Man, wife and 5 children | 10 - 6 |
| Man, wife and child | 6 - 0 | Widow * | 2 - 0 |
| Man, wife and 2 children | 7 - 0 | Widower * | 3 - 0 |
| * And one shilling per child | | | |

**Table 18: Princes Risborough: Examples of Payment of Doles 1833** [4]

| Recipient | £- - s - d |
|---|---|
| Wm. Clark – 3 days sick (*presumably had wife and 4 children*) | 5s-3d |
| Sarah Gomme – husband gone for soldier | 1s-6d |
| Thomas Meaks – ill | 2s-0d |
| Sam. Hughes unemployed: mill broke down: wife + 4 children | £1-0s-0d |
| John Hister for keep of 22 people in workhouse for 2 weeks | £6-12-0d |

**Table19: Princes Risborough - Supplementary Assistance to Paupers c. 1829** [5]

| Assistance | Cost |
|---|---|
| M.Lacey for part of a wooden leg for Joseph Bristow | 4s-0d |
| Two women for laying out J. Walker | 3s-0d |
| Thos Meade to Wycombe for medicines by order of the vestry | 6s-0d |
| Mrs Shard for a pair of blankets | 15s-0d |
| Order for removal of Mrs Hunt and daughter | 16s-0d |
| Summons for John East for his refusal to pay poor rates | 4s-0d |
| Mary Bailey's bastard | 1s-6d |

The Speenhamland System, on which the dole (Table17) was calculated, had one major advantage: it protected the worker and his family from actual starvation. It had three disadvantages. Firstly, there was no inducement for the labourer to work harder to secure higher wages, or for farmers to vary their labourers' wages according to their age, effort and ability. Under Speenhamland, ability and effort were irrelevant. Whatever the man earned, if it was less than his due under Speenhamland, a dole was paid to make it up to that level. Secondly, the 'upper classes' maintained that the allowances for wives and children encouraged early marriages and large families. Finally, even an *unemployed* labourer still received the full Speenhamland dole. Due to this, some workers ensured their own unemployment by deliberately antagonising the farmers with sheer idleness and verbal abuse, knowing that they would still get the full dole from the parish, and have plenty of time for gardening, poaching, etc..[6]

### The Workhouses before 1834

Under the poor law the parish vestry could use the poor rate to provide communal accommodation for its poor. It was variously known as the Parish House (at Marsworth), the Poorhouse (at Wingrave), and the Workhouse (at Aylesbury). Such houses varied greatly in size. In the early 19th century, Wingrave's workhouse accommodated up to ten parishioners, who were totally destitute, and usually elderly, whereas Aylesbury's house held forty. It was the houses with no segregation between the aged, the idiots, the senile, the children, etc., which gave the institution the bad name perpetuated by Crabbe: [7]

> *Theirs is yon house that holds the village poor*
> *Where walls of mud scarce bear the broken door.*
> *There children dwell who know no parents' care;*
> *Parents, who know no children's love, dwell there!*
> *Heartbroken matrons on their joyless bed,*
> *Foresaken wives and mothers never wed.*
> *Dejected widows with unheeded tears,*
> *And crippled age with more than childhood fears,*
> *The lame, the blind and, far happier they*
> *The moping idiot, and the madman gay!!*

Too many such monstrosities did exist, but Eden's monumental study of the poor at the end of the 18th century makes it clear that this was the workhouse at its worst. Many small village poorhouses were much less forbidding and Wingrave was fairly typical. Built of brick in Church Street, on a corner of the churchyard, the poorhouse faced onto the Village Green, from which one walked straight into the fields. The familiar sounds of the farm animals, church bells, the blacksmith's hammer and the threshers' flails were clearly heard, and for those who were still mobile the smithy, the village pond and the Rose and Crown were all nearby. The inmates would have known one another since childhood. Their family and friends could visit them. They could attend the church in which they had worshipped since childhood, and they had long known the vicar, the vestry and the overseers, who had long known them. Neither was the regime particularly harsh, as the Overseers' Accounts indicate: see Table 20.

Neither were all workhouses tumbledown wrecks. In 1815 Marsworth spent £83-14s-6½ on repairs to its poorhouse. Even so, as Frederick Eden pointed out, there was massive prejudice against poorhouses:

> *Although it is certain that in the workhouse the Poor are far better provided with the important necessaries of food, clothing, habitation and fuel than they could be by their most industrious exertions at home, this mode of receiving parochial relief is universally disliked. Many distressed families prefer the chance of starving among relatives, friends*

*and neighbours in their own native village to the mortifying alternative of being well-fed, well-lodged and well-clothed in a Poorhouse amongst a motley selection of idiots, vagrants and the sick.*[9]

Of course, if they refused to enter the workhouse, there was still outdoor relief, which (at the discretion of the Overseers) might include payments for home nursing. [10]

**Table 20: Wingrave and Rowsham: Expenses of Ye Poorhouse –1811** [8]

| Nov 15 | Vegetables | 1s-6d |
|---|---|---|
| Nov 22 | Vegetables 1/-  Ashes 6d | 1s-6d |
| | 5 persons Tea and Tobacco | 3s-6d |
| | Pd  Mr Hunt for cheese to bill | £1-7s-11d |
| | Pd  Mr Maltby for a side of bacon 73lbs at 10½d | £3-3s-10½d |
| | Pd  Mr Griffin for bread to bill | £9-12s-11½d |
| | Pd  Mr Grace to bill | £1-9s-7½d |
| | Pd  Mr Mortimer to bill | 5s-4d |
| | Pd  Mr Maltby for milk  4 wks at 1s-9d per week | 7s-0d |
| | Pd  Humphrey for potatoes | 3s-4d |

## SOLVING THE PROBLEMS
### The Non-payment of Poor Rates
Throughout England the poor rates rose. At Doddershall, they were under £16 in 1776 and £84 in 1822. At Great Horwood the poor cost nearly £41 in 1774, but £836 in 1819. By 1827 Aylesbury's rates reached £4,640. In 1827 Mr Richard Gurney, an Aylesbury farmer, was summoned to explain why he did not pay his poor-rate.[11] He told the Justices that he wanted to be summoned so that he might explain how matters were managed in his parish. First, they had had five rates since Easter. Next, due to unemployed labourers being paid the full dole, he could get no men to work for him. So his corn could not be harvested. The Bench quickly solved the problem. They informed Mr Gurney that they did not make the poor laws, and he must pay, which he did at once. He was fortunate to be able to do so. Many farmers were abandoning their tenancies, because their funds had run out. As a result it was becoming difficult to let land. In 1830 a good farm of 270 acres at North Marston was *"on its owner's hands"* for want of a tenant. Just one quarter's poor rates had cost the owner £40. By October 1831 a further 300 to 400 acres of land were unoccupied, and eighty able-bodied men were unemployed. By 1833, 42 farms near Aylesbury were vacant. People said, *"The poor law has eaten all the farmers up."* It became difficult for the Overseers to collect enough rates.

### Private Initiatives to Help the Poor [12]
By 1816 the distress due to unemployment was so great that public collections for the poor were organised in Aylesbury, and many of the county's leading citizens made individual contributions. For instance: in 1822 the Aylesbury churchwardens distributed nearly £100 to the poor, obtained from various town charities; in 1823 the late Duke of Bridgwater left £6,000 per annum to employ and improve the Ashridge poor; in 1826 the Rev. John Dell distributed the carcases of six sheep among the Walton poor; in 1827 Aylesbury vestry purchased 100 tons of coal, for sale at a reduced price in the winter; and in 1830 the Duke of Buckingham distributed coals to the poor of Stowe, Hillesden, Ratcliffe and Finmere. What we don't know is what proportion of the poor this generosity relieved.

### The Provision of Work for the Unemployed [13]

The authorities found this very difficult to provide but, as the following examples show, some jobs were created. In 1823 the Aylesbury Vestry rented land and re-let it to paupers in allotments. In 1827 paupers were employed to clear Aylesbury's streets of pigs and vagrants. By 1830 a twice daily attendance at roll-call was required, and anyone not answering was fined half-a-day's pay: it was said that some were too idle to turn up. In 1831 ninety men and boys were employed at a cost of £24 per week to *"grind away birch brooms in a pretence of sweeping the streets"*. In 1830 Buckingham's surplus labourers were sent to a stone-pit about two miles away. Each man returned carrying a great stone. This was the morning's work. It was repeated in the afternoon. In 1834 Buckingham Parish acquired 103 acres to let out in small allotments. In 1831 Waddesdon and Stone employed 130 men repairing the roads.

### Early Emigration

By 1830 many agricultural labourers had lost both patience and hope, and began to consider emigration. The following is one of many departures recorded by Robert Gibbs, a local historian:

> In 1832 there was some stir in the Aylesbury Wharf Yard, as eighty emigrants "embarked" for the United States. They were mostly from Waddesdon, from which village they were brought in by Benjamin Crook's waggon. These folks were stowed away in Mrs England's boats and dragged up the canal at the rate of about two miles an hour, and in this or some other as miserable a style have to make their way to Liverpool. There is hardly a district in the county of Bucks in which families are not packing up, their intention being to emigrate this spring to the U.S. or a colony. [14]

**Fig. 107: The Emigrants' Farewell.**

Even after the train service to Euston began in June 1839, most of the Vale's emigrants had to begin their journey by road to the station in Aylesbury.

In these early years it is remarkable that so many people were prepared to emigrate: the journey took over three months; the destination was virtually unknown; modern communications didn't exist and letters to relatives at home took twelve weeks. The journey absorbed what little savings they had, because parish vestries (composed largely of farmers) were reluctant to assist emigration, fearing that wages would increase as farmers competed for the reduced supply of labour. The Poor Law permitted Boards of Guardians to assist emigration, but it was not mandatory: nationally, between 1834 and 1845, an average of only 800 to 1000 were sent out each year.[15]

## THE PROTESTS MOUNT

Emigration, charity and job creation, certainly helped, but the supply of labour still much exceeded the demand. As the plight of the paupers worsened, their protests became more desperate.

> *In February 1833 fifty or sixty paupers went to the home of Mr Vincent Corbet, the overseer for Haddenham, and insisted on entering. They said they would have money or food before they left. One sat down in an armchair and smoked his pipe. Another made the fire up. Another asked the way to the cellar. Another ordered his supper and asked for some ham to be fried for him. Mr Corbet sent for the constables, but they were useless when they came. Mrs Corbet was very much frightened and was taken seriously ill as a result of the incident. Eventually, being remonstrated with, the intruders left. They did not display the least violence. Even so, some of them were brought before the Aylesbury magistrates, and were bound over to appear at Quarter Sessions.[16]*

Despite the penalties, which were horrendous, some of the poor and the paupers turned to crime, and the numbers convicted of poaching, common theft, and burglary escalated.[17] The following examples were typical. In July 1822 two men were sentenced for robbing the Rev. Dell's house in Walton, Aylesbury. One was transported for seven years and the other imprisoned for one year. In March 1824 several men were convicted of stealing 38 sheep from John Dodwell of Long Crendon. They were all sentenced to death, but the sentences were later commuted to imprisonment. In May 1825 some prisoners from Aylesbury Gaol were transported to the colonies: they had been convicted of crimes ranging from killing men to killing ducks! By December 1826, of 172 prisoners in Aylesbury gaol, over fifty were there for poaching. In June 1827 the papers were full of burglaries and the like. In February 1828, at the Lent assizes at Aylesbury, Robert Saunders was tried for burglary at Radnage. He was 22 years old, and was one of four ruffians who broke into, and ransacked, the home of Rev. Jones. Saunders was convicted, and sentenced to death, *"without hope of mercy"*.

As the years passed with no improvement in their condition, the labourers' protests became more violent. In November 1830 incendiary fires and machine breaking were reported by farmers at Nash, Wavendon, Sedrup, Stone, Winchendon, Long Crendon, etc.. Another farmer stated that he had met a mob of eighty men near Winchendon, who told him they intended to break all the machinery they could get at. Altogether, in the Vale and North Bucks. in excess of 31 machines were lost in 16 machine-breaking attacks. In a lecture at Waddesdon in 1884 Mr Robert Gibbs of Aylesbury remembered:[18]

> *Mr Roads of Winchendon had his machinery set fire to and destroyed. A mob went to Mr Ballard's of Upper Winchendon, took possession of a new thrashing machine, heaped straw upon it and burnt it to ashes in the presence of the owner, who dare not interfere to save it. On the night of the 26th thirty men went to Blackgrove Farm, on the road to Aylesbury, and called to Mr Rickard's bailiff that they would burn him out if he did not appear. They demanded and obtained all the machinery on the farm, piled it up, and then fetched a large quantity of straw from the rick-yard, and finished by setting the whole lot on fire.*

## Recollections J: Sentencing the Machine Breakers *

*15th January 1831* On the last day of the special assizes at Aylesbury, the final sentences dealt with cases involving force or intimidation. In 17 such cases, in the judge's words:

*The sentence of death will be recorded against you, instead of being formally passed. This means that your lives will be spared, but on what terms it is for His Majesty to determine.*

Neither of the remaining two prisoners appeared to be prepared for the sentence that awaited them. And so, when the judges placed on their heads the square pieces of black cloth, commonly called black caps, the wretched men shrank instantly and appeared confounded. Then Mr Justice Park addressed them.

*Prisoners, we have struggled anxiously to prevent the sacrifice of any human life; but on the deepest and fullest consideration we found it impossible to spare yours. You, Thomas Blizzard, are a most guilty person by your own confession. You have been convicted . . . of a most serious offence at Mr Lane's mill; and you have admitted yourself to be . . . the most active and violent in the destruction of the machinery at Mr Davis's, Mr Allnutt's, Mr Plaistow's and Mr Hay's mills. You took the most active and violent part in the business, and excited others to mischief. In addition, nothing of character has been given to you. As to you, John Sarney, yours is a case of extreme wickedness. You were engaged at Mr Davis's, Mr Allnutt's and Mr Plaistow's mills. You had come out with the intention to do what you were engaged in, and you were determined to persevere till you had destroyed every machine. Moreover, it appears that you threatened the most gross personal violence; that you attempted to knock out the brains of one of the coroners of this county while on his knees struggling with the rioters; and that when a hammer was taken from one of your associates, you held up a rod of iron and threatened to knock out the brains of the man who had seized it. We think that you are a fit subject for capital punishment because yours is an aggravated case. I therefore beseech you to prepare for your appearance at the bar of your heavenly judge.*

While passing the awful sentence of death, his lordship was completely overcome by painful emotions and wept aloud. Very few could contain their tears. The effect on the prisoners was remarkable. They seemed struck dumb with grief and astonishment. Sarney cried bitterly, and Blizzard also wept, but no sound broke from either. Then the trap door was opened and the prisoners were led down the ladder into the underground passage that leads to the gaol. A petition seeking mercy for Sarney and Blizzard was signed by over 200 people including most of the jurymen and six clergymen. A second petition was signed by a farmer whose threshing machine had been destroyed, and by seven paper manufacturers, including three whose mills had been attacked.

*24th January 1831* The governor of Aylesbury Gaol received from the Secretary of State for the Home Department a respite for the condemned men. He passed on this news to Sarney and Blizzard. Their joy was excessive. They muttered broken prayers, wept, gave thanks to God, and declared their gratitude to the King for his great mercy. Their pardon was conditional upon their being transported for life. Blizzard was transported, but received a conditional pardon in 1838. Sarney was not transported. Following a petition in his favour, he was pardoned in 1836 after serving 5 years in a prison ship.

\* Compiled from The Bucks Gazette, and The Times.

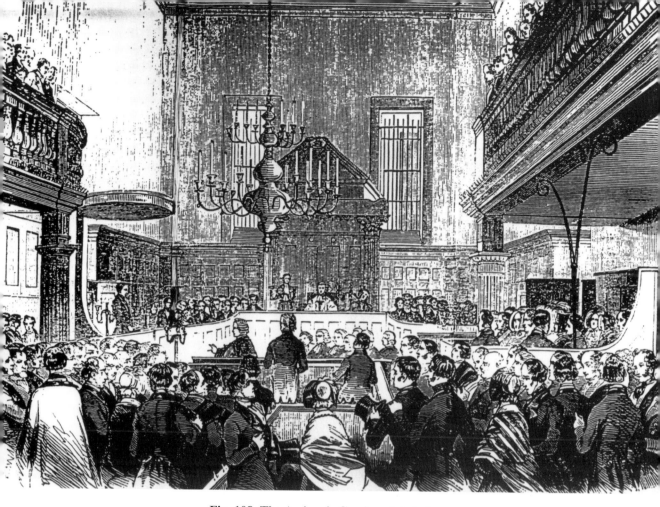

**Fig. 108: The Assizes in Session at Aylesbury.**
The scene depicted was sketched during the trial in January 1845 of John Tawell for the murder of Sarah Hart. However, it was the same court-room that accommodated the machine breakers' trial, and the packed court was typical of a trial which might lead to capital punishment. Such trials always attracted crowds, sometimes so great and so noisy that the business of the court was delayed.

Meanwhile, in the Wycombe area, there was a sudden surge of mob violence, which came to a head at the end of November 1830 with attacks on paper mills in the Wye Valley. On Monday the 29th of November there was a major confrontation at Lane's Mill, only a quarter of a mile from Wycombe. A mob of over 50 men, armed with axes, sledge hammers, crowbars and pickaxes, attacked the stout wooden door which blocked the entrance to the mill, and eventually smashed holes in it, through which one of the defenders threw a gallon of acid, and another fired a gun. This produced a respite while some of the mob retired to the mill stream to wash off the acid. Soon they were back, and having broken down the door, crowded into the mill and began smashing the machinery. This success persuaded 200 or more waverers to join in, and the mob smashed the machinery at two more mills, before pausing at the nearest inn for some liquid refreshment. Two mills further on, the authorities caught up with them. Throughout the morning, special constables had followed the mob, so that they could report on its activities and speculate as to its future targets. Now reinforcements arrived in the form of thirty special constables from Beaconsfield, and a party of ten horsemen. They charged the mob, only to be driven back by a flurry of stones. At this point

Colonel Vyse, the High Sheriff of Buckinghamshire, arrived with a number of gentlemen, and called on the mob to disperse. They answered with a further volley of stones. Meanwhile 20 men from the mob got into the mill and destroyed its machinery. Finally the tide was turned by the arrival on horseback of a party of His Majesty's Staghounds. A further charge into the rioters left the authorities in control, and holding a number of prisoners. The rest melted away, but 20 were later caught at a local inn. Soon a party of Guards from Windsor, and a strong force of special constables from Eton, arrived, which helped to reduce the general tension in the area. With the magistrates overwhelmed by sheer numbers, special assizes were held at Aylesbury to try the machine breakers. There were 126, many of whom had no criminal record. So, on the fifth day, when the sentences were pronounced there was a wide range of penalties. Some were transported, others received various terms of imprisonment, while some were simply fined and discharged. The court dealt very leniently with the simple cases of breaking machines, but where there had been force or intimidation the sentences were severe: see Recollections J. [19] For the present, the crisis was contained.

**C24 and C25: Harvesting with Modern Equipment**

The combine harvester cuts the crop and threshes it. The grain is blown into a lorry, or (as here) into a container drawn by a tractor, though the latter is hidden by the combine. The straw is ejected, and later picked up by a baler. This forms it into a cylindrical or rectangular bale, which can easily be moved and stacked by a tractor or JCB fitted with a spike.

To left
**C26: "As Prolific as Poppies"**
This floral display was probably the result of a year's set-aside: to reduce an over-production of crops (see Chapter 19). The very same field can be seen at a distance in Plate C31.

Below
**C27: Rape Dominates the Scene**
in parts of the eastern Vale. After the oil has been extracted, the residue of the seed is made into rape-cake for animal feed.

**C28: An Arable Panorama**

The BSE epidemic and the high cost of providing for the collection of milk by tankers severely reduced the Vale's herds of cattle. Many farmers turned to arable crops, as this picture demonstrates.

**C29: Winslow's Sheep Market**

The rearing of sheep continues to be important in the Vale, as this scene from Winslow's sheep auction indicates. Huge lorries ship the animals by the hundred to distant destinations.

### C30: Scenes like this are now quite rare

According to a friendly farmer, Vale farmers in general have little confidence as to the profitability of milk and meat, and in consequence are concentrating on arable crops. The white tower on the skyline belongs to Wingrave church.

### C31: Housing Development at Princes Risborough

Development within villages and towns is kindest to the countryside. Even large estates are better than the ribbon development of pre-war times, but they do create an urban 'feel' to the countryside as this view from the Chilterns demonstrates.

## Chapter 16

# A TIME OF LAST RESORTS

### THE POOR LAW AMENDMENT ACT 1834

We have seen that the years from 1815-1834 were desperate times for the agricultural labourers of the South Midlands. There was worse to come. In 1834, encouraged by the defeat of the Wycombe machine breakers, the government introduced the Poor Law Amendment Act. This draconian measure had two fundamental flaws. It falsely assumed that pauperism was due to a character defect which generated idleness, unreliability, drunkenness, financial incompetence and violence. It also assumed that all able-bodied men could find employment if they tried hard enough. To ensure that they did try, the new law reduced the parish poor rates firstly by reducing the weekly doles; secondly by limiting outdoor relief (doles to people living in their own homes) to the aged and infirm; and thirdly by giving relief to the unemployed only if they and their dependants entered a workhouse, where life would be made as unappealing as possible.

> *For many labourers the Act was the final confirmation that landowners, farmers and clergymen placed their own selfish economic interests before those of the wider community. With this realization came sullenness and a desire for revenge.[1] It became a matter of congratulation among the men . . . that they had succeeded in 'doing' a person in a better position, or even if they had 'sloped summat' from the well-to-do.[2]*

This Act was the last straw, and the labourers soon returned to their last resorts: arson, theft and emigration.

### Pinching the Paupers and the Poor

The cuts in the doles began what contemporaries called *"a pinching time"* for the paupers and the poor, who (by 21st century standards) were already severely pinched! Even before the new Poor Law Amendment Bill had passed its second reading in the Commons, the Aylesbury Vestry decided to reduce its poor law doles with immediate effect. There were immediate repercussions.[3]

> *On the 18th April 1834, able-bodied paupers collecting their doles at the Workhouse at Aylesbury, rioted and several were summoned before the magistrates. On July 1st nine Aylesbury paupers were indicted for riot. The prisoners challenged every farmer called on the jury, which caused some delay. Mr J.K.Fowler was the principal witness. He stated that the Select Vestry had thought it expedient to reduce the pay, and that when the able-bodied paupers were offered their money, they would not take it. About 50 or 60 assembled and refused to leave the Workhouse, nor would they allow anyone to go in or out. He saw Mr John Gurney holding a man of the name of Webb, and many scuffling to rescue Webb. When he went to Mr Gurney's assistance, a brickbat was hurled at him. The men were all convicted, but the Select Vestry recommended mercy, and they were each sentenced to 14 days' imprisonment and to find bail for good conduct for 12 months.*

### THE WORKHOUSE TEST

To administer the new law, parishes were combined into groups called Unions. The authorities believed that if all the paupers of a Union were housed in one building, there would be savings through such things as bulk buying of food and clothing, better use of staff time, lower legal expenses per inmate, etc.. However, in each Union the *existing* accommodation consisted of

**Figs. 109 (a) and 109 (b): The Leighton Buzzard Workhouse in the 19th Century:
The Elegant Facade and the Obnoxious Interior.**

It is extremely difficult to find illustrations of conditions inside workhouses before 1850. These engravings which turned up quite unexpectedly in a collector's album illustrate just two of the reasons why 19th century workhouses were dreaded, viz. gross lack of privacy, and segregation by sex rather than family.

small poorhouses scattered over a large number of parishes, but none of them large enough to cope with the unemployed from the whole of the Union. At this time the best that could be said was that new centralised workhouses *"were contemplated throughout the county"*. In reality it was 8 years before the new Aylesbury Workhouse came into use. Desperate to reduce the poor rate, the authorities were not prepared to wait so long. So, years before new workhouses had been built, some Unions decided to close their smallest workhouses and transfer the occupants to parishes with spare capacity. Thus, it was decided to transfer the inmates of the Chesham Workhouse to the Amersham Workhouse. Matters came to a head on the day of removal.[4]

> *On the 23rd May 1835 there was a pauper riot at Chesham. It was occasioned by the removal of the pauper inmates of the parish workhouse to a distant one which it would be difficult for friends and relatives to visit. Stones were thrown indiscriminately, and the horses were forcibly taken from the conveyances by which the paupers were to be removed. Mr Fuller, the magistrate, received a tremendous blow from a stone. The workhouse was attacked, and the windows broken. The metropolitan police were sent for by express. In July 1835 the ringleaders were tried at Aylesbury Quarter Sessions. Mr Joseph Heath spoke of the fury of the mob. Mr Maltby, on behalf of the prisoners, explained that their intention was not mischief, but to show their detestation of the new Poor Law Act. The Chairman pointed out to the jury that they were not there to try the merits of the Act, but to decide if the prisoners had broken the law. A verdict of guilty was returned and the prisoners were sentenced to various terms of imprisonment.*

### Less Eligibility

In case paupers did apply for indoor relief, the authorities deliberately made conditions in the workhouse worse than that of an *"independent labourer of the lowest class"*, a deterrent known as *'less eligibility'*. In practice, the authorities found it very difficult to impose *'less eligibility'* because the condition of starving agricultural labourers *outside* the workhouse was so low that it was hard to provide anything worse inside, without abandoning both humanity and decency. Even so, the authorities tried hard!

The old Leighton Buzzard workhouse is an example of the workhouse at its worst. Looking at its exterior (Fig. 109), who would suppose that it would subject its residents to the gross abuse

**Fig. 110: The New Aylesbury Union Workhouse**
It was erected in 1844/45, and the buildings are still in use as part of Tindal Hospital.

of privacy depicted in Fig. 109 ? It makes one wonder what the sublime exterior of Aylesbury's new workhouse concealed (Fig. 110). Many of the *new* workhouses had an elegant public face, disguising the policy of *less eligibility* carried out within. What makes it certain that Aylesbury's new workhouse also pursued this policy, is what kept all workhouses pursuing it, namely the fact that it was government policy, which was *rigorously* imposed by the Poor Law Commissioners in London. They were so domineering that they were nicknamed *'the three bashaws of Somerset House'*, a title richly deserved as their correspondence with local workhouses demonstrates. For instance, at the Aylesbury Workhouse the management was prepared to provide the elderly with a limited quantity of small beer with their supper, but it had to apply to the London Commissioners for permission, and it took an extended correspondence with them before approval was received: see Table 21 and note 11.

A lack of privacy was only one element in *"less eligibility"*. Another element was the segregation of the sexes, and the new centralised workhouses were planned so as to implement this. A contemporary view of them has survived.[5]

> *Here are not only large and small sleeping rooms but water closets, and a Chappell to promote (the inmates') spiritual welfare . . . but when I entered the building and saw the rooms with the closets, and beheld how you had provided for them in every way, I thought – this building is fit for a nobleman to dwell. But upon enquiry I found that these rooms were not for different characters, but for the separating of single familyes into four parts, thus cruelly tearing asunder man and wife, parents and children, and breaking those bonds that nought but death should break.*

Segregation was sometimes taken to such an extreme that there were separate exercise yards for husbands, wives, sons and daughters. In 1836, in his evidence to the Select Committee on Agricultural Distress, William Cox, a Buckinghamshire farmer of 1800 acres in the Vale, was asked about this:[6]

> **Questioner:** *Should you say that the regulation contemplated under the new Poor Law Act, with respect to the separation of the sexes, could be carried into effect without difficulty?*
>
> **Cox:** *I think not. Anything that does violence to human nature would be attended with difficulty.*

In many workhouses unmarried mothers were consigned to canary wards, so-called because they were forced to wear a distinctive yellow uniform. Even worse was the practice of removing the new-born babe from the mother, who only saw the child when she breast-fed it.

Another tactic intended to achieve *'less eligibility'* was the particularly hard and unpleasant work that was expected of the inmates of all workhouses. Breaking stone, picking oakum and crushing putrid cattle bones for fertiliser were some of the worst jobs. General William Booth of the Salvation Army described the stone-breaking requirement as *"Monstrous. Half a ton of stone from any man in return for partially supplying the cravings of hunger is an outrage."*[7] This regime was still in force in 1890 when Booth wrote about it. Picking oakum was an unpleasant task, for oakum was the loose fibre obtained by untwisting and unpicking old rope for use in caulking the seams of wooden boats. A third tactic was to impose strict rules, and punish breaches by prosecution in the courts. For example, relatives had to contribute to the cost of the inmates:[8]

> *In 1875 George Badrick of Wingrave was charged by Aylesbury Union with not contributing to the support of his aged mother, Sarah Badrick, who was chargeable to the common fund of the Union. He was ordered to pay 1/- per week and the costs of the prosecution.*

The inmate who failed to do the work expected of him was also prosecuted and could expect a sentence of 21 days or a month with hard labour. Also, it might be easy to get into a workhouse, but it could be more difficult to get out. Inmates were not allowed to go outside the workhouse unless they sought *"leave of absence"*, which was not readily given, even if the inmate wanted to go in search of work for a couple of days. As Thomas Pitkin of Swanbourne told the Commission on Old Age Pensions in 1894, *"It is the confinement that causes the great dislike (of the workhouse) as much as anything"*. The pauper's family had to go into the workhouse with him, and they were also subjected to severe restrictions. The Union's first priority was to put them to work. For the children this usually meant farming them out to a local employer, without so much as a *"by your leave"* to the parents. Groups of youngsters were sent from Aylesbury Workhouse to the silk mill at Tring, where they not only worked but lived. Their pay went to the workhouse. Yet another route to 'less eligibility' was the workhouse diet. Table 21 is a fair sample. It was predictable and it was boring. 62% of the meals consisted of bread and gruel, or bread and broth or just soup. There was no friendly neighbour to call with a plate of innards from the pig-killing, or some fruit or vegetables from their garden. In some workhouses not enough food was provided to sustain the workers. An extreme example was the Andover Workhouse scandal of 1845, which revealed that able-bodied paupers, employed in crushing putrid bones for manure, were so hungry that they gnawed the bones for the marrow.[9] Finally, the fabric of the building was impersonal, and the routine inviolable: there was a fixed bed-time, and one might have to share a bed with a stranger. For most inmates, distance was a bar to regular visits from friends and relatives. One had no privacy, and was separated from one's family. Especially when the running of the workhouse was contracted out to private enterprise, the management could be extremely petty and mean. A favourite economy was to refuse to pay for the ringing of a mourning bell at a pauper's funeral. In some houses there were no chairs with backs for the inmates, but only backless benches.

**Table 21: Aylesbury Union Workhouse: Weekly Diet, June 1837** [10]

| Breakfast | Bread and gruel |
|---|---|
| Dinner | Cooked meat and potatoes (4 days per week)<br>Soup (2 days per week)<br>Suet or rice pudding (1day per week) |
| Supper | Bread and broth (4 days per week)<br>Bread and cheese (3days per week)<br>Small beer daily if aged 60 years upwards (men: one pint; women: half pint) [11] |

### *Outdoor Relief Survived*

The abolition of outdoor relief was one of the principal aims of the 1834 Act, and was backed up by repeated orders from the Poor Law Commissioners in London. As one abolitionist remarked:

> *Let the Poor see and feel that their parish, although it will not allow them to perish through absolute want, is yet the hardest taskmaster, the closest paymaster, and the most harsh and unkind friend that they can apply to.[12]*

Nevertheless, the attempt to abolish outdoor relief failed. Nationally, by 1846 nearly 300,000 *able-bodied* adults were still receiving outdoor relief, [13] if only because outdoor relief was cheaper. It was cheaper because Overseers of the Poor were encouraged to reduce the rates of outdoor relief; and given low doles the unemployed labourer had an incentive to find work, and to take advantage of private charity. Consequently, in 1860 for example, in the eastern counties unemployed labourers cost 3s-5½d a week if taken into the workhouse, but only 1s-9d if relieved outside.

The reductions in the parish poor rates throughout the Aylesbury Union bear silent witness to the misery of both the paupers and the poor. For instance, the average annual expenditure for all the parishes forming the Aylesbury Union before the 1834 Act was £25,221. In the following year it was £13,234. The cost of the poor in Aylesbury parish in 1833/4/5 was £3623, and in 1836/7/8 was £1739. The rate-payers of other parishes seem to have benefited similarly.

**Fig. 111: Alms-houses at Quainton.**

The alms-houses with their two handsome porches, fine chimneys and many gables were built of warm red brick in 1687. Especially after 1834, it is important to distinguish between workhouses and alms-houses, which were quite different. The latter were usually funded by a local benefactor (often by a bequest in his will) to help the aged poor. Quite often the vicar and one or two members of his vestry, plus the local squire's lady formed a committee to administer the bequest and vet applications when a house became vacant. In today's terms it was sheltered accommodation, and was not affected by the 1834 Act. Although the tenants lived under the same roof, the building was really a terrace of separate houses, each with its own entrance. So tenants could come and go, prepare meals to their own liking, and entertain friends and relatives just as they pleased. The rent (if any) was very low. The main disadvantage of alms-houses was the shortage of places in them, especially after the passing of the 1834 Act, which had made workhouses extremely unpopular: see also Plate C23.

## THE LAST RESORTS

The transportation, imprisonment and fines which had been meted out to the machine breakers in 1830 had taught the labourers some realities. It became clear that, especially in rural areas, faces, names and addresses were known. So it was foolish to operate in the daylight, whereas night-time arson required just one man, who would be concealed by the darkness, yet could move around easily since he knew the countryside like the back of his hand. And arson needed only a rasp or two from an inconspicuous tinder box, as opposed to the considerable noise from the very visible sledgehammers and pickaxes of the machine breakers. Also, a mob recruited with too much persuasion or too many pints introduced a weak element, which would quickly betray the rest just to save its own skin. So arson became the main weapon of the protesters. In the Vale and North Bucks., for the period 1834 to 1880, Gibbs records 68 cases of arson, but only 4 of machine breaking. However, this underestimated the scale of the problem, for quite often, in between specific statements, Gibbs simply generalises, as in December 1847 when we are told,[14]

> *the reports of so many incendiary fires in the neighbourhood of Aylesbury cause great alarm.*
> *A fire brigade is to be established at Aylesbury.*

**Fig. 112: The Leighton Buzzard Fire Brigade.**
The Aylesbury version would have been similar.

Farm fires could do much more than destroy farm buildings. If barns were fired, machinery and stocks of grain awaiting threshing could also be lost. Hay stacks were a popular target. In one fire at Olney a cow-house was destroyed, and the Northampton Herald reported, *"The cries and bellowings of the animals were terrible"*. When Dr Reynold's stables at Thame were fired in 1845, two horses were burned to death. In another fire two men lost their lives trying to rescue animals. If property were not insured, arson could ruin the owner. A major problem was the prevalence of thatched rooves, for fire, thatch and a strong wind were a deadly mixture. At Dinton in 1858, due to arson, the farm buildings of Mr Howlett were destroyed by a fire which spread to the Boot public house, and two cottages. At Wendover in 1858 a fire on the farm of General Sir James Watson destroyed farm buildings worth £4,000. Sir James had recently, for the first time, used a steam engine to thresh his corn. By this time farmers knew that they were the targets of a definite campaign. In March 1850 most of Brill's farmers received threatening letters. The farm of Mr Fuller, of nearby Dorton, was fired three times in three weeks. Farmers were so alarmed by the large number of fires that they persuaded their nearest towns (Aylesbury and Leighton Buzzard, for example) to establish fire brigades. (Fig. 112) Arson may have satisfied the hot-heads amongst the labourers, but it did absolutely nothing for the income of the poor. Indeed, since the property that was destroyed had to be replaced, it may have made the farmers more careful with their money. [15]

There was also a fresh wave of sheep stealing, poaching and petty crime. In fact, there was so much sheep stealing that these reports were also often generalised. In 1836, *"There is much sheep stealing in and around Aylesbury"*. In 1837, *"Sheep stealing is again rife"*. In 1838, *"More sheep stealing"*. As late as November 1841 sheep stealing continued to increase. Where just one or two sheep were taken, the thefts were probably carried out by agricultural labourers desperate to feed their half-starved families. Indeed, some only took the prime joints, leaving behind the mangled carcase,[16] which might provide evidence of theft if disposed of near home. However, at times the number of sheep stolen in a single theft (numbers such as 12, 15, 20 and 38 appear in the records) suggests that a black market had been established. *"It is a regular trade!"* Gibbs concluded. By 1844, professional thieves were using a horse and cart to go round Quainton farms picking up sheep. Yet after 1854 the reports of sheep stealing cease completely.

In the 1820's death was commonly the punishment for theft, but in the 1830's it was sometimes commuted to imprisonment or transportation to the colonies. Even so, in 1837 at least two poachers were hung at Aylesbury. In the same year, for stealing a penny loaf, a man was jailed for 12 months, while in 1842 a boy was gaoled for four months for stealing apples valued at ½d. However, as the years passed, sheep stealers, horse thieves, house breakers and the like were increasingly sent from Aylesbury for transportation. It was not only a punishment, but a way of freeing space in the jail. In 1844 Sir Harry Verney had forecast that they were building a jail for poachers! Sure enough, in just 2 weeks in November 1846 a record 26 poachers were sent to Aylesbury's new gaol. Problems were not limited to the countryside. According to Gibbs, *"Petty thefts occur at Aylesbury almost every night and great pilfering from shops goes on after dark"*.

Despite the arson and the thefts, the hardships suffered by the poor and the paupers were recognised *"by those who can afford to be charitable"*. There were reports from all districts of the distribution of meat, coal and clothing. Certainly the usual donors of charity like the Rev. John Dell, Mr Rickford, the Earl of Buckinghamshire, and the Aylesbury Vestry continued to function, but there were also contributions from a much wider circle. Private charity probably reached a peak during the winter of 1845/6. Particularly notable were 400 blankets distributed to the poor of Thame and Risborough, 2,000 hundredweights of coal made available to the poor at 6d per cwt., and the free distributions of the Aylesbury Relief Committee: 2,224 quarts of soup, 1,310 loaves and 1,150 cwts. coal. Unfortunately, there is no evidence as to how far it went. Even Mr Gibbs had to qualify his enthusiasm with a generalisation, *"The sufferings of the poor in agricultural villages are great"*.

### The Settlement Laws

Although they were not part of the new poor law, the Settlement Acts still applied, and the Guardians of the Poor enforced them rigorously. The original act of 1662 complained that the poor and the paupers,[17]

> go from one parish to another and endeavour to settle themselves in those parishes where there is the best stock, the largest commons or waste to build cottages, and the most woods for them to burn and destroy; and when they have consumed it, then to another parish.

To counter this, the Act required that any stranger settling in a parish be removed if he or she was likely to require support from the poor rates. In practice this meant that virtually all labourers were tied to the parish in which they were judged to be settled. However, the 1662 Act was modified in 1795, so that a poor person moving to another parish could not be sent back to his original parish just because he or she only *looked likely* to require doles from the poor rate, but only if he or she *actually applied* for doles. But this only helped the poor, if they did find work. As the Bledlow labourers explained,[18]

*The Justices tell us they can do nothing. The Guardians tell us they can do nothing. We have looked for work in vain. We have gone here and there and can find none. And when we leave our parish in the fruitless search, we are deprived of the little allowance which the parish gives us. Ready as we are to work, the parish can give us no work.*

And if their search for a job in another parish *did* prove fruitless, steps would immediately be taken to return them to their original parish. Fortunately, the laws of settlement were modified in 1850, severing the last tie that bound people to one particular spot.

### Surviving Under Reduced Doles

In 1836 at his appearance before the Select Committee on Agricultural Distress, William Cox, a Vale farmer, was asked a number of questions relating directly to the Poor Law Amendment Act.[19]

**Questioner:** *Supposing a rise (in the price) of provisions to take place from unfavourable seasons, ought not there to be a greatly increased attention paid to that circumstance, to prevent the new Poor Law becoming a measure of great severity?*

**Cox** (his answer illustrates the gap between the masters and the labourers): *Yes, but they have their remedy. They can go into the workhouse if they like. (The Justices) will always give them an order, if they are dissatisfied with the pay, to go to the workhouse.*

**Questioner:** *Are they not well clothed and well fed in the workhouse?*

*Cox: Yes, but they have a prejudice against it.*

**Questioner:** *Do you know any persons that have been removed from a cottage of their own to a workhouse?*

**Cox:** *I know several that have petitioned their neighbours and friends to assist them to keep out of the workhouse.*

**Questioner:** *Sooner than go to the workhouse they will use every exertion to remain in their cottage?*

**Cox:** *Yes. The weekly allowance is 4/- for an elderly man and his wife out of the work-house.*

So paupers were faced with an unpleasant dilemma: either semi-starvation, ragged clothing, and no medical attention, but a familiar environment amongst friends and relatives; or a better diet, the workhouse 'uniform', and medical attention, at the expense of incarceration, a divided family, distance from friends and relatives, and the rigorous workhouse environment in the company of strangers. Their natural inclination was to stay out of the workhouse. In practice, much would depend upon family circumstances.

### Maximisation of the Family Income

In the 1840's the typical Bucks. household was very different from that of today. Despite the high infant and child mortality, the average family was much larger. With no compulsory education and no restriction on employment, children were expected to contribute to the family income from four or five years of age. Usually this contribution continued until they married, for many children remained at home until then. The resultant overcrowding was an accepted part of life. A family of twelve might have to bed down in a two-bedroomed cottage. The generations would usually be separated by a sheet pegged onto a rope strung across the room. If sheets could not be afforded, the sleeping arrangements might provide some sex education for insomniac teenagers. However, it was quite common for older 'children' to take live-in jobs as domestics, or to lodge with relatives. They were usually welcomed by grandparents, aunts and uncles and young married brothers and sisters, for the family was more important than privacy.

Many villages had a cottage industry of straw plaiting or lace making. In the Vale straw plaiting for the hat industry of Luton and Dunstable flourished. At three, four or five years old most children started straw plaiting in one of the village plaiting 'schools'. From as young as six or seven the lads would look for work with a local farmer, but for girls plaiting usually became a life-long occupation.

All this meant that with good health, with agricultural work available, and with plait in reasonable demand, an agricultural labourer's family could expect an income from more than one source. The family whose weekly budget occupies Table 22 funded it from father's wage of 7s-0d from the farm, mother and daughter's income of 3s-0d each from plaiting straw for 12 hours a day, and the son's 'crow-starving' for 2s-0d. For 1840 the budget is quite impressive, but some of its attractions are illusory. The income of 15s-0d assumes regular employment and stable prices, but in practice neither could be relied upon. Father and son could be laid off due to bad weather, seasonal variations in labour demand, or simply a drop in farm income. Similarly, the income of wife and daughter was at the mercy of the volatile plait market in which the season of the year, current fashions and competition from imports caused major variations in the worker's income. Also, in a scarce year potatoes could be six times as expensive as in a plentiful year, while the price of wheat could double in a poor year. And if income fell or prices rose, the first things to be cut were the star attractions: meat, butter and beer. Still, the budget does include potatoes, now known to be rich in starch and calories, and a valuable source of vitamin C, the antidote for scurvy. When the potato crop failed in 1846-7, there was an immediate outbreak of scurvy. Conspicuous by their absence are milk, eggs,

**Table 22: The Budget of a Family with Working Dependants 1840** [20]

| | | | | | |
|---|---|---|---|---|---|
| 5 Quarten (4 lb) loaves | 3s - 9d | | | B/fd | 10s - 8d |
| 5 lbs meat | 2s - 1d | | 1 lb butter | | 7d |
| 7 pints small beer | 1s - 0d | | 1 lb soap and 1 lb candles | | 5d |
| ½ cwt coal | 10d | | Rent | | 1s - 0d |
| 40 lb potatoes | 2s - 0d | | Sundries | | 2s - 2d |
| 3 ozs tea and 1lb sugar | 1s - 0d | | Schooling | | 2d |
| C/fd | 10s –8d | | | Total | 15s - 0d |

green vegetables, fruit, oily fish, salt, footwear, clothing and savings to cope with rainy days. Despite these reservations, the families of labourers with working dependants were among the most fortunate.

### The Problem Households

For **the young farm labourer** it was starting a family which caused problems. The first child considerably reduced the wife's income for several years. She could rock the cradle with her foot while continuing to plait, but plaiting was quite incompatible with breast feeding, nappy changing, baby washing, and quite a lot of household tasks. The next two children eroded the wife's income still further. However, from the age of four or five, the children contributed to their keep by plaiting, and by sharing in the household chores. This 'all-hands-on-deck' policy certainly improved the family's income, but with wages being so low, even two or three incomes did little more than pay the rent, fend off starvation, and provide for such unavoidables as repairing the fieldworker's boots. If unemployment reduced the husband's income, the family's main options were the workhouse or emigration.

**The elderly** (those over 60) **and the infirm** were either at or rapidly approaching the time when agricultural labour was just too strenuous for them. Of sixty-one cases recorded in Wingrave in 1851, thirteen had moved in with a married child. A further eighteen were still living in their own homes, supported by unmarried sons and daughters, two-thirds of whom were over thirty years of age, which suggests that some had postponed or foregone marriage in order to assist their parents. Eight elderly couples had found lodgers, leaving twenty-two households (36% of the total) struggling along without any visible assistance. With no savings and no families to support them, their remaining options were either to accept the uncertain charity, and the inadequate outdoor relief, or to enter the dreaded workhouse.

### The Increase in Emigration

Emigration thrived. If unemployment and the 1834 Act were the sticks, then free and assisted passages, and encouraging letters from earlier emigrants were the carrots. Successful emigrants were anxious to spread the good news. Here is Charles Payne, formerly of Wingrave, trying to persuade a friend to join him in Australia. His letter, written in 1849, was unsuccessful, but in many homes in the Vale and North Bucks. such a letter was the rainbow at the end of the yellow brick road.[21]

> *My Ever Dear Frend*
>
> *I now write these few lines to let you know that we are safe Arrived at sydney And a most beautiful contery that ever was seen. My Dear Isebela never stop in that Lousey cuntery and se yourself starve. com to sydney my Dear were we can save a litel money to keep us when we get in years with out beolding to aney body and this is the place ware we could Do it. If you can com for it is a place ware you could hurn more money then I could. A good cutter out in the Dres making can have aney money thay like to ask for in thear work. I am satesfide that you will never Repent coming to sydney.*
>
> I remain your Ever Dear frend and well wisher,
> Charles Paine

#### Fig.113: The Discovery of Gold in Australia

In 1851 gold was discovered near Bathurst in New South Wales. Later in 1851 it was also discovered in Victoria. Thousands of people went to Australia seeking gold. Many were unsuccessful. In 1855 Charles and Edward Payne, formerly of Wingrave, spent 20 months at the Louisa Creek diggings unsuccessfully trying to make their fortune.

In January 1842, a party of young agricultural labourers from Risborough left Aylesbury station for Sydney. In the autumn of 1843, two groups totalling 200 people emigrated, mostly from Chinnor. That must have upset some employers! At about this time the Aylesbury Workhouse Union began to help paupers to emigrate. Groups left Aylesbury twice in March 1844, twice in 1845 and in April 1847. Some were *"of a respectable class of labourers"*. Usually there is no record of the numbers.

### The State of Agricultural Labourers in the Vale in 1867
In Table 23, 11/6d is the average family income. Some of the differences in the husbands' earnings were due to the nature of their work. Carters, cowmen and shepherds received an extra 1s. or 2s because they had to work on Sundays. [22] The Betts have been more closely scrutinised because their family budget (Table 24) is included in the records. The main item in their diet was bread, home-made by Mrs Betts: a little over one loaf *each* per day. *"Give us this day our daily bread"* reflected the reality of 19th century poverty. [23] The only protein was a pound of pork, the meat from which would not go far when shared between a family of six, three of whom had long hours of outdoor work. As in medieval times, a large pot of vegetable broth would be a popular hot meal, made cheap by the use of

**Table 23: Weekly Incomes of Farm Labourers & their Families in the Vale 1867** [24]

| Village | Labourer | Ch'n | Allotment | Husband | Wife | Ch'n | Total |
|---|---|---|---|---|---|---|---|
| Swanbourne | Rowe | 0 | Nil | 11s-0d | | | 11s-0d |
| Waddesdon | Timms | 3 | Nil | 11s-0d | | | 11s-0d |
| Princes Risboro' | Smith | 4 | ¼ acre | 13s-0d | | 3/- | 16s-0d |
| Cuddington | Betts | 4 | 20 poles | 12s-0d | 9d | 4/-* | 16s-9d* |
| Oving | Clever | 7 | ½ acre | 11s-0d | | 5/9d | 16s-9d |
| Stewkley | Smith | 6 | Nil | 13s-0d | | 5/- | 18s-0d |
| Princes Risboro' | Lonun | 2 | Nil | 12s-0d | | 8/- | £1-0s-0d |
| Worminghall | Chudbone | 7 | Nil | 10s-0d | 3s-6d | 11/6d | £1-5s-0d |

\* Weekly average over the year

**Table 24: Comparison of the Budgets of an Agricultural & an Industrial Labourer**

| The Betts of Cuddington [25] | | The 'Dyers' of Manchester [26] | |
|---|---|---|---|
| Weekly Budget | s – d | Weekly Budget | s – d |
| Flour (bushel) [26] | 11 – 4 | Bread | 3 – 6 |
| Rent (house) | 1 – 0 | Meat | 2 – 3 |
| Rent (allotment) | 3 | Beer | 6 |
| Pork (1 lb) | 8 | Cheese | 8 |
| Tea (¼ lb) | 6 | Butter | 2 – 0 |
| Sugar | 7 | Milk | 4 |
| 1 cwt coal | 1 – 0 | Tea and Sugar | 2 – 6 |
| Washing materials | 6 | Potatoes and other vegetables | 1 – 0 |
| Sewing materials | 3 | Soap, candles and salt | 1 – 0 |
| School | 2 | Clothes | 1 – 6 |
| Sundries | 6 | Surplus | 1 – 0 |
| Weekly Income | 16 – 9 | House (rent and fuel) | free |
| | | Weekly income | 16 – 3 |

the allotment's produce. However, with little meat and no dairy produce this was a deficient diet, and even worse in winter for, according to Mrs Betts, "*When the boys can't get work, we can't buy pork or as much tea and sugar*". Hopefully, the allotment provided enough vegetables to make good some of the deficiencies. By comparison, the Dyers' free house and fuel increased their income by 2/- per week, which enabled them to buy so much butter. Their budget is also far better balanced, having more meat plus cheese, milk, beer and provision for clothes: see the right-hand column of Table 24. The startling fact about this comparison is that the Betts' budget is for 1867, whereas the Dyers' budget is for 1795! In other words, the Bucks agricultural labourer of 1867 could still not afford the essential items enjoyed by the northern factory worker 72 years earlier. And the Betts were a typical southern family rather than an exceptional case. For instance, the income of the family of Mr Clever (also in Table 23) was identical, but Mr Clever somehow found the energy to cultivate a much larger allotment. The family were lucky to have a teenager in full-time work, but they also had three more mouths to feed. Consequently, as Mrs Clever pointed out, "*It has been awful bad with us lately. We have no potatoes now and I don't know when I did have any butter or meat*". The problem was that in the South Midlands and agricultural areas such as the Vale, despite emigration, the supply of agricultural labour still exceeded the demand. A comparison with the labourers' situation in areas with industrialised towns makes this absolutely clear.[27] In those areas (like the West Midlands, and parts of Lancashire and Yorkshire) where industrial development had drawn surplus labour from the countryside, some say that farm labourers were able to earn three times what they could in the south. However, the parliamentary investigation of 1867 saw these matters in a very different light. [28]

> *The northern labourers' earnings are very little higher than those of any fairly industrious man in Bedfordshire or Bucks., and yet he is mentally and physically a superior animal, treating his family in a manner which three or four times the difference in wages would not account for. What then are the causes operating in his favour? His hiring is a yearly hiring and his wages are paid when he is sick as punctually as when he is at work. His own earnings and those of his family all go to the family purse, and suffer very little variation. It is not his habit to drink beer. Except at the annual hiring, he hardly knows what a beershop means, and his children suck at the milk bowl instead of himself at the beer jug.*

**Fig. 114: The Gawcott Labourers.**

We have seen how poverty, including semi-starvation, drove agricultural labourers to violence and crime. Nevertheless, even at this late stage, there were still those who hoped that reason and negotiation would prevail. Amongst these were the Gawcott Labourers, who publicised their plight in the following pamphlet.

209

# GAWCOTT LABOURERS

**We, a few working Men, desire to lay before a discerning Public the following facts. We are poor men, and wish to have the facts fairly stated, as the only thing that can give us a standing in the sight of the Public.**

For a long time we have complained and stated our position to our Employers. In some cases we have been laughed at, and had indefinite promises . We would have them remember "Whoso mocketh the poor reproacheth his Maker". We have worked all winter at nine and ten shillings per week; we are willing to take the sum of twelve shillings per week; (these last few weeks some have had eleven shillings) other places they have had twelve all winter. What has a man to spend when he has paid

    Rent,1s. 6d.              Firing, 1s. 0d             Bread at 7d per loaf.

We leave these facts with you and your families. We have nothing for the Clothier, Draper, Butcher, and Shoemaker, etc. Where are we labourers with our industry? On the verge of pauperism! The men we work for, some have grown well-to-do within our recollection.

We are sober men----Home loving men----Wish to be honest men----We have cried unto our God, and we trust he has heard us-----We appeal to you fathers of families for sympathy---- There is enough for all of us in this land-----We appeal to you Christian men-----We appeal to you Ministers of Religion, you who preach to us and tell us, in the House of God to say " Our Father," and tell us he is your "Father" and " my "Father" and all ye are "Brethren." "The rich and the poor meet together, and the Lord is the Maker of them all." "Thou shalt not kill (starve)." We ask you to stand forth, and preach against oppression, tyranny, and for universal brotherhood from the pulpit, and come down with us to the stern realities of life. We ask that we may live, not as paupers, but by our own industry. We are willing to work, in order that our families may live. All we now ask is twelve shillings per week, and those who work on Sundays, one shilling more. For this application, some of us have had part of our week's wages put into our hands, and dismissed there and then. Will this advance of one shilling bring ruin upon our Employers? We know it will not, but it will enable us to have more to eat, in order for us to do our work to their satisfaction. Your friend,

**Edward Easter, for Gawcott Labourers**    March 11th, 1867.

# Chapter 17

## LIFE & DEATH IN A VALE VILLAGE

Today death in the first ten years of life is very unusual. Less than 1% of children die before the age of one year, and only 2% fail to reach ten years of age. Of the survivors, less than a quarter die before their 65th year, and half live beyond 75. Things were very different in the Vale in the 19th century when, from the day of one's birth, Death's door was wide open (Table 25: 1841-75). One out of every five infants died in their first year, and by the age of ten years two out of every five children had been buried. Only half of the population survived to 25 years of age, and only 12% reached the age of 75 years.

### Table 25: Parish of Waddesdon with Westcott and Over Winchendon

Percentage of Population Dead by the Age Stated

| Age in Years | 1 % | 10 % | 25 % | 35 % | 45 % | 55 % | 65 % | 75 % | Total Burials |
|---|---|---|---|---|---|---|---|---|---|
| 1841 – 1875 | 22 | 40 | 50 | 56 | 61 | 66 | 73 | 88 | 1058 |
| 1876 – 1910 | 19 | 31 | 37 | 42 | 47 | 54 | 66 | 82 | 956 |
| 1921 – 1955 | 4 | 7 | 10 | 13 | 17 | 23 | 38 | 65 | 715 |
| 1956 – 1990 | 1.7 | 2 | 3 | 4 | 7 | 10 | 25 | 52 | 631 |

Source: Burial Registers of the Parish by kind permission of the Vicar

Although some consciences were stirred, little was done to improve matters. Indeed, in the 1830's and 40's the Poor Law Commissioners attributed sickness and death among *"the labouring classes"* to:

> *noxious vapours arising from damp or imperfect drainage and decaying vegetable and animal substances . . . If a drain be out of repair it is usually left untouched . . . and if the privy becomes full, it is left uncleaned until the increase in the contents renders the accommodation inaccessible. To the state of the privies in the cottage gardens is attributable more illness than to any other cause.* [1]

Only gradually, in the second half of the 19th century, were the major causes of the carnage revealed: poor quality and overcrowded housing, contaminated food and water, medical ignorance and inadequate diet. Critical in this exposé was the Sanitary Act of 1866. Prompted by outbreaks of cholera in 1854 and 1865/6 Parliament compelled local authorities to appoint sanitary inspectors, to identify problems and to enforce solutions. We now consider what they found, in Waddesdon and thereabout.

### HOUSING

Until 1875, when the first Housing Act enabled the inspectors to close, without compensation, houses "unfit for habitation", people's housing needs were still at the mercy of speculative builders and rapacious landlords, who could provide whatever quality of house gave them the greatest profit. Most of the cottages at Waddesdon, Long Crendon, Haddenham, Chearsley, Cuddington, Dinton, Stone, Ludgershall, Grendon Underwood and Twyford were built of a special kind of earth called witchert, meaning white earth. It was obtained by digging out the subsoil, usually one to four feet below the surface of the land, where it consisted of decayed Portland limestone

**Fig. 116: Thatched Witchert Cottages in Malthouse Yard, Long Crendon.**
Dilapidated cottages were commonplace in most Bucks villages until the Acts of 1866 and 1875 (see text).
Such cottages were usually built from layers of witchert, two of which can be seen, where the rendering
has fallen off on the extreme right. The exposed witchert is then broken down by rain and frost. See also
Plate C37.

and clay. When thoroughly mixed with water and chopped straw, this produced a walling material
of high quality, *provided certain conditions were met*. The main conditions were summed up in
an old saying, *"All an earth wall needs are good boots and a good hat to keep it dry"*. For damp was
the earth wall's enemy. To prevent damp from rising into the wall by capillary action it needed
substantial footings of stone (known in the Vale as grumplings) built to a height of 18 to 24
inches. The witchert was then laid on the foundation to a depth of no more than two feet and left
to dry. This was repeated until the wall reached the desired height. Walls over 20 feet high were
built for houses and cottages. Such walls would be two feet thick at the base, and taper up to one
foot. They provided the building with a high thermal insulation. Finally the building must be
provided with its 'good hat' which, in practice, meant a thick over-hanging thatch. Unfortunately,
both grumplings and thatch were prime items for economy by a penny-pinching builder. For if
moisture got into an earth wall it could rot the straw, create soluble salts and change the character
of the clay. Loosened window and door frames would let in both draughts and rain, the latter

212

GRANNY SMOKE A PIPE

## Fig. 117: Granny 'Smoke-a-Pipe'

At the end of the 19th century those elderly who refused to enter the dreaded workhouse suffered levels of poverty unknown in the 21st century, for it embraced everything: food, clothing, health and accommodation. Despite this, Granny 'Smoke-a-Pipe' is said to have lived to the age of 103.

## Fig. 118: Two Elderly Neighbours

Chatting contentedly on their doorsteps, they illustrate important reasons why the 'Union' was dreaded, for they are both free to do as they please, and go where they please. Of course, if she didn't attend to her endless straw plaiting, and he to his garden, there would be less in the larder. Admittedly plaiting was poorly paid, but at least it could be done amongst friends, for 70 years ago they may well have learned plaiting in the same 'school'. He has his hand on his knee, for it helped to ease the pain from joints worn out by a lifetime of hard labour in the fields. Even so, with a struggle, he will coax a year's vegetables from his garden.

creating damp patches and mouldy growths on walls. At worst a wall could collapse. Some did, as the sanitary inspectors reported in 1890, when quite two-thirds of the cottages were newly built.

> *There are some ruinous fallen cottages in the Quainton Road (Waddesdon), which are totally unfit for habitation. A house at Waddesdon is ruinous and unfit for occupation, but still occupied.*

Another economy was not to pave the ground floor of the cottages, which therefore contained all the vegetable matter that is a natural part of the top soil. Over time it also acquired food scraps, faeces from domestic animals, and a mixture of dung and dirt from the local farmyards, all ground in by the family's boots, and extremely difficult to remove. It was a particular menace to crawling babies with their tendency to suck their fingers.

It was not the builder's fault if some families overcrowded their cottages. One small cottage with just two beds was occupied by a man and wife and children of 7, 9, 11,13, 15, 18, 22 and 24 years ! Did they sleep in shifts, or sleep on the floor? Both these things did happen! At Monks Risborough a cottage with four small rooms housed 14 people: a man, his wife and 7 children, 3 old men, and a girl (a notorious prostitute) with a bastard child. In 1841, in the parish of Wingrave, 33 labourers and their families averaged 8 per cottage. Remember that the typical cottage had no more than two bedrooms (sometimes only one), and these were not only limited in floor area, but also (due to low ceilings) in cubic capacity, and (thanks to tiny windows) in ventilation. This created ideal conditions for the spread of infectious diseases by direct contact, and by airborne droplets propelled by coughs and sneezes. Little wonder that there were epidemics of cholera, typhoid fever, diphtheria, smallpox, measles, scarlet fever, diarrhoea and whooping cough.

Yet another of the builders' economies was a failure to provide adequate drainage to cope with sink and slop water, the effluent from pigsties, storm water, and domestic faeces and urine. For the latter a primitive lavatory was constructed. This was a small wooden hut variously known as a privy, a latrine, a closet, or (to many working class villagers) a shit-house. Inside was a bench with one (or two !) holes cut into it. For preference it was built on the edge of a stream, so that the faeces and urine fell onto its bank. In dry weather it simply lay there, and accumulated and stank until rain came. Then the rain and the higher level of the stream carried some of it away. In 1886:

> *a frequently recurring nuisance is the Waddesdon stream, which receives the bulk of the sewage of the village. It is slow-flowing and has an uneven bed. Consequently, in hot weather pools form which are very offensive.*

Of course, not everyone could have direct access to the village stream. In such cases a hollow was excavated immediately behind the closet, and this filled up with faeces, urine and rainwater to form a pond which if long and narrow was known as a moat, and if round was known as a cesspool. The trouble with these, in addition to the smell, was that in wet seasons they overflowed. At worst the overflow spread onto the yard behind the cottage(s). Quite often the yard was not paved, and the residents had to wait for the overflow to soak into the ground, leaving on the surface of the yard such solids as had been floating in the cesspool or moat before the overflow began. Sometimes the floor of the cottage was lower than the yard, and the revolting residue invaded the cottage. Whenever possible the overflow was directed into the nearest ditch, but ditches only 'ran' in times of heavy rain, and for the rest of the time they just stank to high heaven. Selected extracts from the minutes of the Rural Sanitary Authority fill in the details. [2]

> *In several places (in Waddesdon) the drainage is very imperfect, consisting of drains which have been put in from several properties to suit the convenience of the builders but without much regard for sanitation. These drains empty into culverts (i.e. artificial channels) which have been put in by the sides of the public roads. The culverts empty into the open brook*

*which runs through the village from Mill Pond eastwards to Warmstone. This brook has long been notorious for its foul condition, as it also receives the overflows from pig sties (of which there are many), from the cowsheds and dunghills of farmyards, and the washings and blood from slaughterhouses.*

At the end of May 1892 Waddesdon's ditches were still in a deplorable state:

*The ditch in the High Road is in a foul and filthy condition, there being a mass of stagnant sewage along its whole course, creating constant filthy stenches. The sewer entering the ditch in Baker St. is full of stagnant sewage. Mr Copcutt's cottage has the main drain running immediately under the living room, giving rise to frequent bad smells. The moat at the back of Moscrop's cottages ought to be at once filled in as the stench is abominable.*

In one case the smells were so bad that the stench was perceptible 200 yards away, and so unbearable at close quarters that people had to leave their houses on account of it.

## THE CONTAMINATION OF FOOD AND WATER

The cesspools, the moats, the blocked drains, the stagnant ditches and the sewage-laden streams disposed of much of their load in two ways: by soaking downwards into the earth where it contaminated the ground water that fed the wells; and flooding sideways across the ground when the polluted liquid drained into the many wells with damaged sills.

*At Post Office Cottage, Waddesdon, there is an old, shallow, objectionable well liable to filtration from adjacent sources of contamination.*
*The suspected cause* (of the current outbreak of typhoid) *is water from a well contaminated by surface water.*
*A well supplied by rainwater from the roof provides the only drinking water.*

By whatever route the liquid drained away, there was always solid matter left for the flies to breed on. And breed they did, there being always plenty of raw sewage draining down from the primitive closets. Due to the efforts of the sanitary inspectors, these were slowly being replaced by earth closets, which were only an improvement if the accumulated contents were regularly dug out of the closet and into the garden. This was an unpleasant job and was often neglected. In the meantime a thick sludge composed of earth, faeces and urine oozed out over the surrounding area, some of which was inevitably carried on boots and shoes onto the earthen floors of the cottages. And, in practice, it was not only the flies but also the people, who carried the bacteria from faeces to food and drink, for the closets were communal. There was always some excuse for delaying the cleaning of the floors and the seats, and the shortage of water discouraged the washing of hands. So the inspectors' complaints continued.

*The closets are filthy, and too close to the house.*
*At Waddesdon the closets are still in the same foul and filthy condition.*
*While inspecting 31 properties, 10 cases of bad drainage or bad privy accommodation were identified.*

The contamination of food was a common cause of gastroenteritis, varying in severity from mild to fatal. In the Aylesbury Union in 1884 half the deaths from infectious diseases were from "infantile summer diarrhoea". In three months in 1893 in the rural sanitary district which included Waddesdon there were 48 cases of infectious diseases, but *"practically no mortality"*. The satisfied tone of the quoted remark seems rather misplaced until one considers 1884-7 when the **deaths** from infectious diseases totalled 721, an average of 45 in each three months.

Clean water for drinking and washing was scarce in Waddesdon until late in the 19th century. Before this - unless you could collect rainwater - all drinking water had to be carried from Spring

Hill, a distance of some half a mile from the village. Then, with the building of Waddesdon Manor by the Baron Ferdinand de Rothschild, the pipeline from the Chiltern Hills Water Company to Aylesbury was extended to Waddesdon, and standpipes were installed in the village. Waddesdon was lucky. Many Vale villages had to wait until 1940 for piped water. Rothschild also ensured that cottages built for estate workers had *"a wholesome supply of water"*. Despite this, even in 1894 some new houses were being built without a water supply.

## MEDICAL IGNORANCE

Bacteria had been discovered in the 17th century, following the development of the microscope, but it was not until the mid-19th century that Louis Pasteur established beyond doubt that they were the cause of many diseases. Of course, this knowledge did not in itself reduce disease. However, medical and sanitation officers, in their efforts to suppress the *"noxious vapours"* thought to be causing disease, attacked the foul drains, the overcrowded cottages with their ill-ventilated bedrooms, the contaminated water supplies, and the filthy communal privies that really were spreading disease. Remember that, when Gibraltar was devastated by cholera, the Medical Officer at Aylesbury had the cottages thoroughly cleaned by fumigating and limewashing, and had *"the pestiferous ditch behind them containing filth of every description"* filled up with layers of earth and lime. Chloride of lime kills bacteria. On another occasion at Wing one cottage had to be limewashed four times before it was regarded as clean. Often all the bedding and any clothing worn by those who were infected was burned. Infectious diseases were not admitted to the County Infirmary in Aylesbury, but were isolated in a separate building. Over the second half of the century the cleansing of privies and drains, the isolation of the sick, and the testing of water supplies to prevent further cases by identifying contamination became standard practice. However, it was not until around the mid-20th century that antibiotics, antibacterials, vaccines, antiseptics etc. began dramatically to reduce infectious diseases which were formerly common. For example, penicillin was discovered by Andrew Fleming in 1928, but it was not until 1940 that Florey and Chain showed how effectively it could cure diseases.

## "THE GREATEST FOE TO HEALTH AND LONG LIFE IS POVERTY"

So quoted the medical journal The Lancet in 1843, when reporting *"a lecture on the laws which govern the mode and rate of decay in the human frame"*. Five years earlier, **Dr Ceeley, a much-respected Aylesbury surgeon**, was convinced of the link between poverty and disease:

> *The health of the poor is greatly diminished by the inefficient diet. Their diet is bread and a little animal food, and what they have of that is bacon. The poor are compelled to be frugal: their means are very limited. In consequence they have more ills than the wealthy, and need more medical care. Better diets would lead to quicker recovery.*

He was certainly right about the nature of their diet. **Harriet Gibbs, a plaiter of Wingrave,** was the eldest of the six children of Henry Alcock, who was employed as a farm labourer. So the family were poor, but they were not paupers. Harriet was born circa 1823, and she claimed to have had a happy childhood, but her diet was certainly that of a poor family:

> *We only saw meat once a week: a toad in a hole, or sometimes a bit of fat bacon and a few potatoes. We ate the pudding on Sunday and left the meat for Father to take to work all the week. Buttermilk, coarse home-made bread and black treacle was good to us in them days. We never tasted cake, and as for all they new sorts of fruits as there is now, we'd never heard of sich things.*

**The Bledlow paupers**, whose budget for a typical family was published in the Bucks Herald in 1834, had to suffice upon *"eight quartern (4lb) loaves and one smallish piece of pork per week"*, and admitted,

*"When the day's work is at an end, we are very much pinched . . . On Fridays and Saturdays we have scarcely any bread remaining in the house, and no money to buy more."*

In 1833 **Sir Harry Verney of Claydon** reported to the Poor Law Commissioners that Steeple Claydon had 50 able-bodied labourers receiving poor relief. He thought they were poor workmen, due to:

*low wages and consequently poor food, which does not give the requisite strength . . . Indeed, a labourer had told him, "I'd much rather have parish work, which does not exhaust my strength, than farmers' work and another shilling a week".*

When, in 1834, people prayed, *"Give us this day our daily bread"*, it was heartfelt, because for many agricultural labourers and their families bread was their principal food. In Chapter 16 (Table 24) we record (from a Parliamentary Paper) the weekly budget of the Betts of Cuddington. However, we had doubts as to its authenticity, for the only food which they could afford to buy, apart from a pound of pork, was a bushel of flour. A bushel, the Oxford Dictionary told us, was 2,218 cubic inches of flour. We converted it to the standard bags of flour used in our home baking machine, and found that a bushel of flour would yield about 48 loaves of the size produced by a home baker. If the Betts' loaves were just 12.5% larger, which they quite probably were, having been baked in a 19th century bread oven, their bushel would yield 42 loaves, which was just what a family of 6 required for one loaf per person per day for one week. Even after an exhausting day in the fields, fuelled by not much more than one loaf, Mr Betts could find enough energy to cultivate a sizeable allotment. Many couldn't even get an allotment, and their diet suffered accordingly. So much for the Good Old Days!

## HOW DID THEY FARE AT WENDOVER?

We know that Waddesdon was not an exception. The 19th century life-span at Wingrave was very similar to that at Waddesdon. But maybe Wingrave was just another exception. So we took a closer look at Wendover.

Although its population was much smaller in the 19th century, Wendover was by no means a run-of-the-mill village. Trade came to it from several sources. Centuries earlier, King John (1199-1216) had granted it the right to hold a market. It came and went over the centuries, and was most recently revived in 1988, after an absence of nearly a hundred years. Local farmers looked to the village for at least some of their needs. Situated at the northern end of a gap through the Chiltern Hills, it is on a main route from Aylesbury to London, and became a calling point for the horse-driven coaches of the pre-Victorian era, which made good use of its ancient Red Lion Inn, and several lesser hostelries. After the opening of the Grand Union canal, it quickly obtained a branch to it, and acquired a good deal of trade in the process. The opening of the Birmingham to Euston railway killed its long-distance coach trade but, with the completion of the feeder line from Aylesbury, trains to both London and Birmingham were a mere five miles away by hansom cab. So the deep-pocketed businessman could enjoy a retreat in the country without neglecting his business interests. Indeed, by 1892, Wendover had its own station on the newly extended Metropolitan Line, and London was little more than an hour away.

Wendover's situation brought other benefits. The nearest deposits of the mud known as witchert were too far away to build Wendover's cottages economically, but in past centuries the Chiltern woodlands had provided cheap timber for the construction of timber-framed cottages, which could be infilled with bricks, made from Vale brick-earth. Not only were they *very* much longer lasting than the witchert-walled cottages, but they also looked very much better. In 19th century picture postcards, villages with a lot of witchert cottages look rather drab. Besides, labouring families could just about afford the rents of Coldharbour's cottages. Fine-looking and more commodious houses, both ancient and modern, line the Aylesbury Road.

The Chilterns also provided excellent spring water, available in quantity all the year round and free of pollution for those sufficiently near to the source of the water. Admittedly most people had to bucket it home from spring, stream or well, but this was trifling compared with the problems of water supply in many Vale villages. Unfortunately the disposal of sewage was still very primitive, and as the village expanded away from the foot of the Chilterns onto the flat land of the Vale, sewage began to pollute the local streams. This became a serious problem with the invention of the water closet, which was installed by the wealthier members of the village in the larger houses on the Aylesbury Road. Their sewage was discharged into the Mill Stream, which stank abominably. In October 1894 the recently elected Parish Council agreed to contribute a third of the cost of clearing out the stream, on condition that the residents of Aylesbury Road stopped pouring their sewage into it. A scavenger was employed to cleanse the stream, empty the earth closets twice a week and empty cesspits periodically. Despite this, by July 1895 the stream was in a worse condition than before, largely due to the lack of cooperation by the Aylesbury Road residents. Five years elapsed before the problem was solved by Wendover being created a special drainage district, and soon afterwards opening its first sewage works.

Table 26: Parish of Wendover
Percentage of Population Dead by the Age Stated

| Age in Yrs | 1 % | 10 % | 25 % | 35 % | 45 % | 55 % | 65 % | 75 % | 85 % | Total Deaths |
|---|---|---|---|---|---|---|---|---|---|---|
| 1841 - 1875 | 11 | 31 | 40 | 46 | 52 | 58 | 69 | 83 | 97 | 1099 |
| 1876 - 1910 | 12 | 23 | 28 | 34 | 40 | 49 | 61 | 80 | 97 | 940 |

A comparison of Table 26 with Table 25 shows that during the period 1841-1910 Wendover's inhabitants outlived Waddesdon's by a significant margin. For example:

| 1841-1875 | Waddesdon | Wendover |
|---|---|---|
| Buried by the age of 10 years | 40% | 31% |
| Buried by the age of 25 years | 50% | 40% |
| Buried by the age of 55 years | 66% | 58% |
| Still alive at 75 years of age | 12% | 17% |

| 1876-1910 | Waddesdon | Wendover |
|---|---|---|
| Buried by the age of 10 years | 31% | 23% |
| Buried by the age of 25 years | 37% | 28% |
| Buried by the age of 55 years | 54% | 49% |
| Still alive at 75 years of age | 18% | 20% |

Clearly, throughout the years 1841-1910, Wendover was a healthier place to live. Even so, by 1901-1910, Waddesdon was rapidly closing the gap, and even overtaking Wendover as the final (emboldened) figures indicate:

| 1901-1910 | Waddesdon | Wendover |
|---|---|---|
| Buried by the age of 10 years | 11% | 6% |
| Buried by the age of 25 years | 22% | 15% |
| Buried by the age of 55 years | 44% | 42% |
| **Still alive at 75 years of age** | **24%** | **21%** |

Fig. 119: Sheep in the High Street

Fig. 120: The Old Village Pump

**Fig. 121: The Red Lion Hotel in the High Street**
The high-ceilinged passage leading to the stables at the rear is typical of coaching inns (see Plate C17).

**Fig. 122: The Anne Boleyn Cottages in Tring Road**
There is an unconfirmed story that they were part of the royal estate, and were given to Anne by Henry VIII. They are also known as the Coldharbour Cottages: see Plate C33.

## Chapter 18

## SOME GLIMMERS OF HOPE

### THE LABOURERS' FRIEND

In 1872 Edward Richardson, a young schoolmaster at Dinton, resigned his post in order to establish the Aylesbury District branch of the National Agricultural Labourers' Union. Eventually, due to his efforts, there were at least eighty Vale villages with a NALU branch. Due to the failure of strike action, Richardson began to see emigration as the most realistic solution to the labourers' problems. Fortunately, the new state of Queensland urgently needed labour and was offering farm workers free passages, if they paid £1 for their 'ship kit'. In addition, twenty-five million acres had been set aside for emigrants to purchase at 9d per acre. Despite this, the labourers were slow to take up the offer. Richardson understood their reluctance. Over the years they had come to accept their lowly place in society. If they spoke their minds, they might well be considered *"too uppity"* and lose their jobs. Many men had been sacked simply because they had dared to join *"the obnoxious association"* as farmers called the Union.[1] And if you lived in a tied cottage, losing your job meant losing your home. In the few cases when employers made a concession they did so reluctantly and resentfully. When the Claydon labourers succeeded in getting the unmarried labourers' pay raised from 3s-6d to 5s-0d a week, Sir Harry Verney said this *"made the farmers more angry and discontented than the labourers had been."* [2] Usually, even a request for a wage increase resulted in dismissal, as happened at Gawcott, Sherington, Wingrave, Chinnor and elsewhere.[3]

At first Richardson concentrated on recruitment for the Union, and the defence of its members. For instance there was a dispute between Wingrave farmers and their men. About twenty-five men from the village demanded a rise of 1/- a week. This was refused, so with Richardson at their head, and sympathisers from elsewhere, they organised a five-day march in the hope of gaining support. Carrying banners, they passed through Aston Abbotts, Weedon, Whitchurch, Quainton, Waddesdon, Brill, Long Crendon, etc., singing their Union songs. One favourite was sung to the tune of God Save the Queen:

> *Lord of the earth and sky,*
> *Hear now the poor man's cry,*
> *Stand by our cause.*
> *Content shall then abound,*
> *Where want may now be found.*
> *Send up a mighty sound,*
> *And God will hear.*

They *"generally met with a hearty reception from the country folk"*. On Saturday afternoon they returned to Aylesbury and marched into the Market Square. Each man wore the blue rosette of the Union, and had a card stuck in his hat, bearing the message, *"Locked Out"*. Then Richardson addressed the crowd, said to number three thousand, and a collection was made for Union funds. At the meeting George Griffin, of Manor Farm, Wingrave, defended the farmers' position. The *"Locked Out"* notices should read, *"On Strike"*. He was quite willing to pay his best men fourteen shillings a week, but not everyone, regardless of ability.[4] The Wingrave labourers *'stand'* soon collapsed, because the farmers *"locked the men out"*, and the Union could not provide financial support. With the harvest over, some farmers retaliated by laying off men for the winter.

## EMIGRATION TO QUEENSLAND, AUSTRALIA.

**QUEENSLAND GOVERNMENT OFFICES,**
82, CHARING CROSS, LONDON.

OWING to the great demand in the Colony for labour, the Agent-General will grant, under the New Immigration Act, passed on the 2nd August, 1872,

### FREE PASSAGES

TO AGRICULTURAL LABOURERS,
Married and Single, and to
FEMALE DOMESTIC SERVANTS,

without undertakings to repay the cost of passage ; and

### ASSISTED PASSAGES

to Mechanics and other eligible persons, at lower rates than the cost of Passages to Canada or the United States.

£20 Land Order Warrants, per Adult, issued to Persons paying their own full passage to the Colony.

Further information on application.

☞ Appointed Agent for Aylesbury, Mr. S. G. PAYNE, 1, New Road Terrace.

**Emigration** was attractive to men who had been laid off for the winter, but so far it had been haphazard and small scale. Richardson decided that it was time to actively recruit emigrants, and personally escort parties to Queensland. So, in just 20 months (1873 to 1874) 7,931 people left the Vale, and this was just to Queensland.[5] It seems that emigration improved most of their lives. Unlike the Vale, Australia had too few labourers for the available land, and competition for it pushed up Australian wages. Henry Slade from Quainton was typical. He worked for a Queensland builder at 8s. a day plus his keep.[6] *"I never was more happy in my life than I am now"*, he wrote. *"It is a fine country."* Solomon Sawyer of Long Crendon also wrote cheerfully from Queensland of the high wages, and ended,[7] *"I wish I had been here 20 years ago."*

**Fig. 123: Emigration Adverts**
During the Winter of 1872-3 this advert appeared in every issue of the Bucks Advertiser, which had a wide circulation in the Vale.

**Fig.124: The Indus in the Thames**
In the 1870's there were at least 20 ships carrying emigrants to Queensland. The Indus was the third largest, and held nearly 600 passengers.

The **Rothschilds first** arrived in the Vale in 1798, and by 1833 the family were renting Tring Park for the summer. The Vale, with its extensive pastures and lack of woodland, was the ideal place for Nathan's four sons to indulge their passion for hunting. By 1890 seven Rothschild estates had been established in the Vale, all within a radius of seven miles. Even by today's standards, the Rothschilds were immensely wealthy, and their personal expenditure alone gave a fillip to business throughout the Vale. Their mansions and gardens provided employment for hundreds of people. Their estates extended over thousands of the Vale's acres, and they were regarded as model landlords, especially noted for their generous rebates of rents in difficult times. They did much for the agricultural labourers of the Vale. Their rates of pay were always 10% or so above the general level, and they refused to lay-off workers in slack times. They set a new standard for working class housing, and their extensive building of 'cottages' was not confined to estate workers. Their gifts to the community of village halls, schools and reading rooms encouraged the down-trodden labourers to aspire to better things. They supported every charitable cause, and all sorts of personal appeals. They entertained at the highest social level, but also gave teas, concerts, etc. for ordinary folk. **Waddesdon Manor**, designed and built for Baron Ferdinand de Rothschild, to house his family, his visitors and his collections of objets d'art is overwhelming proof of the Rothschild's incredible wealth, and their readiness to spend it. Now owned by the National Trust, it is regularly open to the public (Tel: 01296-653211). **It is well worth a visit.**

**New Industry** created jobs, and many men, who stayed in the Vale, simply left the agricultural labour pool. The railway workshops at Wolverton eventually provided 2,000 jobs. In 1863 some local people formed the Aylesbury Market Company, which built a cattle market, market house and corn exchange next to County Hall in Aylesbury. In 1870 the Aylesbury Condensed Milk Company opened a factory on the Tring Road, employing 150. Hazell, Watson and Viney's printing works, which opened in 1879, employed 400 more. In the 1880's Webster and Cannon set up business as builders in Cambridge Street complete with a large clay-pit and on-site brickworks. By the 1930's the firm employed nearly 500 people. Hunt Barnard, another printing company, arrived in 1898. Twelve years later came the Bifurcated and Tubular Rivet Company. Many workers needed housing, and this created more jobs for the building trades. The increased population generated increased attendances at church. The new churches included the Congregational Church in the High Street (1874), St John's Church in Cambridge Street (1883; extended 1895), [8] and the Methodist Chapel in Buckingham Street (1894). All this completely changed the occupational balance. In 1861 there were 18,703 farm labourers and shepherds in Buckinghamshire. By 1901 there were 10,899.

**The Franchise** was granted to the townsman in 1867, but still denied to rural house-holders. Not until December 1884 did the agricultural labourers, through their union, gain the vote.

**King of the Road** was the chap with a bicycle. Throughout the early 1900's bicycles were increasingly seen in villages, though it was some time before they became commonplace: many people just couldn't afford one. It was probably the Great War which accustomed villagers to travelling and working outside their parish. In many cases it was **the Temperance Movement** which, by persuading labourers to reduce their expenditure on beer, provided the funds for 'extras' such as the bicycle.[9] Once obtained, there was no doubt that the bicycle was *"king of the road"*. It provided transport precisely when its owner demanded it. It operated from home to destination, and it was cheap. You could get a new bike for £5 or so, and a second-hand one for much less. There were virtually no running costs and, if an Aylesbury job paid 4/- to 5/- per week more than a village job (see below), the cost of a bicycle could be recovered in less than six months. As the years went by, more and more people acquired one. No longer was the labourer tied to a job on the local farms, or anywhere in the village for that matter. In 1905, Mr George Elliott, a tenant farmer renting 316 acres in Hulcott, gave evidence to the Tariff Commission, on the availability

**Fig. 125: The Five Arrows Hotel, Waddesdon.**

It was built for Baron Ferdinand de Rothschild, whose great wealth enabled him to satisfy his liking for elaborate and excessively ornate architecture. One can imagine young Victorian dandies describing the Five Arrows as "a really jolly jape". In fact, it is named after the crest adopted by the original 5 Rothschild brothers from Frankfurt.

**Fig. 126: Mentmore Towers**

It was designed by George Stokes, under the supervision of his father-in-law Joseph Paxton (the architect of the Crystal Palace), for Mayer Amschel Rothschild. It was Meyer's daughter, Hannah, who provided Wingrave with a new infants school, rebuilt its derelict cottages and added 20 more. The Towers was just one of the seven mansions owned by the Rothschilds in the Vale.

of labour locally.[10]

*The supply of labour in my district does not exceed the demand. We have no-one out of work in the neighbourhood I live in, that I know of. The young men have been going away for some years. They prefer the clean work and the town work so much . . . and are receiving 4/- or 5/- per week more ready cash. If they can get into the building trade, they prefer to stop there.*

The problem for local employers, and especially for the farmer, was that everyone now had a much wider selection of jobs. In 1999, an old lady remembered,

*When I left school at 14, I did housework. I biked the six miles into Aylesbury to Youngs, who had a toy shop there. I had to set off in the dark on winter mornings, but sometimes I rode with a neighbour, who worked at the County Offices. The Youngs treated me as one of their own. I was over ten years with them, and their daughter still keeps in touch.*

**Table 27: United Kingdom - Growth of Food Imports** [11]

| Commodity | 1856-62 | 1905-11 | Increase |
|---|---|---|---|
| | £ 000 | £ 000 | % |
| Wheat and flour | 17,876 | 48,104 | 269.1 |
| Potatoes | 174 | 1,570 | 902.3 |
| Other vegetables | 121 | 2,477 | 2,047.1 |
| Meat | 3,584 | 48,042 | 1,340.5 |
| Butter and marg. | 3,217 | 25,783 | 801.5 |
| Cheese | 1,249 | 6,902 | 552.6 |
| Eggs | 408 | 7,247 | 1,776.2 |
| Raw fruit | 839 | 9,073 | 1,081.4 |

**Cheap Food** arrived in the late 19th century, when railways and steamships dominated international trade, and carried vast surpluses of food cheaply from the Americas and Australia. After 1875 prices tumbled as this food flooded in from both the New World and Britain's colonies. In 1893 a Hitchin grocer found an invoice of 1812 and published it alongside his current prices. Cheap food transformed the diet of the working classes. The fall in

**Table 28: Comparative Food Prices**

| | 1812 | 1893 |
|---|---|---|
| Tea | 10s-0d  lb | 1s-10d  lb |
| Candles | 1s-0d  lb | 4d  lb |
| Moist sugar | 10d  lb | 2d  lb |
| Loaf sugar | 2s-0d  lb | 3d  lb |
| Yellow soap | 9d  lb | 3d  lb |
| Coffee | 4s-0d  lb | 1s-0d  lb |

prices due to cheap food from overseas increased the *real wages* of labour. A weekly joint of beef or mutton was now affordable by most families, as were canned meats and fish, coffee, cocoa, currants and fresh fruit. They also benefited from the greater availability of **allotments**. The 1867 Report[12] listed a dozen Vale villages with allotments, but many more were later created. In 1887 local authorities were compelled (if requested) to purchase land for letting as allotments.

**Fig. 127: Surprise, Surprise!**

A visitor to the area, having walked to Lodge Hill from Ashendon, is said to have enquired of an estate worker as to whether this was Waddesdon Manor. *"Certainly not"*, was the reply. *"This is the stables"*. And so it was. It is also a testimony to the Rothschild wealth, though the cost of building them was probably dwarfed by the cost of maintaining them and their occupants.

**Fig. 128: The Rothschild Largesse**

This Village Hall, complete with stage, is just one of Baron Ferdinand de Rothschild's improvements for the village of Waddesdon. He also provided a literary institute with a reading room, a number of cottages and houses all prominently hallmarked with his Five Arrows crest. In addition he modernised the 17th century almshouses, and contributed £600 of the £1500 needed in 1895 for a new school.

# Recollections K: Cooperation in Farming – J. K. Fowler *

When I was at school in 1831, every farm in the parish of Aylesbury was untenanted and in the hands of the landlord, whilst the pitiably bad management of the Poor Law had pauperized nearly the whole working population of the kingdom. I was accustomed to look from my bedroom window at Uxbridge School and often saw three or four blazing homesteads. These troublesome times culminated in the rising of the agricultural labourers. Bodies of lawless men marched from village to village, breaking up every machine invented for the saving of labour. The farmers and the trading classes were powerless to control them. The yeomanry were called out and special constables were sworn in to suppress the Swing Riots as they were styled, probably in allusion to the penalty of hanging for arson.

On taking a farm I determined to improve the position of my labourers. I set aside four acres out of two hundred for them to use as allotments. I am speaking of 1853, and for twenty-six years I found it had a marvellously beneficial effect. I gave the men the very best land on the farm. They were charged the same amount per acre that I paid myself, with the rates and taxes added. No man had less than a rood, nor more than half an acre, as I found that this was quite as much as a man and his family could cultivate, and that it amply supplied the family with vegetables for their own consumption, and often with an abundance over to sell. They had full permission to fetch whatever amount of manure they required from my farmyard. I, on my part, insisted that their holdings should be well-cultivated and kept clean. Each year we had a horticultural show of all the garden produce. I put the rent of their holdings together, which were supplemented by the gift of a sovereign from my landlord and the same from my wife, and I then distributed the amount in prizes for their produce. Their vegetables were splendid, and my labourers were generally most successful in the Horticultural Society's show in the town. I feel sure it benefited me as much as the men, as they were always fresh to their work, and were certain to be on the spot whenever they were wanted.

I encouraged the men to do their best with the machinery I used on the farm. I bought my own set of steam-tackle, and hired an engine from the man who threshed my corn. My ploughman drove the cultivator, and I gave him, on top of his full weekly wage, 3d an acre on all he cultivated. As he did about five acres a day, he earned an extra six shillings a week. All others doing that work, also had so much an acre. Consequently, they worked as long in the evenings as it was possible to see, and started as early as they could in the morning. I purchased a mowing machine. When it arrived, I sent for my carter who, with his gang of five mowers, not only mowed my crops but also my neighbours. Working very hard they earned about thirty shillings a week in haytime, but found their own beer. I told him I was giving him a carriage and pair of horses to drive, and that in future he would earn as much as a coachman as he could by mowing. I told him to prepare a new set of leather reins, and to have ready a pair of his most active horses. Then one day Mr Cranston arrived with the mower, the horses were harnessed to it and, Mr Cranston driving, they dashed into the standing grass, levelling it as they went, to the great surprise of Jem, my carter. Jem now in turn took his seat, and after a few lessons he was mowing upwards of a hundred acres that year, including clover and meadow grass. I gave him 6d an acre and four pints of beer a day. So he earned much more than he could have done by mowing with his scythe, and he was very content.

* Source: J.K.Fowler, Echoes of Old Country Life, Edward Arnold, 1892, pp. 254-257.

**Fig. 129: The Rise of the Building Trades**

Between 1870 and World War 1 there was a substantial influx of industry into Aylesbury. It not only provided jobs for the workers who made its products, but much labour was also needed to build the factories, shops, churches and houses which the workers required. Building was a labour-intensive industry. 25% of the men on this site are just carting bricks to the bricklayers, a job that is now done much more efficiently by two men and a crane. Notice also the primitive timber scaffolding, joined by ropes. Judging from the men's clothing, the picture is from the 1920's.

**Fig. 130: The Benefits of Allotments**

Allotments provided space to keep chickens and even a pig, and to grow food for them as well as the family.

**Fig 131: 'Lord' George's Bounty**

Not until 1925 did the pension rise to 10/- (50p) every week, and even then not everyone was eligible.

Unfortunately, the Aylesbury Sanitary Board only provided *"evasive and unsatisfactory answers"* to requests for allotments! It required private initiatives by the Rothschilds, the Roseberys and local farmers to make such provision, which greatly eased the budgeting of labourers' families. When J.K.Fowler, formerly the proprietor of Aylesbury's White Hart Inn, turned to farming, he showed what an individual farmer with only 200 acres could achieve: see Recollections K. So the shadows of unemployment and starvation had been reduced. Even so, the agricultural labourer was still so poorly paid that saving for old age was almost impossible. It was a time that many old people looked forward to with dread.

**Old Age Pensions** were created by Lloyd George and the Liberal Party. The Old Age Pensions Act of 1908 provided a non-contributory pension of five shillings per week to all persons aged over 70 years, whose income was under £21 per year. No longer would they suffer the indignity of being called paupers. In 'Lark Rise' Flora Thompson describes the impact on its cottagers. [13]

> *They were relieved of anxiety. They were suddenly rich. Independent for life! At first when they went to the Post Office to draw it, tears of gratitude would run down the cheeks of some, and they would say as they picked up their money, "God bless that Lord George!" For they could not believe that one so powerful and munificent could be a plain 'Mr'.*

By introducing an element of compassion into the treatment of the poor, state pensions marked the beginning of the end for the 1834 Poor Law, and pointed the way to the Welfare State.

**Fig. 132: Thomas Pitkin of Swanbourne**

Most people - if they had been told that a farm labourer had helped to persuade the government to grant pensions to the elderly poor - would never have believed it. Of course, it was very unusual for a farm labourer to give evidence before a Royal Commission, but Thomas Pitkin was a very unusual farm labourer. For 13 years he had worked as cowman for Lord Cottesloe at Swanbourne, and for some years had been involved in local politics.

## Recollections L: Thomas Pitkin of Swanbourne

In February 1894 Thomas Pitkin, an agricultural labourer, aged 67, gave evidence at the House of Lords before the Royal Commission on Old Age Pensions.

**Lord Aberdare:** How do people on outdoor relief of 3/- per week contrive to live?

**Pitkin:** I cannot tell how they contrive it.

**Lord A:** Can you not make a guess at how they contrive to live?

**P:** No, I cannot; I do not know how they live. It is a puzzle to me, and always has been. They get on someways, but it is a very poor living. Well, it is not a living at all, Sir, it could not be called so.

**Lord A:** Do you know anything of the treatment of the poor in the workhouses?

**P:** I only know what I have been informed.

**Lord A:** By the inmates themselves?

**P:** Yes. I know there is a great dread of going in.

**Lord A:** But when they are once in?

**P:** Well, there is nobody wants to go in twice.

**Lord A:** What sort of complaints are made to you once they get in?

**P:** I do not know that there is a great deal of fault about the food and the clothing, but it is the confinement that is the greatest evil.

**Lord A:** Suppose they were let out for a few hours every day, would they use it badly?

**P:** I do not think so.

**Mr Henley:** I think a great majority of the old people at Winslow, who are destitute, get out-door relief.

**P:** A great many of them from Swanbourne get outdoor relief.

**Mr H:** I see there were only 8 people over 65 in the (Winslow) workhouse. And at the same time there were 131 old people over 65 years of age receiving out-door relief.

**P:** In the Winslow Union, Sir. I did not know of that.

**Mr Roundell:** You have told us about workhouses and the way in which decent people are mixed up with others, and that they have no liberty to go out. If it could be that the decent people could be kept together, and that there was more liberty to go out, would that lessen the objections to the workhouse?

**P:** I do think so. It is the confinement that causes the great dislike.

**Mr B:** Would people in your part prefer a system of pension paid unconnected with the association of pauperism, and to remain outside the workhouse rather than to go in?

**P:** Yes, I think they would like outside the best; in fact, I know they would.

**Mr Chamberlain:** What do you think ought to be the amount of outdoor relief ; what is the lowest sum that is necessary that a man should be able to live?

**P:** Well, I have thought 5/- you know.

**Mr C:** You think 5/- would be a fair sum?

**P:** Yes, I think so.

**Mr C:** And if every respectable working man who required relief were offered 5/- outdoor relief you would have nothing to complain of the Poor Law system?

**P:** No, I should not.

* The above is a small extract from a lengthy inquisition.

## Chapter 19

## *FARMING IN THE VALE OF AYLESBURY*

### *WHAT A DIFFERENCE A CLAY MAKES!*

As we saw in the Introduction (it will be helpful to check the text and Map 1) the principal 'rocks' in the Vale are the Gault and Kimmeridge Clays.[1] The Gault (the whole of the area containing G's on Map 1) is over 200 feet thick, the Kimmeridge Clay (the whole of the area containing K's on Map 1) is over 100 feet thick, and both are highly impervious, so drainage can be a problem. Fortunately in large areas both have been considerably modified. For instance, in the parishes of Aston Abbotts, Mentmore, Wingrave and Wing, large areas of the Gault hillocks (eg. $G_1$) are capped by glacial drift including Chalky Boulder Clay. This cap is more easily cultivated than the Gault, and arable crops thrive, especially as there is natural drainage. Immediately to its south a belt of pure Gault (e.g. $G_2$) creates a heavy, wet, blackish-grey clay soil with almost no lime in it. It is difficult to work and traditionally has been largely under grass. South of that, as the Chilterns are approached, the Gault becomes increasingly chalky and silty, (e.g. $G_3$) because *"a chalky gravelly sludge, spread out from the (Chiltern) escarpment during a late glacial phase".* [2] In consequence, arable crops are once again important. To the south-west of Aylesbury the Gault is again modified by the almost pure sand (e.g. $G_4$) from strata at the foot of the Chilterns.[3] providing scope for still more arable. North of this the Gault Clay and the equally sticky Kimmeridge Clay are both significantly improved by the sand and lime washed down over the millennia from the ridges and hills of the Portland Beds. [4] Due to this there is often a foot or two of rich earth

**Fig. 133: Part of the Western Vale**

The grey hills on the far skyline are the Chilterns. In the middle distance are the Portland Ridges: on the extreme left is Lodge Hill, the site of Waddesdon Manor; there is a small gap and then the Winchendon ridge sweeps across to the right-hand side of the picture. The picture was taken from the Portland Ridge on which Ashendon stands.

overlying the clay subsoil (e.g. $K_1$).[5] With adequate drainage both these *modified* clays makes excellent grazing. Unfortunately, due to the softness of its clay, erosion has considerably lowered the Kimmeridge part of the Vale, which slows down the drainage, and makes the *unmodified* clay less suitable for grazing beef, though the less nutritious grasses which grow on it are quite adequate for dairying.

It is clearly the *mixed* soils which contribute so much to the renowned fertility of the Vale. These are the soils which produce the fattening pastures – *"the luxuriant and deep-coloured herbage"* [6] – for which the Vale has been famed and, *where adequate drainage is possible*, these same soils are also suitable for arable crops. Even the pure clays, which in earlier times were mostly put to grass, can now support both pasture and arable given really efficient drainage, enough lime to counter acidity, good management, and the benefit of modern machinery. It is important to remember that, for the farmer who lives by his land, what the soil is used for has to be determined by the bottom line on the farm accounts. In the Agricultural Research Council's soil survey of the Gault of the Vale[7] between 1951 and 1957, the top-soil of 24 of the 31 farms sampled was described as loam, which is defined as *"a rich soil composed chiefly of clay and sand with an admixture of decomposed vegetable matter"*. It is a soil which one might expect to be devoted to arable. In fact, 28 of the farms were grazing animals: 22 on permanent grass, and 6 on grass/clover leys. Only 3 farms were arable. In 1997 we asked one Vale farmer just how the soil influenced his choice of crops. *"It doesn't,"* he replied. *"So what does?"* we enquired. *"Government subsidies,"* he replied. As we indicate later, a number of other factors may also influence the farmer's decisions.

To fully appreciate the Vale soils it is only necessary to look at the clay plain immediately to the north of the Vale. It is dominated by the Oxford Clay, about which we can find no writer who speaks kindly. In the 19th century Read referred to the area as: [8]

> *that unhappy portion of the County ... From Marsh Gibbon to Steeple Claydon and Winslow where there is hardly anything but poor wet clays ... tenacious and adhesive ... producing a wretchedly stubborn and barren soil ... chiefly in pasture. Some of these grasslands, dignified by courtesy with the name of pasture, grow nothing but rushes, and are decorated all over with tufts of hassock-grass and numberless ant-hills. .... The whole of this district is used for dairying.*

In 1929 Temple saw no reason to differ. However, three quarters of a century later, even the Oxford Clay responds to chemical supplements, the essential drainage, and informed management, backed by a sufficiency of capital to purchase the vital machinery.

## THE GOOD YEARS 1851-1875

At this time English farmers prospered for, while England's pioneering railways widened the home market, they were protected from foreign competition by distance and wars. Russia was involved in the Crimean War (1854-56) and freeing her serfs, Germany was at war with Denmark (1866), Austria (1866) and France (1871), and the United States was absorbed in the Civil War (1861-65). Abroad, the railways were only just being developed, the steamship was in its infancy and refrigeration only came into commercial use in 1875.

### THE PRODUCTS OF A GRAZING ECONOMY

In the Vale, following the enclosure of the open fields, farmers concentrated upon pasture with a much smaller area under crops (Table 29). This seems to have been a common arrangement. It certainly added flexibility to the Vale's natural advantages. Farmers could choose between sheep or beef cattle or dairy cattle, or a combination of these. If the choice was dairy cattle, there were still more options. The milk could be made into butter or cheese, and the skimmed milk from this could be used to fatten calves and pigs. Milk might also be retailed locally.

The pastures were grazed intensively. For example, at one farm 54 acres of grassland supported forty beef cattle. To prevent the fields from becoming 'poached', cattle were kept indoors over the winter and stall-fed on oil-cake and vast quantities of hay from the waterside meadows. Dairying was even more profitable than beef, especially as dairy cattle could be fed very successfully on the middling and poorer pastures. So dairy cattle were purchased outside the Vale and usually each given 3 acres of grazing, which would maintain a cow for 12 months.[9]

### Table 29: Pastoral /Arable Bias In The Vale Over 150 Years

| Year | % Pasture | % Arable | Acreage Sampled | Determining Factors included | Sources |
|------|-----------|----------|-----------------|------------------------------|---------|
| 1810 | 63.4 | 36.6 | 49,331 | Anglo-French wars | Priest: 1810 |
| 1905 | 75.5 | 24.5 | 50,716 | Great depression | Min of Ag & Fish |
| 1928 | 73.4 | 26.6 | n/a | Inter-war depression | Temple: 1929 |
| 1960 | 78.7 | 21.3 | 13,055 | Govt. subsidies | B.W.Avery: 1960 |

In the middle of the 19th century butter was still a major product of the Vale. Generally, one cow would provide milk for five pounds of butter per week for about forty weeks in the year. The cows were milked by hand twice daily, usually out in the fields, and the milk was carried back to the farm in pails hanging in pairs from a yoke across the shoulders of a labourer (a yokel!). The milk was poured into shallow containers known as 'leads', and left until the cream rose to the top, when it was skimmed off. This was repeated several times. On the larger farms butter was churned twice a week, often powered by a horse. Each churn held about eight dozen pounds, and one horse could turn several churns at the same time. Marketing was quite simple. The butter was patted up into lumps of about two pounds each and packed into baskets made of osiers, and known as 'flats'. Each held from 36 to 120 lbs. Having come to an agreement with a butter factor as to quantity and price, the farmer simply delivered the flats to the nearest point where the factor's carrier passed, and left them by the roadside. Then every month the factor would send payment. Butter-making provided Vale farmers with a good and reliable income.

Pigs were a very profitable sideline for the dairy farmer. They were usually bred in Berkshire, 'stored' in Oxfordshire, and 'finished' in the Vale on the by-products of butter-making: skimmed milk and buttermilk. Without refrigeration, people did not eat pork unless there was an R in the month, these being the cooler months. So from September to April 'porkers' were killed on the farm and either sold to local butchers or (especially when rail transport became available) sent to

### Fig. 134: By Hook or By Crook

This was the medieval way of reaping cereals. It was still in use on a few farms in 1900. On a few other farms the long-handled scythe was still used, it being less back-breaking. Later, but before the days of chemical sprays, both were still in use to clear patches of aggressive weeds like nettles, docks and thistles. Both the methods were extremely labour-intensive, because the cut cereals lay on the ground until teams of labourers followed the reaper to bind the wheat stalks into bundles known as sheaves. These were then collected and stacked upright in groups (6 - 12 in each group) to form stooks in which the wind and the sun dried them out.

**Fig. 135: A Hurdler at Work Making Hurdles**

Before the advent of electric fences, hurdles were popular for controlling animals.

**Fig. 136: Inspecting the Sheep**

Notice the extensive use of hurdles.
It is important that problems like foot rot are identified in their early stages.

London to be sold at market. In the hotter months the pigs were marketed as bacon.

Whether they were to replace their mothers in the farm herd, or to be marketed as beef, calves were another outlet for skimmed milk. In fact, some farmers specialised in rearing beef cattle, and the best grazing was usually devoted to this. The best Vale grass was so good that it was possible to fatten the animals without much additional feeding stuff, except in winter when they were stall-fed to avoid 'poaching' the pastures. Sheep were also important. The production of beef, lamb and mutton for the London market was profitable, with wool as a by-product. In addition, farmers valued sheep for the manure which they provided, whether grazing on pasture or when folded on crops such as turnips, of which they not only ate the leaves, but neatly cleaned out the flesh of the turnip as it lay in the ground. As Vale farmers put it, *"A sheep's fart is better than a cow's turd!"*

In 1839 Aylesbury was linked by rail to the Birmingham/Euston line, and London became just two hours distant. By the 1850's the problem of ensuring that the milk arrived there without curdling had been resolved, and a huge new market was opened up for the Vale's dairy farmers; or more precisely for the *large-scale* dairy farmers. This was because the import of milk into London was controlled by wholesalers, who would only contract for large quantities. Dairy and beef farming were the reason why about a third of the Vale was devoted to arable (Table 29), mainly growing wheat and barley. As a modern farmer explained:

> *Farmers must have straw for their cattle, and they grow wheat and barley because they provide the best straw: wheat straw for bedding, and barley straw for fodder.*

In this context the grain was a valuable by-product, either sold to the local bakers and brewers, or fed to the farm animals. Most farmers really had no incentive to produce corn for the market, when meat and milk were better suited to the Vale, less expensive in labour, and almost entirely without competition from abroad: at this time only salted and canned meat could survive the journey from the New World, and it was greatly inferior to English meat.[10]

> *Canned mutton from Australia was coarse and stringy, each can containing a lump of overdone and tasteless flesh, flanked on one side by a wad of unappetising fat, and surrounded by a great deal of gravy.*

Given this use of grain, and a suitable water supply, running a water mill was a profitable sideline for a farmer, for grain which had been ground was worth more than grain still in the husk. And, with a little adjustment, the same stones could mill the grain fine for baking, and coarse for animal feed. Better still the mill could bring in custom from farmers with no milling facilities. In 1798 Ford End Water Mill at Pitstone could grind 16 (very large) sacks of grain a week. Like the nearby Brookend Mill and the mill at Wendover (both long redundant) it relied upon water from the scarp-foot Chiltern springs.

Milk was extremely important in the Vale, but it was not *universally* important. For instance, in the parish of Pitstone geology ensured that milk did *not* play a major role. Early in the 19th century it was noticed that fruit trees flourished on a narrow belt of land from Weston Turville to Edlesborough, just below the 400 foot contour, where a thin belt of Greensand separates the Lower Chalk from the Gault Clay. By the middle of the 19th century extensive orchards had been established, in which apples, damsons and plums (known as Aylesbury prunes) were especially important. In a good year a single plum tree could yield half a ton of fruit, though such bonanzas occurred only once in four or five years. In many Pitstone orchards 'Aylesbury' ducks were pastured, the trees providing a shady run for the birds. With the development of the railways, plums, apples and ducks were sold to places as distant as Lancashire, London and Brighton. Another geological factor could be exploited, because Pitstone parish extends from the clay of the Vale onto the chalk of the Chiltern Hills. Its downland pasture provided excellent grazing for sheep, though they were also fed on the crops (swedes, rape, turnips, trefoil, sainfoin, etc.) grown on the arable in the Vale. By the 1860's Pitstone Green Farm alone had over 500 sheep.

### THE GREAT DEPRESSION & THE RESPONSE OF FARMERS (1875-1914)

In Chapter 18 we saw that the cheap food, which flooded into Britain from the New World and the British Empire after 1875, was a major reason for the agricultural labourers' improved fortune. However, the labourers' good luck was the British farmers' misfortune. Other European countries stemmed the flood of cheap food from the grasslands of the New World by imposing import duties. Britain alone remained free trade, because cheap food meant cheap labour, and that meant cheap exports of manufactures. Table 27 in chapter 18 shows how one import after another came to harass British farmers. For example, between 1861 and 1895 imports of wheat and wheat flour almost trebled, and as a result the price per quarter of wheat in Britain fell to 23s-1d. It was a disaster for farmers with large acreages of wheat. Meat producers also suffered unless they were producing meat of the highest quality. Nationally: [11]

> a regular panic set in. Some tenants, who had hitherto weathered the storm, refused to renew their leases on any terms, while others continued from year to year at large reductions (in rent).

In the past farmers would have cut their labourers' wages, but with labour already in short supply (due to emigration and the growth of industry) they simply had to cope with their reduced incomes. Some adopted new methods. Some produced different goods. Some economised on farm maintenance: hedging and ditching were neglected; repairs were postponed; outlying fields were allowed to relapse into rough pasture; and (as Table 30 shows) a lot of land went out of cultivation, and was left to return to grass. Even so, most farmers' incomes were much reduced, and many farmers became bankrupt.

The Royal Commission on Agriculture of 1893–97 considered that the most profitable agricultural activities at this time were market gardening for vegetables and salads, fruit growing, dairy farming, flower growing, poultry farming, and – in the Fenland region – potatoes and bulbs.

### Table 30: Great Britain: Changes in Crop Acreages

| Commodity | Millions of Acres  (Dates) | |
|---|---|---|
| Wheat | 3. 60 (1872) | 1.4 (1895) |
| Permanent Grass | 11. 40 (1871) | 21. 80 (1901) |
| Orchards | 0. 15 (1873) | 0. 25 (1904) |
| Soft Fruit | 0. 04 (1881) | 0. 07 (1897) |
| Market Gardening | 0. 20 (1872) | 0. 40 (1913) |
| Green & Root Crops | 3. 60 (1872) | 3. 00 (1913) |

Unfortunately, many farmers did not regard horticulture as 'real' farming, and rather looked down upon it, however profitable it might be, while dairying, which tied the farmer to his farm day in, day out, was considered to be a decided step down the social scale. Even 'real' farmers were often reluctant to move from one specialisation to another: for instance, *"once a sheep man always a sheep man"*. Nevertheless, as Table 30 shows, there were major changes, especially where wheat had been an important crop.

Even Vale farmers, with their smaller acreages of arable, had to make adjustments. For instance, Mr Elliot of Hulcott, whose 316 acres had included 60 of arable, had converted them all to pasture by 1885, as he explained to the Tariff Commission:

**Questioner:** *Gradually throughout the district has there been a conversion of arable land into* *pasture?*

**Elliott:** *A great many farmers have laid down a portion (to grass). Not all, but they have laid down a portion.*

**Questioner:** *About what period did the conversion of arable into pasture take place?*

**Elliott:** *In the eighties I would say. Agriculture began to go wrong about 1878 or 1879. That was when I had my first remission of rent, I know.*

**Questioner:** *What, in your opinion, has been the cause of that change?*

**Elliott:** *Because the corn was not worth growing. You could not make a profit.*

**Questioner:** *Is the conversion into pasture directly traceable to the inability to get a profit from corn growing?*

**Elliott:** *Quite so. You can farm pasture with less labour.*

Farmers were still reeling from the crash in wheat prices when refrigerated steamers and railway carriages began to bring vast quantities of chilled and frozen meat to England. Shipments of beef from the Americas in the late 1870's were followed by mutton from Australia and Argentina in the early 1880's. Although not up to the standard of first quality English meat, it was much cheaper and sold well. By 1895, when imports had risen to over ten million hundredweights, the price of top quality English beef had fallen by 25%, mutton by 17% and pork by 10%. This affected many Vale farmers, as Mr Elliott explained to the Tariff Commission:

**Questioner:** *What has been your experience with grazing in recent years?*

**Elliott:** *Very bad indeed.*

**Questioner:** *Has there been any diminution of profits?*

**Elliott:** *There has been a great loss the last two or three years especially.*

**Questioner:** *That is in beef?*

**Elliott:** *Yes, beef and mutton, but beef principally.*

To farmers generally the depression in farming was *"a great national calamity"*. In their evidence to the Royal Commission on Agriculture they were unanimous as to its chief cause: *"the heavy and progressive fall in the prices of agricultural products"*. This was quite true, but other matters were questionable: the size of the farm; the farmer's ability to produce the most marketable products; the degree to which machinery was used; the farmer's relationship with his workforce; and the willingness of his landlord to share his burden. In 1879 the Rothschilds were returning up to 20% of their farm rents. The following cases show how fortunes could vary even in the Vale.

**John Gibbs of Home Farm, Wingrave** rented its 54 acres from the governors of Berkhamsted School and cultivated 32 acres of it for wheat and beans. He cut hay from the meadows, and we assume that he kept some animals, though they are not mentioned in his papers. In 1896 with an annual rent of £90, he sold his wheat for £50-3s., but had not managed to find a customer for his beans and hay. He seems always to have been on the verge of bankruptcy, and waiting for *"a time when things are better with farming"*. A photograph suggests a man racked by the strain of work, worry and insoluble problems.

His problems were very real. With such a small acreage, a market swamped by imports and the consequent low prices, his output of crops was just too small to generate a viable income. Put in another way, his costs were spread over too few units of output. With land which was ideal for grazing (it is now 100% pasture) a change to dairy farming would probably have increased his income even if, with his small acreage, it did not yield a respectable profit. As with many small farmers, his landlord was prepared to reduce his rent, but only by 6.25%, whereas some of his neighbours' landlords were conceding 30% to 50%.

**Mr Elliott's farm at Hulcott** was also in a prime grazing area, but with six times as much land as

John Gibbs was a very much better sized holding. As he explained to the Tariff Commission (see above) it had not profited him. Sensibly, Mr Elliott had concentrated on grazing. Unfortunately, he was grazing beef cattle, when market prices clearly favoured milk production. It also appears that he had an inflexible attitude to labour problems. *"We used to milk over sixty cows, but the men went on strike, and my father sold some of the cows and we diminished (the herd) gradually until I do not milk at all."*

**Mr Treadwell of Upper Winchenden,** six miles to the west of Aylesbury, rented two farms, of which *"the little farm"* alone was of 200 acres. He obviously studied the market, and adjusted his farming accordingly. He had previously made butter, but it became unprofitable due to the cost of labour, and competition from abroad. So now he sold the milk. Instead of buying cattle cake, he used his own barley, oats and beans as fodder. *"I have made a good bit of money with my milk,"* he told the Royal Commission in 1895. *"Dairying has been the next best thing to sheep."* For he was also a well-known sheep breeder. *"I have been able to sell a good many sheep, besides five rams to go abroad for breeding purposes, so I have made a good deal of money with my sheep."* His landlord had *"very much reduced"* his rent on the larger farm and there was also a reduction of 10% on the smaller one. With a flexible and accurate response to the market, the Depression had not yet touched him. Even so, typically, he was already trying to anticipate the future, and predicted a further fall in the price of mutton.

### THE VALE'S PROTECTION BY DISTANCE

The Vale's farmers, in common with dairy farmers elsewhere in England, were protected from imports of milk, because it soured too quickly to cope with the distances involved. Also, because the price of many foodstuffs had been reduced due to cheap imports, people could afford to buy other things. Between 1895 and 1914 the consumption of milk doubled, and the consumption of eggs and vegetables increased year by year. Fruit was eaten in increasing quantities, and the growth of jam factories provided a market for surplus fruit crops.

The Vale also had the advantage of rapid access to the vast London market for milk. By 1894 the Dairy Supply Company of London was buying in excess of 33 million gallons of milk annually, and one farmer's output was not worth its attention. Fortunately for Vale farmers, the Rosebery Estate's dairy at Mentmore sent its milk to Cheddington Dairies at Notting Hill. It seems that Knight Bruce (Lord Rosebery's agent) also acted for some of the larger local farmers. Thus in 1896 Mark Finch of Rowsham wrote to him:

> *Here I shall milk 40 cows and at Astwell Park 50 or 60, and can deliver by either L&NW, Metropolitan or G W R.. If you are in the market to buy, I shall be glad to treat with you. You can rely on purity and quality.*

There was also a huge demand locally by milk processors. In 1870 the Aylesbury Condensed Milk Company opened a factory close to the terminus of the Aylesbury branch railway line. By the 1880's it was consuming 1¼ million gallons of local milk annually. By 1911 Dominion Dairies was established in Aylesbury, where it processed a considerable gallonage of milk into butter and cheese. Much of its Golden Acres butter was shipped out by rail.

In the Vale, barn butter (as the farmhouse product was known) was still produced by a few farmers, who supplied private families and small grocers in the Vale and London. Otherwise butter from highly efficient and hygienic cooperatives in Denmark, Ireland and Normandy had cornered most of the English market. However, there was still a market for best quality Vale meat, and due to its better flavour and texture it still commanded a higher price than imports.

During World War 1 (1914-18) British agriculture prospered. For example, due to the sinking of merchant shipping, home-grown wheat fetched very high prices, sometimes exceeding 100 shillings per quarter. The maximum output was essential to the war effort, and a considerable degree of state control was exercised over farming. Much grassland had to be ploughed to increase wheat production. And in 1917 a Corn Production Act guaranteed a minimum price for corn, a fixed rent for farmers, and a minimum wage for labourers.

## THE WORLD TRADE SLUMP

In 1921 the guaranteed price for corn ended, and from 1922 to 1929 wheat averaged only 46s-4d per quarter. Then came the world trade slump of the 1930's, and by 1939 the price of wheat had collapsed to 21s-5d. At long last the need to protect farmers from imports was accepted by the British government, and by 1938 the Minister of Agriculture claimed that the government's policy was providing the essentials for efficiency on the land: the regulation of imports; price insurance; and the encouragement of good farming. The continuation of huge imports shows these were largely empty words. For instance, a fall of 0.3% in meat imports was totally meaningless. The establishment of demonstration farms did little to ensure profitable farming, judged by a mere 1% increase over twenty years in the wheat yield. Another failure was the Livestock Industry Bill of 1936 which aimed to regulate imports. Incredibly it was expected that the producers themselves would arrange the regulation. Only if this failed would the Board of Trade take action. Also in 1936 the government announced a subsidy of £5 million for farming. This sounded impressive. Then it emerged that it was to reorganize cattle markets, encourage quality production, increase the wheat acreage, assist growers of oats and barley, and increase soil fertility and land drainage. With thousands of farmers desperately trying to stave off bankruptcy it was just jam spread too thin. The only success story was sugar beet. It was subsidised in 1925, and fixed in price from 1931. Lacking local facilities for processing the beet, it did not appeal to most Vale farmers.

So how did the Vale's farmers survive? Some creative accounting was possible. Very conservative valuations of livestock and feeding stuffs could trim a lot off profits. Many things (from gumboots to cars) which could be charged against profits as business expenses also had non-business uses. Farm products such as meat, poultry, eggs, milk, butter, bacon, vegetables and timber for fires were available from the farm at cost price. For a few shillings a week village lads would come in before school, arriving at 6.30 am to do jobs like stone picking, crow-starving and even milking, and at weekends and holidays they would do whatever jobs were going: they rolled the oats, kibbled the beans, cut the chaff, chopped up the mangolds, carried sacks of chaff and hefted the hay as it was cut from the rick. And all that was just to *feed* the livestock! Farmers cut costs by dealing directly with each other, The markets at Tring, Thame and Aylesbury saw a good deal of bartering and direct dealing. And if any cash was involved it often went from back pocket to back pocket. Finally, some farmers increased their income by retailing milk in the villages, and supplying local shops with meat, poultry, eggs and butter. By cutting out the wholesaler, they got a better price. Even so, it was a struggle just to survive.

Of course, there was another route to an improvement of the farm accounts. Costs per unit could have been reduced by increasing the size of farms and by mechanising production, but this required capital and most farmers either didn't have any, or were understandingly unwilling to invest it with the industry in depression. Besides labour and horses were cheap and plentiful, and a known factor with which both labour and management were familiar, for they were used at every stage of food production. Where mechanisation was used it was not very efficient, and still required a substantial amount of labour. So what were these old methods that were used during the Great Depression?

At the beginning of World War 2 ploughing had changed very little since medieval times. Over the same period broadcast sowing of seed had been replaced by updated versions of the seed drill invented by Jethro Tull (1674-1741): see Fig. 64 in Chap. 11. This machine has revolving spoons in a box at the back of the drill. These spoons pick up the grain contained in the box, and drop it into a row of eight tubes through which it falls onto the ground in neat lines. As the seed began to grow, another of Tull's inventions - the horse-drawn hoe - was used to clean out the weeds growing between the rows. However, the use of these machines spread very slowly and, a century after he invented them, it was said to be unusual to find more than a dozen farmers using them in a given county. Even in 1939 they were usually driven by horsepower.

Even the centuries-old way of harvesting "by hook and by crook" (Fig. 134) was still being used on a few farms as late as 1900. The earliest reaping machines (Fig. 137) just cut the corn, which then had to be picked up and bound into sheaves by hand. These were then shocked i.e. stood in groups upright, and supporting each other, to effect the drying and ripening of the grain before it was carried back to the farm. A later version of this machine not only cut the corn, but bound it into sheaves, (Fig. 138) which made shocking much quicker. The cart used to take the crop back to the farmyard was specially adapted for the job by fitting extensions to the front and rear of a standard cart. Loading it demanded considerable physical strength, because as it filled up the sheaves had to be flipped up on the end of a long-handled, two-pronged fork for as much as six feet above the head of the loader, if they were to land on top of the load. When it reached the yard the load had to be stacked and thatched to protect it against the weather (Fig.140). Then, in such quantities as suited the farmer and his customers, the corn was threshed and winnowed to obtain the grain. However, if customers wanted flour in quantity, the farmer would have the grain milled at one of the numerous water and wind-driven mills. (Figs. 142 and 143) After World War One it became increasingly common for farms with a large acreage to hire a contractor to thresh the whole crop in one continuous operation, using his own machinery (Fig. 141), and the milling was done in a workshop with steam engines providing power, instead of the uncertain wind and water. Today all the farmer's side of the work (including threshing) can be done in a few hours, and much more efficiently, by a combine harvester (Plate C24). If the grain needs drying, this is done in specially designed equipment, thus once again avoiding the uncertainty of the weather.

## *A NEW ERA*

With the outbreak of World War 2 (1939-45) the Great Depression came to an abrupt halt, for food production became a national priority. In 1939 grants of £2 per acre were available for ploughing up inferior grassland to fit it for arable crops. In every county War Agricultural Committees were formed, which could order the ploughing of grass, specify the crops to be grown and the rotation to be observed. Farmers who ignored such orders were removed and replaced, as was one of Wingrave's farmers. In the Vale the Thames Conservancy dredged the rivers and streams, which by increasing the drainage, improved both crops and grazing, and made better use of fertilisers. Between 1939 and 1946 the wheat acreage doubled, the barley acreage tripled and the production of oats greatly increased, while maintaining the production of meat, milk, eggs and animal fodder. The annual value of farm produce rocketed from £290 million to £500 million, which suggests that much was achieved.

Post-war it was government policy to have the maximum amount of the nation's food produced at home. To achieve this the Agriculture Act of 1947 provided farmers with an assured market at guaranteed prices for cereals, potatoes, sugar beet, fat cattle, sheep and lambs, milk and eggs, these products representing nearly 80% of the total value of the agricultural output of the U.K. In addition, agricultural output was to be increased by 20% by 1951-2. Although these new policies converted much pasture to arable, pasture still dominated the Vale (Table 29), and (as pre-war) it was mainly farmed for milk, beef and lamb. Milk was still a major source of income, but most farms also grazed beef cattle and sheep, often with pigs and / or poultry as a sideline. Pigs were ready for sale at 5½ to 7 months, and a steady income could be obtained by selling small batches throughout the year. Poultry could provide an even more regular income. The small amount of arable was used for cereals: wheat, barley and oats in that order.

**Fig. 137: An Early Reaping Machine**

It cut the stalks of the cereals just above ground level, and dropped them on the ground. Consequently, a gang of labourers would have to follow the reaper and bind the stalks into sheaves (bundles) before setting them up in groups (stooks or shocks) to dry.

**Fig. 138: A Reaper/Binder in Action**

The picture shows a 19th century self-binding reaper from the Pitstone Museum collection. At that time it would have been drawn by horses, but for this demonstration a tractor was used. The sails push the wheat into the cutters, and it falls onto a moving belt, where it builds up in quantity. The machine then binds it together, and the labourer riding pillion releases it. The resultant sheaf is thrown out onto the ground, ready to be picked up and stooked.

**Fig. 139: A Typical Scene in the Fields at Harvest**

**Fig. 140: Carrying, Stacking and Thatching at Wingrave**

Carrying meant carting, and the cart in the picture was typical, for a framework extended from its front and over the rear of the horse There was also an extension over the back of the cart. These extensions enabled the maximum load to be carried back to the farm. There the straw, with the ears of wheat attached, was piled up into a rectangular shape, and finally thatched to keep the stack dry, until it could be taken into the barn and thrashed to extract the grain, a job which might continue all through the winter and spring.

**Fig. 141: Mechanical Thrashing at Haddenham**

In the early 20th century, especially on large farms, a contractor might be brought in to thrash the wheat mechanically, using tractors to provide the power, which was transmitted to the thrasher by long belts. It was still labour-intensive. There are at least eleven men in the picture, mainly to stack and thatch the straw, which was valuable for bedding, and for feeding the cattle during the winter.

**Fig. 142: Quainton Windmill**

Windmills had been in use since medieval times. Unfortunately they relied completely upon the wind for their power, and so were often becalmed. Consequently the delivery of the flour could not be relied upon.

**Fig. 143: Ford End Water Mill**

In a summer drought water could also be an unreliable source of power, as drought and even periods of low rainfall could dry up the streams that they relied upon. Ford End was fortunate in that its mill-pond was fed by a stream from the scarp-foot of the Chilterns only a short distance away.

**Fig. 144: Cattle Continue to be a Risky Investment**

In the Vale, cattle were once much more important than crops. In fact, many of the crops were grown just to feed and bed the cattle. The BSE epidemic severely reduced the Vale's herds, due to the loss of capital when animals died, and the loss of income from exports. Meanwhile, the high capital cost of providing facilities for milk tankers reduced milking herds. There are still a few cattle to be seen, but whether numbers will slowly increase is arguable. (Plate C30)

By 1961-62 farm incomes nationally were eight times the 1937-8 level. Indeed, the government had raised agriculture to a level of national importance previously unknown in peace-time. In return farmers revolutionised their industry with a combination of mechanisation, factory farming, toxic sprays, drainage and fertilisers . On the more moisture-retentive soils in the Vale

---

### Recollections M: Farming in the Past at Aston Abbotts *

**Michael** *It was a lot more manual work in the Thirties: hand milking the cows, for instance. We farmed 236 acres and were a really mixed farm. We had sheep, pigs, beef cattle and a milking herd plus poultry, and arable. That consisted of about 40 acres, which was used to grow food for the animals. I think my ancestors would turn in their graves to think of Oxleys Farm without any cattle, because we'd always had cattle. We used to do between four and five hundred a year. The dairy herd was shorthorns. Then, I suppose, it was in the Forties when we swapped to Friesians. The shorthorns were more or less dual purpose: you got good beef cattle from shorthorns as well as good milkers. But the Friesians gave more milk. In the Fifties we had the first milking parlour in Bucks..*

**Phyllis:** *Of course, until 1960 everything had to be done without electricity, only what you made yourself.*

**Michael:** *A typical day started at half-past five. Everything on the farm got fed, watered and bedded up every morning before you came in for breakfast yourself. That was father's rule. Of course, all the cattle were indoors in the winter, so you'd got a fair amount of cleaning out and bedding up. There weren't any bales in those days. The hay was cut, picked up loose, pitched up into the waggon, and put in the Dutch barn or made into ricks which all used to be thatched. In those days all the hay had to be cut out with a hay knife and carried in on your back.*

**Phyllis:** *In winter in the evening you'd come in between 6 and 7. If there was anything such as calving you were up at night or anytime. Last thing before you got to bed was to go round the barns and make sure everything was all right. In the summer you'd start again at 5. 30, but I've known you doing hay and harvest until nearly midnight, and then you'd got to get all the milking done, the milk cooled and out on the milk stand ready for the lorry driver by eight o'clock.*

**Peter:** *This was a dairying area. From Weedon to Aston Abbotts, virtually every farm had a herd of cows . . . I should think that second to the elm trees going, the biggest change in Aston Abbotts parish (farming-wise) is the lack of livestock. (As late as 1989) you could stand on Lines Hill, look to the right and see 200 cows grazing, and you could look to the left and see another 120. In another field you'd see young stock and heifers, and so it looked completely different.*

\* Michael and Phyllis Page, and Peter Knight were interviewed by the Aston Abbotts History Group for 'Aston Abbotts 1000-2000'. Their waiver of copyright is gratefully acknowledged.

---

in excess of 30 cwts of wheat per acre could be obtained in favourable seasons. Although the Vale's natural grasses were highly regarded, the more progressive dairy farms replaced them by specially-seeded leys designed to provide a continuous supply of extra-nutritious herbage for grazing and silage. However, in 1961-62 alone, agricultural subsidies cost the tax-payers £342 million, and the government was criticised for 'feather-bedding' the farmer. By 1965 British farmers were using half a million tractors and sixty thousand combine harvesters. Whereas in 1890 Pitstone Green Farm had employed 18 men, 3 boys and 10 shire horses, by 1960 there were only 3 men and one boy, but 4 tractors, a combine harvester and many other machines. This was typical. So national productivity rocketed, for output was raised despite the reduction in the labour employed. (Plates C24 and C25)

Consumption lagged behind production. When the surpluses created mountains of wheat and beet, and lakes of milk and wine at astronomical cost, action had to be taken. By this time Britain was within the European Community, the farm policy of which was, and still is, extremely contentious. For instance, the imposition in 1984 of EC milk quotas to drain the milk lake[12] was sharply criticised by both politicians and farmers, not least in the Vale. Ironically, just when this curb on milk production was being imposed, many small farmers were *voluntarily* ceasing production due to the considerable capital expenditure, which continuation required. For milk was no longer collected from churns left at the roadside, but by tankers. This required major expenditure on access roads, stainless steel storage tanks and pumping equipment. In 1960 at Wingrave twelve farms produced milk. By 1990 there were just two. In 1988 'set-aside' was invented whereby farmers are given direct grants to take land out of production as a means of reducing surpluses. Originally aimed at cereal farmers it was extended in 1993 to every farm in the European Community, which must set aside at least 18% of its land. At the same time target prices for cereals, beef and dairy produce were reduced by 29%, 15% and 5% respectively. By 1995 these reforms had virtually eliminated the EC food mountains. (Plate C26)

## *THE CHANGING ENVIRONMENT OF FARMING*

In the last decade or so new factors have confronted the farmers, no less in the Vale than elsewhere. The bulk of retailing of meat, dairy products and vegetables is controlled by a small number of large and powerful chains of supermarkets, with whose bargaining power individual farmers cannot compete. This power is strengthened by the supermarkets' ability to source supplies from around the globe. Such a policy could cause problems. For example, according to a government-funded report, the rock bottom prices offered by supermarket chains have forced more dairy farmers than expected to sell up. In the past two years 12½% of the dairy farmers surveyed had quit the industry, while over 16% of those remaining say they might leave within five years. If they do, milk production could fall by one billion litres a year, creating shortages for British producers of butter, cheese and powdered milk, which would necessitate imports.[13]

For farmers in the Vale recent years have brought additional costs and inconveniences. Local cattle markets have closed at, for example, Tring and Aylesbury. Thame still has one, but only because it is owned by farmers. For some Vale farmers the closure of Banbury market was a shock for it was a first-class market, reputed to be the biggest in Europe, and with excellent facilities such as banks and restaurants. An important factor in its closure is said to be problems in dealing with the authorities. In the past local farmers regularly dealt directly with one another. The sale of animals, for instance, might be just be done with a phone call: *"Arthur, send us up forty like we had last year"*. The cattle would be loaded into a couple of lorries which would be sent off, maybe the same day, and a day or two later there would be a cheque in the post, whereas nowadays permission to move the animals would first have to be obtained, with a form to be filled in. And if anything goes wrong, such as the duplication of an ear tag, it is said that *"the Ministry people are difficult"*. The requirements of local authorities, and their support for local objectors (even if they have only recently arrived in the area) are said to be seriously reducing the number of abattoirs: locally Thame and Cheddington have closed, and Westoning is said to be *"under pressure"* for the same reasons. Today, even the traditional muck heap has to satisfy the regulations. A concrete base is required with a brick wall on three sides, to a specified height. Failure to comply could bring a savage fine, and a gang of workmen to remedy the omission, after which a bill would arrive for the work done. This last is part of the increasing pressure on farmers to care for the environment. There is already a ban on the *'burning-off'* of crop stubble, grants are now available to restore hedgerows, and rivers and streams are regularly monitored for

**Fig. 145: The Changing World of Farming: The Farrier**

Shoeing is no longer done by a blacksmith working under a spreading chestnut tree. Nowadays a farrier arrives in a van.

**Fig. 146: The Changing World of Farming; Aylesbury's Market Square about a Century Ago**

Many farmers regret the loss of local markets. Until quite recently the Vale had markets at Thame, Winslow, Aylesbury, Leighton Buzzard and Tring. Today only the first two remain, and Winslow is only for sheep.

contamination from the over-application of slurry and fertilisers. Since 2005 there has been a single farm payment for EU farmers, independent of production, but linked to respect for food safety, animal welfare, and a commitment to keep all farmland in good condition.

In the longer term the greenhouse effect, if it continues, will cause a change in climate which will shift farming zones northwards. For example, in southern England, crops which are currently marginal, such as vines, will be more easily cultivated. There will have to be an increased investment in water supply and equipment for irrigation.

In response to the trimming of subsidies, many farmers are once again selling direct to the public through farm shops, farmers' markets and Pick Your Own farms. Many have entered the leisure market by offering bed and breakfast, camping and caravanning sites, caravan storage, fishing lakes, driving ranges for golfers, rare breeds' farms and children's zoos. But cooperative marketing – the saviour of small-scale farming in many countries – has still not become the norm in England.

There are still large numbers of sheep in the Vale, but by the end of the 20th century the number of cattle in the Vale has declined dramatically, due to the BSE epidemic, very low prices for milk, the high capital cost of the infrastructure for modern milk production, and (what some farmers regard as) unsympathetic and excessive regulation by government agencies. One Vale farmer told us sadly,

> *This used to be a dairying area, and virtually every farm had a herd of cows . . . The milk tanker just drove around calling at all the farms to pick up the milk . . . In 1989 we had a thousand herd of cattle all told, which were divided between the farms at Lower Burston, Dinton, Thame and Norduck. Not now!*

For the first time in two centuries the peace-time countryside of the Vale is dominated by crops of rape and cereals: Plates C27 and C28. There is still a significant amount of sheep farming (Plates C1, C2, C29), but there is little enthusiasm for cattle, though small herds are still to be seen: Plate C30.

**The Pitstone Farm Museum**, housed in farm buildings dating back to 1831, has a large collection of farm implements and machinery, and exhibits relating to rural life, local trades and professions. A visit **is strongly recommended.** (Tel: 01296-668918) **The Ford End Watermill, at Ivinghoe** is the county's only working watermill. It is especially interesting when milling is being demonstrated. (Tel: 01582-600391) **Quainton's windmill** is now in full working order, and open on Sunday mornings, when it mills wheat. (Tel: 01296-655306)

# Chapter 20

## LOOKING TO THE FUTURE

### SOME RECENT THREATS TO 'OUR' VALE

The greatest recent threat to Our Vale was the proposal by the Roskill Commission in 1969 to site the third London Airport at Cublington, for its development would have destroyed the Vale as we know it. The temerity of the planners was incredible. Sir Arthur Bryant spelt out the implications:

> *It is hard to define the beauty of the Vale, for it is compounded of ever-changing light, but whether seen from the Chiltern escarpment or from the hills which rise like islands in the midst of its undulating plain, that chequered landscape of soft greens and browns, enclosed by hedgerow elms, oaks, ashes and sycamores, with reflected clouds and far blue horizons, beautiful villages and a wealth of historic houses and cottages is unsurpassed anywhere in England. . . .* [1] But if the airport came:
> *Cublington, Dunton and Stewkley would be demolished (and) a galaxy of lovely villages unsurpassed anywhere between the industrial Midlands and the Channel coast would be involved in a corridor of continuous noise and uproar: the three Brickhills, Stoke Hammond, Soulbury, Aston Abbotts, Hardwick, Weedon, Hoggeston, Whitchurch, Oving, Pitchcott, Quainton, Dinton, Cuddington, the two Winchendons, Grendon Underwood, Chearsley, Long Crendon, Ashendon and probably the hill town of Brill.* [2]

In addition, it was estimated that 1700 people would lose their homes, and a city housing some 275,000 people would be needed to staff the airport.

The greatest threat aroused the greatest opposition, and the Wing Airport Resistance Association (WARA) was created to organize it. On one occasion 60 beacons were lit enclosing an area of about 300 square miles, on another a five-mile long motorcade bedecked with protests toured the area, and on yet another 10,000 people gathered together in a massive demonstration of opposition. The result of all this was huge publicity both locally and nationally. Even the New York Times chipped in to declare that the fight for Cublington was a fight for mankind! Meanwhile every village organized fund-raising events large and small to pay for legal costs and publicity material. Finally, in April 1971, the government rejected Roskill's plans. [3]

1996 brought an attempt to establish in the middle of the Vale, an airport and training centre for microlights. The training aspect was especially worrying. It involved the use of forty flying 'lawnmowers' (as we dubbed them due to their noisy engines) which would circuit the Vale from dawn to dusk for seven days per week. Fortunately we were able to cooperate with like-minded friends in our village, and with an equally-concerned group at Dancers End. Our main contribution was to deliver several thousand leaflets to Vale villagers, who responded magnificently by swamping the planning authority with nearly 1200 letters of protest. The authority still favoured giving permission for the scheme, so we appealed to the Minister. Meanwhile, the authority decided that it could only give permission for three years' operation, as the land would be needed for housing. At this, the application was withdrawn.

Now the peace of the Eastern Vale could be destroyed by yet another airport proposal, this time to expand Luton airport. For several years its management has been seeking permission to change its flight paths over the Vale. The reason given for this is concern for safety, but the National Air Traffic Service has stated that the existing flight paths are *"extremely safe"*.

**Fig. 148: Stewkley's Villagers Protest**

Like most other villages they were against the proposal to site the third London airport in Aylesbury Vale.

Opponents of the proposals believe that the real reason for the requested change is the airport's ambition to increase the annual throughput of passengers from 7 million to 29 million, which would quadruple the number of flights, the pollution and the extent of the noise in the Vale. Some facts about this matter don't seem to be common knowledge. Firstly, aircraft noise is not confined to the flight path, but spreads out over a much larger area. Secondly, it appears that Luton is the only airport in the south-east with unrestricted night flying, when older and therefore noisier aircraft are often used. Thirdly, it is admitted that aircraft will fly over Vale villages at as little as 3000 feet, but this is 3000 feet *above mean sea level*, and therefore only 2,700 feet over much of the Vale, because this is already 300 feet *above mean sea level*. Fourthly, if the planned expansion of the airport materialises, landings would eventually increase to approximately 440 every 24 hours, which *on average* would mean one aircraft passing overhead every 3¼ minutes. In practice, as there are more day-time flights, the day-time frequency would be greater. Finally, compared with the present minimum level of 8000 feet for commercial flights in this area (and they are few in number) a minimum level of 2700 feet would mean that engine noise on the proposed flight path would be approximately four times (sic) as loud as at present. An earlier proposal for a new flightpath, known as Option 3, which caused outrage in Vale villages, besides upsetting Cranfield Airfield and Milton Keynes' Council was scrapped. However, a revised proposal (Option 3a) was approved to operate from 10ᵗʰ May 2006.

Over the years repeated applications to operate sites for landfill have caused much concern amongst Vale residents. In 1989 Hales Waste applied to create at Grove Farm, Bierton what would have been *"one of the most extensive landfill sites ever developed on virgin farmland in Britain, occupying the equivalent of some fifty football pitches".* [4] Local people roundly condemned it, and the Bierton and Villages Environmental Group was formed to lead and coordinate the opposition. Fortunately, its evidence was sufficient to ensure the rejection of the scheme by the local authority. Later, waste disposal proposals for the Brickhills, Newton Longville and Pitstone were also rejected.

The post-war years have seen a considerable development in farm buildings. Silage towers, white-roofed barns, plastic tunnels, housing for the expensive farm machinery, large milking sheds and buildings for battery hens have mushroomed. Ancient farmhouses have been sold to commuters, while the former owners move into brand new houses on Greenfield sites. Much of this may have been necessary to keep the farm accounts in the black, but – added to new buildings for golf courses, driving ranges, garden centres, etc. – it also raises the spectre of subtopia.[5] So, despite efforts to maintain the Vale in pristine condition, things have changed a bit! Even so, good views can still be had from the Chilterns, but you must pick your spot, for some of the scarp-foot villages of a century ago are now small towns, several with industrial estates. When searching for soft-blue horizons, the eye must first avoid Aylesbury, which is, and will be for some time to come, expanding rapidly. A large new estate, now known as Fairford Leys, has recently been added to its western edge, and work has just started on its northern edge where two new developments (Berryfields and Weedon Hill) will eventually include 3850 houses plus industry, schools, accommodation for 'park and ride', a new railway station and other facilities.

Remember that we have defined 'Our Vale' according to its geology (the Gault Clay, plus the Kimmeridge Clay, plus the Portland beds) and the type of agriculture which it supports. 'Our' Vale is not at all the same thing as the administrative district of the Aylesbury Vale District Council. AVDC's domain is very much larger than 'Our' Vale. Except for Milton Keynes, it covers the whole of Buckinghamshire north of the Chilterns, and so includes Winslow, Buckingham, the delightful Ouse valley, and the northernmost part of the county, where it borders on Northamptonshire. In what follows, this administrative Vale will be called the 'AVDC Vale'.

### AVDC's VISION FOR THE 'AVDC VALE'

Realising that its local plans of 1991 and 1998 were inadequate to deal with new government policies, Aylesbury Vale District Council created a new Local Plan, which applied to the whole of the AVDC Vale. Published in January 2004, it was mainly concerned with two topics: increased urbanisation due to residential development; and the congestion of road transport. What follows is limited to the urbanisation planned for the town of Aylesbury, because this could be very destructive of the countryside of the eastern Vale.

So what is all this about *urbanisation*? The word alarms people, who are concerned for the preservation of the Vale's lovely countryside and delightful villages. Presumably this is one reason why – to provide some reassurance – AVDC's plan establishes the criteria which it thinks should influence future urbanisation, much of it originating from the very firm guidance and advice supplied by the government, its advisory bodies and Bucks County Council.[6] These criteria can be summed up by the two principles emboldened below:

**Minimise the effect on the AVDC Vale of creating large numbers of new homes by:**

re-developing Brownfield sites (i.e. redundant developed sites), which are currently vacant;

only using Greenfield sites (i.e. currently open countryside), as a last resort;

developing at a high density;

concentrating development in existing settlements i.e. mostly at Aylesbury but with some development at Buckingham, Wendover (the Halton hospital site), Winslow and Haddenham (only within the existing boundaries);

enhancing development with landscaping;

restricting development in villages and the countryside.

**Create sustainable communities,**

by ensuring that large scale housing developments include not only essential shops (as in the recent past), but also the full infrastructure needed to provide for leisure, health, social activity, employment and education within or close to the housing, so as to reduce the traffic created when jobs and services are only available at a distance.

Summing-up, a District Councillor said:

*Firstly, we want to maintain the (AVDC) Vale environment as it is now, which means protecting our wonderful countryside and villages. We want to make sure that "all this growth" doesn't destroy our prime asset.*[7]

Meanwhile, the Government had refined *"all this growth"* into more precise (but still very intimidating) targets for AVDC's housing, for they required an additional 23,500 dwellings to be built in Aylesbury Town between 2001 and 2031, and an additional 3,300 dwellings to be built in the rest of AVDC's district between 2001 and 2016.[8] These plans were greeted with horror, and for some time have been under review by the regional planning authority. Its proposals have only recently undergone their Public Examination, which (rather strangely) took place in Reading. These new proposals would require the AVDC to approve a total of 16,000 dwellings for Aylesbury Town between 2006 and 2026. However, the proposals have to be accepted by the government before they become binding upon AVDC. Whether they will be accepted will not be known until after this book has gone to the printers. Look out for news in the local and national press. In the next few pages, as we consider the implications of government housing targets for the Vale's green fields, we assume that the government *will* accept them. En passant, you might assume that the latest figure represents a reduction on the planners' earlier ambitions. In total maybe, but notice that the **annual** rate of building in Aylesbury for the 2001 to 2031 period was 758, whereas the new figure of 16,000 for 2006-2026 yields a rate of . . . . . . . 762 !

**Table 31: Aylesbury Town - Housing Developments Nearing Completion, In Progress and Under Scrutiny**

| * | Development | Dwellings | Employ't |
|---|---|---|---|
| G | Fairford Leys | c 2000 | Yes |
| G | Berryfields  (210 hectares = 504 acres) | c 3000 | Yes |
| G | Weedon Hill   (50 hectares = 124 acres) | c 850 | Near |
| G | Aston Clinton Rd (Employ't + Park & ride) | Nil | Yes |
| G | Circus Fields | 152 | |
| | **Sub-total for Greenfield Dwellings** | **c 6002** | |
| B | Tring Road | 100 | Near |
| B | Bearbrook House | 50 | Near |
| B | Territorial Army Centre | 76 | Yes |
| B | Ardenham Lane | 50 | Near |
| B | Park Street | 25 | Yes |
| B | Waterside (Exchange Street site) | 200 | Yes |
| B | Part of the old ABC Brewery site | 70 | Near |
| B | Viridian Sqr (former council offices + c/park) | 214 | Near |
| B | Grand Central (Schwarzkopf site) | 391 | Near |
| B | Nestlé | 136 | Near |
| B | Gatehouse Quarters | 370 | Yes |
| B | Stocklake West and East | Tbd | Yes |
| B | Telford Close | Tbd | Yes |
| B | Hampden Hall | 150 | Yes |
| B | Big Hand Mo | 24 | Near |
| B | Dayla (High Street) | 38 | Yes |
| B | Petrol Station (Oxford Rd / Buckingham St) | 19 | Yes |
| B | Jansel Square, Bedgrove | 24 | Near |
| B | The Green (Persimmon site) | 140 | VeryLtd |
| B | Stoke Mandeville Hospital Site | 330 | Very Ltd |
| | **Sub-total for Brownfield Dwellings** | **2407** | |

The areas to be used for Greenfield housing are assumed to be sufficient for **sustainable development** (ie. also to provide jobs, social facilities, health services, education, etc.) as defined earlier in this chapter.

Under 'Employment' *Yes* means within or adjacent to the housing, while *Near* means up to a mile from the housing. Very Ltd means very limited.

* G = Greenfield Site; B = Brownfield Site; Tbd = To be determined; c = circa
The sources for Table 31 are AVDC and the press. However, some schemes are at an early stage of consideration, and subject to rejection or amendment as the planning process proceeds.

As Table 31 shows, AVDC is authorising (as the government requires it to do) a considerable redevelopment of urban Brownfield sites for housing.[9] Such Brownfield development is now regarded as an important way of concentrating urbanisation in existing towns instead of disfiguring the countryside with it, as often happened in the Twenties and Thirties. As Table 31 indicates, AVDC has identified many Brownfield sites (Fig. 150 and Plate C32), for which it is in process of finding developers. However, agreeing with its owner a suitable development for a Brownfield site can be a difficult and time-consuming task with no guarantee that the eventual oucome will favour the Local Authority. For instance, the Castle Cement Works at Pitstone (Fig. 149) had long been more than a local eye-sore. With its extensive and very ugly factory buildings, glaring white quarries and tall chimneys (one was 350 feet high) it dominated the landscape for miles around, and was particularly destructive of views from the Chiltern ridge. So no tears were shed when, in 1991, the company closed the site. It then submitted proposals for its redevelopment: 275 houses, buildings for light industry, and the use of one quarry for landfill with household refuse for twenty years. This quarry was immediately at the foot of the Chilterns and therefore in the forefront of views from its crest. Its operation would have involved a major increase in road traffic. This created strong objections from amenity groups, and from Buckinghamshire and Bedfordshire County Councils, and this proposal went to a public enquiry. The Inspector ruled in favour of the company, but the Minister for the Environment overruled him and rejected the landfill part of the application.[13] The result is that only the housing and environmentally acceptable industry is being developed. It is also proposed to convert one of the offending quarries into a park.

The intensive development of Brownfield sites is a relatively new idea and so, up to the present, there has been a substantial backlog of sites available. However, once this backlog has been utilised, it seems to us that the future supply will be greatly reduced. There are three reasons for this. In the last quarter of the 20th century many Brownfield sites were created because redundant industry deserted them. It seems that in Aylesbury much of this redundancy has been part of the general movement in Britain from somewhat heavier industry to lighter and service industry.

**Fig. 149: The Castle Cement Works at Pitstone**
The buildings have now been demolished, and the site has been developed for housing and light industry.

With most of the exodus completed, fewer abandoned sites will become available. Secondly, the Brownfield sites at present identified include several which have been deemed suitable for multi-storey development for 'flats'. Indeed, the information obtainable at present suggests that between 1000 and 1500 of the dwellings at present proposed for Aylesbury Town's Brownfield sites will be of this type, [10] which use land economically, but can easily destroy the amenity of nearby residents. AVDC's local plan promises to respect this. If so, it follows that in a town like Aylesbury, dominated by 2-storey development, further sites suitable for multi-storey flats will become increasingly rare, thus reducing the contribution of Brownfield sites to the housing target. There must also be concern as to the future size of the market for flats, especially in multi-storey developments. Thirdly, so as to reduce commuting, there is a desperate need for more jobs in Aylesbury, and this means that housing competes with industry and commerce for Brownfield sites. This has already happened in the case of the "Gatehouse Triangle" (also known as "Gatehouse Quarters"), where AVDC wanted an exclusively commercial development, but (on appeal) the planning inspectorate insisted on a mixed housing/commercial scheme.

### The Brownfield - Greenfield Debate

In October 2005, during a visit to Aylesbury, the Government's commitment to Brownfield re-development was confirmed to the Press by **Yvette Cooper, Minister for Housing:**

**Reporter:** *Will the building of thousands of new houses mean the Government will be concreting over the Vale's much celebrated countryside?*

**Minister:** *That is why we changed the planning guidance to ensure that far more homes are built on Brownfield sites. 57% (of homes) were to be built on them, and now it is over 70%. We are very clear that we should be regenerating old sites, old buildings and areas left derelict, and that should be the priority in the way we build new homes. [11]*

To us, the Minister's answer to a quite specific question clearly implied that we need not worry about our celebrated countryside. All AVDC had to do is to arrange for 70% of Aylesbury's new homes to be built on Brownfield land and that will resolve the problem. Unfortunately, the Minister apparently forgot to ask a rather important question: "How much Brownfield land do you have in Aylesbury?" Bearing in mind that the Government wants at least 11,200 homes (i.e. 70% of 16,000) built on it, the answer has to be, "Not enough, by far!" (see Table 32, rows A and C, and the following paragraph)

**Table 32: Likely Land Usage for 16,000 Homes in Aylesbury Town 2006–26** [12]

| Row | Brownfield as % of Total Homes | Brownfield Homes (acres) | Greenfield Homes (acres) | Total Homes (acres) |
|---|---|---|---|---|
| A | 70 | 11,200 (504) | 4,800 (783) | 16,000 (1,287) |
| B | 28 | 4814 (216) | 11,186 (1825) | 16,000 (2,041) |
| C | 14 | 2,407 (108) | 13,593 (2,218) | 16,000 (2,326) |

As row A of Table 32 indicates, if 11,200 homes could be built on the Brownfield sites of Aylesbury town, (ie. 70% of the 16,000 total) the remaining 4,800 homes (needed to meet the target of 16,000) would require only 783 acres of the Vale's green fields. "Only!" you cry. Well, if you think that is a lot, consider the present situation. Although AVDC has done a pretty thorough job in identifying Aylesbury town's present crop of Brownfield sites, its pronouncements and publications to date indicate that these sites will accommodate only 2407 homes (including one-bedroom flats): see the emboldened sub-total for Brownfield sites at the bottom of Table 31. Assuming that there are no more Brownfield sites to be had in Aylesbury town, Table 32 row C shows the result: the remaining 13,593 homes required to raise the total to the government's target of 16,000 will have to be on Greenfield sites, and that means that no less than 2,218 acres of the Vale's fair fields (an area capable of supporting 22 hundred-acre farms) will have to disappear under bricks and mortar. Can nothing be done to remedy Aylesbury's shortage of Brownfield sites? Well, the year 2026 is a long way off. If we are very optimistic, we could assume that in the meantime sufficient additional Brownfield sites will become available to double the present total of Brownfield homes, raising it to 4814 homes. For the result refer to Table 32, row B, which shows that even with this improvement we still have to sacrifice 1,825 acres to Greenfield housing. We would not expect an increase in the availability of Brownfield acres to go beyond a doubling of the present figure, unless industry were driven out to make more room for Brownfield houses. As jobs are already in short supply in Aylesbury we don't think that this will happen due to AVDC policy, despite the recent case of the "Gatehouse Triangle" referred to earlier.

In view of the importance of adequate modern housing to family life, it could be that some people would consider the loss of around 2000 Greenfield acres, an unfortunate but essential sacrifice. If so, it is important to remember that Tables 31 and 32 do not spell out the whole future of housing development in the Vale and North Bucks.. Also scheduled for the period 2006 to 2026 are 4,400 new dwellings in the AVDC area, but away from Aylesbury Town. A substantial proportion of these are to be erected in Buckingham (700+), Wendover (300+), Pitstone (355), Winslow (250+) and Haddenham (100). In addition, there is the possibility of substantial overspill into the Vale and North Bucks from Milton Keynes and Leighton Buzzard.

When considering figures for Greenfield housing, remember that they are (as they should be) figures for housing **and infrastructure**: roads, pavements, and facilities for education, health, transport, leisure, shopping and employment. All this is not only to convenience the residents, but also to reduce the number of journeys on our crowded roads created by commuting, the school

**Fig. 150: A Brownfield Site being Cleared for Redevelopment**

At Aylesbury the major disadvantage of Brownfield sites is their relative scarcity. In this case the Nestlé factory will be replaced by 136 flats. Such sites are also desperately needed for industrial and commercial development.

256

run, and town centre shopping. Hopefully, if viewed in a long-term and national context, this will also reduce accidents, $CO_2$ emissions and the use of finite resources such as oil. However, much of this infrastructure is not only expensive to provide, but is a voracious devourer of land.

What happens after 2026 will depend largely on the size of Britain's population. Ironically, we find that it is often the people who want the most liberal immigration policies, who are most adamant that no green fields should be sacrificed to housing and its voracious infrastructure. Unfortunately, even in the 21st century you can't have your cake and eat it. And that adage certainly applies to the green fields of the Vale.

It is sometimes said that when you are 'down', the only way out is 'up'. Unfortunately, in planning, this means tower blocks with all the disadvantages that have come to be associated with occupying flats in them.[13] For some people they are aesthetically unpopular. Thus Aylesbury's older residents have never forgiven Fred Pooley (then County Architect) for his eleven-storey accommodation for the County Council, which for many years afterwards was dubbed 'Fred's Folly' or 'Pooley's Plonker'. Since then high-rise flats have often been condemned as breeding grounds for anti-social behaviour amongst the young, and distress amongst the elderly. Researchers have even devised laboratory experiments in an effort to find explanations for these problems. In one it was shown how the behaviour of rats deteriorated if too many were crowded together. However, another study attributed problems amongst the elderly to isolation due to the lack of communal facilities. In desperation several local authorities have simply demolished their tower blocks. Nevertheless, high-rise buildings can do much to improve housing densities, as is illustrated by Aylesbury's Nestlé site for which planning applications to provide up to 209 dwellings in blocks of up to 7 storeys have been dismissed, and replaced by a scheme providing just 136 flats in a more moderate 4-storey format,[14] but with a loss of about 70 dwellings. It will be interesting to see how Aylesbury residents (and the buildings' tenants) react to the re-development of the Schwartzkopf site with 391 dwellings in four blocks of from three to six storeys.

### The Arguments for the Denser Development of Cities and Towns

Some planners think that the government's Brownfield target is a GOOD THING, and would be pleased to see it raised. **The architect Lord Richard Rogers, a member of the Government's Urban Task Force**, believes that the Government should be doing even more to ensure that this really happens. He is reported as saying, for instance:

> *Countryside sprawl has produced acute social problems in urban areas, as better-off families move out to areas where it is cheaper to build new homes . . . Continuous outward movement causes environmental damage, the loss of Greenfield, traffic congestion, the fragmentation of urban communities and the loss of social cohesion. The concentration of low skills and sharp racial divisions in cities and towns means the poor are left behind, and newly arrived groups move into the spaces created by the outward exodus.*

He also points out that by favouring the re-use of Brownfield land instead of Greenfield sites, people had started moving back into city centres: in 1990 there were fewer than 1000 people living in the centre of Manchester, but by 1995 there were 25,000; and the population of central Liverpool had increased fourfold. Nationally, he believes that 75% of new development should be on Brownfield sites. [15]

Told of the Minister of Housing's remarks **Dr John Wilson, Buckinghamshire chairman of the Campaign to Protect Rural England,** commented: [16]

> *We are totally in favour of building on Brownfield sites and if what she* (the Minister) *said about 70% being built on Brownfield land is true, that is not bad news at all.* (However) *we are concerned we will see a disappearance of Greenbelt land, and I don't understand how all these houses can be built without that happening.*

*The Argument For More Greenfield Development*

Some planners think that the Government's high Brownfield target is a BAD THING and want it to be severely reduced. *"Houses with Gardens, not High-rise Hell,"* is the call for change by **Professor Sir Peter Hall, chairman of the Town and Country Planning Association, and also a (dissenting) member of the Government's Urban Task Force.** He describes the proposal to raise the number of homes built on Brownfield sites as, *"unnecessary, unworkable and potentially a housing disaster"*, and adds:[17]

> *Not everyone believes that everyone should be forced to live in high-density housing, crammed into cities Hong Kong style. It is ridiculous to expect families to squeeze into clogged cities, sacrificing their privacy, enduring a lack of sunlight and fresh air, and being forced to send their children out to play in the street. We have a dreadful lesson from Paris (the riots of November 2005) on what can happen in these conditions.*

Professor Hall has called for more houses to be built on low-quality agricultural land, of which, he says, there is a surplus in the South-East. He adds that there has been an unprecedented increase in the construction of apartments. Figures from the house builders confirm this. The proportion of apartments to houses built had soared from 36% in 2003 to 55% in 2005. Builders are now warning that the market for apartments has reached saturation point across the country, but particularly in the South-East. [18]

**Geoff Ball, chairman of Cala Homes,** a leading builder, commented:[19]

> *The drive to build apartments has been overdone. We need more houses. We are building fewer houses than anywhere else in Europe. We are building smaller ones, too!*

So far as Aylesbury is concerned, if the sharp decline which we expect in the availability of Brownfield sites in the future does occur, then the demands upon our green fields will increase with similar inevitability. Once the supply of Brownfield sites dries up, the choice is simple: either green fields are lost or less dwellings are built.

Although in the body of the Local Plan we are told that Greenfield sites will be used only as a last resort, the foreword admits that "the development of Greenfield land is inevitable". It is not only inevitable, but has already happened at Fairford Leys, and the latest developments at Weedon Hill and Berryfields are also on Greenfield sites. Moreover, there has already been a recommendation that, once the estates to the north of Aylesbury have been completed, the next large phase of Greenfield development should be on the southern edge of Aylesbury,[20+21] within an arc stretching from the A41 to the A418, and a public consultation period will be in full flow between July 19th and August 30th 2007, with a further period scheduled for 2008.

So far as the Vale of Aylesbury is concerned, far from being used as a last resort, its Greenfield sites are currently being used as the premier and principal source of land for housing. By 2006 the current score for sites completed and contemplated is almost the exact opposite of that proposed by the government:

|  | Brownfield | Greenfield |
|---|---|---|
| Government target. | 70% | 30% |
| AVDC achievement | 27% | 73% |

However, the shortage of Brownfield sites in Aylesbury is no indictment of AVDC!

## *ENJOYING THE VISUALS OF THE VALE*

So, the development of Aylesbury town could destroy a substantial acreage of the green fields at present surrounding it. In practice still more fields will be required to provide sites for the 4,000 new office and factory jobs *on new sites* that will be needed by 2011[22] if the commuting to

**Fig. 151: Song-Thrush Feeding Young: see Plates 38 and 39**

The thrushes suffered from a surfeit of pesticides on arable land. The population crashed, but is slowly recovering.

**Fig. 152: Skylark Nesting**

Formerly, grass was cut for hay in June/July after the nesting season. Now the grass is cut for silage in May/ June which is during the nesting season, exposing the nests to predators like magpies and crows.

other areas is to be reduced. Add in the possibility of incursions for housing by Milton Keynes and Leighton Buzzard, and the Vale vistas which we cherish will be considerably reduced. If it all happens!!! For much can change in a quarter of a century: faced with electoral uncertainties, governments have been known to perform a u-turn on their own policies; attitudes to immigration could change with all that that implies for population growth; attitudes to the expansion of urban development in the south-east could harden; etc., etc.. Or things could get even worse. In the meantime let's enjoy what we've got. Despite the creeping urbanisation as Aylesbury expands and villages infill, the Vale still has some of England's most attractive villages and viewpoints.

We wonder why more people don't visit the western Vale. Its hill-top villages of Brill, Ashendon, and Chilton offer wonderful views, though you do need a map to know what you are looking at. Fortunately Britain has the world's best maps. Try the Ordnance Survey Explorer Series, obtainable at most booksellers. Each map covers a large area and, at 2½ inches to the mile, provides such useful information for walkers as field boundaries and public footpaths. Brill offers extensive views in all directions. **Brill's 17th century windmill is a particular attraction:** see Plate C35. It is situated on a common, pock-marked by ancient claypits, now a jumble of grassy humps and hollows, which are great fun for children. From the 13th to the 19th century the clay was used to make bricks, tiles and pots. Brill used the bricks in its own buildings. The Elizabethan Manor House in The Square has rows of the long, narrow bricks of that period, laid in a pattern known as English Bond, for which rows of bricks laid lengthwise (known as stretchers) alternate with rows of bricks laid endwise (known as headers). In Tudor times the poorer villagers still built their houses with timber framing infilled with lath and plaster, and reserved the narrow bricks for making their chimneys fireproof. In the High Street and Temple Street there are many of these buildings, though their fronts have been updated in later styles. In such cases the chimneys may reveal their true age: look out for square chimneys set on the diagonal and, of course, built with the narrow bricks. In the late 17th century the narrow bricks were used, even in the less expensive houses: notice the lower walls of 2, Temple Street. In the 18th century blue vitrified bricks became available, and builders created a chequered pattern, using alternate blue headers and red stretchers as at 1, The Square. Even more striking patterns can be seen in Rose Cottage near the east end of the church (Plate C36), at Bernwode House in the High Street, and at the Old Vicarage. Sir John Betjeman was fascinated by the Vale's bricks. [23]

> *The Vale has real country, where the farms and villages are the gradual growth of centuries: red brick farms, houses and barns, the brick varying from the dark brownish red of Tudor times, to the dark red brick patterned with sanded headers popular in the 18th century, and the pale red and yellowish brick of the early 19th century.*

Elsewhere in the western Vale many of the villages for centuries used a quite different building material, known locally as witchert. In chapter 17 we noted its composition, its production, its use in building and the villages where most witchert cottages are to be found. Of these, Haddenham's narrow old streets and lanes are well worth a visit.

For bright, inquisitive children (and their parents!) Aylesbury Museum has a good display on bricks, and Shire Publications of Princes Risborough publish a book on the subject. It is part of an excellent series of cheap, well-illustrated paperbacks, many of which deal with countryside topics such as fields, hedges and ditches; straw plait; thatching; vintage tractors; horse shoes and harness; farms and farming; etc.. So far over 400 titles have been published. [24]

### *Is Eco-Farming [25] An Achievable End?*
The second half of the 20th century has not been a good time for wildlife, and this is just as true of the Vale as it is of the rest of England's agricultural areas. For instance, changes in agricultural practice have resulted in a drastic reduction of farmland birds. Thus it was discovered that silage

**C32: A Development of Flats on Part of the Old Aylesbury Brewery Site**

**C33: The Anne Boleyn Cottages at Wendover**
They are an attractive reminder of earlier times: see also Fig. 122 in Chapter 17.

**C34: College Lake, a BBOWT (Berks., Bucks., and Oxon/ Wildlife Trust) Wildlife Centre.**
It is an outstanding venue for wildlife enthusiasts. Its facilities include several well-places hides.

**C35: Brill Windmill**

The windmill is one of several prime viewpoints around the village. Adjoining it are the pits and hollows of the diggings which provided clay for Brill's pottery and brick industry.

## C36: Rose Cottage, Brill

A few steps from the windmill are houses and cottages built from the local bricks, as they developed over the centuries. Notice in buildings like the Old Vicarage, Rose Cottage and Bernwode House how bricks of different colours (obtained by differences in firing) have been brought together to make patterns.

## C37: Building with Witchert at Haddenham

The Methodists of Haddenham were justly proud of the high witchert walls of their chapel. Then in 2001 one of its main walls collapsed. It was replaced with a wall of cob: a west country version of witchert. Six years later this also collapsed. However, most of Haddenham's witchert heritage remains intact, as this picture shows.

## C38: The Kingfisher

It is heavily dependent on the state of rivers and streams for these birds are quickly affected by pollution. In the last 30 years river water has, on the whole, improved due to better surveillance, and larger fines.

## C39: The Goldfinch

This bird feeds on weed seeds such as thistle and groundsel. So farmers' use of herbicides reduced its numbers. However, set-aside and the popularity of garden feeders have helped it to survive.

(grass cut green and stored in pits or silos) is much more nutritious than grass dried into hay. Unfortunately this meant that the grass had to be cut earlier in the year, and this clashed with the ground-nesting favoured by birds such as the skylark, whose nests were either destroyed before their young could fly, or exposed to predators such as magpies and crows.

Before the arrival of the combine harvester, much corn was stored and thrashed in the autumn, winter and spring, whenever the grain was required for use or for sale. This meant that old-fashioned storage in sacks or ancient bins, plus the residue from repeated bouts of thrashing, left a generous supply of grain for the rats and mice. The latter were particularly active at night, just the right time to be picked off by the barn owls. Nowadays, better storage and faster marketing of the grain keep away the rats and mice, and their absence keeps away the owls, which now have difficulty in finding alternative roosts and adequate food for their nestlings. Moreover, the use of poisonous sprays (against weeds, blights and destructive insects) on farms has also reduced the population of harmless flying insects, small mammals and common weeds, on which many birds fed. Spraying littered the countryside with toxic corpses, which spread the poisons as one level in the food chain fed on the level below it. Fortunately, research into the causes of the decline in wildlife led in 1982 to a ban on the use of DDT, and has persuaded farmers to use safer pest controls. The barn owl, sparrow hawk and goldfinch were all very badly affected, to the point of extinction, by the sprays, but are now gradually recovering (Plate C39).

Some of the results of human activity have had quite unexpected results. For instance, better land drainage combined with drier springtimes have robbed the swallows and martins of the mud to build their nests. The demolition of old farm buildings has reduced the number of nesting places, while the machine cutting of hedges, irrespective of season, and often with a reduction in hedge height, has made them less attractive to all hedge-nesting birds. Meanwhile the reduced flow in rivers and streams, and their pollution, has adversely affected kingfishers (Plate C38).

Despite the above, local experts assure us that in the Vale much wildlife is gradually recovering.

### Accessing the Vale

A car will access the Vale's villages, and many of its viewpoints, but walking takes you into the heart of the countryside. Sadly, many folk are put off walking by uncertainty as to where they have a right to walk. The Ordnance Survey Explorer maps mentioned earlier are a great help, and include an information panel, which sets out clearly the public rights of way, and other footpaths which the public can use. Where a public right of way meets a road there should be a clear sign marked Public Footpath. You have as much legal right to walk along these footpaths as along your local High Street, and if the farmer allows his crop to grow on the path it is he who is at fault: you are perfectly entitled to walk through it. Even seasoned walkers find that books of walks with their detailed guidance are a valuable aid. Such walks are used more often and so are not usually blocked by vegetation or wire, and are often way-marked with small plastic discs bearing an arrow to indicate the direction taken by the next section of the path. A selection of such books is stocked by most booksellers. They are invariably written by experienced Vale walkers such as Diana and Peter Gulland. Both Bucks and Herts County Councils have also published pamphlets providing detailed instructions for local walks.

County Councils are responsible for seeing that paths are maintained and kept open but, funds being in short supply, they rely largely on information from walkers. Paths in some areas are served better than others. Thus, in August 2005, the Ramblers' Association reported that: [26]

> *Northamptonshire footpaths are in a dismal state. Just 52% are classified as 'easy to use'. Cambridgeshire and Bedfordshire fare little better at 58% and 62% respectively, whilst more than 30% of Buckinghamshire's paths are below standard.*

To report problems, obtain advice, or view the definitive maps with the latest information about public rights of way, contact the Rights of Way Officer at your local highway authority. In the Vale this is Bucks County Council. For guided walks contact the **Ramblers' Association**, (Tel: 0207-339-8500), whose local branches are active and welcome new members.[27] Larger branches, as at Aylesbury, are more easily able to provide walks for both beginners and experienced walkers. **The Friends of the Vale** also have an annual programme of walks and talks. Tel: 01844-290441 (evenings and weekends). If you want to know more of your own village or parish, many have active groups, which welcome new members. For a concentrated exposure to local wild-life **College Lake Wildlife Centre** (off the B488 just to the east of Bulbourne) is good. It occupies a 160 acre worked-out chalk quarry, which includes a large lake, several well-placed hides and a two-mile wildlife walk. It is managed by BBOWT (Berks, Bucks and Oxon Wildlife Trust). Tel: 01865-775476. For young children a visit to the Mead Open Farm at Billington (01525-852954), or the Bucks Goat Centre at Stoke Mandeville (01296-612983), which has other animals besides goats, might be a useful introduction to the countryside. From 2008 the Goat Centre will be called the Bucks Mini Zoo.

**Fig. 153: College Lake, a BBOWT Wildlife Centre**
This is a worked-out chalk quarry which has been turned into a nature reserve and is particularly interesting for its birdlife. It has a large woodland and marshy area plus ponds and a large lake. A five acre field is given over to growing rare cornfield flowers, and is a spectacular sight in the summer. See also Plate C34.

# Notes and References

PP    = Parliamentary Papers
BRO   = Buckinghamshire Record Office, County Hall, Aylesbury
AVDC  = Aylesbury Vale District Council
VCH   = Victoria County History of Buckinghamshire

## Introduction: 'Tis the Far Famous Vale

1.  Read, C. S: Report on the Farming of Bucks., Jnl. of the Royal Agricultural Society of England, 1856, pp. 269-322.
2.  MacDonnell, A: England, Their England, MacMillan, 1942, p. 222.
3.  Donald, J.H: VCH Bucks., vol. 1, p. 399.
4.  Gault is a local word of unknown origin, but the Portland Beds and Kimmeridge Clay are named after the locations at which they were first identified.

## Chapter 1: Early Times

1.  Chatwin, C.P. (British Regional Geology, East Anglia, H.M.S.O., 1954, p.78) points out that early man may have inhabited the area even before it was invaded by ice sheets.
2.  Akeman Street follows the route of the A41 through Aston Clinton and Aylesbury to Fleet Marston.
3.  Records of Bucks., vol. 28, 1986.
4.  Anglo-Saxon boys of the aristocratic warrior class were trained from around seven years of age for a military role. For much interesting detail, especially on their training, see Hawkes, S.C.(ed.): Weapons and Warfare in Anglo-Saxon England, Oxford University Committee for Archaeology, Monograph 21, 1989.
5.  After the Roman legions had withdrawn in A.D. 407, the kings of British tribes tried to administer their territories and repel invasion, still using the Saxon mercenaries. Whether, after the Saxon invasions of A.D. 450 onwards, the mercenaries remained loyal to their British masters is a matter of debate. There may have been some doubt about their loyalty, for at least one Saxon garrison was moved back from the eastern frontier with the invaders so as to avoid a possible conflict of interest.
6.  The location of Mount Badon is not known.
7.  Some earlier writers believed that an enclave inhabited solely by Britons had survived to 571 in the area just north of the Chilterns. Note, for example, Mawer and Stenton, Buckinghamshire Place Names, CUP,1925: "There is no archaeological evidence in this quarter of early Saxon settlements", and "The objects recovered from the numerous burial grounds suggest that most settlements in central Buckinghamshire were established after the Saxon victory of 571". This has been challenged by Michael Reed. (The Buckinghamshire Landscape, Hodder and Stoughton, 1979, p.66). He accepts the date of military conquest but suggests that there had been earlier peaceful penetration of the area by Saxon peasant farmers.
8.  The Anglo-Saxon Chronicle is ambiguous about this. The Parker version attributes the victory to a Saxon named Cuthwulf, while the Land version attributes it to Cutha and identifies him as the brother of Ceawlin, the Saxon King (561-591). See G.N.Garmonsway (trans/editor), The Anglo-Saxon Chronicle, Dent, 1953.
9.  Davis, K.Rutherford: Britons and Saxons chap. 8 argues the case for Bedford as the location.
10. The small number of British words to be found in the Anglo-Saxon language suggests that the Anglo-Saxons overwhelmed the existing population.
11. Davis, K.Rutherford: Britons and Saxons, Phillimore, 1982, p.55. See also Mawer and Stenton in Buckinghamshire Place Names, CUP., p.xiii: "The objects recovered from the numerous burial grounds suggest that most settlements in Central Buckinghamshire were established after the Saxon victory of 571."
12. Reed, M: The Buckinghamshire Landscape, Hodder & Stoughton, 1979, p.63.
13. Figure I includes place names which (in Reed's opinion) could have been found only in the earliest period of the English settlement. However, these are only the names which have survived unchanged. There are also well over thirty place-names in the county which are composed entirely of topographic elements and which are likely to be just as old. They include, in our area, Stone, the Stratfords, the Linfords, Horwood, Swanbourne, the Claydons and Twyford.
14. The base-line was usually a local stream which could be navigated in the Anglo-Saxon shallow-draught boats.
15. Bailey, K.A: Buckinghamshire Parish Names, Records of Buckinghamshire, vol.40, p.69.
16. Reed, M: A History of Buckinghamshire, Phillimore, 1993, p.59. Dr Richard Gem considers that St. Mary's, Aylesbury was earlier.
17. Jackson, E.D.C. & Fletcher, E.G.M: The Apse and Nave at Wing, Bucks., Journal of the British Archaeological Association, 3rd Series, 25, (1962). Stenton, Sir Frank (p. 145 Anglo-Saxon England) regarded Wilfrid as "certainly one of the greatest men of his generation".
18. The queen of King Egfrith of Northumberland referred pointedly to 'Wilfred's countless army of followers'.

(Colgrave, Bertram: The Life of Bishop Wilfred by Eddius Stephanus, Chap 24, pp.48/49).

19. It seems likely that many of the monasteries in Wilfrid's 'empire' observed (though not strictly) the rule which he had introduced viz, the Benedictine Rule. Godfrey, C.J: The Church in Anglo-Saxon England, CUP 1962, pp. 144,148-9 and 156 refer.

20. Mercia does not appear clearly in the early records until the time of Penda c. 634-656. (D.P.Kirby: The Making of Modern England, p.61).

21. Colgrave, Bertram: The Life of Bishop Wilfred by Eddius Stephanus, Chap XIV, 1927.

22. Stenton, Sir Frank: Anglo-Saxon England, 3rd Edition, O.U.P., 1971, p. 67.

23. It seems quite unrealistic to assume that the building was completed by 669, when Wilfrid left Mercia to act as bishop in western Deira. In the same year Archbishop Theodore made Wilfrid Bishop of all Northumbria. (Stenton, op. cit. p.132) As an active, many-faceted character, Wilfrid would surely have delegated supervision of the work at Wing to one of his trusted followers. It would thus most likely have been completed at some time in the final quarter of the 7th century. In any case, Wilfred may not have been quite so welcome in Mercia soon after 674, when King Wulfhere was defeated in battle by Egfrith of Northumbria. (Campbell, James: The Anglo-Saxons, Penguin, 1982, p.73)

24. Stenton, F: op.cit., p.143.

25. Morris, Richard: Churches in the Landscape, Phoenix, 1989, p.129.

26. The Venerable Bede in a letter to Egbert, Bishop of York in 734 quoted in Haddon, A.W. and Stubbs,W: Councils and Ecclesiastical Documents, Oxford 1871, iii, 316; also in Whitelock, D: English Historical Documents, c.500-1042, London 1955, 737.

27. Debilitated by a variety of parasites, as evidenced in the Coppergate excavations at York in the 1970's.

28. Morris, Richard: op.cit. p.146. By the time of King Stephen (1135-1154) Aylesbury is referred to as 'a former minster'.

29. Reed, Michael: History of Buckinghamshire, Phillimore, 1993, p.59. Others are to be found outside Bucks..

30. Campbell, James: The Anglo-Saxons, Penguin, 1991, pp. 72 and 88.

31. Morris, Richard: op.cit., p.149.
Christie, H., Olsen, 0., & Taylor, H.M: The Wooden Church of St. Andrew at Greensted, Essex, 1959, pp.92-112.

32. Reed, Michael: The Buckingham Landscape, Hodder & Stoughton, 1979, p. 67.
Taylor, H.M. and Taylor, J: Anglo-Saxon Architecture, 1965, Vol. 3, Appendix D.

33. Baines, A.H.J: The Lady Elgiva, St Aethelwold and the Linslade Charter, Records of Bucks, Vol.25, p.128.
Also Stenton, Sir Frank: op.cit., p.322n.

34. Kirby, D.P: The Making of Early England, Batsford, 1967, pp. 85-6.

35. Baines, A.H..J: Lady Elgiva, Chess Valley Archaeological and Historical Society, 1999, pp. 28 and 34.

36. Baines, A.H.J: ibid. p.35.

37. Baines, A.H.J: ibid. pp.23 - 4.

38. Godfrey, C.J: The Church in Anglo-Saxon England, CUP, 1962, p.174.

39. After Taylor, H.M. and Taylor, J: op. cit., vol. 2, pp. 665-671.

40. We have no direct evidence of such activities at Wing, but the cost of building a stone church at that time would require more than parochial needs to justify it. Elgiva's use of the crypt to house her relics and so create an attraction for pilgrims was such a justification.

41. Baines, A.H.J: ibid., pp.26-27
Baines, A.H.J: The Lady Elgiva, St. Aethelwold & the Linslade Charter of 966, Records of Bucks. Vol.25, pp.110-38.

42. Kirby, D. P: The Making of Early England, Batsford, 1967, p.29.

43. Taylor, C: The Making of the English Landscape-25 Years On, Local Historian, Vol. 14, no.4, pp.195-201.

44. The basis of representation is disputed. One expert says, "One per hundred families", while another says, "All free tenants".

45. Baines, A.J.H: The Lady Elgiva, St. Aethelwold , etc., op. cit., pp.110 –12 8.

46. Campbell, Jas: op. cit., p.181.

## Chapter 2: An Anglo-Saxon Village

1. The extent of Saxon Wingrave (as of all villages) was measured in hides. In theory, in eastern England, each hide was 120 acres of ploughland, and this is the conversion rate which we have used. By Edward the Confessor's reign, the hide was essentially a measurement of the value of land, rather than its area. Thus if Wingrave's land were of above average quality, 100 acres in Wingrave might be called a hide simply because it could produce as much as 120 acres of average land. However, the precise meaning of the hide has long been – and still is – disputed. For example, S. P. J. Harvey, 'Taxation and the Ploughland in Domesday Book' (in Sawyer, P: 'Domesday Book: a Reassessment') claims, "that the ploughlands here (in Bucks.) are based on the actual arable is indisputable". The ploughland was another unit of measurement for land. It was the area capable of being tilled by one plough-team of eight oxen in a year. See chapter 3, note 12 for a comment on the hide in Norman times. Note that the area of ploughland was 1800 acres in Wingrave in King Edward's time, which with the addition of water meadows, common meadows, common

grazing and waste would be roughly comparable with the 2421 acres of Wingrave in 1798.

2. In Domesday Book and the Victoria County History the name is Suen. The Phillimore translation is Swein.
3. Banishment included loss of property, and Swein certainly was deprived of at least some of his property, but there is no indication as to whether or not this included his Wingrave land.
4. According to Peter Sawyer: Domesday Book - A Reassessment (Edward Arnold, 1985, pp.72-3), "It is possible that other references to Brictric . . . . were to the same man, but that cannot be proved."
5. The oldest known Anglo-Saxon version of the Bible was made in the 900's.
6. Morris, J (Ed): Domesday Book (Bucks), Phillimore, 1978, 12.9, 23.21 and 23.22.
7. Fisher, D.J.V: The Anglo-Saxon Age, pp.260-61.
8. Page, R.K: Life in Anglo-Saxon England, pp. 93-6.
9. Stenton, Sir Frank: Anglo-Saxon England, 3rd edition, Oxford (Clarendon), p. 315; .Loyn, H.R: Anglo-Saxon England and the Norman Conquest, Longmans, 2nd edition 1991, p.167.
   Rowley, T: Medieval Field Systems in Cantor, L: The English Medieval Landscape, Croom Helm, 1982.
10. Quoted by Wood, M: Domesday – A Search for the Roots of England, BBC, 1986, pp. 109-110. The estate was at Hurstbourne Priors, to the east of Andover in Hampshire. The 10th century document read:
    *for every hide forty pence at Michaelmas, 6 large buckets of ale, 3 pounds of barley, 4 cartloads of split wood, 3 measures of wheat for bread, and 16 poles for fencing. They must also plough 3 acres in their own time and sow them with their own seed, and bring the sheaves to the barn. And at Easter give 2 ewes with 2 lambs . . .*
11. In Saxon times the social classification was more detailed, and the nomenclature varied with time and location. For more information consult Sir Frank Stenton, ibid.. In this case we have used the Domesday names.
12. Teams of two and four oxen were also used on lighter soils.
13. In theory the individual peasant could protect his plots with hurdles, but in practice this was unrealistic due to the amount of labour needed to make so many hurdles, and to install them, and the fact that the fallow field was ploughed twice.
14. Garmonsway, G. N (ed.): Aelfric's Colloquy, 1938.
15. Munby, L. M: Review of Beresford and Hurst's "Deserted Medieval Villages", in Local Historian, vol. X, p. 150.
16. The earliest bye-law from a Bucks village appears to be for Cheddington in August 1275.
17. Milling and baking often had to be done at the lord's mill and in his oven.

## Chapter 3: The Normans as Conquerors
1. Anglo-Saxon Chronicle 1085.
2. Morris, J: Domesday Book – Buckinghamshire, Phillimore, entries 14.23 and 2.3.
3. Baring, F.H: The Domesday Tables, Appendix A, 1909.
4. Stubbs, Wm: Select Charters, 9th edition, Oxford. 1929, p.101.
5. Until Baring's work was published, Berkhamsted was always cited as the location of William's meeting with the deputation from London. Baring produced persuasive evidence that it was really Little Berkhamsted.
6. Stenton, Sir F: Anglo-Saxon England, p.556.
7. Baker, T: The Normans, Cassell, 1966, p.41: Baker identifies it as the earliest known example of such a summons. Aethelwig was a regional governor.
8. Wace, a Channel Islander, writing a century later on the basis of information from his father. Quoted by Baker, T. op.cit.
9. Domesday Book Studies, Electo Historical Editions, 1987, p.34.
10. The tenants-in-chief were all given estates exceeding £100 in annual value. Many estates vastly exceeded this.
11. Andresen (ed.): Roman de Rou, vol. 2, p.126.
    Parker, John: The Giffards, Records of Buckinghamshire, vol.7, pp 475-510.
    Tillyard, V: Domesday People, 2002, pp 70-72.
12. In Norman times the 'hide' was a basis for taxation rather than a measure of area. However, in the eastern shires (including Bucks.) it seems to have been generally accepted as 120 acres, but was much smaller in the west. However, in Bucks, over very large areas (i.e. thousands of acres) a hide seems to equate roughly to 180 modern acres. This may be because the medieval hide included only the cultivated area of the village, whereas the modern acre takes into account the whole area of the parish, including what were formerly woodland, forest, waste, roads, tracks, water, and the very numerous baulks, headlands, and other non-productive areas. See chapter 2, note 2, for a comment on the hide in Saxon times.
13. Morris, J: Domesday Book (Buckinghamshire): Lands of Walter Giffard.
14. Victoria County History (Bucks), vol. 2, p.44.
15. The Anglo-Saxon thane was a noble of lower rank than eorl (= earl), or ealdorman (a noble of the highest rank). The thane was one who held land by service, but not necessarily military service.
16. Morris, J: op. cit., entry 14.45.
17. Morris, J: op. cit., entry 17.16.
18. 'Hundred' was a division of an English county, originally said to contain one hundred families.

19. Wood, M: Domesday – A Search for the Roots of England, BBC, 1986, p.161.
20. Chibnall, M: Anglo-Saxon England 1066-1166, Blackwell, 1986, p.141.
21. Ault, W. O: Open-Field Farming in Medieval England, Geo. Allen and Unwin Ltd., 1972, pp.18-19. The earliest roll for English manors is dated 1246. According to Ault early rolls are not rare because so few have survived, but because the practice of recording the proceedings of the manorial courts did not become general until more people could read and write. This increase in literacy did not begin until around 1200.

## Chapter 4: The Norman Bequests

1. Brown, R.A: The Castles of the Conqueror, in Domesday Book Studies, p. 69.
2. The buhr was a settlement usually surrounded by a high defensive bank and ditch, into which the population of the local countryside could retire when the enemy was approaching. Invented by King Alfred and completed by his son Edward, the buhrs formed a network of primitive fortresses which were defended by local villagers. In our area buhrs at Oxford and Wallingford defended the approaches to the western Vale.
3. Lipscombe, History and Antiquities of Buckinghamshire, 1847.
4. Crook, D., Jurhowaki, M., Smith, C. L: Lay Taxes in England and Wales 1186-1688, PRO, Handbook 31, 1998.
5. Slighted = made unusable as a military stronghold.
6. List of Scheduled Ancient Monuments, July 2000.
   List of Buckinghamshire Sites and Monuments.
7. Morris, R: Churches in the Landscape, Phoenix, 1989.
8. Extending the period to 1189 takes us into the reign of Henry II, who was not Norman but Plantagenet. However, he was a grandson of William the Conqueror. The vast majority of his tenants-in-chief had spent much of their lives under the rule of Norman kings, and it was those same tenants-in-chief, who instructed and paid the masons. They didn't necessarily change their architectural preferences just because a new dynasty ruled the kingdom. So if a church built as late as 1189 (the death of Henry II) exhibited sufficient Norman characteristics it was counted as Norman. But Norman fonts on their own have not been regarded as a determinant; neither have vague dates for a building such as "the late 12th century"; or the presence in later stonework of minor items allegedly from Norman times.
9. In calculating the number of years, 1066 was ignored, as William was not crowned until Xmas 1066.
10. The figures for the Vale and North Buckinghamshire are based upon views expressed in:
    Victoria County History for Buckinghamshire, vols. 1-4, 1905-1927
    Royal Commission on Historical Monuments: vols. 1and 2, 1912-13
    Department of the Environment, Buildings of Special Architectural or Historical Interest, 1974-85
    Pevsner, N. and Williamson, E: The Buildings of England – Buckinghamshire, Penguin, 1944
    The King's England: Buckinghamshire, Arthur Mee (ed.), 1940
    Keyser, C.E: Norman Doorways in the County of Buckingham, Records of Buckinghamshire
11. Based on Smith-Masters J. E: St. Michael's Church, and Mee, A. (Ed): The King's England-Buckinghamshire, Hodder and Stoughton, 1965, pp. 184-5.
12. Powell, K: A Brief History of Bradwell Abbey (pamphlets 1-7). City Discovery Centre, Bradwell Abbey, Milton Keynes, 1994. A survey of the abbey after closure in 1524, but before demolition, is available at the National Archive (PRO / E36 / 165 pp. 37-55). The document is a nightmare to read due to its archaic script, scrawl, and excessive abbreviation. The best transcript is in the Milton Keynes Journal of Archaeology and History, no. 3, 1974. See also Lipscombe, History and Antiquities of Buckinghamshire, 1847, vol. 4, pp. 41-44.
13. The site of the Ashridge house was then in the county of Buckinghamshire.
14. Bucks County Museum Information Leaflet 1: Monasteries in Bucks.
    List of Scheduled Ancient Monuments.
15. Useful sources include: Rowley, T: The Norman Heritage, Routledge and Kegan Paull, 1983; Bateson, F.W: Brill – A Short History, Brill Society, 1966; and Broad, J. and Hoyle, R. (eds.): Bernwood, Harris Papers 2, University of Central Lancashire, 1997.
16. Baker, T: The Normans, Cassell, 1966, p.161.
17. Broad, J. and Hoyle R: op. cit., p.5.
18. Poole, A.L: From Domesday Book to Magna Carta, Oxford, 1955, p.32.
19. Whitelock, D. (ed.) et al., Anglo-Saxon Chronicle, Eyre and Spottiswoode, 1961, p.165.
20. Ordericus Vitalis quoted by M. Wood, Domesday, BBC, 1986, p.159.
21. Strong, R. The Story of Britain, Pimlico, 1998, p.56.

## Chapter 5: The Decline of Feudalism

1. Most of these examples come from Victoria County History (Bucks), vol.2.
2. Rose, Walter (ed: Rose, E.M. and Gulland, P.): Reflections on Life in Haddenham, 1980.
3. Parts of this section have been considerably influenced by John Hatcher's book, 'Plague, Population and the Economy 1348-1530, MacMillan, 1977. For a fuller consideration of the topics the book should be read in its entirety.

4. VCH (Bucks), vol. 1, p.291.
5. From 1346/7 to 1348/9 six courts were held, involving a total of 42 jurymen. Of these 18 (43%) died of the plague.
6. Presumably the penultimate sentence should read, "Custody granted to Richard Martyn junior (son of Richard Martyn senior) until his (i.e. Richard, son of John atte Halle's) coming of age.
7. H. Knighton: Chronicon Henrici Knighton.
8. From 1346 -1352 there are no manorial rolls for Cuxham.
9. Court of Survey of Sir John Fortescue, Lord of Winslow Manor.
10. Clear, A: The King's Village in Demesne, being The History of the Town and Manor of Winslow, 1894.
11. King, P: The Development of the English Economy to 1750, MacDonald & Evans, pp. 289/1.
12. Chibnall, A.C: Sherington, CUP, 1965.
13. The story varies in detail. According to one account the handmills were used for paving the abbey kitchen.
14. Poulsen, Chas: The English Rebels, Journeyman, 1984.

## Chapter 6: Deserted Villages

1. As is the case at Cublington.
2. Beresford, M: The Lost Villages of England, Lutterworth, 1954: p.237, Table 6; p.251, Table 7.
3. Department for Culture, Media and Sport, batch no. 10341, file ref. AA60114, National Monument 29412.
4. Records of Bucks, vol.14, Early Taxation Returns.
5. Nonarum Inquisitiones, Record Commission 1807, p.340, quoted by Beresford, op. cit., p.314.
6. BRO: Court Rolls of Winslow.
7. According to N.A.Saving: Glimpses of Past Days, 1973: "Most of the legends of King Offa stem from the pen of Matthew Paris, a monk who entered the monastery of St. Albans in 1217, and was historian of the monastery from 1236 until his death in 1259.
8. Census 2001.
9. Reed, M: The Buckinghamshire Landscape, Hodder and Stoughton, 1979, pp.148-151.
10. The 25" map for 1898 shows only two farms at Salden.
11. Winslow Manor Roll, 11.11.1359 under Isabella atte Tonne.
12. The Act was to apply to owners of houses let to farm with 20 acres or more of land within the three years preceding the Act, or at any time.
13. A fief is a property or estate held from a superior lord on condition that the holder does homage and service to him.
14. Leadam, J.S: Domesday of Enclosures, Kennikat, 1897, pp.162/3.
15. Leland: Itineraries.
16. Browne Willis: Bodleian Library, Ms 30, folio 14.
17. A ha-ha was a wide trench containing a sunken fence so as to form a barrier to animals without interrupting the view.
At Burston only the trench has survived.
18. Map 7 was compiled after considering existing maps, an aerial photograph, and making a visit to the site.
19. Nellist, E: Burston- A Deserted Medieval Village in Buckinghamshire.
20. Dept for Culture, Media and Sport: Batch 10306, File AA 62492/1.
21. Feudal Aids (Inquisitions and Assessments Relating to), 6 vols., 1891-1920. It is likely that this early enclosure took place after 1428, because in that year all parishes with fewer than ten householders were exempt from the parish tax and Quarrendon did not apply.
22. Everson, P.E: Peasants, Peers and Graziers, Records of Bucks., vol. 41, 2001, pp. 1-45.
23. Adapted from "The Journeys of Celia Fiennes", Ed. C.Morris, 1949, p.30.
24. Page, M: Destroyed by the Temples – The Deserted Mediaeval Village of Stowe, Records of Buckinghamshire, vol. 45, 2005, pp. 189-204. Page argues convincingly that the depopulation of Stowe started in the 17th century, and was only completed in the 18th century. We are particularly indebted to the author, whose thesis corrects earlier misconceptions.
25. Reed, M: op. cit., p.145.

## Chapter 7: Life in a Medieval Village

1. Chibnall, A.C (Ed): Early Taxation Returns, Bucks Records Society, Vol. 14, pp. xi-xvii, 1-2, 65-7.
2. Crook, D., Jurkowski, M., Smith, C., L: Lay Taxes in England and Wales 1188-1688, PRO Handbook 31, 1998, pp. xxx-xxxi and 37-8.
3. Mitchell, R.R: British Historical Statistics, CUP. The prices quoted are from Exeter market.
4. Ault, Warren O: Open-field Farming in Mediaeval England, Allen and Unwin, 1972. Amercement = fine.
5. Maitland, F. W: The Court Baron, Selden Society, p.75.
6. Chibnall, who edited the tax assessments, insists that because they were implements of husbandry, "there would be no mention of plough-oxen in the rolls". Despite this, 23 oxen and 9 steers are mentioned. We have no explanation

for this.

7.  Bennett, H. S: Life on the English Manor, Cambridge, 1937, p. 150.
8.  Well wiste he = He knew well; hyne = steward; sleight = cunning; covyne = deceitful tricks.
9.  Useful sources for the late-medieval reeve include: Woods, Wm: England in the Age of Chaucer, p. 38; Saul,N: Medieval England, p.150; Loyn, H.R: Anglo-Saxon England and the Norman Conquest, pp. 200 & 356; Salzman, L.F: English Life in the Middle Ages, p. 59.
10. Field, R.K: Worcestershire Peasant Buildings, Household Goods and Farming Equipment in the Later Middle Ages, Medieval Archaeology vol. 9, 1965. Also Eames, P: Furniture in England, France and the Netherlands, 12th to 15th Centuries, Furniture History Society Journal, vol.XIII, 1977.
11. Harvey, P.D.A: A Medieval Oxfordshire Village, 1965
12. All possessions with a price attached have been taken from the Winslow Court Roll for April 1329, item 13.
13. Lipscombe refers to, "Margaret daughter of William Pipard of Wingrave". So it appears that the Pipards were resident in Wingrave at least for some time in the 14th century.
14. Lipscombe has Margaret (John Pipard's grand-daughter) married to Gerard Lord Lisle. In Victoria County History she is married to Sir Warin Lisle on the evidence of Chan. Inquisition Post Mortem, 38 Edwd III, no. 35, and we have adopted that version.
15. Dugdale, William: The Baronetage of England, 1675.
16. Coulton, G.G: Chaucer and His England, Methuen, 8th Edition, pp. 174-177; also, Smyth, J: The Berkeley Papers, Bristol and Gloucester Archaeological Society.
17. Woods, Wm: England in the Age of Chaucer, Hart-Davies, MacGibbon, 1976, p.57.
18. Wells, Henry, W (Ed.): Langland, Wm: The Vision of Piers Plowman VI, p. 64.
    Hamilton, H: The History of the Homeland, Geo. Allen and Unwin, 1947, p.64.
19. Calendar of Charter Rolls, 1257-1300, p.430.
20. Trevelyan, G.M: Illustrated English Social History I, p.54.
21. BRO: Winslow Court Rolls, View of Frankpledge, May 1353.
22. Hamilton, H: op. cit., pp 83 & 92.

## Chapter 8: The Reformation

1.  To be more precise, Henry sought an annulment of his marriage, declaring that in marrying Catherine he had married his sister-in-law, which was contrary to church law, even though the Pope had allowed it.
2.  VCH Bucks 1, p. 347; Bucks. County Museum Information Sheet 1; Pevsner N., and Williamson E: Buildings of Britain, Bucks., Penguin, 1994.
3.  Tomkeieff, O. G: Life in Norman England, Batsford, 1966, chap. V.
    Salzman, L.F: English Life in the Middle Ages, OUP, 1966, pp. 122-133.
4.  Lipscombe: History of Bucks., vol. 1, pp. 219-228.
5.  A carucate was as much land as could be tilled in a year by a plough and eight oxen.
6.  The ancient diocese of Lincoln included Buckinghamshire.
7.  VCH Bucks 1, p. 378.
8.  VCH Bucks 1, p. 377 and 377n.
9.  VCH Bucks 1, p. 299.
10. Hooton, T: Chearsley, 1994, p. 27.
11. Wright, Th: Suppression of the Monasteries (Letters Relating To) from Ms Cotton, Cleop. E, iv, folio 225. The writer of the letter was Dr John London, one of Cromwell's agents.
12. Letters and Papers of Henry VIII, xiii (2), 246.
13. Scott, G.G: Proposed Restoration of All Saints' Church, Records of Bucks. IV, pp. 309-325.
14. Lipscombe: History of Bucks, vol.1, p. 231.
15. As 14 above.
16. Wright, Th: op.cit. Ms Cotton, Cleop. E, iv, folio 225.
17. Sir Thomas Brabant was the organist at Woburn.
18. Woodman, A.V: Accounts of the Churchwardens of Wing, Records of Bucks., vol. 16, pt. 5, p. 316.
19. Lysons: Magna Britannica, vol.1, p. 547.
20. BRO/D/X/644: Letter on Long Crendon Manor from E.C.Hohler, June 1977.
21. VCH Bucks I, p. 389 (Latin version); Todd, History of Ashridge, p. 5 (Translation).
22. Clifford, Henry: The Life of Jane Dormer, Duchess of Feria, Burns and Oates, 1889, p. 60.
23. Clifford, Henry: op.cit., p.61.
24. Dickens, A.G. and Carr, DD: The Reformation in England, Arnold, 1967, p. 38.
25. Salzman, L.F: op. cit., p.113. A visitation of 17 parishes in Berkshire in 1222 showed that 30% of the clergy could neither translate nor sing the mass.
26. Wells, Henry, W. (ed); Langland, Wm., The Vision of Piers Plowman.
27. Salzman, L.F: op. cit., p. 57.

## Chapter 9: The Anglican Emergence

1. Chadwick, Owen: The Reformation, Hodder & Stoughton, 1965, p.117.
2. The Sepulchre was a recess, normally in the north wall of the chancel, or a structure placed in it to receive the reserved sacrament and the crucifix from Maundy Thursday or Good Friday until Easter. (Chambers 20th Century Dictionary)
3. The "washing-out" was intended to obliterate the Doom, but slight traces of it were found in 1933.
4. Woodman, A.V: The Accounts of the Churchwardens of Wing, Records of Bucks., vol. 16. Few places have comparable Accounts for this period, but see Croscombe, Somerset.
5. For more information on the Dormers see later references, and VCH Bucks. on the parishes of Wing, Wingrave and Aston Abbotts.
6. Advouson is the right to present a candidate for an ecclesiastical office.
7. Chadwick, Owen: op. cit., p. 123.
8. The "Rode" refers to the rood cross, which probably included the figure of Christ. If so, this would account for the high cost. The rood (i.e. the rood cross) and the rood loft were above the rood screen, which separated the nave from the chancel. Access to the rood and the rood loft was usually by stone steps, built into the walls of the church. Many churches have evidence of the existence of rood screens, etc.. For example:
   Hoggeston: rectangular opening at the east end of the nave.
   Soulbury: the arch to the rood-loft stairs is in the north-east corner of the nave.
   Edgcott: the nave has the upper door to the rood-loft stairs.
9. The pax was an oscutary: a tablet with a projecting handle and a carved representation of the Crucifixion, which was kissed by the priest and (in medieval times) also by the congregation at Mass.
10. Chadwick, Owen: op. cit., pp. 127-8.
11. At Wing, from 1559 on, there is no account of the mending of any vestment but the surplice. However, the Act left some doubt as to exactly what priests should wear.
12. The summoner was a petty official, who summoned people to appear at court, tribunal or meeting.
13. The altar stone at Wing was embedded in the church floor, where it lay for nearly three centuries, only to vanish during a restoration of the church in 1849-50.
14. VCH Bucks I, p. 314.
15. VCH Bucks I, p. 314.
16. VCH Bucks 1, p. 314.
17. VCH Bucks I, p. 314, notes 7 and 8.
18. Verney, Sir H: The Verneys of Claydon, Maxwell, 1968, p. 255.
19. Smith-Masters, J.E: The Parish Church of Stewkley, 1923, p.34.
20. Peters, N: Priests in Hiding, Bucks. Life, March 1970.
21. VCH Bucks I, p. 315.
22. Chadwick, Owen: op. cit., p. 290.
23. Clifford, Henry: op. cit..

## Chapter 10: Nonconformism in the Vale

1. Verney, F. P. and M. M. (eds.) : Memoirs of the Verney Family During the 17th Century, pp. 246-7.
   Dix, K: Benjamin Keach and a monument to liberty, p. 15.
2. Hamilton, Henry: History of the Homeland, Allen and Unwin, 1947, p. 267.
3. Clear, Arthur: History of the Town and Manor of Winslow, 1894. Saving, N.A: Glimpses of Past Days, etc., 1973, pp. 13, et seq.. Dix, K: op. cit..
4. Crosby, Thos: History of the English Baptists, 1739, vol. ii, p. 185.
5. Rose, W: Haddenham Quaker History, ms. 1916, edited and printed 1988.
   Crump, G.C: The History of Thomas Ellwood, 1900.
6. Broad, J. (ed.): Buckinghamshire Dissent and Parish Life 1669-1712, Bucks Record Society, vol..28, p. 43.
7. Luton and Leighton Monthly Meeting Register.
8. Based on McLaughlin, Eve: The Baptist Chapel in Princess Risborough.
9. As note 6.
10. BRO/NQ/1/6/1: The Quaker Book of Sufferings for Buckinghamshire.
11. BRO/NB/16/3
12. McLaughline, Eve: Nonconformist Ancestors, p. 19.

## Chapter 11: The Enclosure of the Open Fields

1. BRO: BAS map 72.
2. It seems that most of that enclosure had occurred before 1485, which was the earliest date for which Cardinal Wolsey's Commission could take action.

3. BRO: BAS map 72, The Open Fields of Soulbury, 1769.
4. BRO: PR67/1/2. Village of Dunton Field Orders.
5. BRO: PR67/1/2 Village of Dunton Tithe Procedures. The words in brackets have been added to clarify the original text.
6. Hollowell, S: Enclosure Records for Historians, Phillimore, 2000, p. 4.
7. BRO: IRM/10/1 Agreement for opposing the Enclosure Act of 1772.
8. House of Commons Journal, vol. 58.
9. BRO: Quarter Session Documents Epiphany Ssssions 1.
10. At least 66.7% to 80% by value was needed to petition Parliament successfully. At Stewkley the figure was 83%.
11. BRO: IRM/10/2 Enclosure Act 1811.
12. BRO: IRM/10/ 4b: Extracts of Claims and Petitions.
13. BRO: IR/110/B
14. The Enclosure Act allowed up to 10 acres for this purpose.
15. BRO: IR/114A The Stewkley Award.
16. Turner, M: Parliamentary Enclosures in Buckinghamshire, 1738-1865, Typescript.
17. As note 16.
18. BRO: IRM/10/ 6: Commissioners' Accounts and Bills.
19. BRO: DX / 362 Account Book of Joseph Mead.
20. BRO: I R / 114A - Joseph Mead Fencing Award.
21. Morley, Ken and Margaret: The Great Upheaval, 1994, p. 53.

## Chapter 12: The Revolution in Transport

**The Roads**

1. Green, J.R: Town Life in the 15th Century.
2. Coulton, G.G: Medieval Village, Manor and Monastery, Harper, 1925, p.35.
3. Markham, S.F, and Hyde, F.E: History of Stony Stratford, 1948, p.100.
4. Webb, S.& B: English Local Government – The Story of the King's Highway, pp. 195-6.
5. Quoted in Wolverton Express, 31/1/1947.
6. BRO: D/X/1099/4 Valuation of the Earl of Chesterfield's estates.
7. Fay, C.R: Great Britain from Adam Smith to the Present Day, Longmans, 1945, p.176.
8. Scott, J: Digests of the General Highways and Turnpike Laws, 1778.
9. Gibbs, R: History of Aylesbury, Gibbs, 1885, p.339.
10. Webb, S. & B, op.cit., pp.119 – 20.
11. BRO: T/1/10, Appointment of Surveyors by Trustees of the Turnpikes, 28/6/1810.
12. BRO: Turnpike records.
13. BRO: T/1/10 Letter (undated) from the turnpike surveyor to Thomas Fleet.
14. Webb, S &B: op.cit., Pamphlet of 1825, p.38.
15. Letter from John Cresset to a postmaster in the country, in 1672.
16. Based on Margetson, S: Journey by Stages, Cassel, 1967.
17. Verney, M, M: Memoirs of the Family, vol.1, 1892.
18. Marsh-Edwards: J.C: The Tantivy Trot through Buckinghamshire's Leafy Lanes, Bucks and Berks Countryside, December, 1973.
19. Gibbs, R: op. cit., entry for 9.12.1821.
20. Chibnal, J: The Roads of Buckinghamshire 1675 –1913, p. 77.

**The Canals**

21. For technical reasons the mechanisation of the production of woollen cloth came later.
22. Bull: Transport and Communication in North Bucks.. Bucks Collection L000.38.
23. Markham, Sir F: A History of Milton Keynes and District, White Crescent, 1973, vol. I, pp. 311-324.
24. Wilson, R.J: Life Afloat, 1976.

**The Railways**

25. Mr Delmé Radcliffe on fox hunting in 1830.
26. Alum shale contains iron sulphate, which decomposes and ignites spontaneously.
27. Osbourne: London and Birmingham Rail Guide, p.52.
28. Based upon Thompson, F.M.L: Victorian England, the Horse-Drawn Society, Bedford College, 1970, p. 13.
29. The building was later dismantled and re-erected at Sydenham in South Bucks..

## Chapter 13: Education

1. Clear, A: The King's Village in Demesne (an account of Winslow), 1894, p .99.

2.  Robert Lovett, Grandson of Sir Robert Lovett, High Sheriff of Buckingham, and Lord of Soulbury Manor.
3.  Charity Commissioners' Report, 1825.
4.  BRO: DX/719/3.
5.  Religious Census (Bucks), 1851, p.58.
6.  Bucks Record Society: The Letters of Thomas Hayton, 1821-1887.
7.  BRO: DX/785/9.
8.  BPP: XVIII Commission Enquiring into the Employment of Children, Young Persons and Women, 1867.
9.  Lewington, Honor: A Tale of Two Schools, typescript, May 1998. Hulcott's earliest National School still stands in Hulcott Lane. No. 1 is the Old School House formerly the schoolmaster's house. No. 2 is the Old School Cottage formerly the schoolroom.
10. As note 8.
11. Lambeth Palace Library, National Society Records.
12. Bucks Herald, 1.9.1849.
13. Bucks Record Society: vol. 16, Letter Books of Samuel Wilberforce 1864-2.
14. As note 11.
15. BRO: E/LB/59/1 Log book of Cuddington School.

## Chapter 14: The Rise and Fall of the Cottage Industries
1.  Morris, C: The Journeys of Celia Fiennes from Wolesley through Warwickshire to London, 1947, p. 119.
2.  Pennant, T: Journey from Chester to London, 1783, p.355.
3.  The Gentleman's Magazine, 1785, vol. 55, p. 938.
4.  White, I.E: in evidence to the Children's Employment Commission, 1862.
5.  BRO/PR11/12/2: Overseers' Accounts of Aylesbury 1670-1683.
6.  PP vol. 13, Evidence to the Children's Employment Commission, 1863, pp. 258 and 260.
7.  Hickman, Daphne: Bucks Family History Society, December 1996.
8.  Donald, J: Long Crendon, A Short History.
9.  PP13, Children's Employment Commission, 1863, evidence of Thomas Gilbert.
10. Gibbs, R: A History of Aylesbury
11. PP: op. cit., p. 256.
12. Adams, D: Elsie Turnham, Lace Collector.
13. Robinson, F.E: The Story of Aylesbury, Home Counties Magazine, vol.3 1901.
14. Cook, Wm: Ducks and How to make them Pay.
15. Rose, Walter: Good Neighbours, 1942, chap. 7.
16. Priest, Rev. J: op. cit., adapted from p.331.
17. Rose, Walter: op. cit..
18. Cook, Wm: op. cit..
19. Wright: The Book of Poultry.
20. Records of Bucks., vol. 19, p.10.
21. Shrimpton, William: Notes on a Decayed Needle-land, p. 21.

## Chapter 15: Desperate Times:
1.  May, T: Economic and Social History of Britain, Longman, 1987, p.89.
2.  BRO: PR175/11/3 Princes Risborough Overseer Accounts, 1826-31.
3.  Gibbs, R: Local Occurrences in Bucks, vol. 3, at date in text.
4.  BRO: PR175/12/1 Princes Risborough Overseers Accounts, 1833.
5.  BRO: PR175/11/3 Princes Risborough Overseers Accounts, 1826-31.
6.  PP: First Annual Report of the Poor Law Commissioners, Mr Gilbert's Report from Bucks., 15/6/1835, pp. 241 etc..
7.  Crabbe, The Village, 1783.
8.  BRO/235/12/2: Expenses of the Wingrave Poor House.
9.  Eden, Sir E.M: The State of the Poor, 1797, pp. 57-8.
10. BRO: PR13/12/2 Overseers' Accounts for East Claydon in 1828.
11. Gibbs, R: op. cit., vol. 3, at dates in text.
12. As note 11.
13. As note 11.
14. As note 11.
15. May, T: op. cit.. p.197
16. As note 11.
17. As note 11.
18. Bucks and Aylesbury News, April 5th, 18 84

19.  For a fuller account see also Chambers, J: The Buckinghamshire Machine Breakers, published by the author at 54, Chagny Close, Letchworth, Herts., SG6 4BY, 1991.

## Chapter 16: A Time of Last Resorts

1.  Jones, D: Rural Crime and Protest, in Mingay, G. E. (ed.) The Victorian Countryside, vol. 2, Routledge, Kegan Paull, 1981, p..569.
2.  Holdenby, C: Folk of the Furrow, 1913, pp. 26/7.
3.  Gibbs, R:. Local Occurrences in Bucks., vol. 3, at dates in text.
4.  As note 3.
5.  Tate, W.E: The Parish Chest, CUP, 1969, pp. 238/9.
6.  PP: 3rd Report from the Select Committee appointed to Enquire into the State of Agriculture, 1836.
7.  Booth, Wm: Darkest England and the Way Out, 1890.
8.  Bucks Herald, 12/6/1875. By this time the rule had been in operation for 30 years.
9.  May, T: An Economic and Social History of Britain 1760-1970, Longman, 1987, p. 124. A Select Committee investigated and the three London-based Commissioners were replaced by a Poor Law Board presided over by a Minister of the Crown.
10. PRO (K): MH12/406.
11. PRO (K): MH12/405. Letters dated 13th and 26th July, and 1st August 1837.
12. Eight Letters on the Management of our Poor, by an Overseer, Newark, 1822, p.4.
13. May, T: op.cit., pp124/5.
14. Gibbs, R: Local Occurrences in Bucks., at dates in text.
15. As note 14.
16. Gibbs, R: op. cit., vol. 4, p.13.
17. Statute 14 Car II, c 12.
18. Bucks Herald 13/12/1834.
19. See note 6.
20. Bosanquet, S.R: The Rights of the Poor and Christian Almsgiving Vindicated, 1841.
21. Tomlinson, G: Bring Plenty of Pickles, 1986, pp. 16-17.
22. The percentage was calculated from the original table of 18 incomes.
23. A bushel of flour really does yield approximately 48 loaves of the size produced by a home baking machine. If the Betts' loaves were just 12.5% larger, which they probably were, their bushel would yield 42 loaves, as required for one per person per day.
24. PP XVIII Commission Enquiring into the Employment of Children, Young Persons and Women in Agriculture, 1867.
25. See note 24.
26. Eden, Sir E.M: The State of the Poor, 1797, p. 358. The Dyers' rent-free house and free fuel increase their weekly income by 2s-0d, and account for their ability to buy as much butter. Nevertheless, their budget is still better balanced having much more meat, cheese, milk, beer and an allowance for clothes.
27. Milburn, J. R. and Jarrott, K: The Aylesbury Agitator, Bucks County Library, 1988, p. 5.
28. PP XVIII Commission Enquiring into the Employment of Children, Young Persons and Women in Agriculture, 1867.

## Chapter 17: Life and Death in the Victorian Villages of the Vale

The principal references were:
Hart, L: Health in the Vale of Aylesbury, 1979.
PP: The Sanitary Conditions of the Labouring Population, 1842, Local Reports.
Waddesdon Parish Church: Burial Registers
Moreton, C. O: Waddesdon and Upper Winchendon, SPCK, 1929.
The Lancet 1842-3, Vol. ii, 1/4/1843, pp. 1-10.
PP: Vol. xxviii, Commission of 1864, pp, 776-780.
PP: Second Report of the Royal Sanitary Commission 1874-90, Vol. iii, Part 2, pp218-219.
AVDC: Advisory Guide "How to look after your Wichert Building".
1.  PP: 4th Annual Report of the Poor Law Commissioners 1837-8; Local Reports July 1842.
2.  BRO/DC2/ 39/1: Rural District Sanitary Authority Minutes 1882-92.
    BRO/DC2/1/1: Rural District Sanitary Authority Minutes 1892-1902

## Chapter 18: Some Glimmers of Hope

1.  The Labourers' Union Chronicle, July 1874.
2.  Bateman, F.W: A Short History of Steeple Claydon.

3.   See note 1.
4.   Bucks Advertiser and Aylesbury News, 18.7.1874, p. 4, col. 5.
5.   The Aylesbury Agitator, Appendix VI, p. 97 details 20 voyages.
6.   Labourers' Union Chronicle, 5.9.1874.
7.   Labourers' Union Chronicle, 10.1.1874.
8.   Demolished in 1970.
9.   There was a National Temperance League which, through lectures and public meetings, encouraged the formation of Total Abstinence Societies, whose members signed a pledge to abstain from alcoholic drinks.
10.  Agricultural Committee of the Tariff Commission: Minutes of Evidence 6.2.1905.
11.  Knowles, L.C.A: The Industrial and Commercial Revolutions in Great Britain, p. 373. The figures are annual averages over seven years.
12.  PP XVII Enquiry into the Employment of Children, Young Persons and Women in Agrculture, 1867: General Evidence from Buckinghamshire, pp. 522-538.
13.  Thompson, Flora: Lark Rise, OUP, 1939.

## Chapter 19: The Vale of Aylesbury

1.   Temple, M.S: The Soils of Bucks, 1929, Reading University.
2.   Avery, B.W: The Soils and Land Use of the District around Aylesbury and Hemel Hempstead, HMSO, 1964, p.21.
3.   This stratum is the Upper Greensand, which in this district is not green.
4.   Morley-Davis, A: Buckinghamshire, CUP, 1912, p.41.
5.   Read, C.S: Report on the Farming of Bucks., J'rnal of the Royal Agricultural Society of England, 1856, pp. 269-322.
6.   Read, C.S: op. cit., p. .281.
7.   Avery, B.W: op. cit., chap. iv.
8.   Read, C.S: op.cit: p. 282.
9.   Read, C.S: op.cit..
10.  Drummond, J.C. and Wilbrahem, A: The Englishman's Food, London, 1964.
11.  PP: The Royal Commission on the Agricultural Depression, 1895, Final Report, p.8.
12.  The Minister of Agriculture (Mr Jopling) during the debate in the Commons on July 3rd.
13.  Daily Telegraph 16/08/2005. Article based on report by Dr David Coleman of Manchester University.

## Chapter 20: Looking to the Future

1.   Commission on 3rd London Airport, vol. 5, Cublington: Pa;ers and Proceedings, pp.1174 -5.
2.   Commisson as above, p. 1174.
3.   For the account of the campaign against the third London airport at Cublington we are greatly indebted to the Aston Abbotts' History Group and their excellent History of Aston Abbotts, chap. 13; to David Perman's book, Cublington: A Blueprint for Resistance, Bodley Head, 1973; and to the Commission on the Third London Airport's Proceedings, vol.5.
4.   Griffin, M. and Thurston, R: The Story of Bierton, 1994, p.56.
5.   Architects and planners have coined subtopia as the opposite of utopia.
6.   Bucks County Council etc., State of the Environment Report for Buckinghamshire, 1997.
     Regional Planning Guidance for the South-East.
     The Milton Keynes and South Midlands Study.
     The Milton Keynes and South Midlands Sub-regional Strategy.
     Tym, Roger, and Partners: Milton Keynes and Aylesbury Growth Area Studies, Final Report, May 2003.
     Tym, Roger, and Partners: Milton Keynes and Aylesbury Growth Area Studies, Executive Summary, May 2003.
     Bucks County Council: Bucks County Structure Plan 2001-2016, A Housing Study, Technical Paper 5, Rural Areas.
     Planning Policy Guidance Notes eg PPG 6, 7, 9, 13, 15, 16.
7.   Bucks Herald 7.9.2005, Section 1, p. 6, col..4.
8.   Milton Keynes and South Midlands Sub-Regional Strategy, March 2005.
     Bucks County Council: The South East Plan, Sept/Oct 2005, p.5.
9.   AVDC Local Plan para. 3.11 (1), p. 14.
10.  The Sub-Regional Strategy – Aylesbury Vale District Council, 14.09.2005, p.5.
11.  Bucks Herald, 5.10.2005.
12.  The figures in Table 32 were calculated as follows, but bear in mind that although largely from official sources they may change in the course of the planning process. The figures have been rounded up where appropriate to simplify the presentation. According to information from their publications AVDC thinks that at present Aylesbury Town can accommodate 2,407 dwellings on Brownfield sites, and this is complemented by 6,002 dwellings on Greenfield sites. (Table 31 refers). In order to speculate on the capacity of Brownfield and Greenfield sites, the following calculations

were made, using ongoing, likely and possible developments to provide figures. We assume that the figures for the Greenfield sites include land for the creation of sustainable communities, as promised in the AVDC Local Plan.

Typical Brownfield Acreages are based upon: the following sample of sites:

| | | |
|---|---|---|
| Keir Place (flats only) | 70 dwellings on | 0.92 acres |
| Dayla High St. (flats only) | 38 dwellings on | 0.70 acres |
| Buckingham St. / Oxford Rd. (flats only) | 19 dwellings on | 0.37 acres |
| Hampden Hall (flats and houses) | 150 dwellings on | 13.60 acres |
| Nestlé (flats only) | 136 dwellings on | 3.00 acres |
| Total | 413 dwellings | 18.59 acres |

Therefore the typical acreage per Brownfield dwelling is 18.59 ÷ 413 = 0.045 acres.

Typical Greenfield Acreages are based upon the following sample of sites:

| | | |
|---|---|---|
| Berryfields: | 3000 dwellings occupying | 504.0 acres |
| Weedon Hill | 850 dwellings occupying | 124.0 acres |
| Total | 3850 | 628.0 acres |

Therefore the typical acreage per Greenfield dwelling is 628 ÷ 3850 = 0.1632 acres

The difference between Brownfield and Greenfield developments in acreage per dwelling is obviously due to the large proportion of flats in multi-storeyed buildings on Brownfield sites, which are usually within a town with an existing infrastructure, whereas when a Greenfield site is being developed, the infrastructure also has to be provided.

13. Power, N: The Forgotten People, 1965.
14. Aylesbury Society Magazine, no. 128, p. 7.
15. Clover, C; Environmental Editor, Daily Telegraph, 23.11.2005, pp. 1 and 4.
16. Bucks. Herald, 5.10.2005, Expansion Plan to provide More Affordable Housing.
17. Daily Telegraph, 23.11. 2005, p.1, and 28.11.2005, p.12.
18. McGhie, C: Flat on its Face, Weekend Telegraph, 17.12. 2005, pp.16-17.
19. Clover, C: Environmental Editor, Daily Telegraph, 28.11.2005, p. 12.
20. Tym, Roger, and Partners, Milton Keynes and Aylesbury Growth Area Studies, Final Report, May 2003.
21. Jackson, A: Second Fire Station for Town? Bucks Herald, 14. 12. 2005, p.12.
22. AVDC Local Plan 2004, Part 1, Table D and paras. 4.47 and 4.48, page 31.
23. Commission on 3rd London Airport, vol.5, Cublington, Papers and Proceedings pp. 1176-7.
24. Shire Publications, Church Street, Princes Risborough, Bucks., HP27 9AA.
25. Eco-farming is farming which is compatible with the habitats and environment of living creatures.
    Fenton, B: Halcyon Days for the Marsh Harrier, Daily Telegraph 19.05.2006. p.9.
    Scott, V: Lecture to Friends of the Vale, AGM 2006.
26. Ramblers' Association, letter dated 17.8.2005 .
27. Ramblers' Association, 2nd Floor, 87-90, Albert Embankment, London, SE1 7TW. Tel: 0207-339-8500.

# INDEX

## Presentation Copies

Emma Bowes Romanelli
Julian Hunt
Edward Stamp
Norman Groom (Pitstone and Ivinghoe
    Museum Society)
Staff of the Centre for Bucks Studies
Gillian Donald
Tony Wells

## Subscribers' Copies

Len & Madge Adams
Mark & Kate Adams
Geoffrey & Hilary Aldridge
Samantha Allen
Lesley & John Alexander
Ken & Meg Anderson
Linda & Cliff Ashall

Eric Bateman
Stuart Bell
Bill & Irene Best
Roger Betteridge
Alec & Sue Bignell
Ian & Nancy Blood
Michael & Vivien Borley
Norman & Sylvia Brackley
John and Jill Branham
Bucks Archaeological Society

Patricia Cafferata
Mike & Pamela Callaghan
June Cannon
Margaret E. Cattell
Celia Childs-Evered
Isobel Clark
Helen & Peter Cleasby
Mrs & Mr Cole
Ann Cook & Joe Fairlie

Mrs Audrey Copelin
John & Sheila Cotton
Mrs Avis M. Cousins
Mike & Ann Curry

Pauline Darvill
Carol & Peter Davey
Mrs Laura Davis
Hazel Doughty
Betty & Geoffrey Dunn and Marian

Alphonse and Jackie Elsenburg
John & Jennifer Evans
Martin & Jackie Evered
Mrs Barbara Evered

Sally, Mick, John & Samantha Foot
Mrs Shirley Ford
Clare & James Fox
Ken & Sylvia Francis
Alan & Janet Frost

Jill & Barry Garland
Margaret & Peter George
Dave & Valerie Godfrey
David & Linda Ginnane
Mrs Christine Goodley
Prudence & Derek Goodwin
Edward Francis Griffin
Diana & Peter Gulland
Ethelie Gutteridge
Nigel Gurney

Robert Hammond
George & Jean Harper
John Hawkes
David, Ruth and Gary Hewitt
Kristian, Gemma & Toby Ben Hewitt
Peggy & Ray Hewitt

Simon, Vikki & Daryl Hewitt
Mrs Linda Hodges
Veronica Hollings
Brenda & Tony Horne
Gerald & Isabel Howe

Mr & Mrs A. Jackson
Linda &  Paul Jauncey
Hazel & Keith Jinks
Mrs Celia Jones
Peter & Jean Jones
Simon Jones & Sarah and Dave Gore-
    Clough

Richard & Jean Keighley
Judy & Nigel Kennedy
Mrs Margaret E. Kennedy
Marie King
Fred Kirby
The Kirkup Family

Caroline Lane & Gordon Smith
Marie Lawton
Marlene  Lee (Archivist-Cheddington
    History Society)
Bruce & Honor Lewington
M. E. Liggett
Gerald W. Line
Andrew & Margaret Liversidge

Mrs Margaret Main
Thelma & Alan Mallett
M. Malone
Prof. W. R. Mead
Chris & Rosemary Meddows
Tom Meddows
Robin & Dominique Moat
Liz & David Morgan
David Morley

Peter & Lani Morley
Mary Mountain
Jane & Andrew Muir

Paul & Vanessa O'Carroll

Elizabeth Philipps
John & Valerie Philpott
Bill & Gladys Phillips
Nicola Place
Sandra & Doug Purrett

Shirley Raw
Colin Rickard
Pat Roberts
Bryan & Joyce Round
Derek & Rosemary Rowe

Joyce  Sinnott
Richard & Christine Skidmore
Peter & Roberta Smith
Isobel Smith-Creswell
Dr David Snow
Paul Stearns
Stone Local History Group

Alan R. Tanner
Rev. Siv & Mike Tunnicliffe

Rev. Ann & Julian Varker

Frank & Joan Watson
Doug & Rachel Webb
Alice, Grace, Emma & Jas. Whitehead
Steven, Carol & Alice Whitehead
Michael Whitney
Lesley & Keith Williams

Audrey Yea

# CHANGES IN OUR LANDSCAPE

## Aspects of Bedfordshire, Buckinghamshire

## And the Chilterns

## 1947-1992

### The photographic work of Eric Meadows

In the post-War years, this once quiet rural backwater between Oxford and Cambridge has undergone growth and change – and the expert camera of Eric Meadows has captured it all.

We see an enormous variety of landscape, natural and man-made, from yesteryear and today – open downs and rolling farmland, woods and commons, ancient earthworks, lakes and moats, vanished elms, quarries, nature reserves and landscape gardens. Here are many building styles – churches of all periods, stately homes and town dwellings, rural pubs, gatehouses and bridges. Secluded villages contrast their timeless lifestyles with the bustle of modern developing towns and their industries.

Distilled from a huge collection of over 25,000 photographs, this book offers his personal selection of over 350 that best display the area's most attractive features and its notable changes during nearly 50 years. The author's detailed captions and notes complete a valuable local history.

# JOURNEYS INTO BUCKINGHAMSHIRE
## Anthony Mackay

This collection of searching ink drawings depicts the buildings and landscape of the county of Buckinghamshire. Four years of work has culminated in a personal choice of images, reinforced with compact historical notes on almost every settlement. It becomes clear, as one explores the pages of the book, that this often neglected part of England is still deeply rural. Ancient market towns predominate in a landscape characterised, for the most part, by the hedges and fields of an agricultural economy. The county is further enriched by countless attractive villages linked by a web of narrow country lanes.

The broad watery basins of the River Great Ouse and the Thames are offset by the striking chalk ridge of the Chilterns whose towering beechwoods and steep north facing escarpments create the only dramatic experiences.

London is very close and yet has failed to quench the pastoral qualities of this subtle blend of the domestic and the wild. Stately homes and modest manor houses coexist comfortably with clusters of simple cottages and mellow farmhouses. Every village has its parish church, which tells the story of the community through its sculpture, stained glass, furniture, memorials and wall-paintings. Windmills, bridges and canals speak of the more recent industrial past and newly planned communities strive to blend into this evolving physical drama.

The companion volumes on Bedfordshire, Hertfordshire and Oxfordshire receive widespread acclaim and admiration.

286

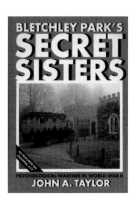

# BLETCHLEY PARK'S SECRET SISTERS

## Psychological Warfare in World War 11

### John A. Taylor

Bletchley Park will be forever associated with the secret intelligence activities of World War Two. Yet in addition to the incredible achievements of the code breakers, only a few miles away several other secret organisations were also achieving clandestine success, with operations that were conducted from centres hidden in the local countryside. This region had been chosen by the Government because it was remote from the London Blitz yet still maintained good road and rail communications with the Capital - but what did these secret organisations do?

In a highly subversive campaign, propaganda played an early and effective role, selecting recruits from amongst the refugees fleeing Nazi oppression. Gathered in large, local houses, there they would write and rehearse propaganda scripts for radio broadcasts to enemy territory. At a secret studio, these broadcasts were then recorded onto discs and taken by the Secret Service to radio transmitting stations, hidden in the local countryside.

Under the control of the Communications Section of the Secret Intelligence Service, another radio station transmitted decoded information from Bletchley Park to Allied military commanders overseas. Further radio stations maintained contact with secret agents, sent on missions deep inside Occupied Europe. In hidden workshops, advanced radio equipment for their use was designed and manufactured and in various country houses specialised training schools were set up.

Later in the war, not far from Woburn Abbey an ultra modern recording and broadcast studio was then built which, when linked to the most powerful radio transmitter in Europe, began use in sophisticated operations that would completely deceive and confuse the Germans.

This book now tells the little known story of all these other secret activities, the fascinating story of Bletchley Park's 'Secret Sisters'.

The Book Castle

# BUCKINGHAM AT WAR

## Pip Brimson

The people of Buckingham adapted well to a state of war. Their stories reflect courage, humour and occasional pathos.

How they coped with A.R.P., gas masks, blackout, mobilization and the secrets of Bletchley Park, followed by the formation of the Home Guard, Land Girls, and the jobs women were directed to. The progress of the war through those early years, which included rationing and evacuation, individual efforts by those at home and fund raising events in the town are all related in this book. The collection of salvage took a large part – as did the knitting of comforts for the Forces by local women's groups. Everything was geared for eventual Victory, however long it might take.

When at last the end of the War approached, the blackout was lifted; the Home Guard, their job finished, stood down, and prisoners of war overseas began to return home to great rejoicing, which culminated on V.E. and V.J. Days. Servicemen too, were slowly beginning to demobilize.

Finally, everyone could sit back and take stock - attend to their losses and sadness, but feel proud of what had been achieved – and then, begin to prepare for the problems and happiness Peace would bring, after long years of struggle and endeavour.

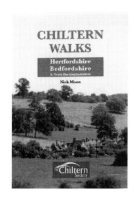  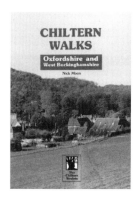

# CHILTERN WALKS
## Hertfordshire, Bedfordshire and North Buckinghamshire

# CHILTERN WALKS
## Buckinghamshire

# CHILTERN WALKS
## Oxfordshire and West Buckinghamshire

## Nick Moon

A series of three books providing a comprehensive coverage of walks throughout the whole of the Chiltern area (as defined by the Chiltern Society). The walks included vary in length from 3.0 to 10.9 miles, but are mainly in the 5-7 mile range popular for half-day walks, although suggestions of possible combinations of walks are given for those preferring a full day's walk.

Each walk gives details of nearby places of interest and is accompanied by a specially drawn map of the route which also indicates local pubs and a skeleton road network.

289

# THE CHILTERN AREA'S LEADING SERIES OF MAPS FOR WALKERS
## by Nick Moon

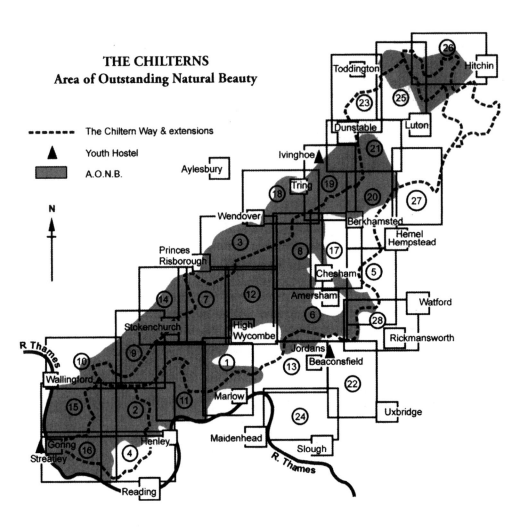

**THE CHILTERNS**
**Area of Outstanding Natural Beauty**

Legend:
- ▬ ▬ ▬ The Chiltern Way & extensions
- ▲ Youth Hostel
- ▩ A.O.N.B.

This expanding series of currently 28 maps at a scale of 2½ inches to the mile depicts footpaths, bridleways and other routes available to walkers, riders and cyclists across the Chilterns, as well as pubs, railway stations, car parking facilities and other features of interest. Several suggested walks also appear on the back of each map. New titles appear regularly and will extend coverage of the area.